SKATE FARM

volume one

Special Scholastic Edition

SBK
publishing, LLC

Skate Farm, Volume 1
Special Scholastic Edition
Created by Danny Neiman, John Stauffer and Barzak
Original graphic novel by Barzak

Published by SBK Publishing, LLC
7172 Hawthorn Ave., Suite 110
Los Angeles, CA 90046-3282
www.skatefarmcomics.com

Editor and Publisher: Richard E. Johnson:
rej@skatefarmcomics.com
Über-Consultant: Extreme Steve, aka John S. Dalton
SBK Publishing LLC Members incl:
Peter "PT" Townend
Tosh Townend
Pre-Press Manager: Paul Sizer

If you know what's good for you, visit:
www.skatefarmcomics.com

ISBN-13: 978-0-9789026-1-2
$9.99 USA/$12.99 CAN

Printed in Canada

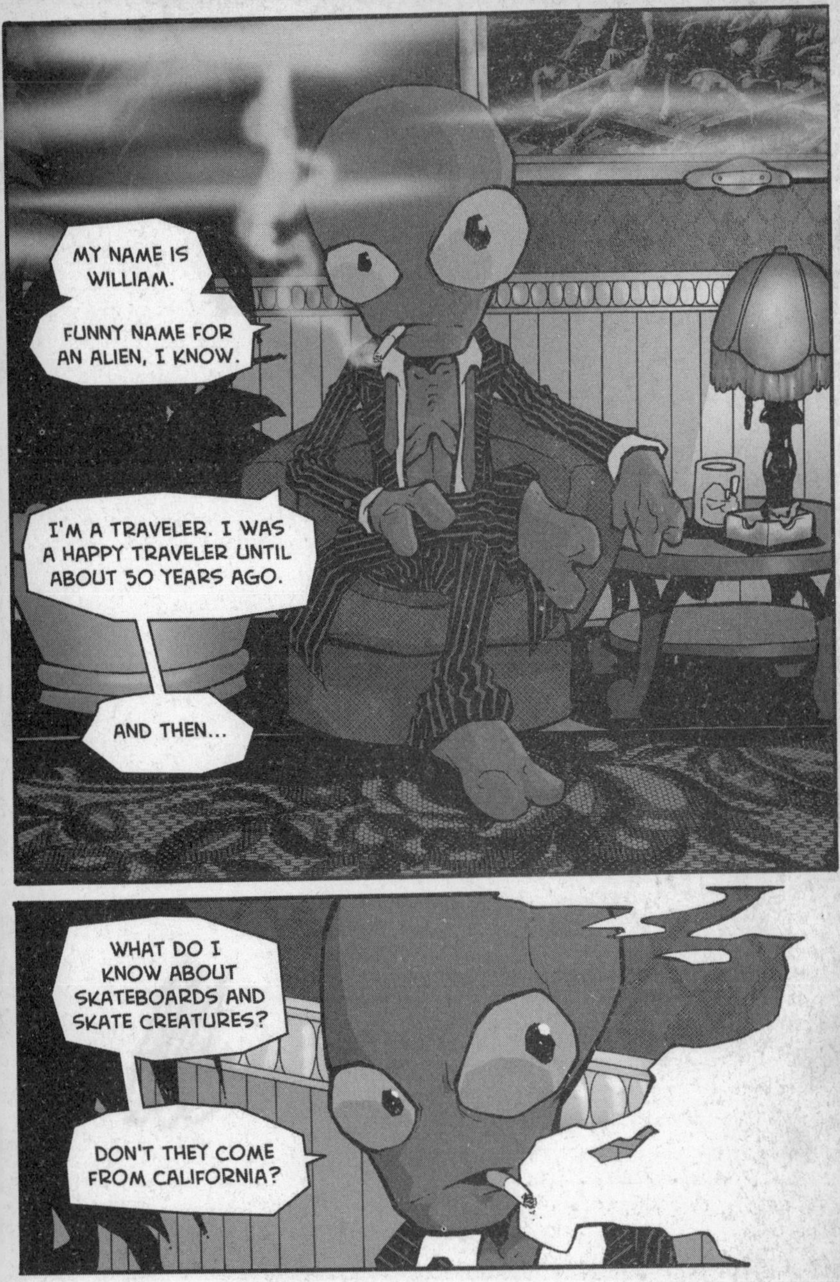
MY NAME IS WILLIAM.
FUNNY NAME FOR AN ALIEN, I KNOW.
I'M A TRAVELER. I WAS A HAPPY TRAVELER UNTIL ABOUT 50 YEARS AGO.
AND THEN...
WHAT DO I KNOW ABOUT SKATEBOARDS AND SKATE CREATURES?
DON'T THEY COME FROM CALIFORNIA?

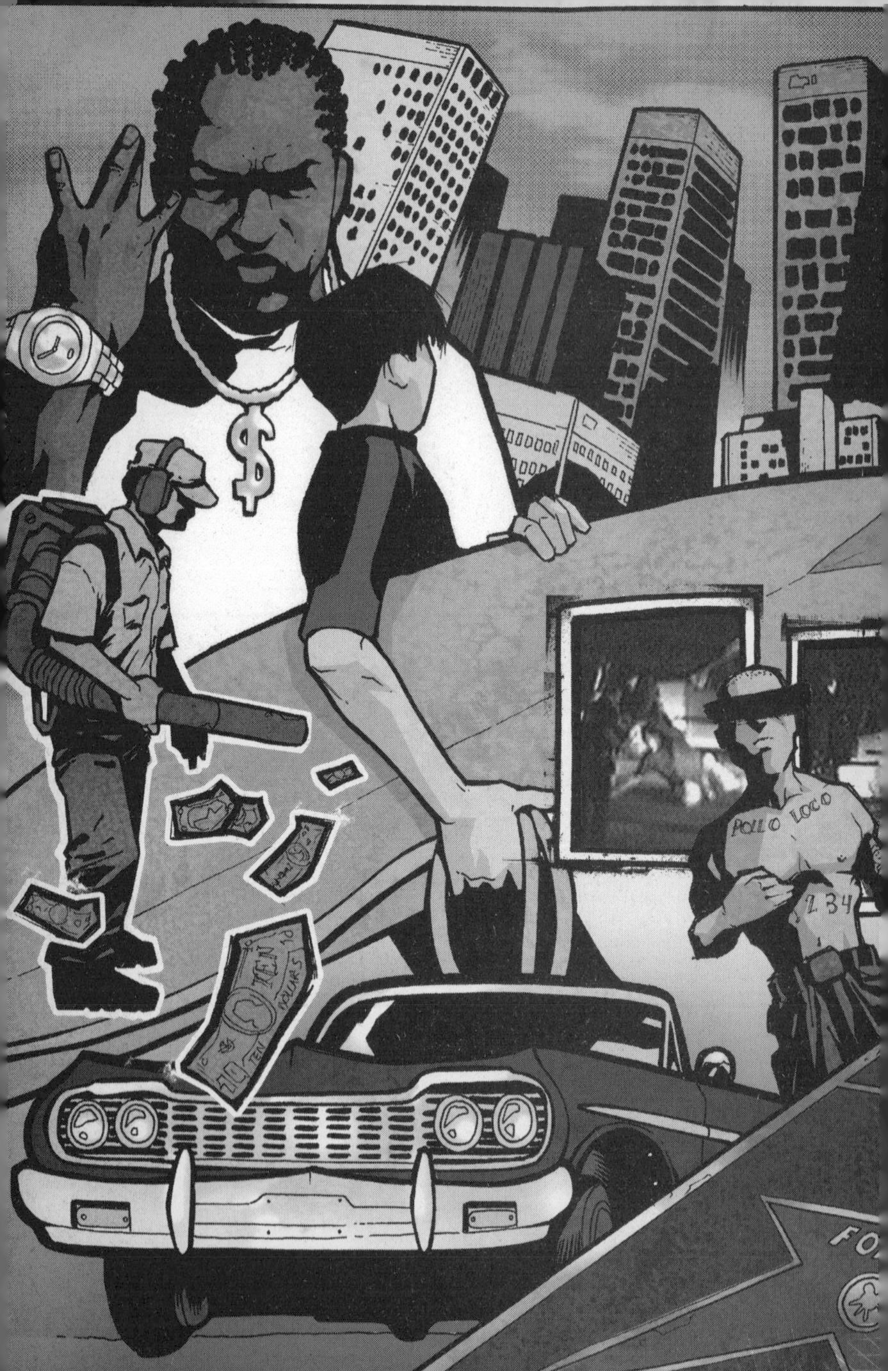
POLLO LOCO
234

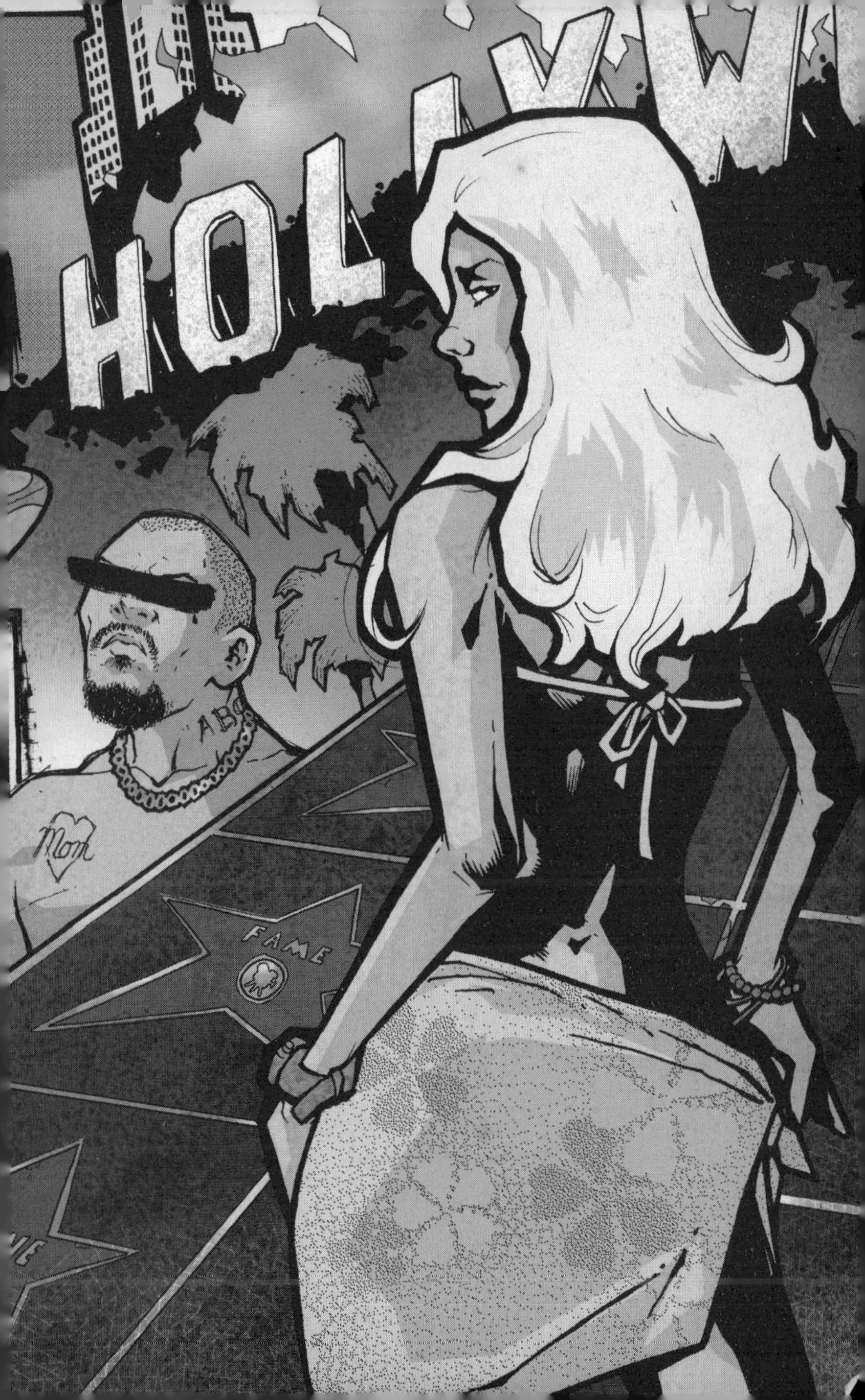
HOL
Mom
FAME

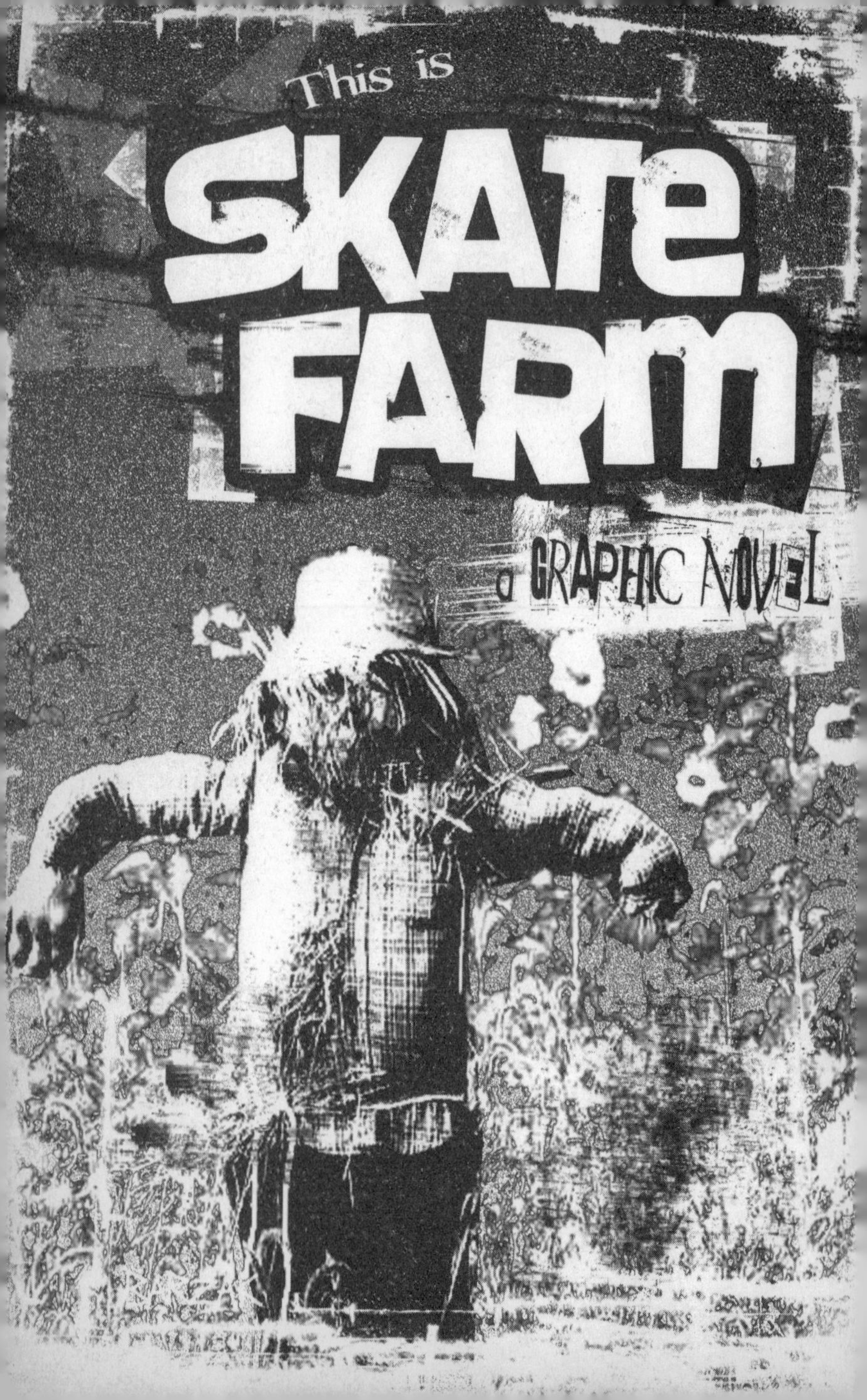
This is
SKATE FARM
a GRAPHIC NOVEL

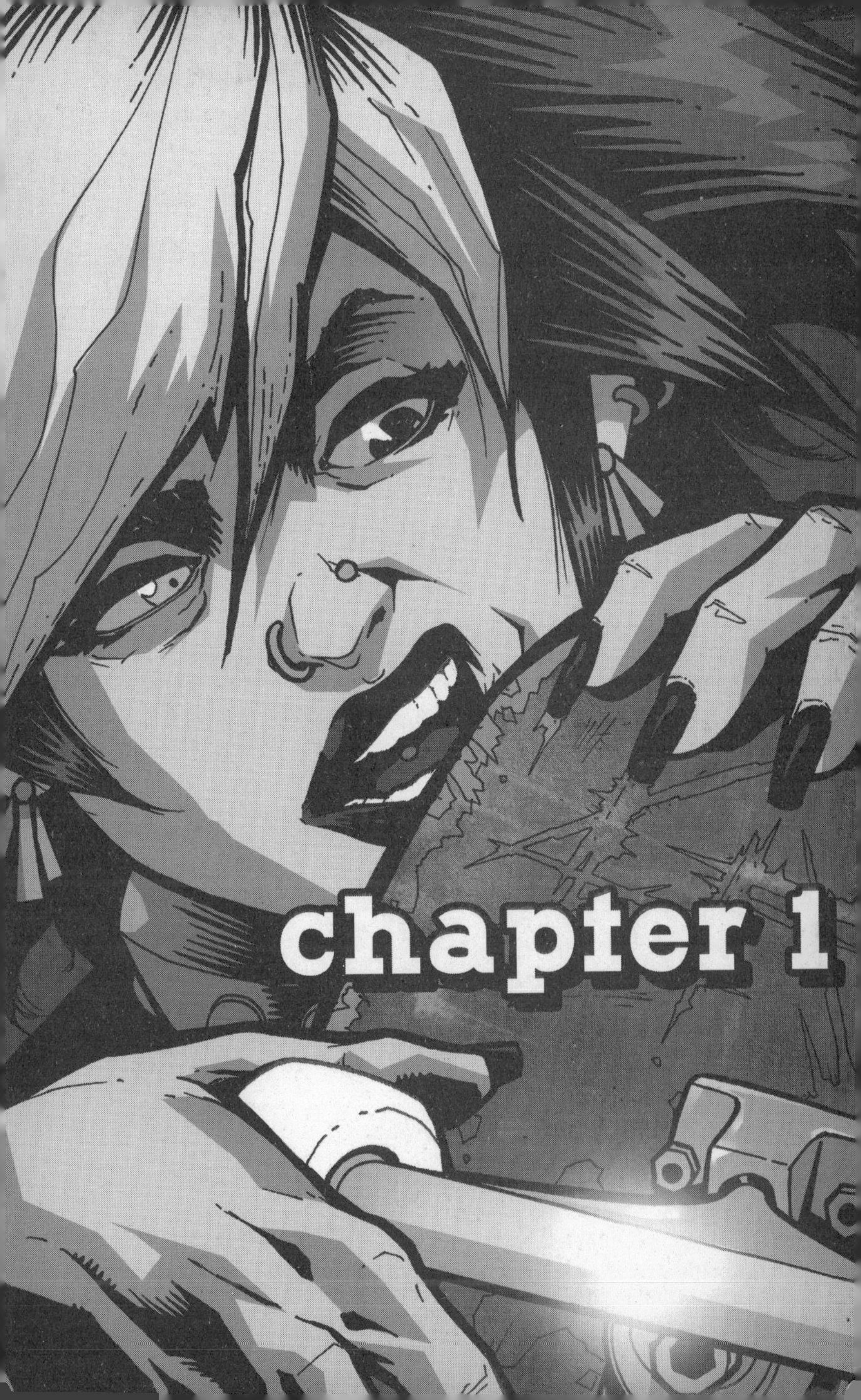
chapter 1

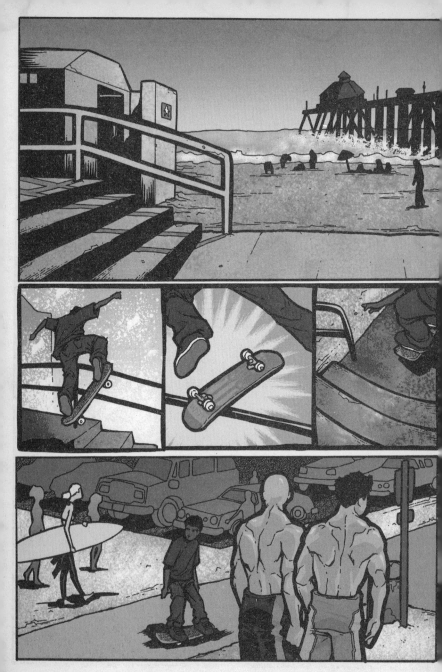

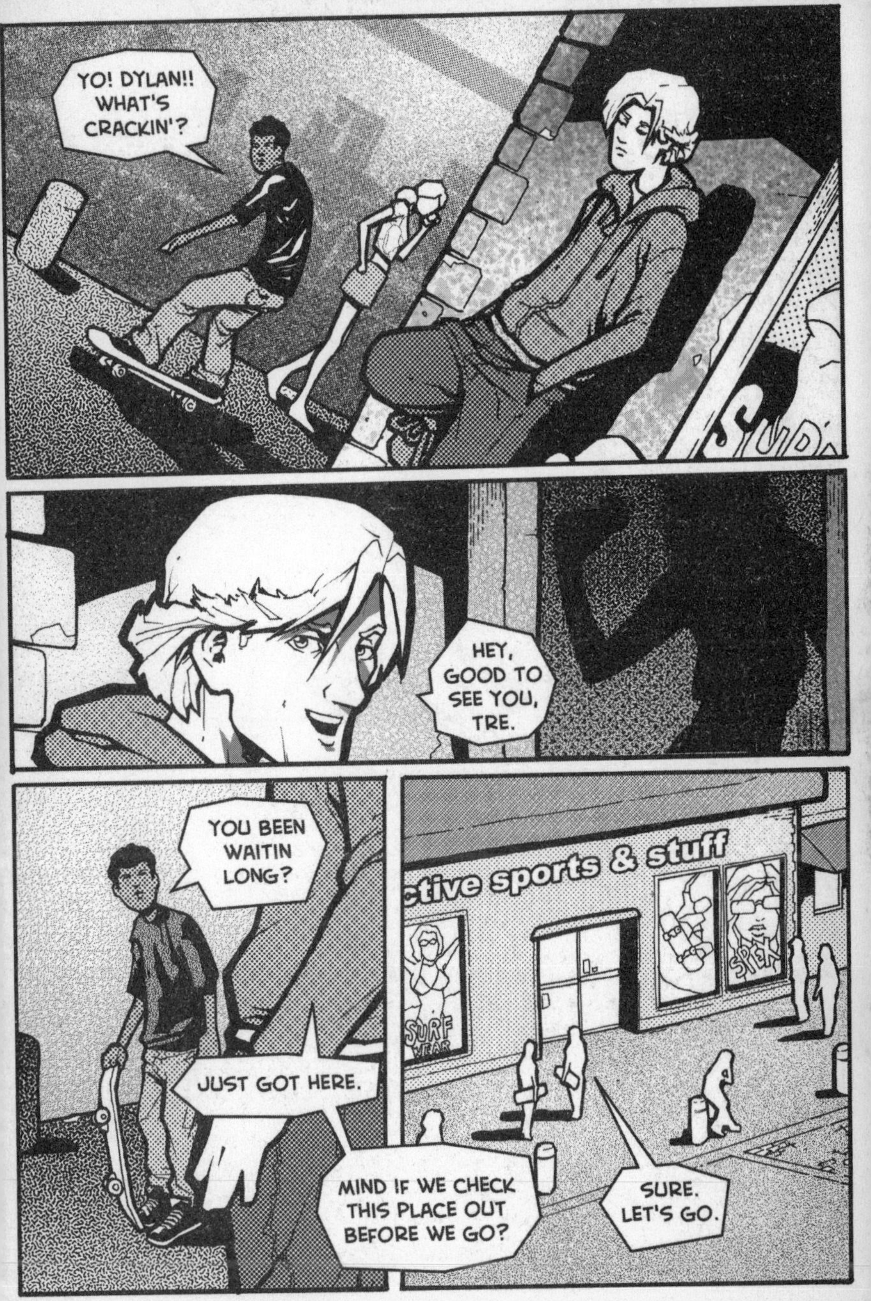
YO! DYLAN!! WHAT'S CRACKIN'?
HEY, GOOD TO SEE YOU, TRE.
YOU BEEN WAITIN LONG?
JUST GOT HERE.
ctive sports & stuff
SURF WEAR
SPEX
MIND IF WE CHECK THIS PLACE OUT BEFORE WE GO?
SURE. LET'S GO.

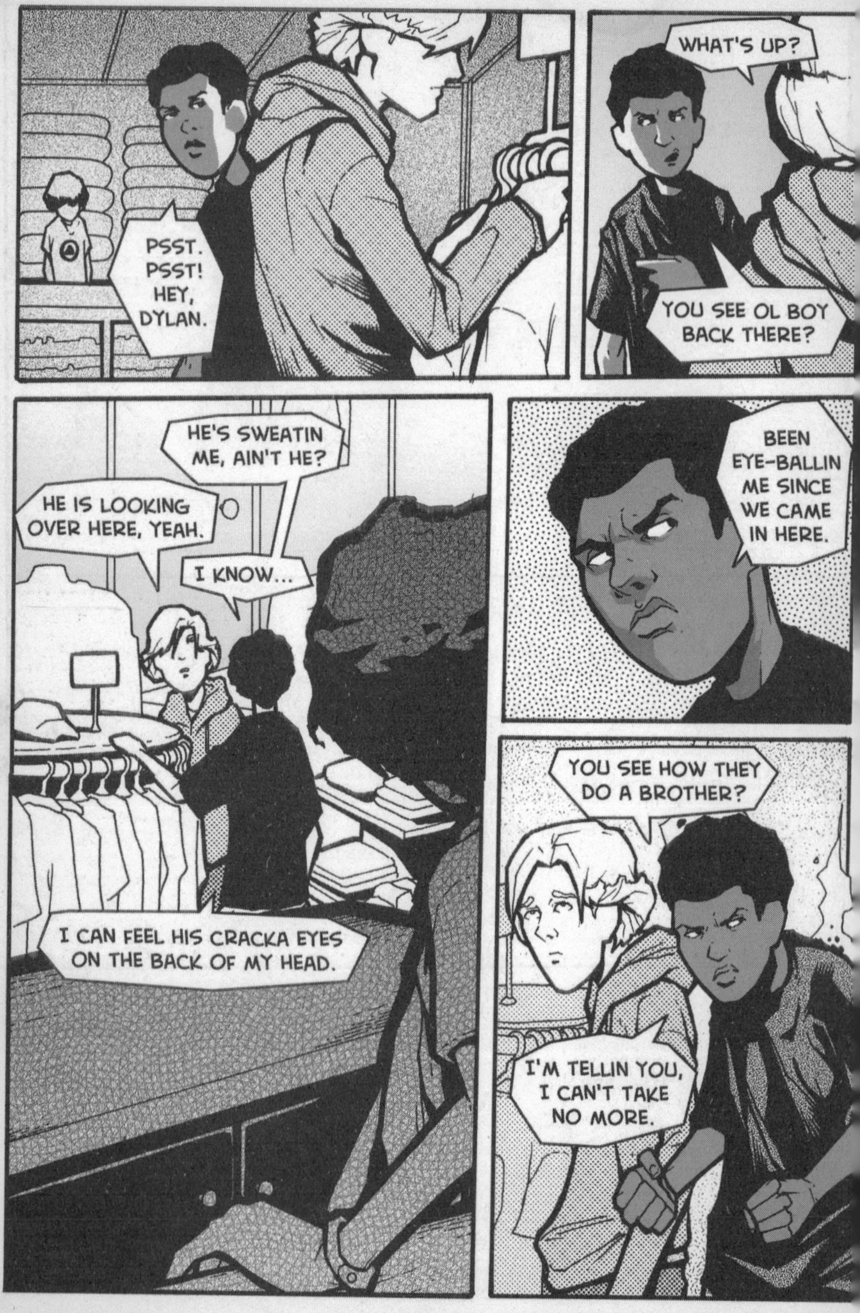
PSST.
PSST!
HEY,
DYLAN.
WHAT'S UP?
YOU SEE OL BOY BACK THERE?
HE'S SWEATIN ME, AIN'T HE?
HE IS LOOKING OVER HERE, YEAH.
I KNOW...
I CAN FEEL HIS CRACKA EYES ON THE BACK OF MY HEAD.
BEEN EYE-BALLIN ME SINCE WE CAME IN HERE.
YOU SEE HOW THEY DO A BROTHER?
I'M TELLIN YOU, I CAN'T TAKE NO MORE.

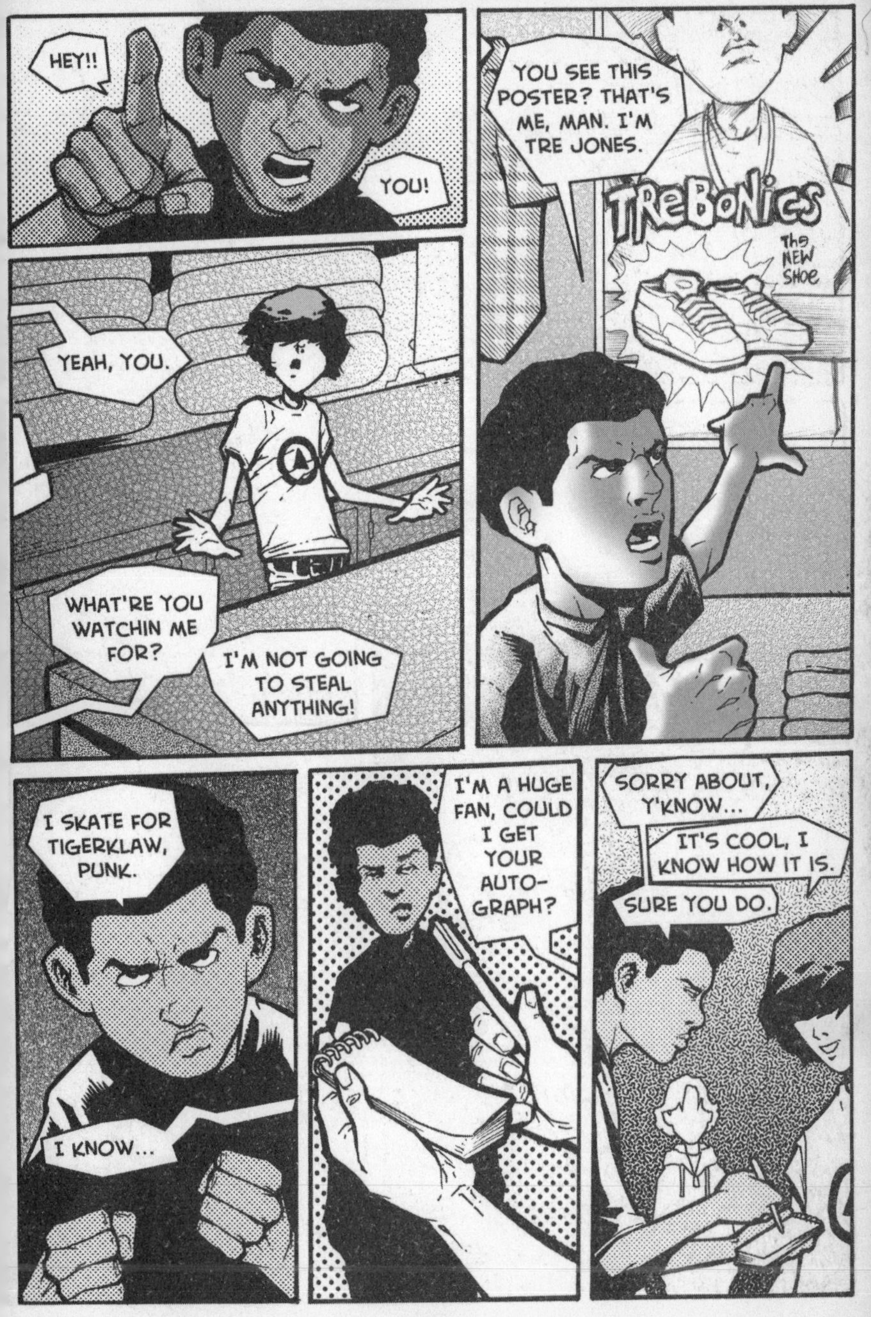
HEY!!
YOU!
YEAH, YOU.
WHAT'RE YOU WATCHIN ME FOR?
I'M NOT GOING TO STEAL ANYTHING!
YOU SEE THIS POSTER? THAT'S ME, MAN. I'M TRE JONES.
TREBONICS
The NEW SHOE
I SKATE FOR TIGERKLAW, PUNK.
I KNOW...
I'M A HUGE FAN, COULD I GET YOUR AUTO-GRAPH?
SORRY ABOUT, Y'KNOW...
IT'S COOL, I KNOW HOW IT IS.
SURE YOU DO.

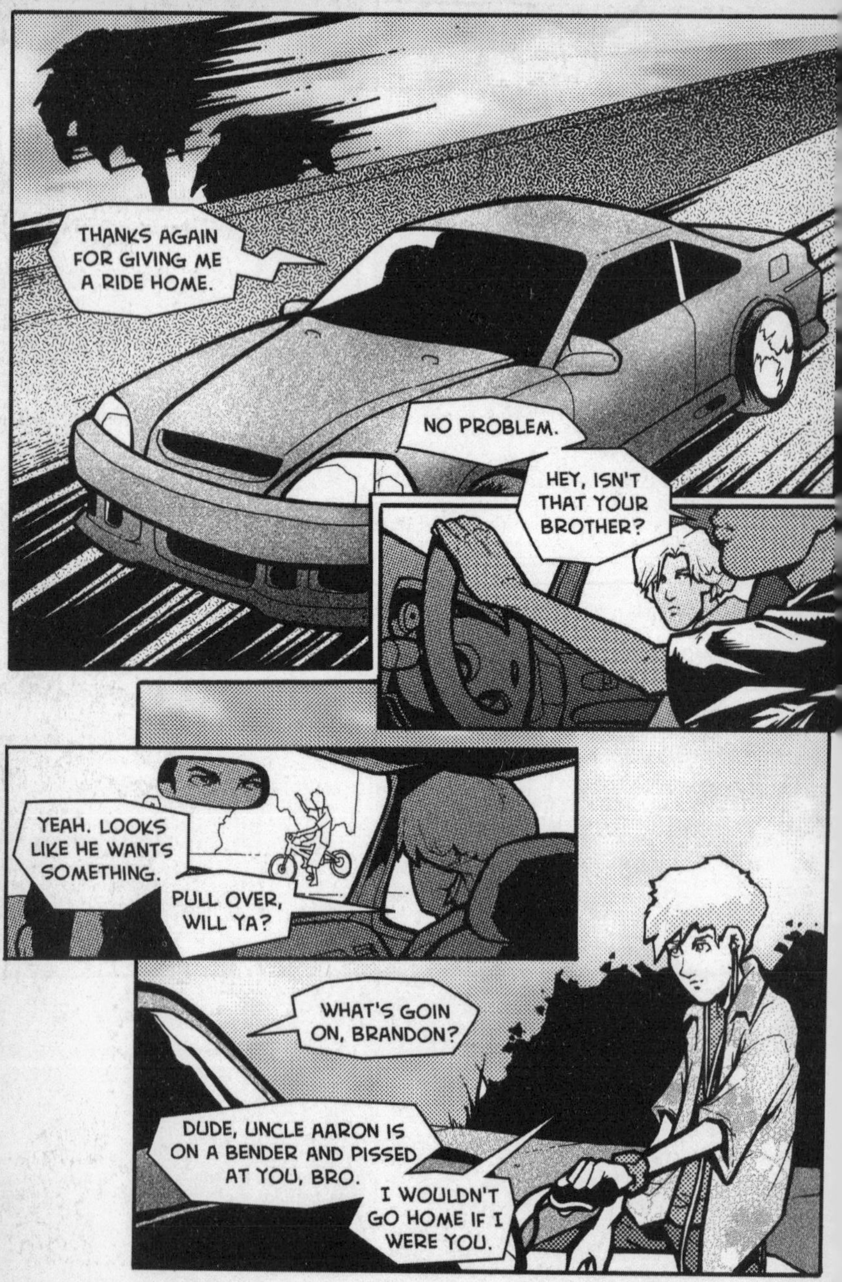
THANKS AGAIN FOR GIVING ME A RIDE HOME.
NO PROBLEM.
HEY, ISN'T THAT YOUR BROTHER?
YEAH. LOOKS LIKE HE WANTS SOMETHING.
PULL OVER, WILL YA?
WHAT'S GOIN ON, BRANDON?
DUDE, UNCLE AARON IS ON A BENDER AND PISSED AT YOU, BRO.
I WOULDN'T GO HOME IF I WERE YOU.

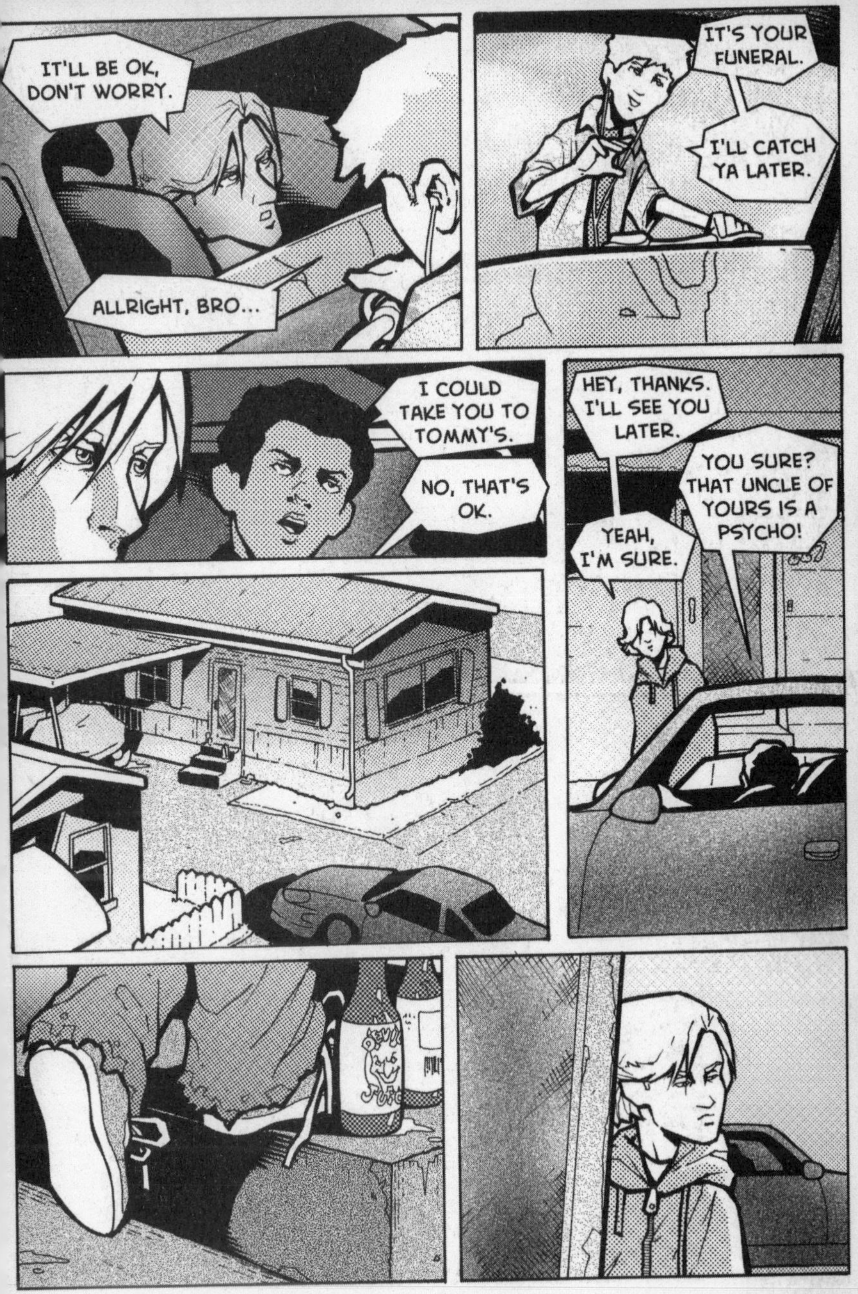
IT'LL BE OK, DON'T WORRY.
ALLRIGHT, BRO...
IT'S YOUR FUNERAL.
I'LL CATCH YA LATER.
I COULD TAKE YOU TO TOMMY'S.
NO, THAT'S OK.
HEY, THANKS. I'LL SEE YOU LATER.
YOU SURE? THAT UNCLE OF YOURS IS A PSYCHO!
YEAH, I'M SURE.

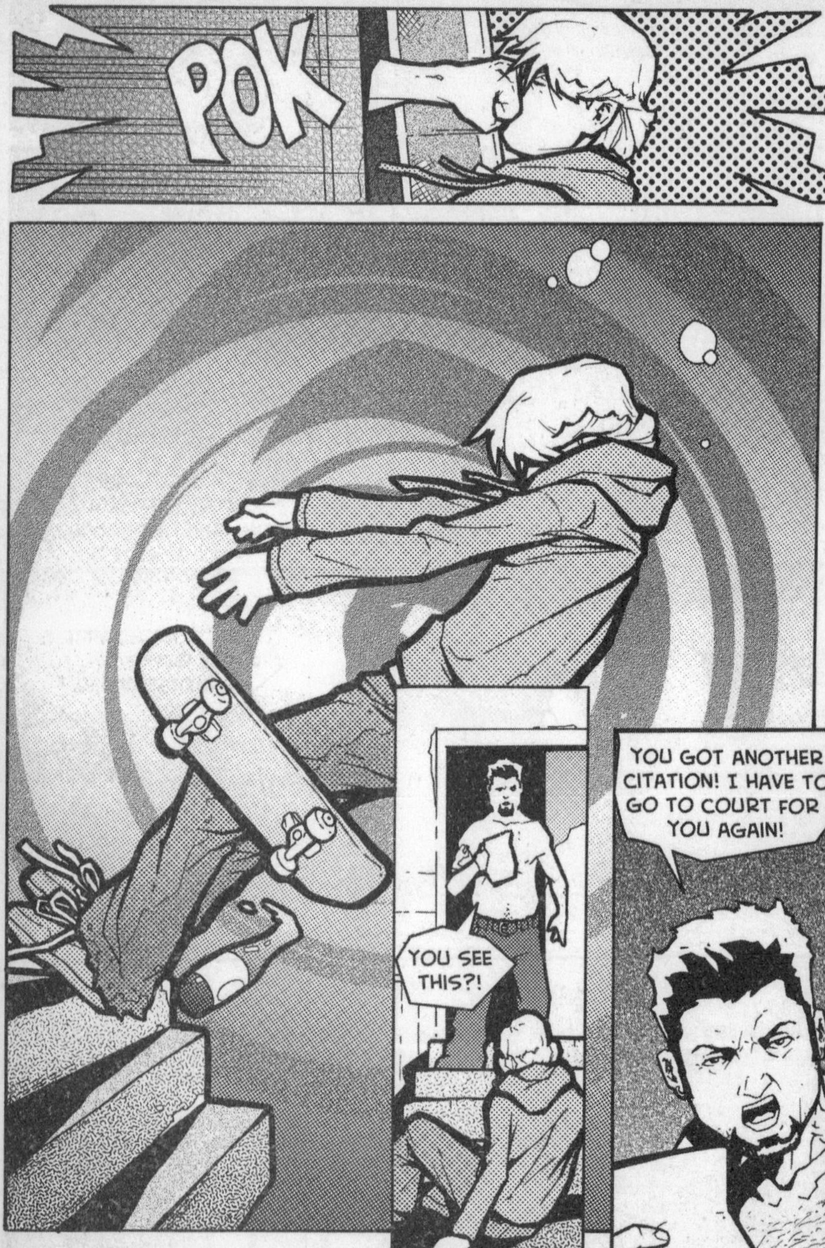
POK
YOU SEE THIS?!
YOU GOT ANOTHER CITATION! I HAVE TO GO TO COURT FOR YOU AGAIN!

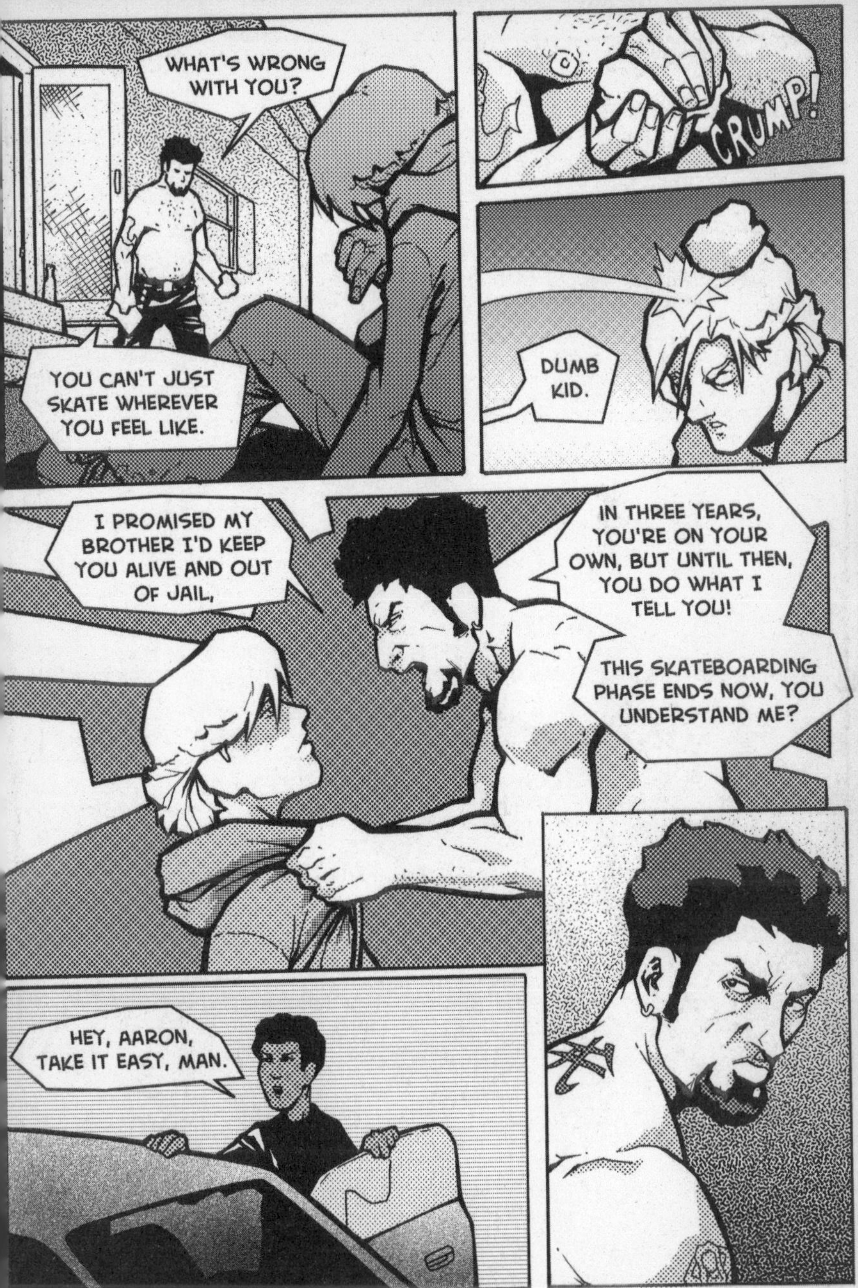
WHAT'S WRONG WITH YOU?
YOU CAN'T JUST SKATE WHEREVER YOU FEEL LIKE.
CRUMP!
DUMB KID.
I PROMISED MY BROTHER I'D KEEP YOU ALIVE AND OUT OF JAIL,
IN THREE YEARS, YOU'RE ON YOUR OWN, BUT UNTIL THEN, YOU DO WHAT I TELL YOU!
THIS SKATEBOARDING PHASE ENDS NOW, YOU UNDERSTAND ME?
HEY, AARON, TAKE IT EASY, MAN.

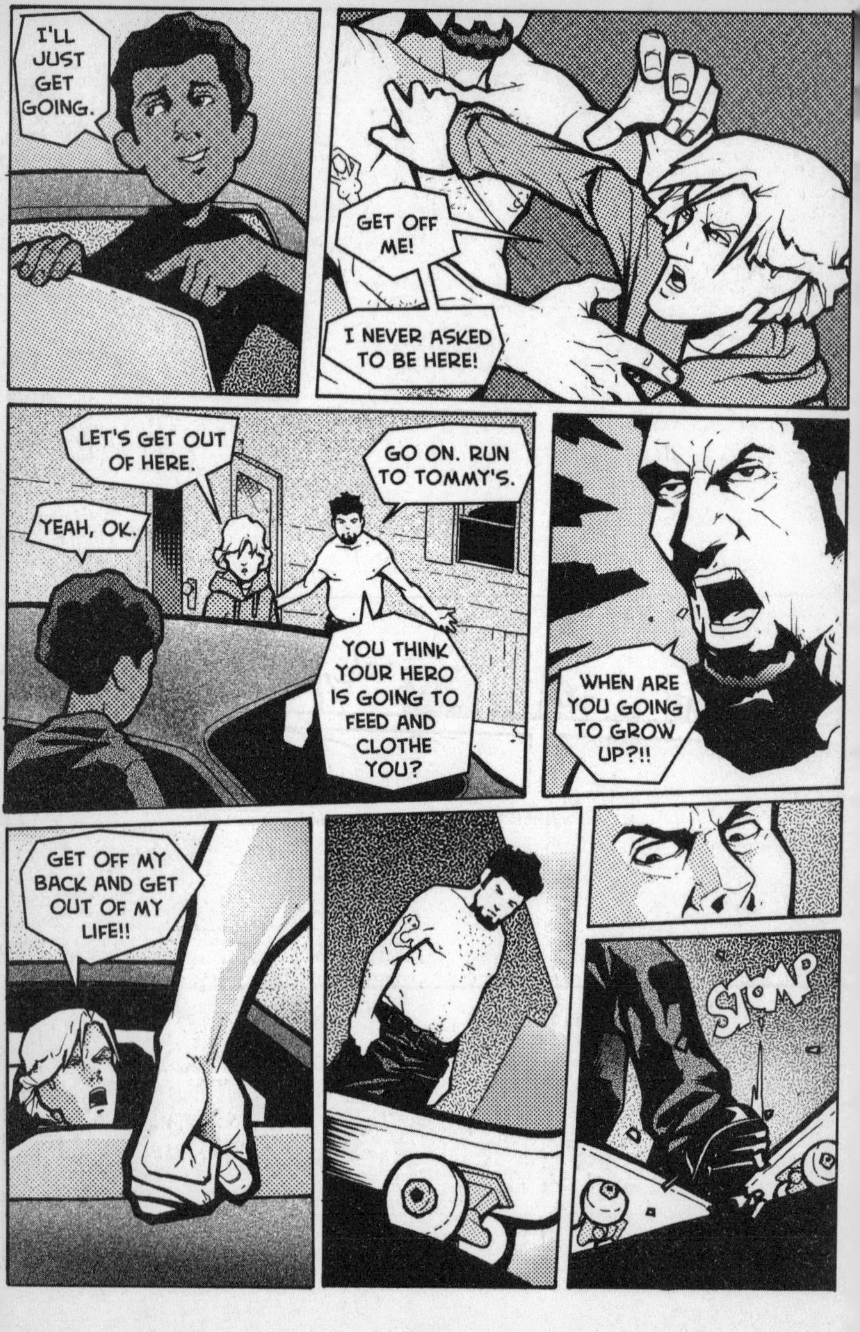
I'LL JUST GET GOING.
GET OFF ME!
I NEVER ASKED TO BE HERE!
LET'S GET OUT OF HERE.
YEAH, OK.
GO ON. RUN TO TOMMY'S.
YOU THINK YOUR HERO IS GOING TO FEED AND CLOTHE YOU?
WHEN ARE YOU GOING TO GROW UP?!!
GET OFF MY BACK AND GET OUT OF MY LIFE!!
STOMP

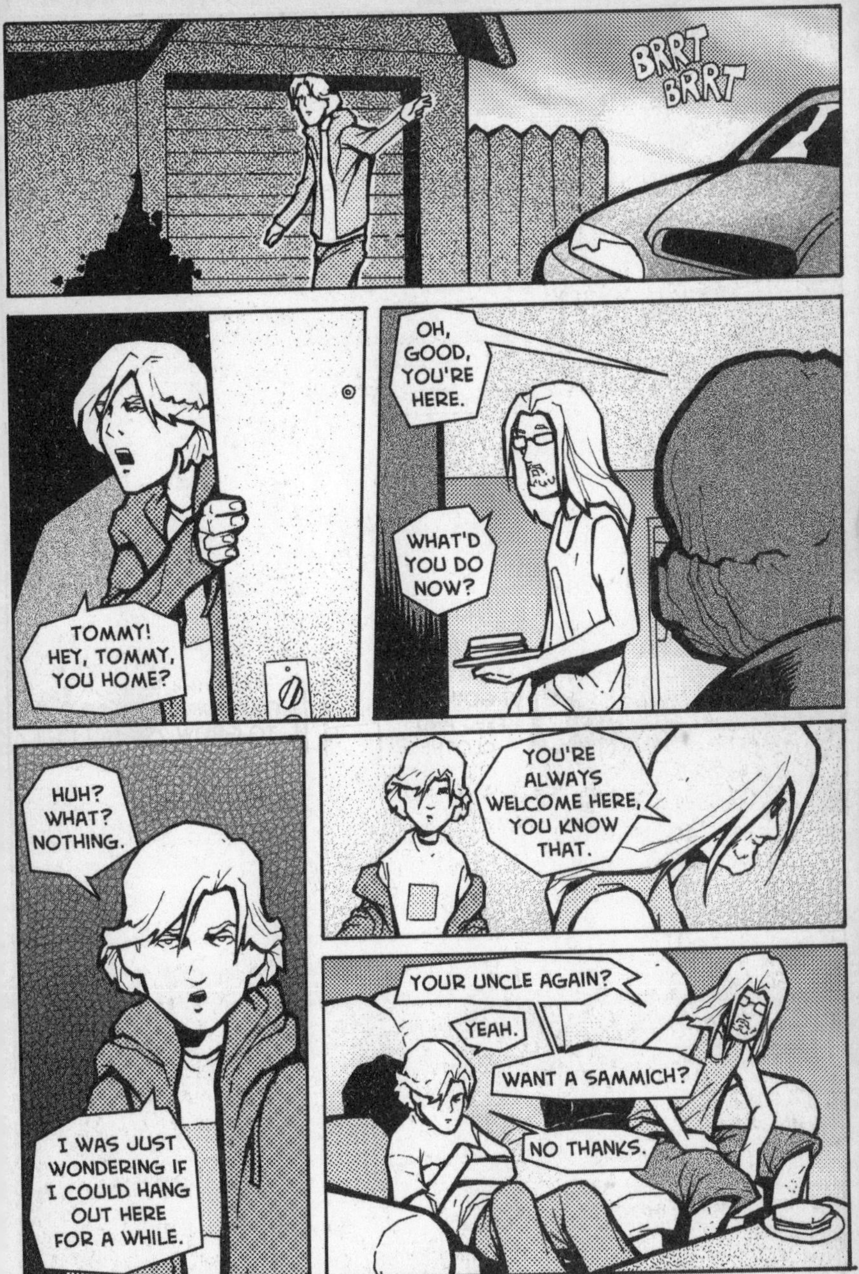
BRRT BRRT
TOMMY! HEY, TOMMY, YOU HOME?
OH, GOOD, YOU'RE HERE.
WHAT'D YOU DO NOW?
HUH? WHAT? NOTHING.
I WAS JUST WONDERING IF I COULD HANG OUT HERE FOR A WHILE.
YOU'RE ALWAYS WELCOME HERE, YOU KNOW THAT.
YOUR UNCLE AGAIN?
YEAH.
WANT A SAMMICH?
NO THANKS.

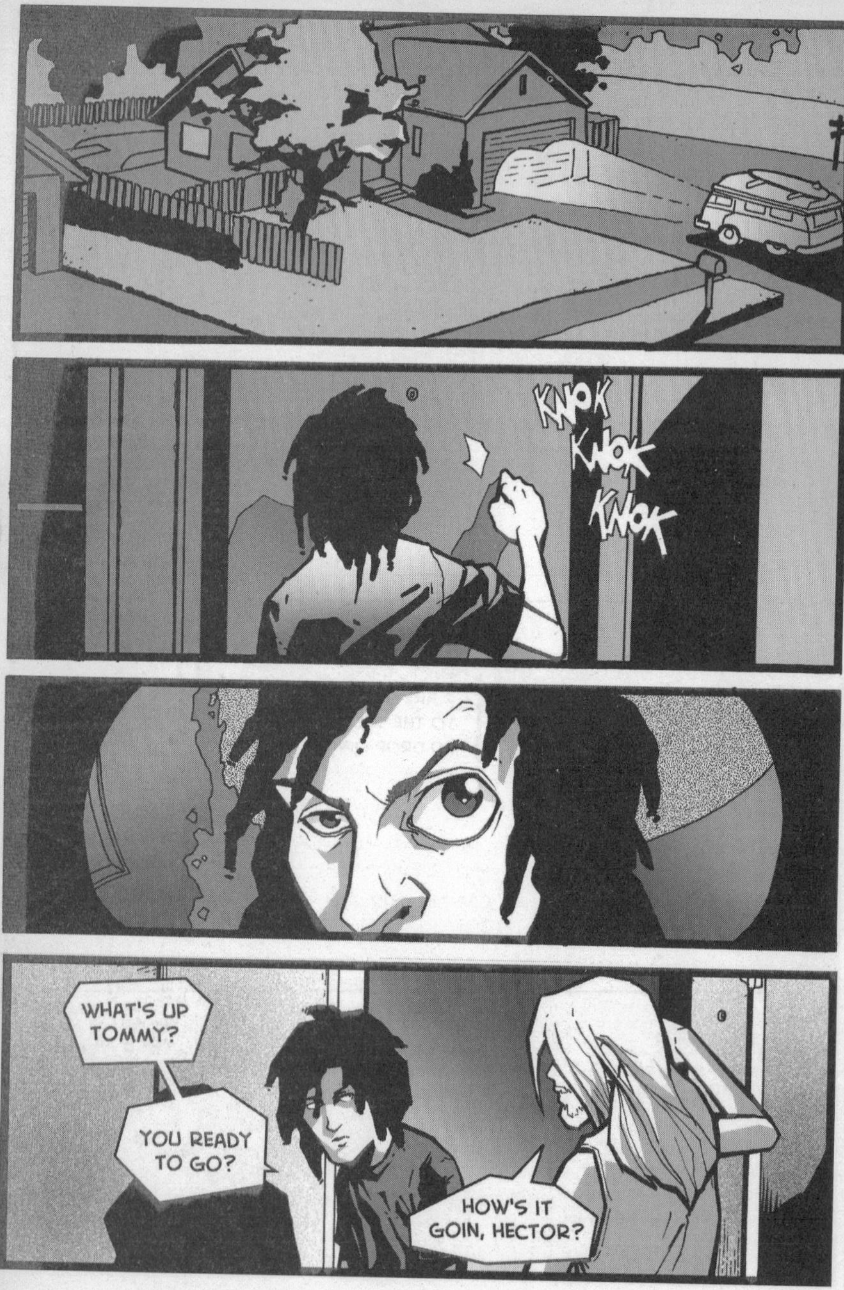
KNOK
KNOK
KNOK
WHAT'S UP TOMMY?
YOU READY TO GO?
HOW'S IT GOIN, HECTOR?

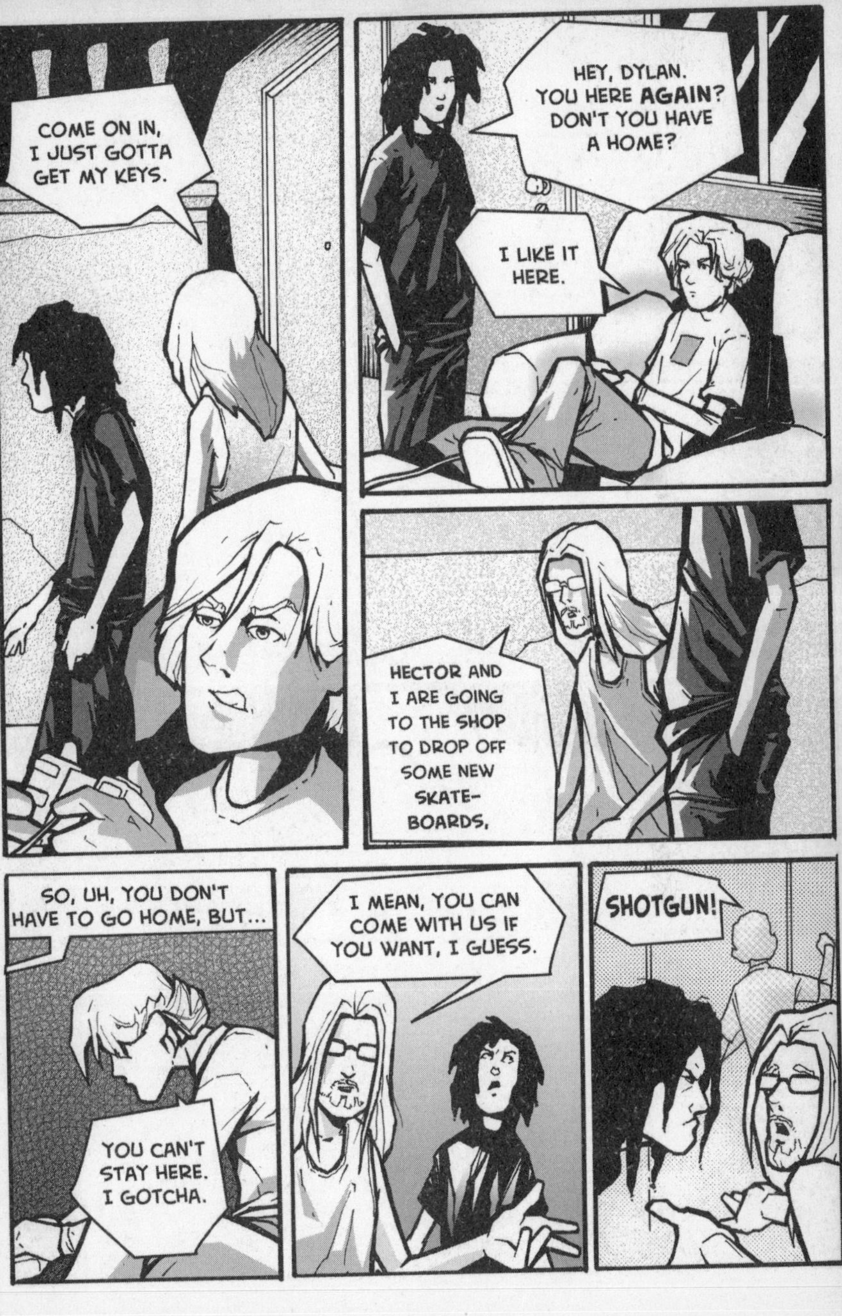
COME ON IN, I JUST GOTTA GET MY KEYS.
HEY, DYLAN. YOU HERE AGAIN? DON'T YOU HAVE A HOME?
I LIKE IT HERE.
HECTOR AND I ARE GOING TO THE SHOP TO DROP OFF SOME NEW SKATE-BOARDS,
SO, UH, YOU DON'T HAVE TO GO HOME, BUT...
YOU CAN'T STAY HERE. I GOTCHA.
I MEAN, YOU CAN COME WITH US IF YOU WANT, I GUESS.
SHOTGUN!

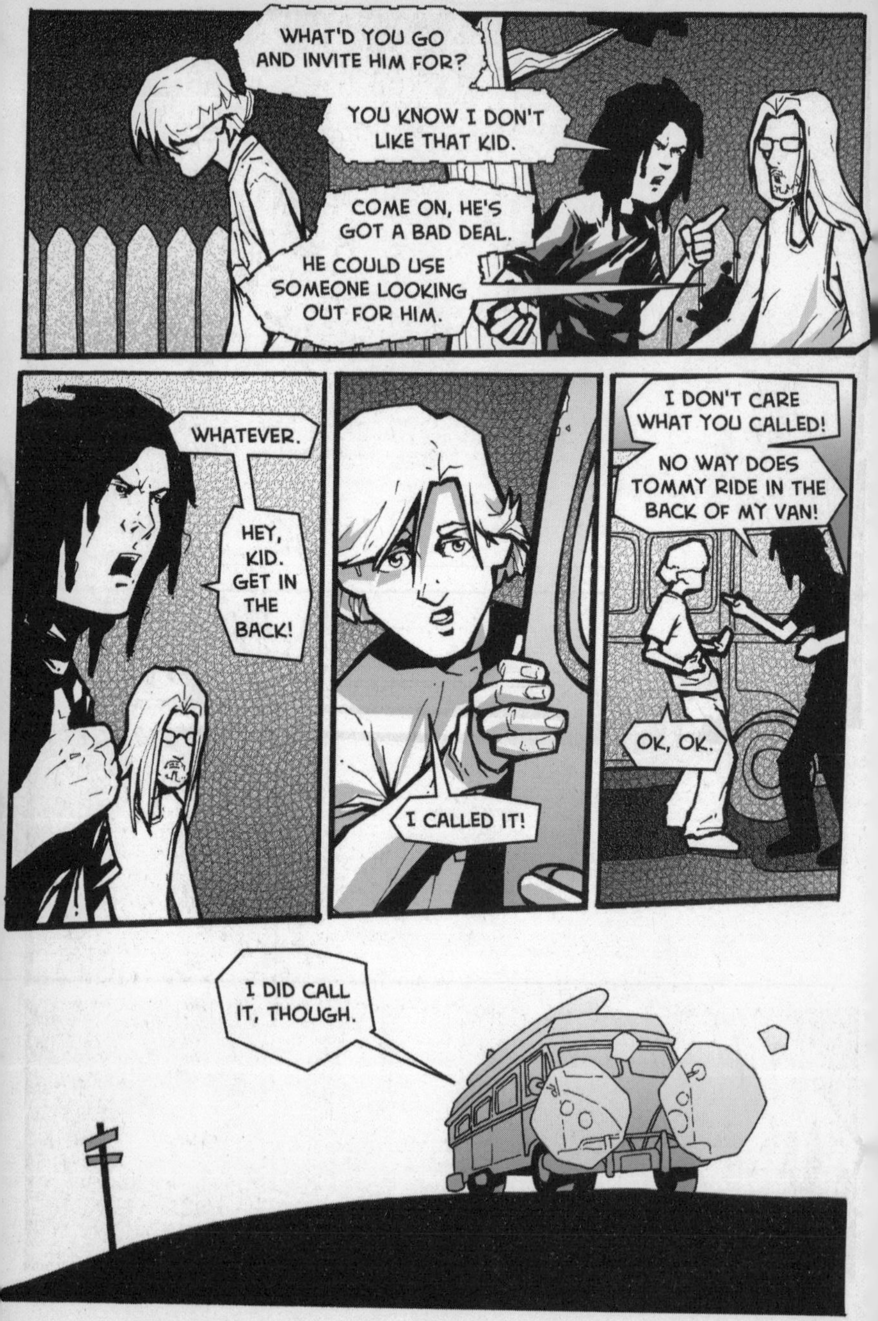
WHAT'D YOU GO AND INVITE HIM FOR?
YOU KNOW I DON'T LIKE THAT KID.
COME ON, HE'S GOT A BAD DEAL.
HE COULD USE SOMEONE LOOKING OUT FOR HIM.
WHATEVER.
HEY, KID. GET IN THE BACK!
I CALLED IT!
I DON'T CARE WHAT YOU CALLED!
NO WAY DOES TOMMY RIDE IN THE BACK OF MY VAN!
OK, OK.
I DID CALL IT, THOUGH.

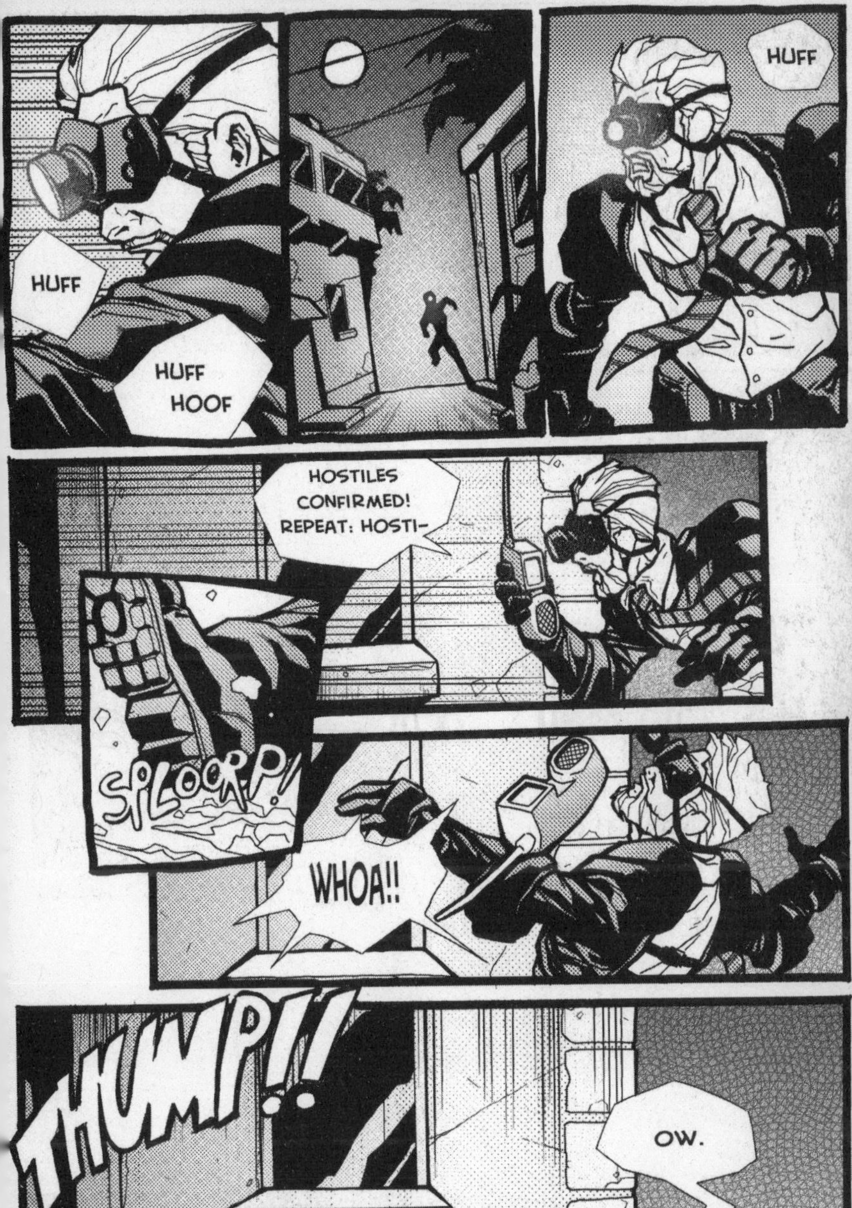
HUFF
HUFF
HOOF
HUFF
HOSTILES CONFIRMED! REPEAT: HOSTI-
SPLOORP!
WHOA!!
THUMP!!
OW.

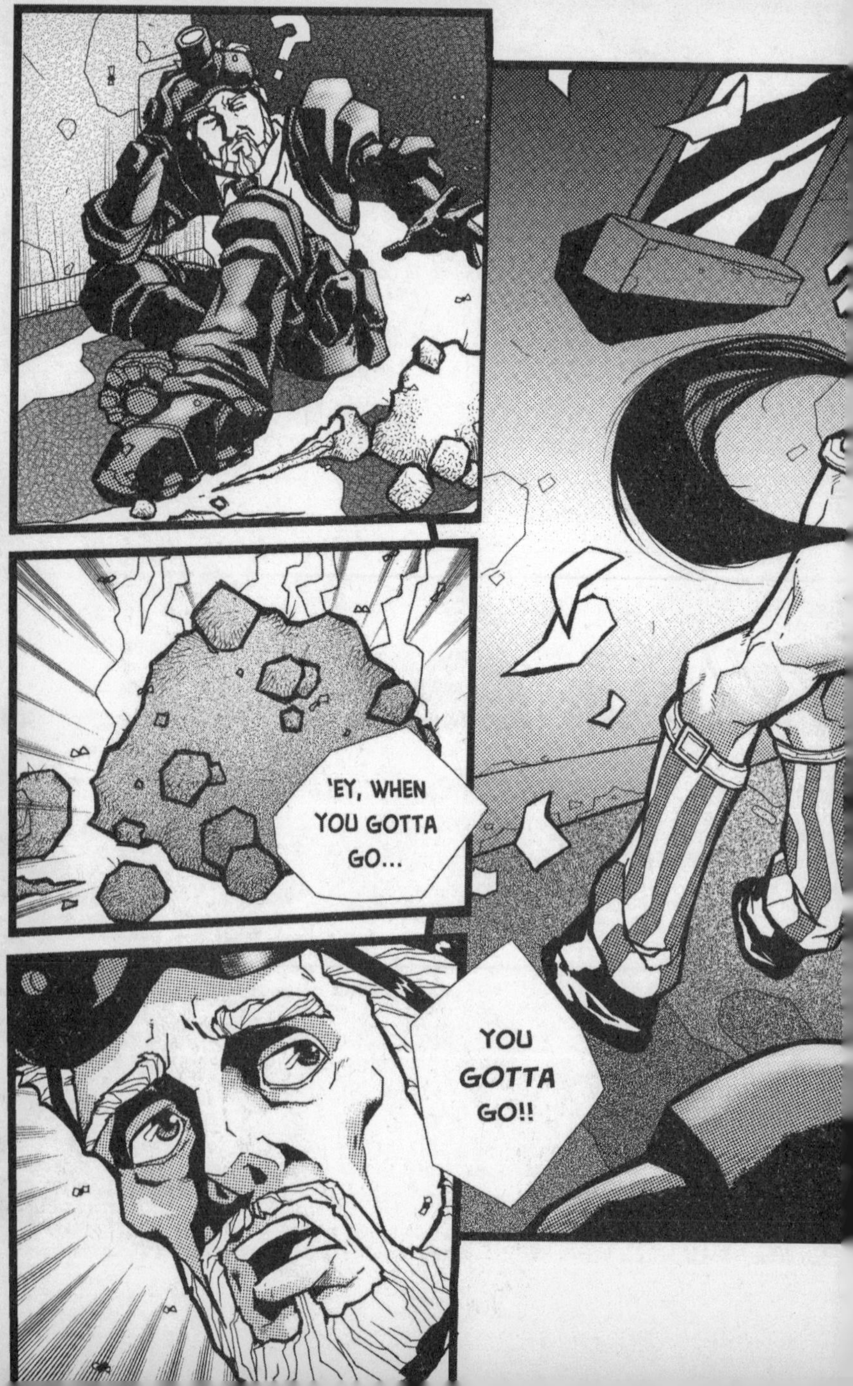
?
'EY, WHEN YOU GOTTA GO...
YOU GOTTA GO!!

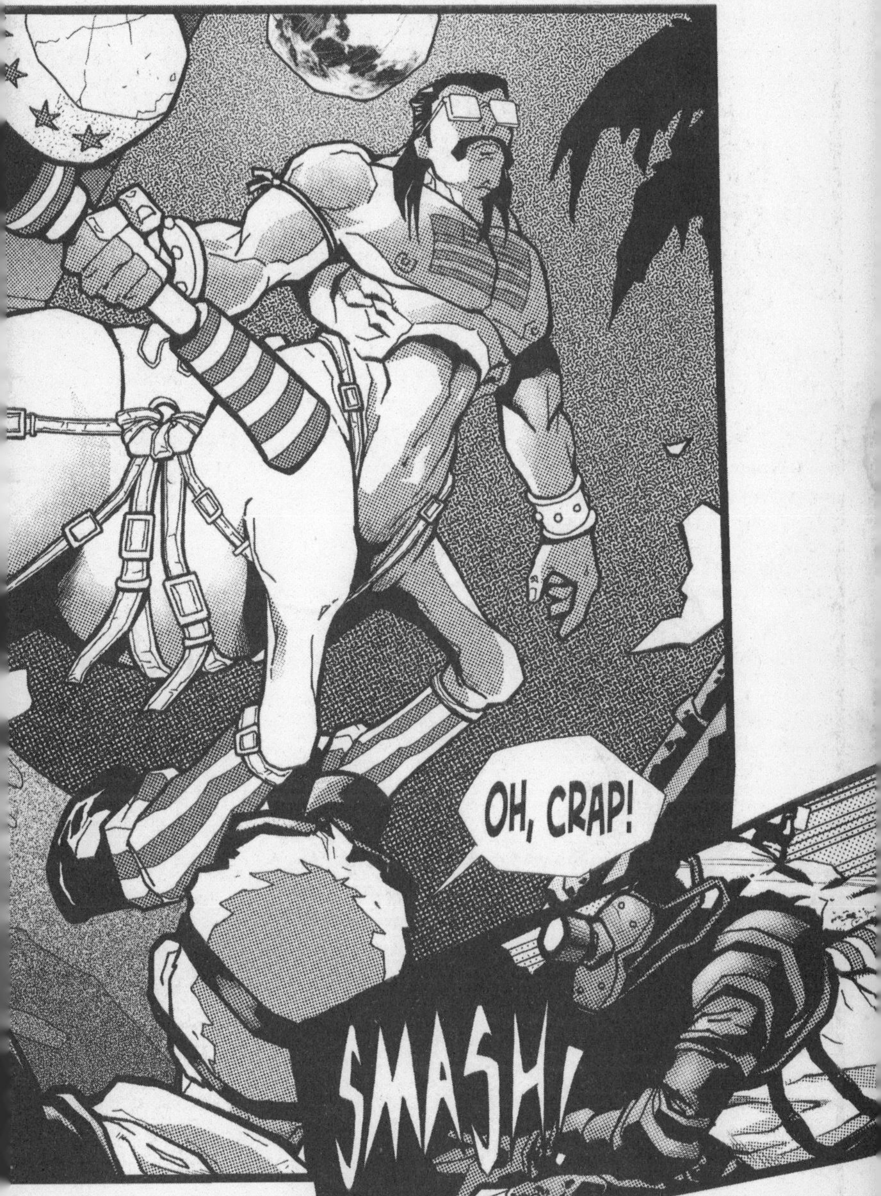
OH, CRAP!
SMASH!

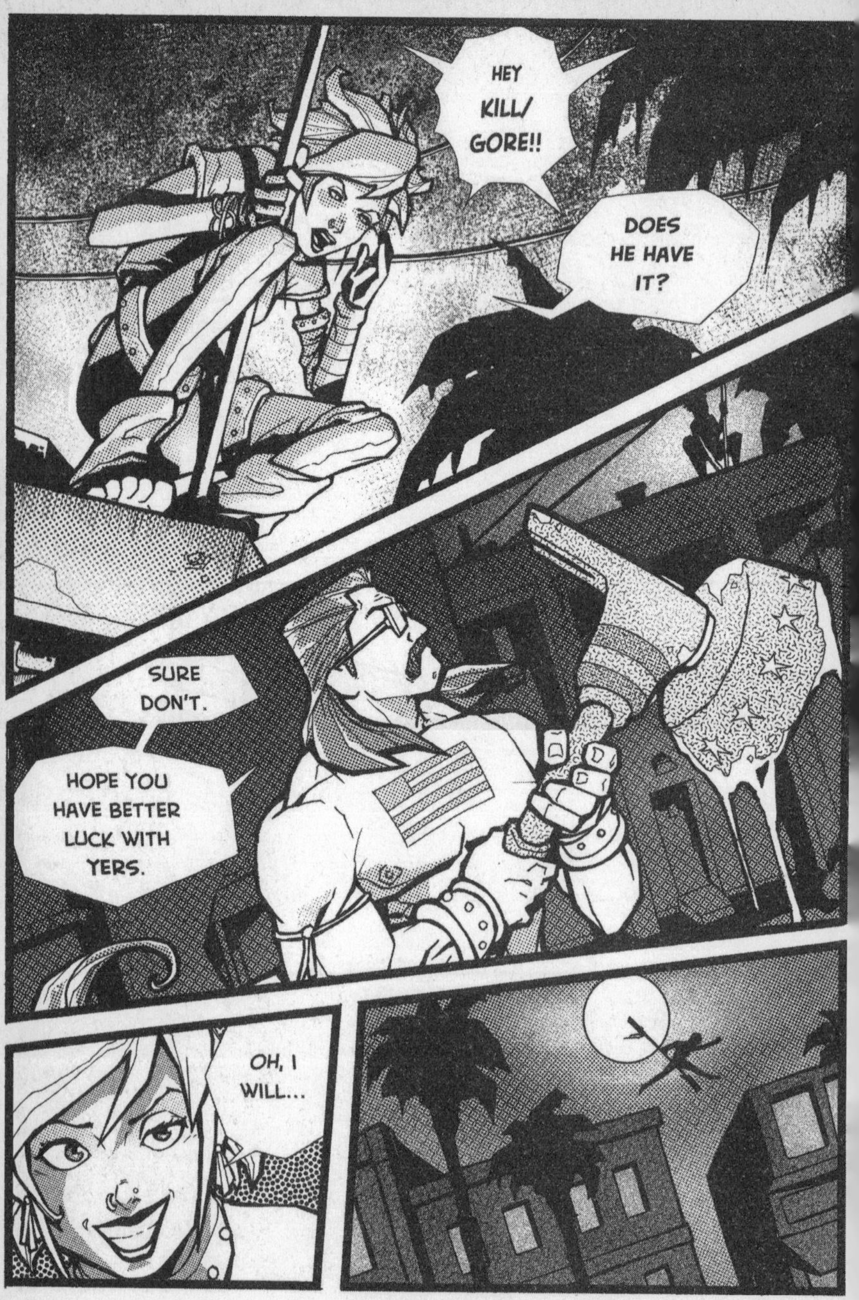
HEY KILL/ GORE!!
DOES HE HAVE IT?
SURE DON'T.
HOPE YOU HAVE BETTER LUCK WITH YERS.
OH, I WILL...

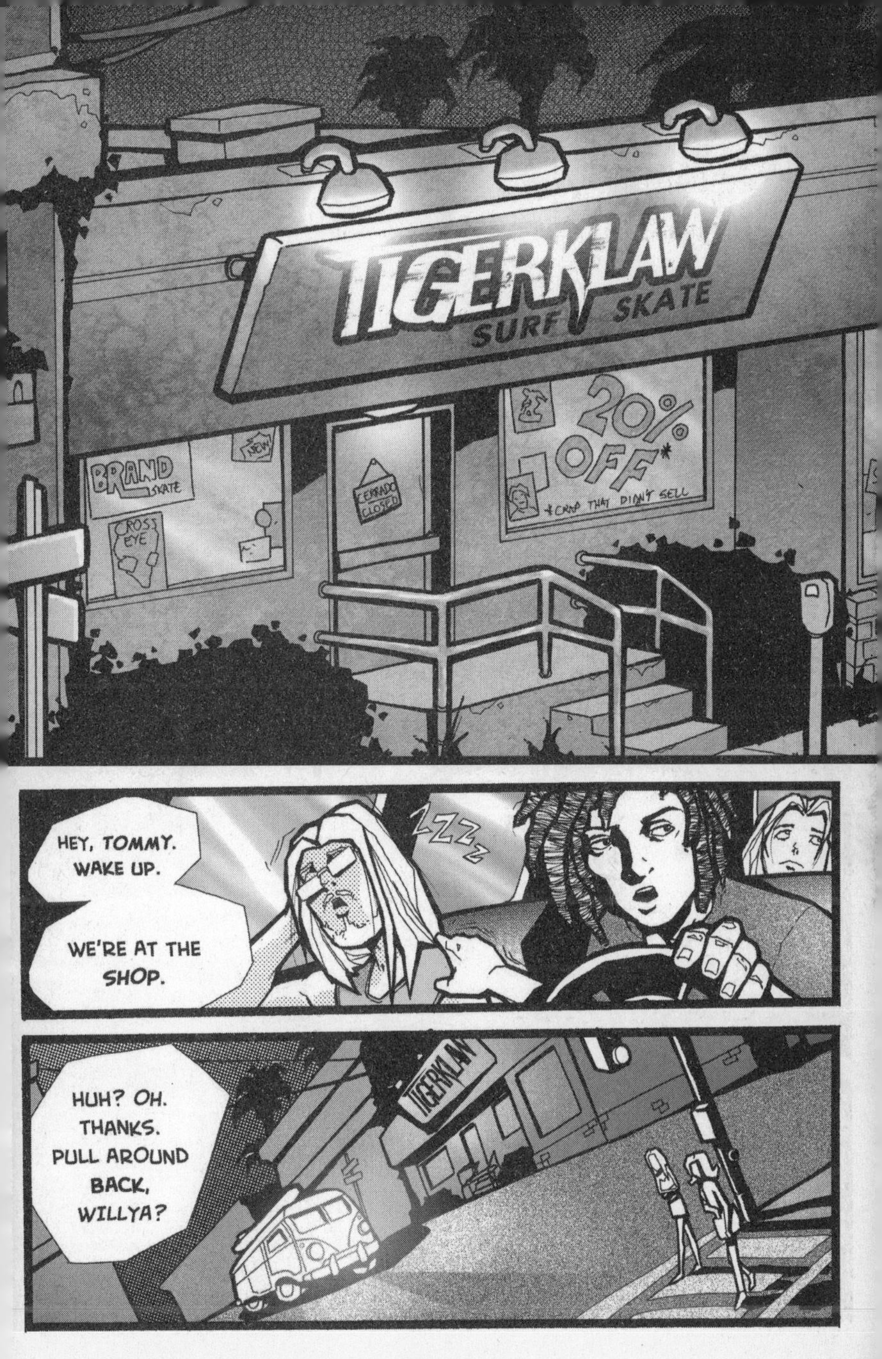
TIGERKLAW
SURF SKATE
BRAND SKATE
NEW
CROSS EYE
CERRADO CLOSED
20% OFF*
*CRAP THAT DIDN'T SELL
HEY, TOMMY. WAKE UP.
ZZZZ
WE'RE AT THE SHOP.
TIGERKLAW
HUH? OH. THANKS. PULL AROUND BACK, WILLYA?

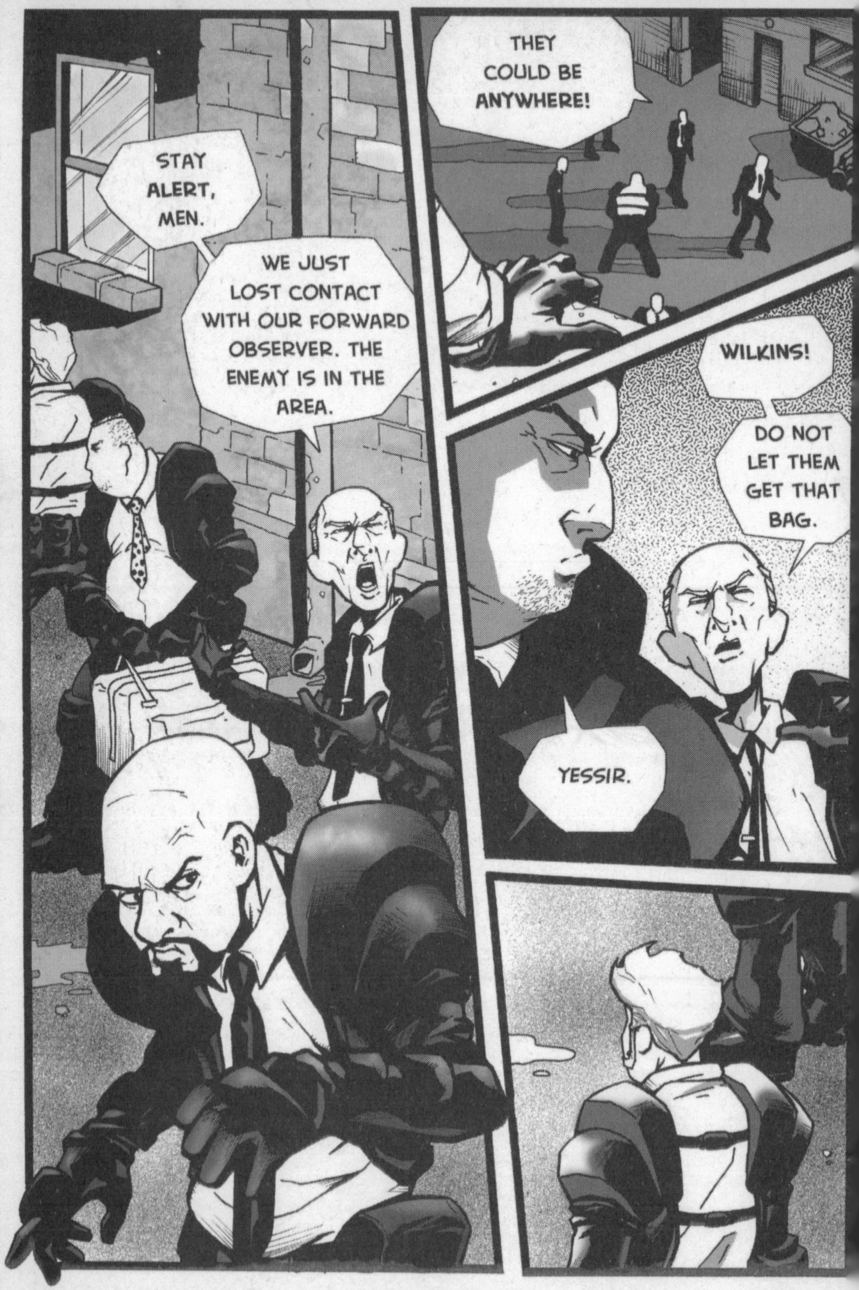
STAY ALERT, MEN.
WE JUST LOST CONTACT WITH OUR FORWARD OBSERVER. THE ENEMY IS IN THE AREA.
THEY COULD BE ANYWHERE!
WILKINS!
DO NOT LET THEM GET THAT BAG.
YESSIR.

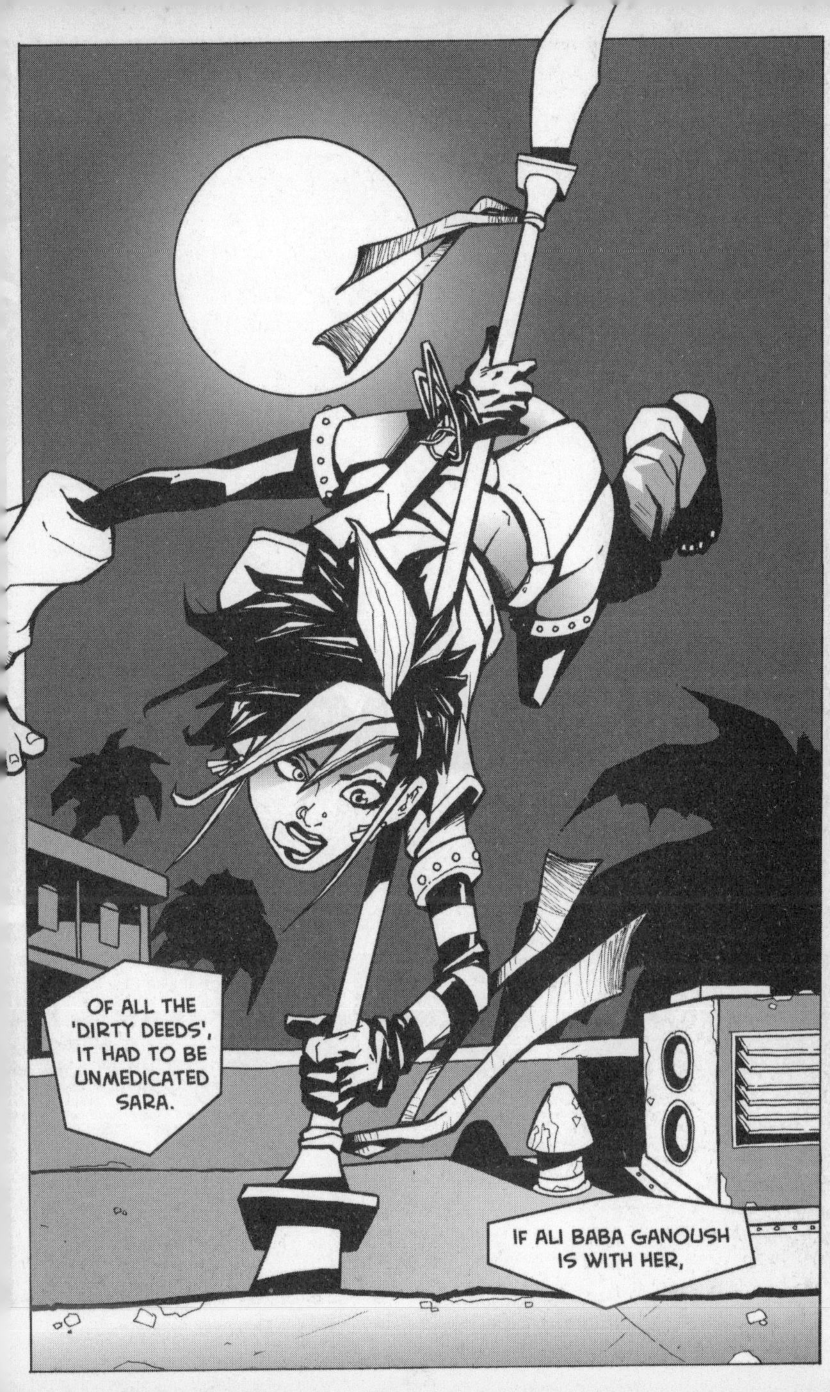
OF ALL THE 'DIRTY DEEDS', IT HAD TO BE UNMEDICATED SARA.
IF ALI BABA GANOUSH IS WITH HER,

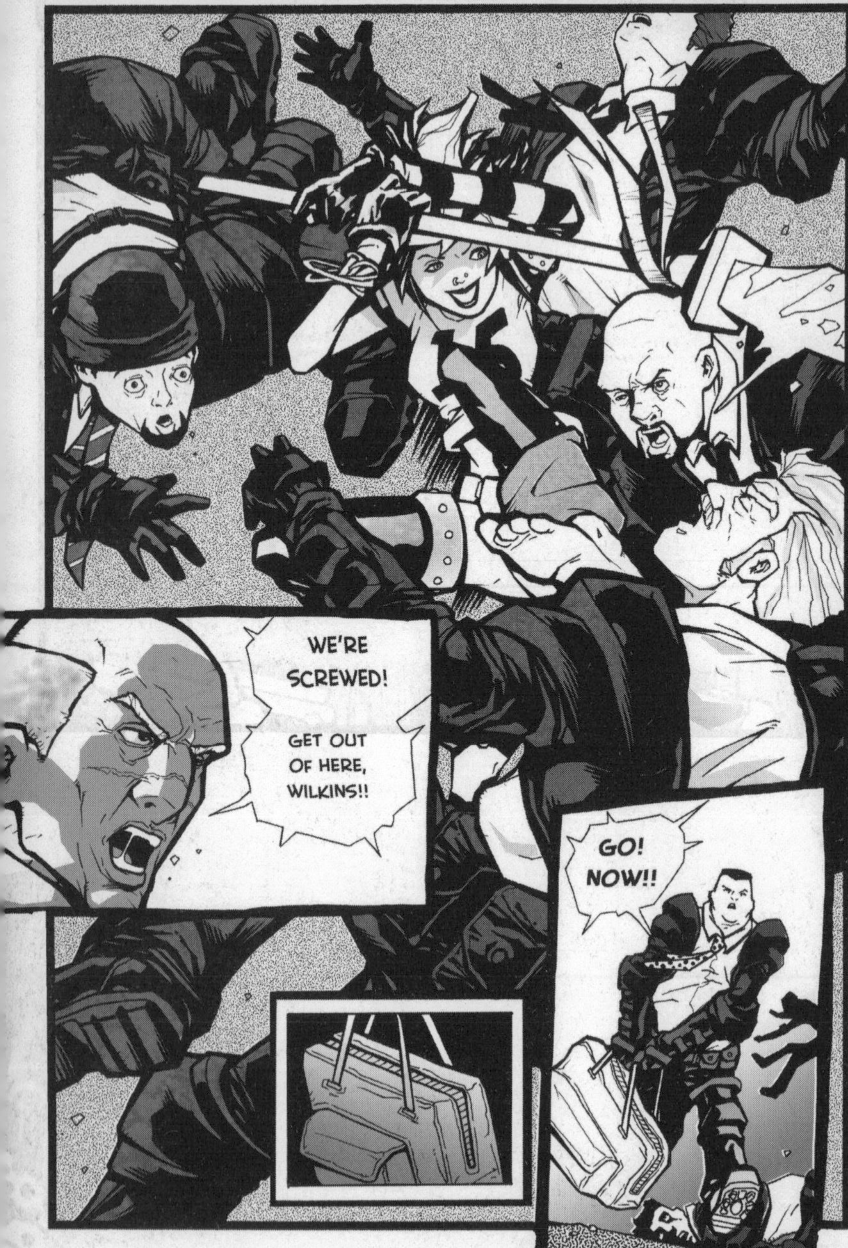
WE'RE SCREWED!
GET OUT OF HERE, WILKINS!!
GO! NOW!!

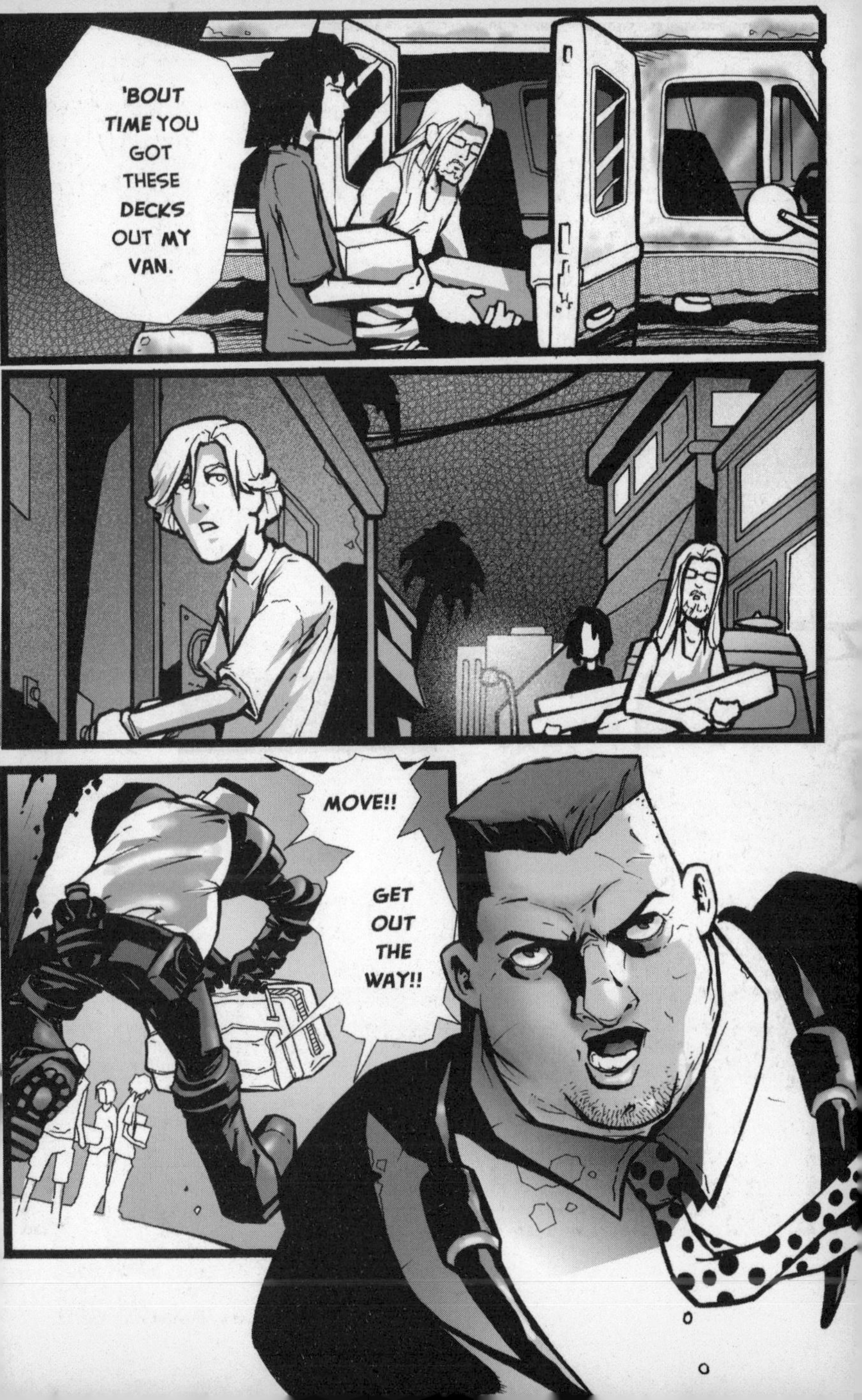
'BOUT TIME YOU GOT THESE DECKS OUT MY VAN.
MOVE!!
GET OUT THE WAY!!

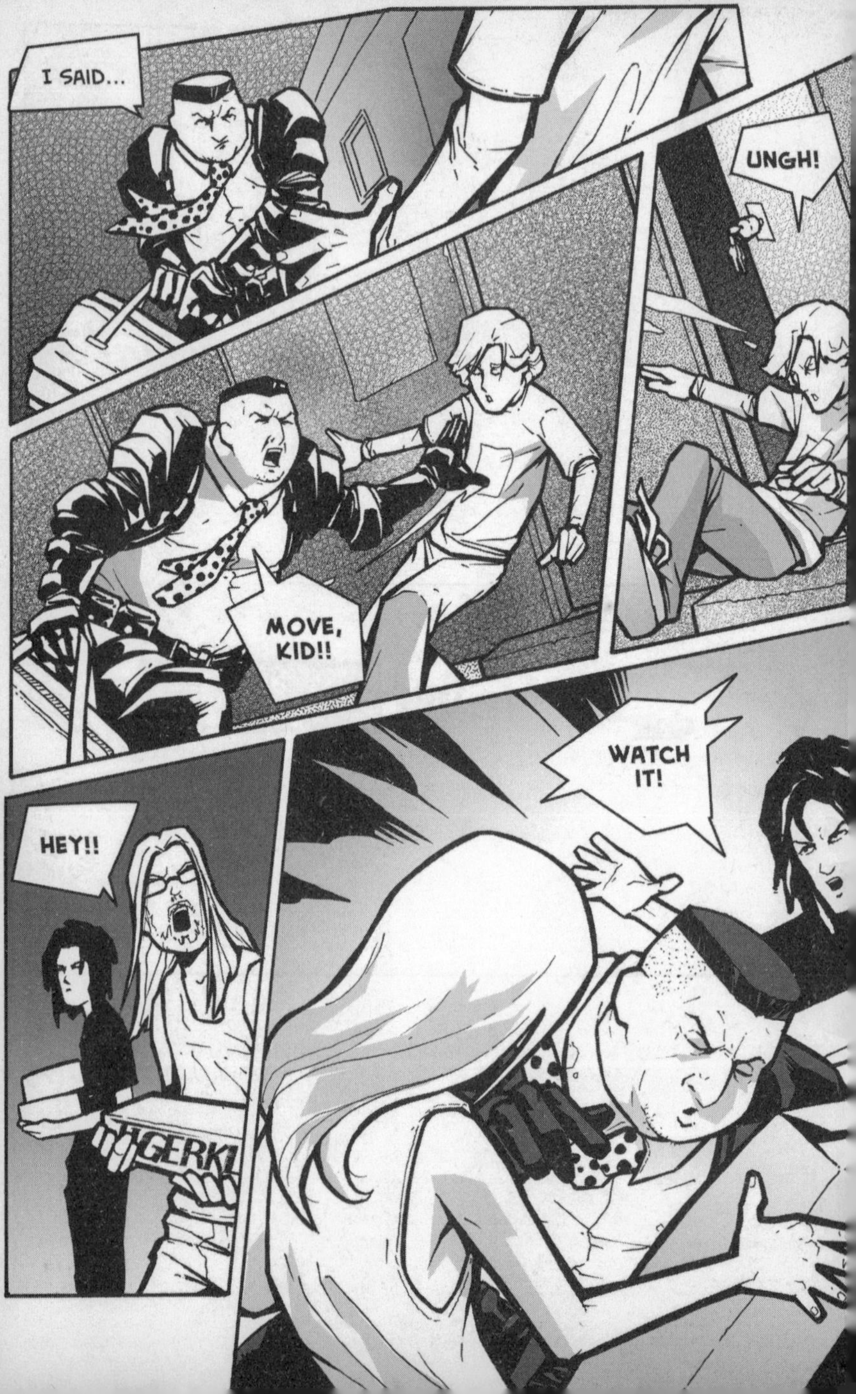
I SAID...
UNGH!
MOVE, KID!!
WATCH IT!
HEY!!
GERK

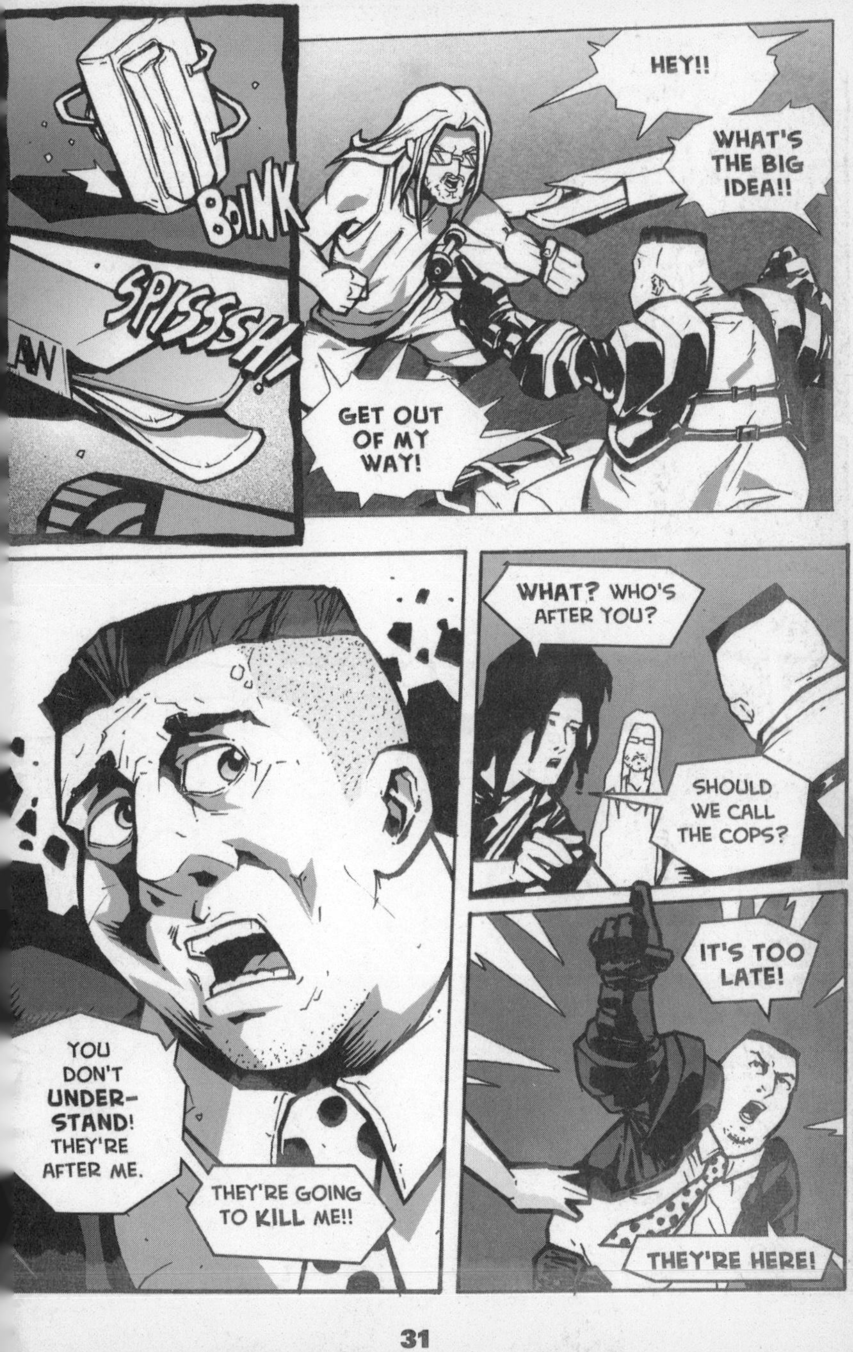
BOINK
SPISSSH!
AW
HEY!!
WHAT'S THE BIG IDEA!!
GET OUT OF MY WAY!
YOU DON'T UNDER-STAND! THEY'RE AFTER ME.
THEY'RE GOING TO KILL ME!!
WHAT? WHO'S AFTER YOU?
SHOULD WE CALL THE COPS?
IT'S TOO LATE!
THEY'RE HERE!

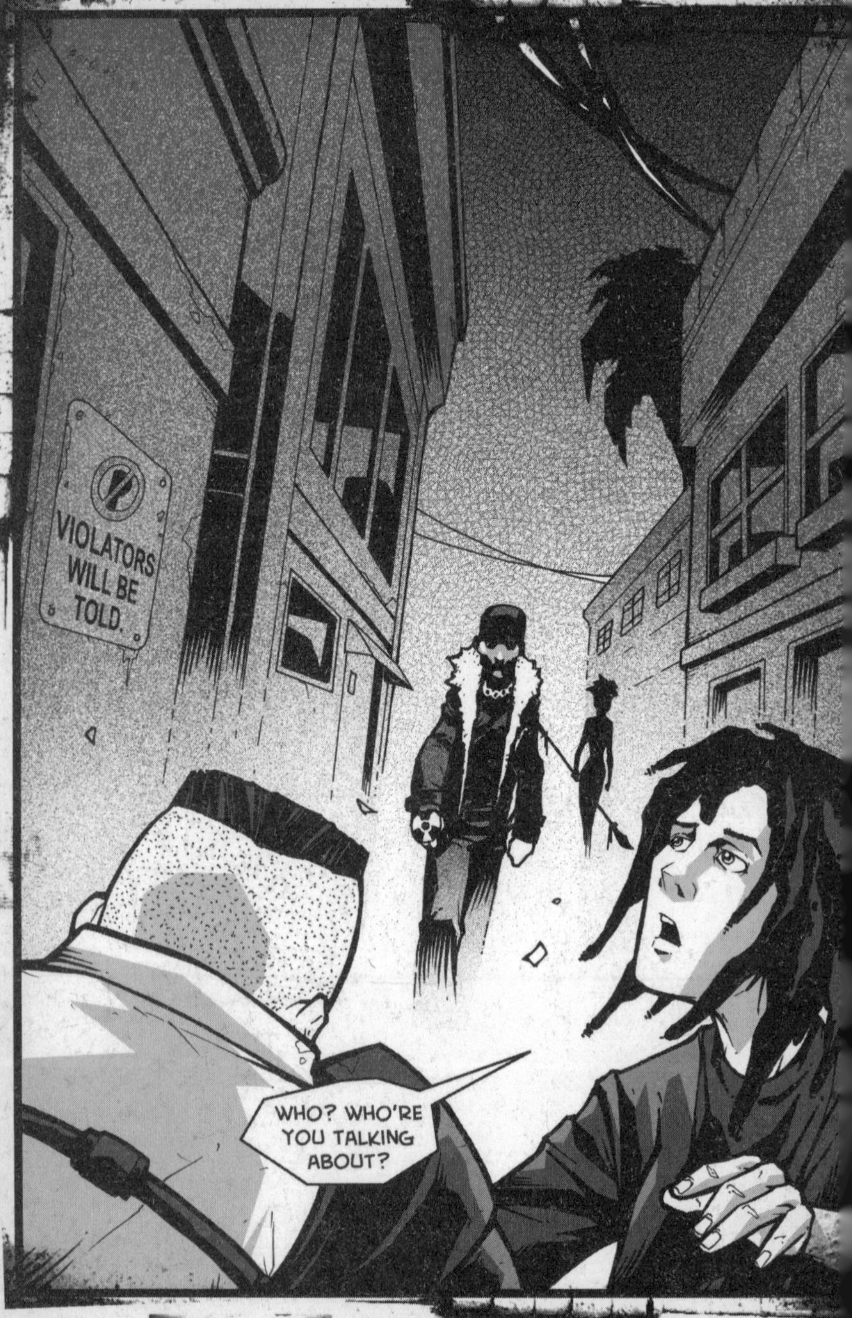
VIOLATORS WILL BE TOLD.
WHO? WHO'RE YOU TALKING ABOUT?

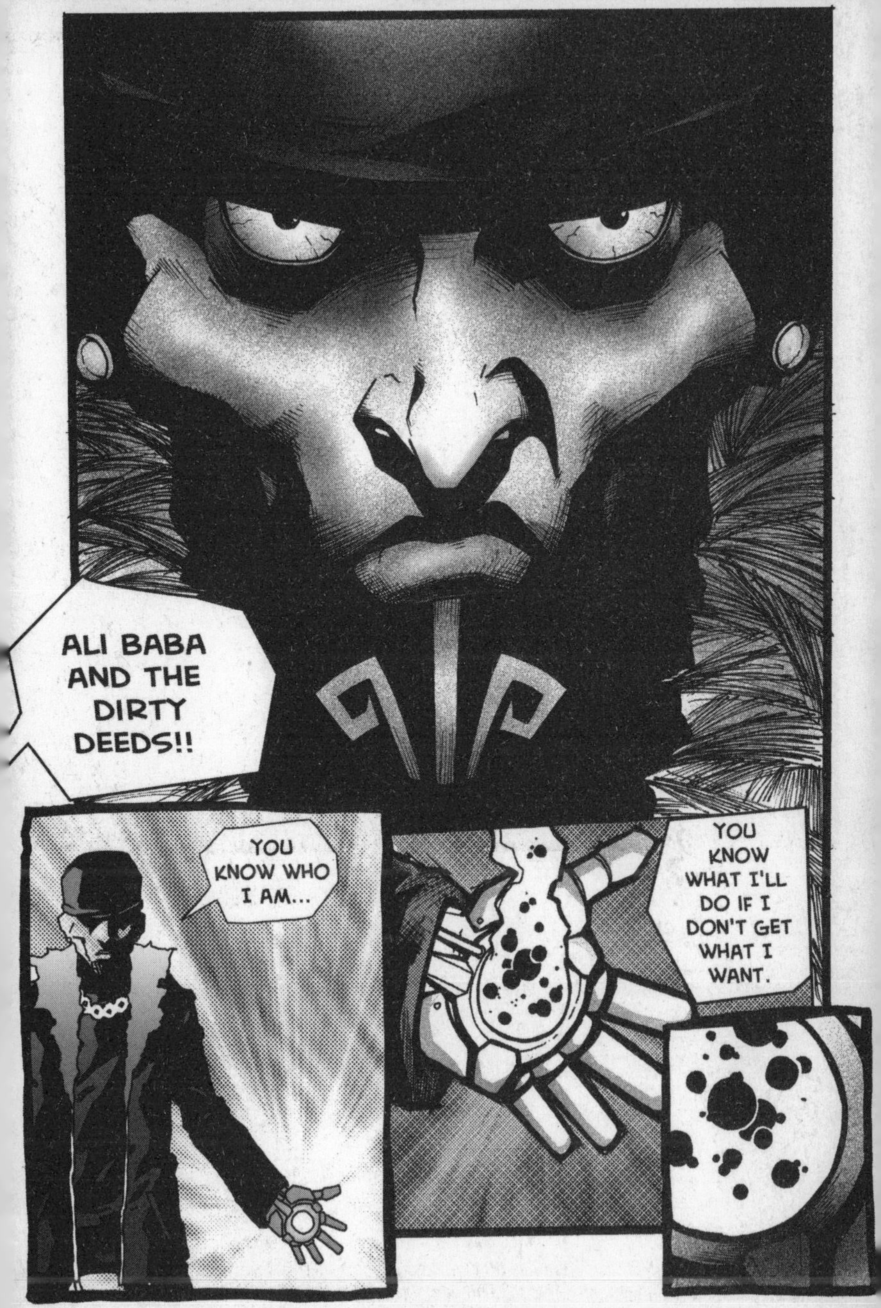
ALI BABA AND THE DIRTY DEEDS!!
YOU KNOW WHO I AM...
YOU KNOW WHAT I'LL DO IF I DON'T GET WHAT I WANT.

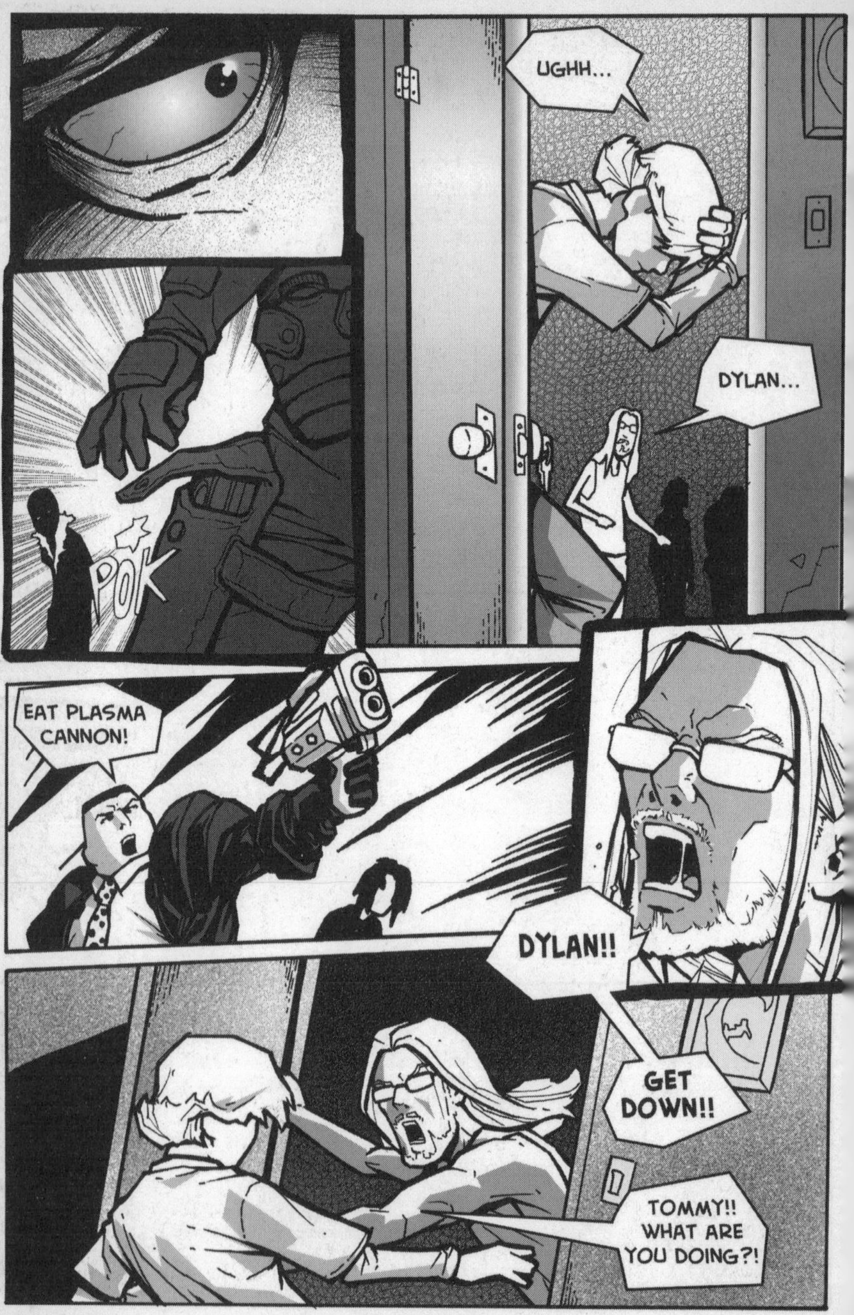
UGHH...
POK
DYLAN...
EAT PLASMA CANNON!
DYLAN!!
GET DOWN!!
TOMMY!! WHAT ARE YOU DOING?!

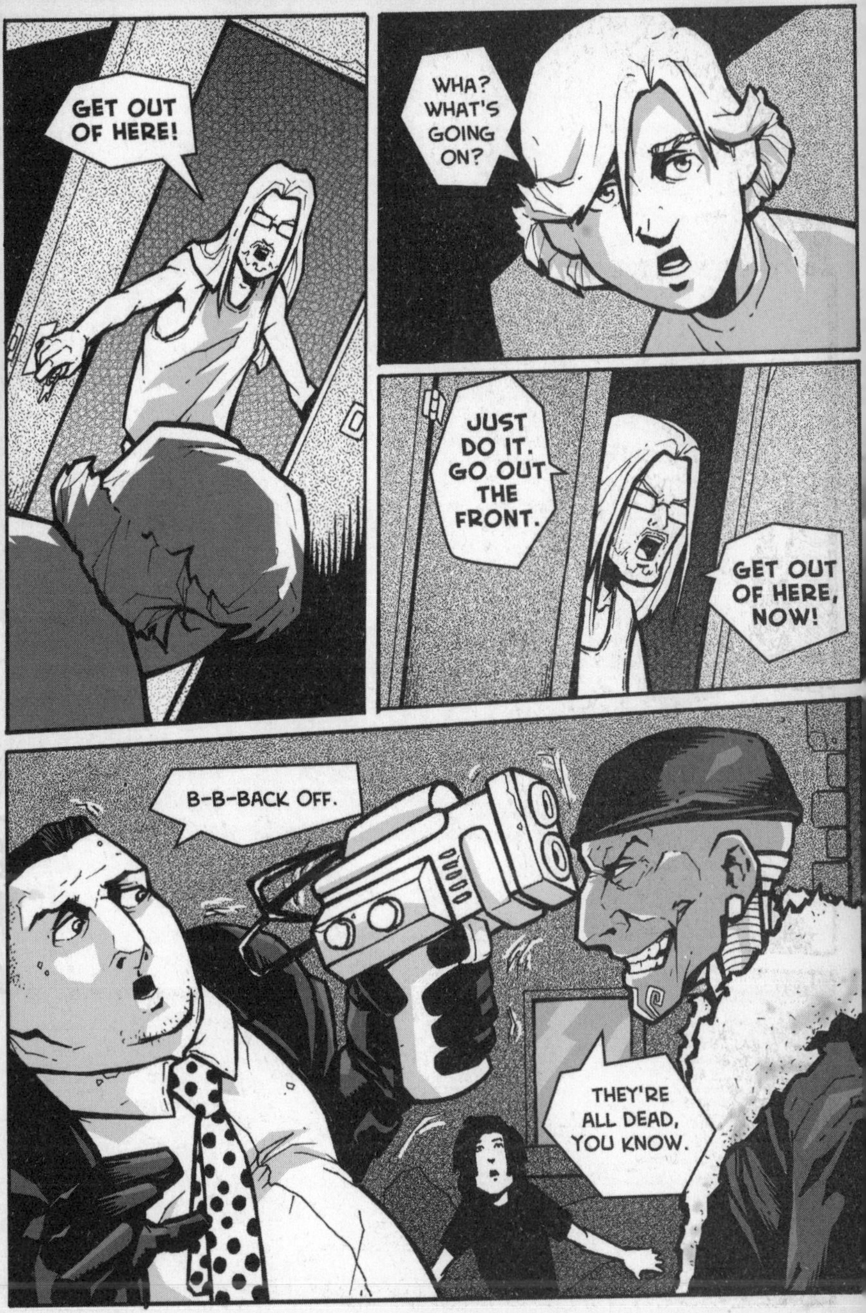
GET OUT OF HERE!
WHA? WHAT'S GOING ON?
JUST DO IT. GO OUT THE FRONT.
GET OUT OF HERE, NOW!
B-B-BACK OFF.
THEY'RE ALL DEAD, YOU KNOW.

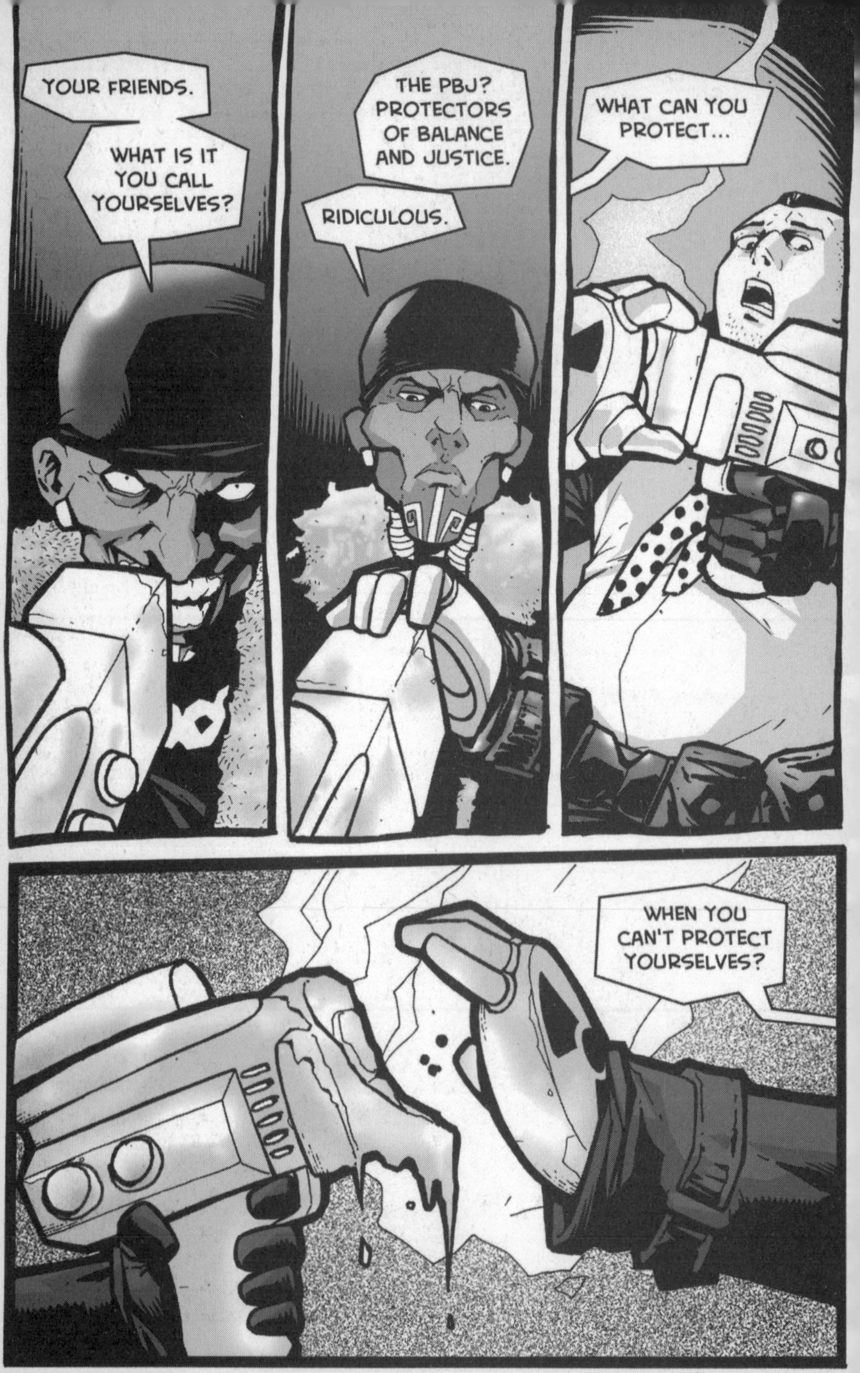
YOUR FRIENDS.
WHAT IS IT YOU CALL YOURSELVES?
THE PBJ? PROTECTORS OF BALANCE AND JUSTICE.
RIDICULOUS.
WHAT CAN YOU PROTECT...
WHEN YOU CAN'T PROTECT YOURSELVES?

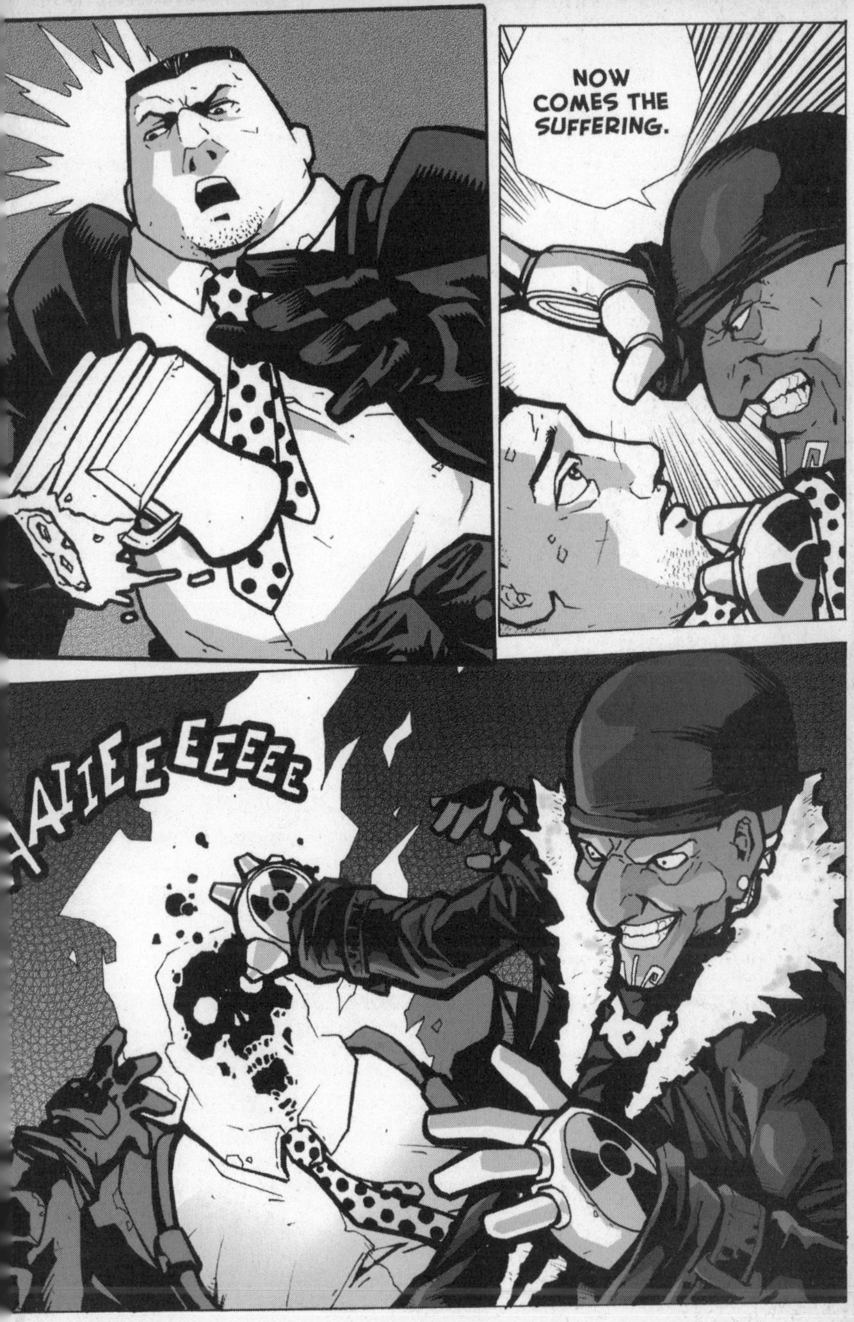
NOW COMES THE SUFFERING.
AIIEEEEEEE

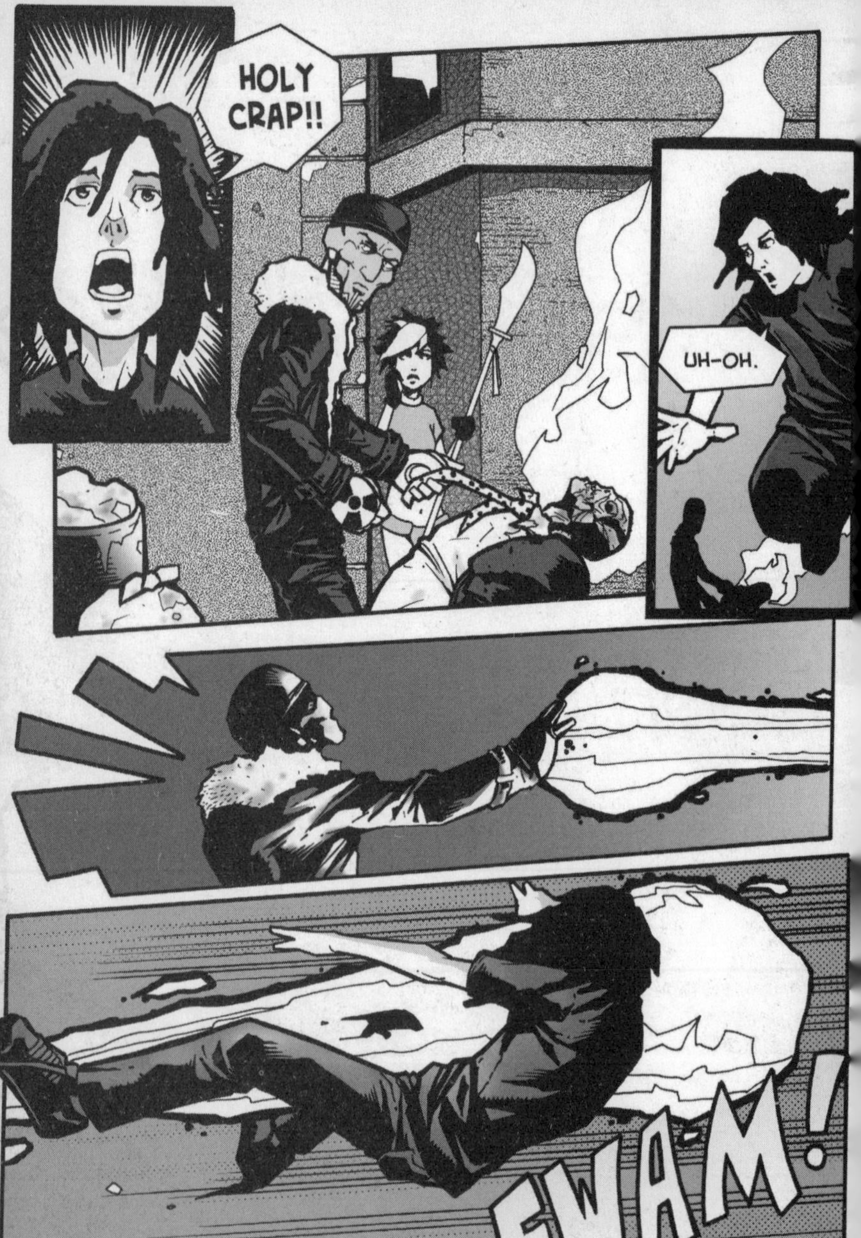
HOLY CRAP!!
UH-OH.
FWAM!

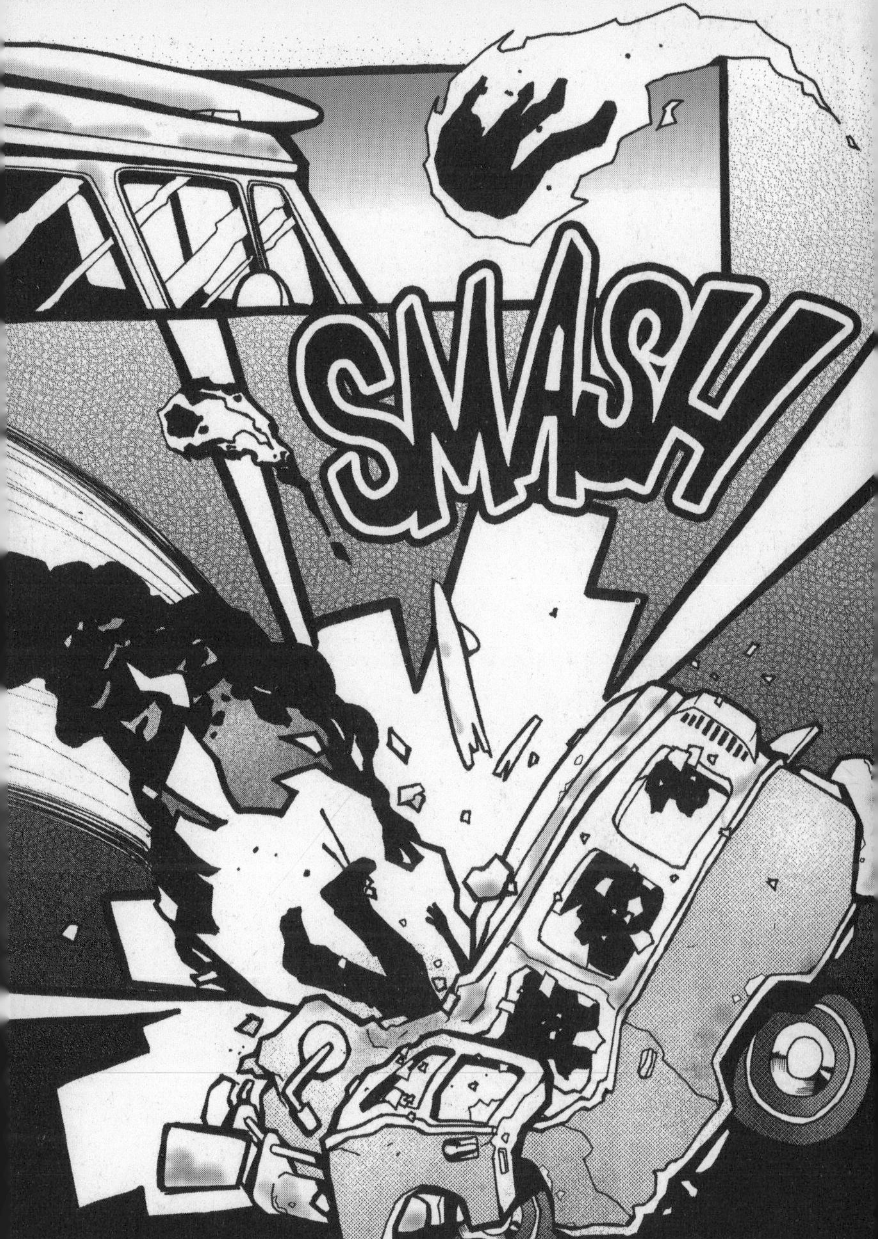
SMASH

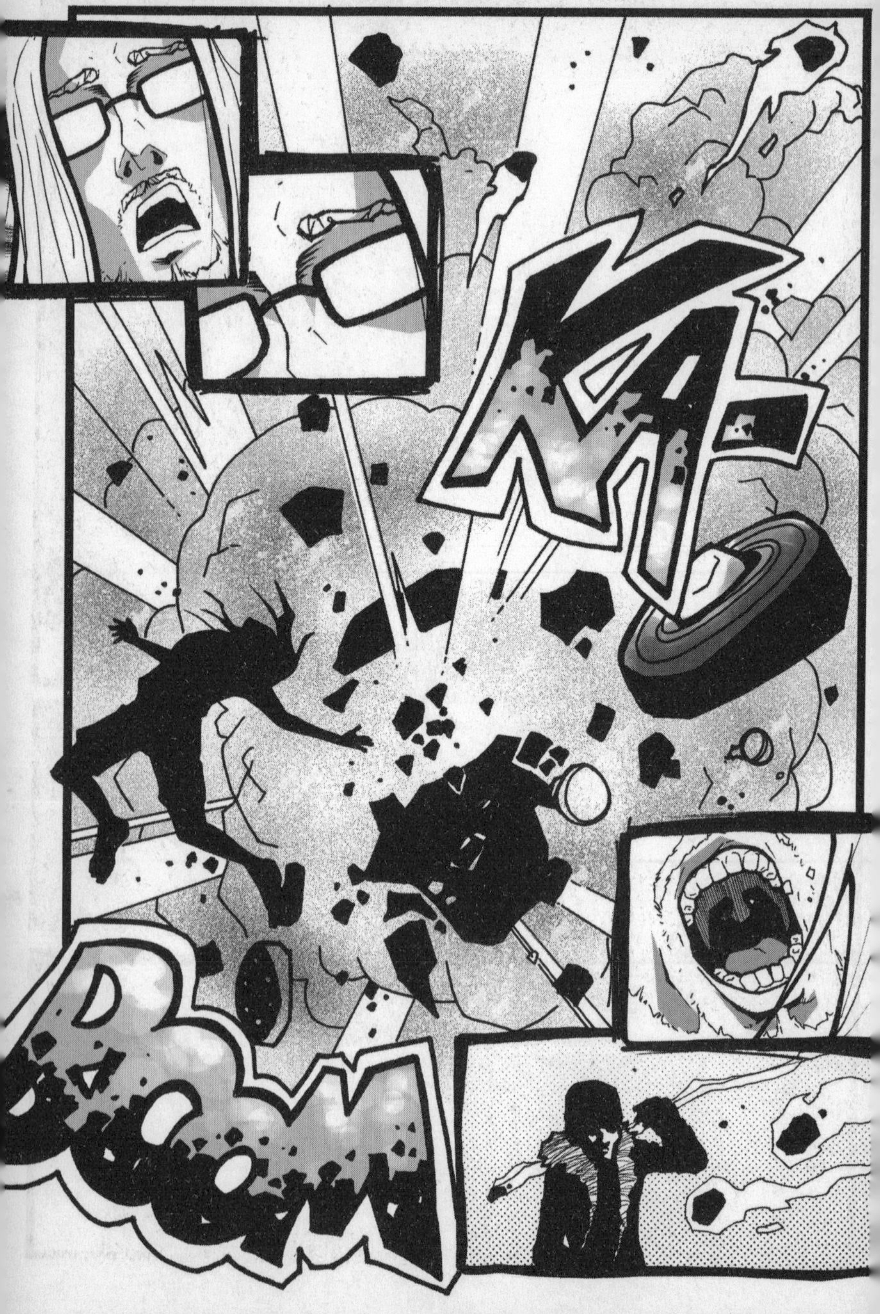
KA
BOOM

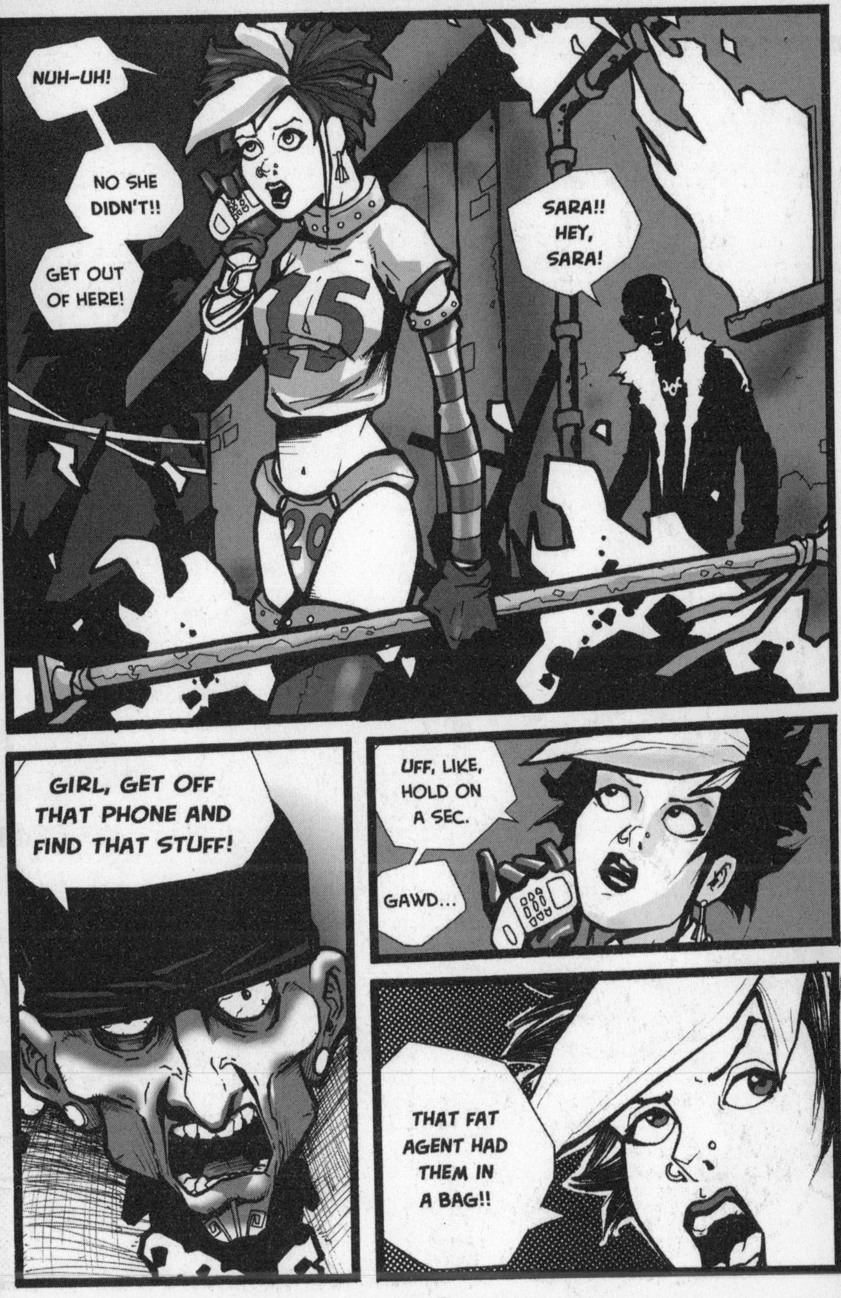
NUH-UH!
NO SHE DIDN'T!!
GET OUT OF HERE!
SARA!! HEY, SARA!
GIRL, GET OFF THAT PHONE AND FIND THAT STUFF!
UFF, LIKE, HOLD ON A SEC.
GAWD...
THAT FAT AGENT HAD THEM IN A BAG!!

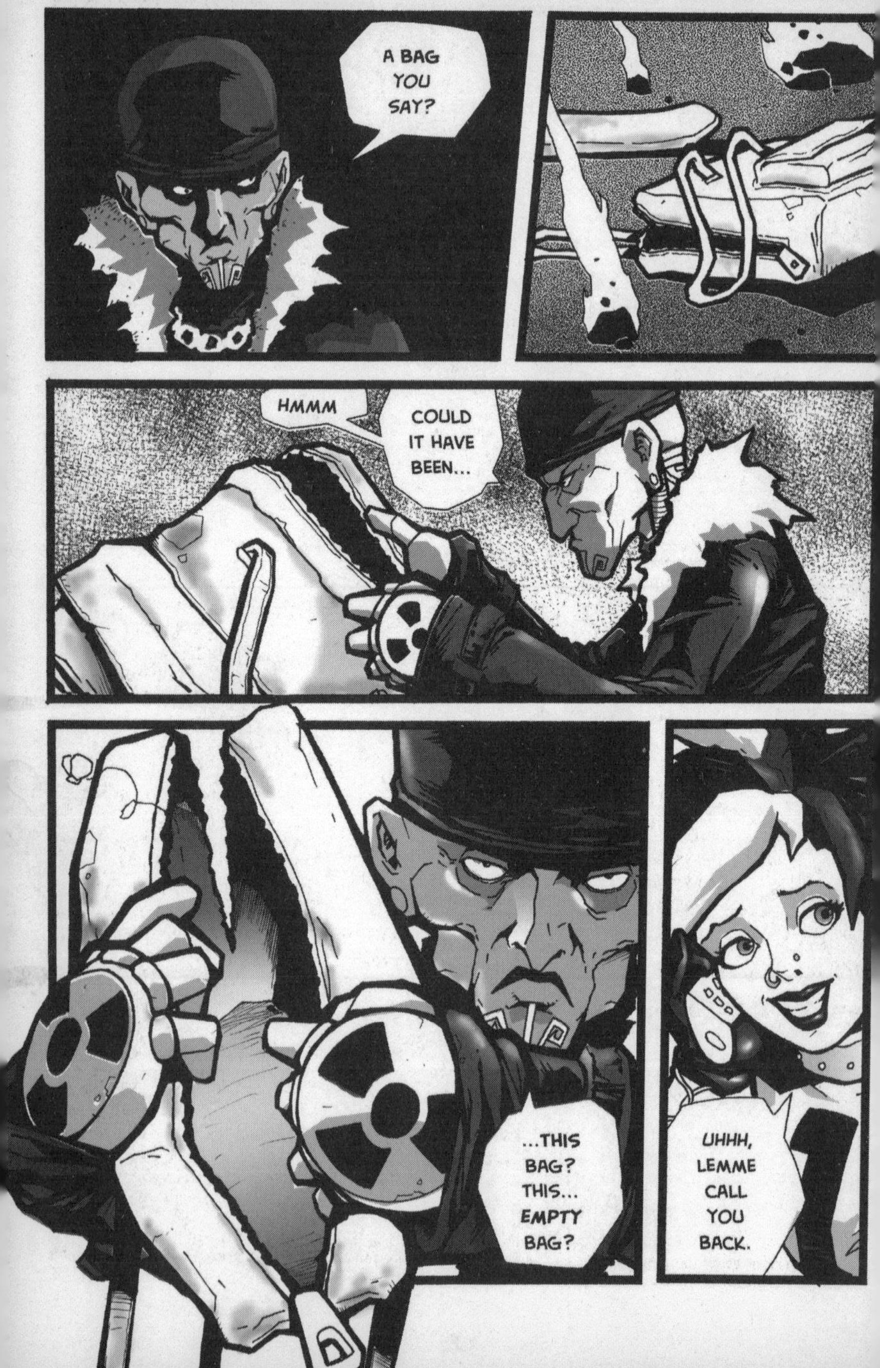
A BAG YOU SAY?
HMMM
COULD IT HAVE BEEN...
...THIS BAG? THIS... EMPTY BAG?
UHHH, LEMME CALL YOU BACK.

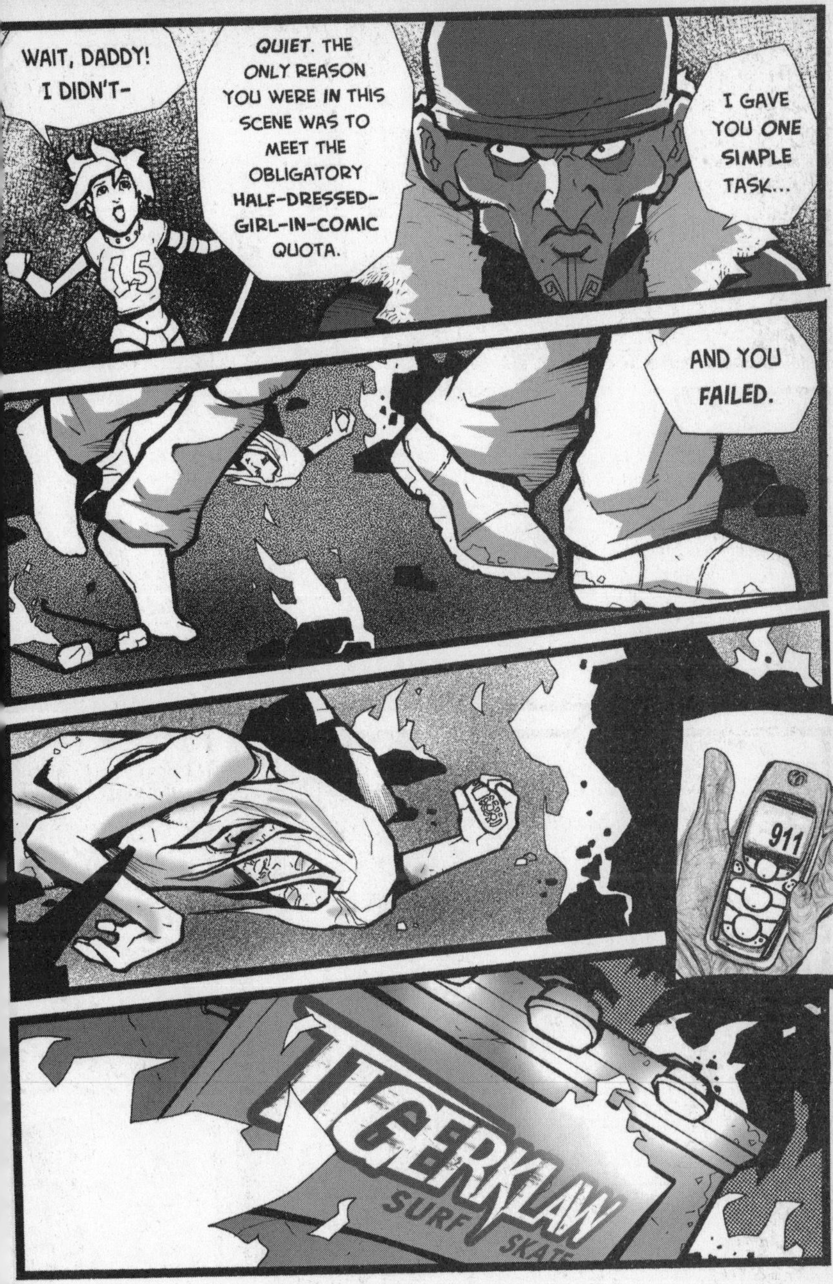
WAIT, DADDY! I DIDN'T-
QUIET. THE ONLY REASON YOU WERE IN THIS SCENE WAS TO MEET THE OBLIGATORY HALF-DRESSED-GIRL-IN-COMIC QUOTA.
I GAVE YOU ONE SIMPLE TASK...
AND YOU FAILED.
911
TIGERKLAW
SURF
SKATE

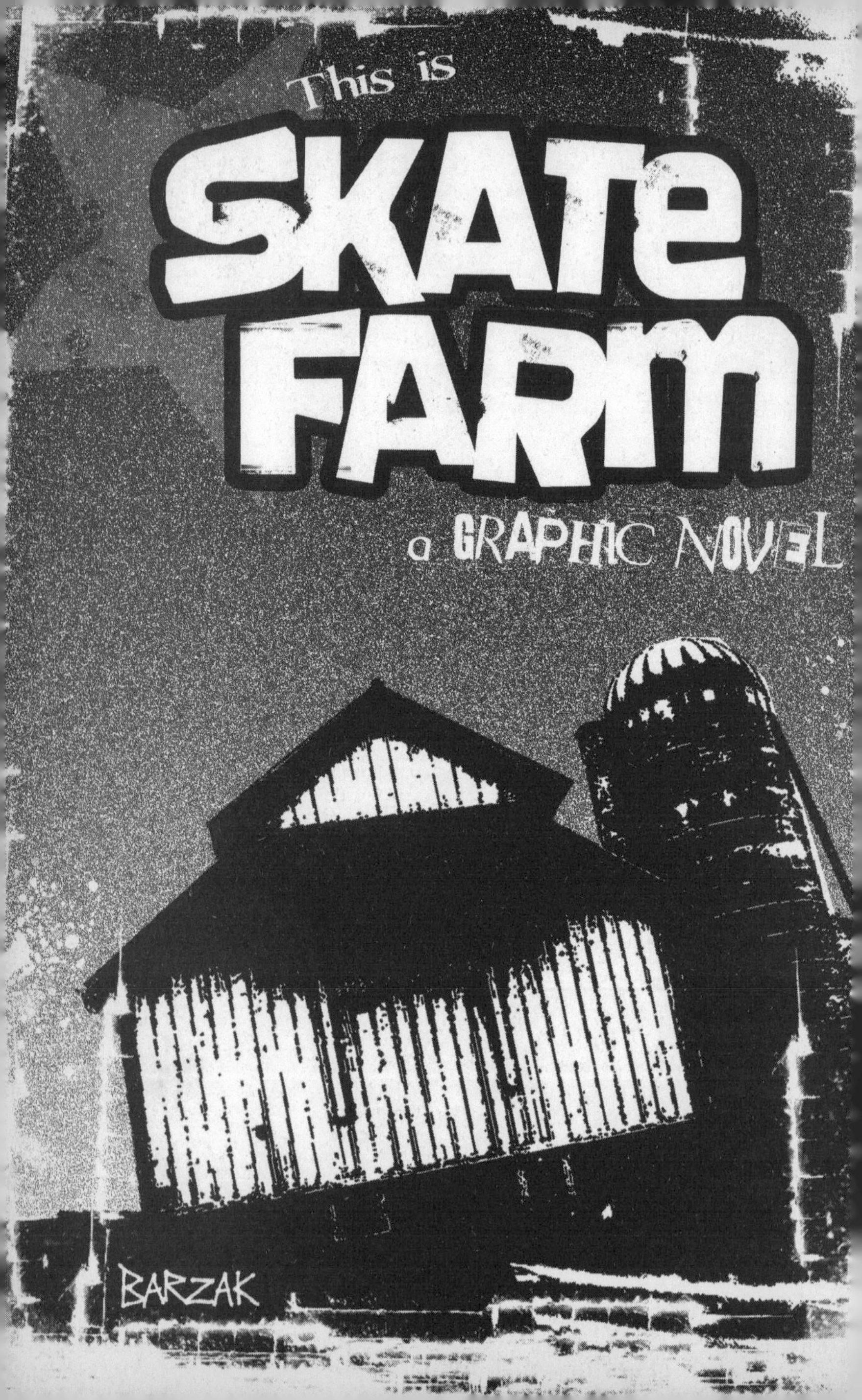
This is
SKATE FARM
a GRAPHIC NOVEL
BARZAK

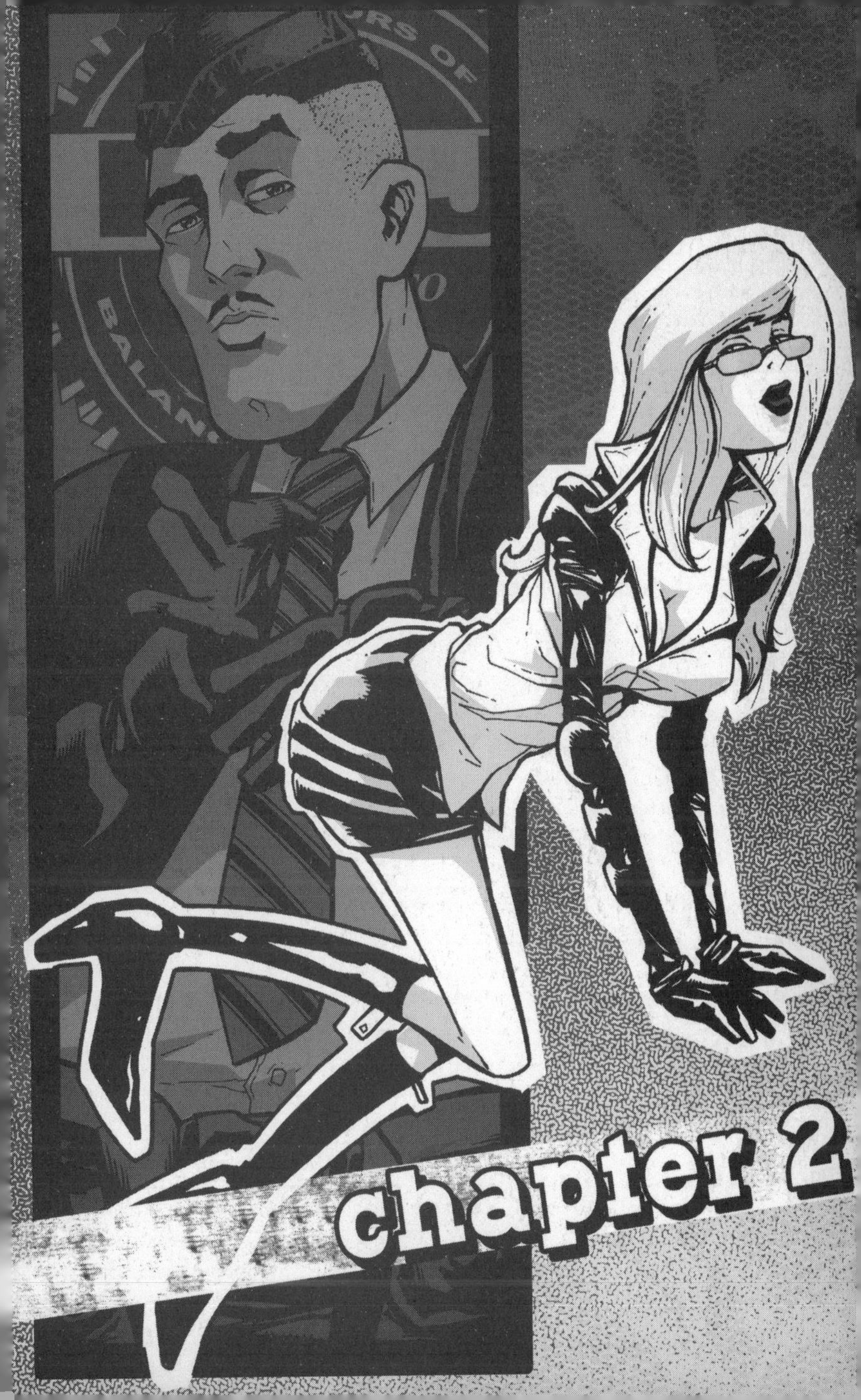
chapter 2

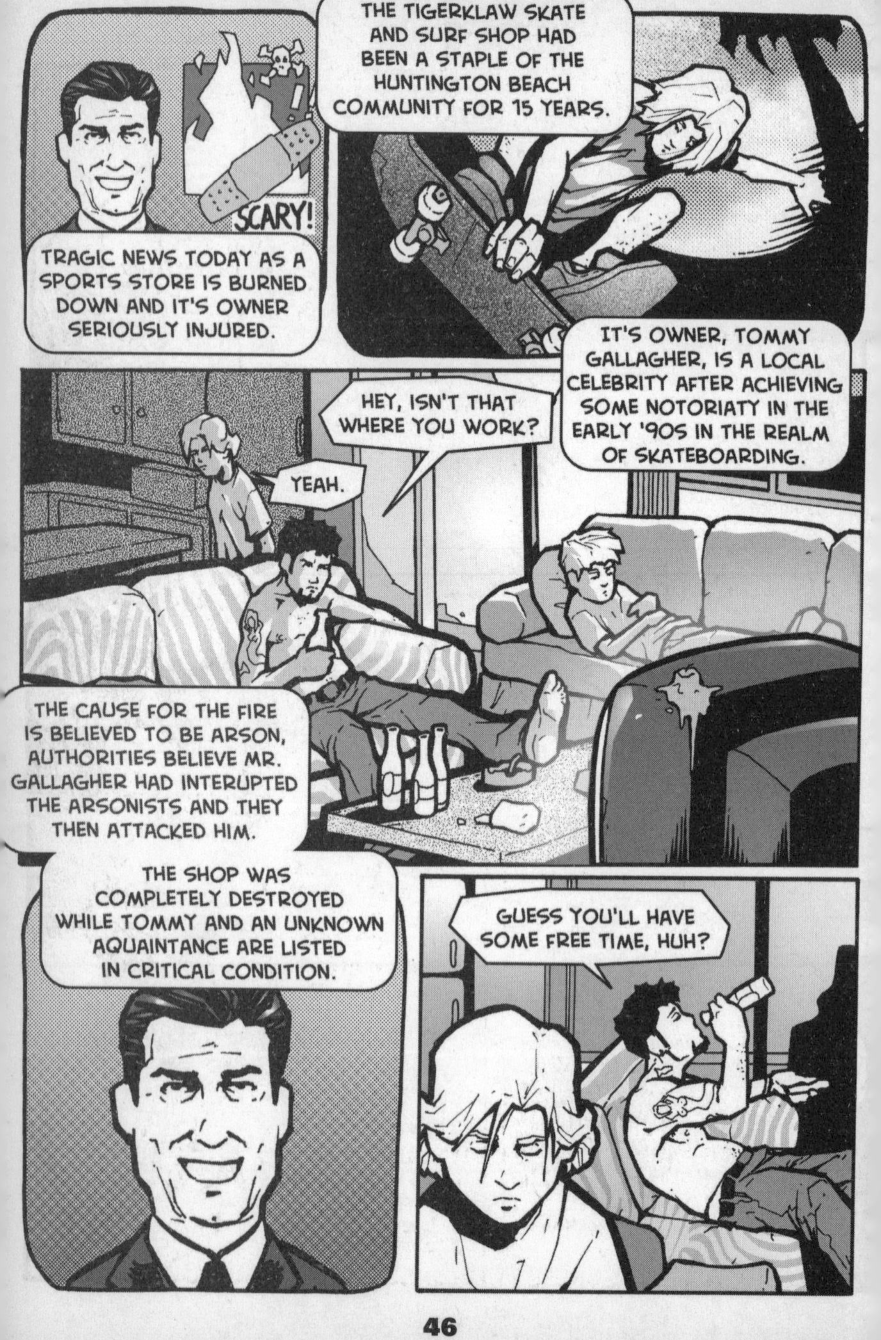
SCARY!
TRAGIC NEWS TODAY AS A SPORTS STORE IS BURNED DOWN AND IT'S OWNER SERIOUSLY INJURED.
THE TIGERKLAW SKATE AND SURF SHOP HAD BEEN A STAPLE OF THE HUNTINGTON BEACH COMMUNITY FOR 15 YEARS.
IT'S OWNER, TOMMY GALLAGHER, IS A LOCAL CELEBRITY AFTER ACHIEVING SOME NOTORIATY IN THE EARLY '90S IN THE REALM OF SKATEBOARDING.
HEY, ISN'T THAT WHERE YOU WORK?
YEAH.
THE CAUSE FOR THE FIRE IS BELIEVED TO BE ARSON, AUTHORITIES BELIEVE MR. GALLAGHER HAD INTERUPTED THE ARSONISTS AND THEY THEN ATTACKED HIM.
THE SHOP WAS COMPLETELY DESTROYED WHILE TOMMY AND AN UNKNOWN AQUAINTANCE ARE LISTED IN CRITICAL CONDITION.
GUESS YOU'LL HAVE SOME FREE TIME, HUH?

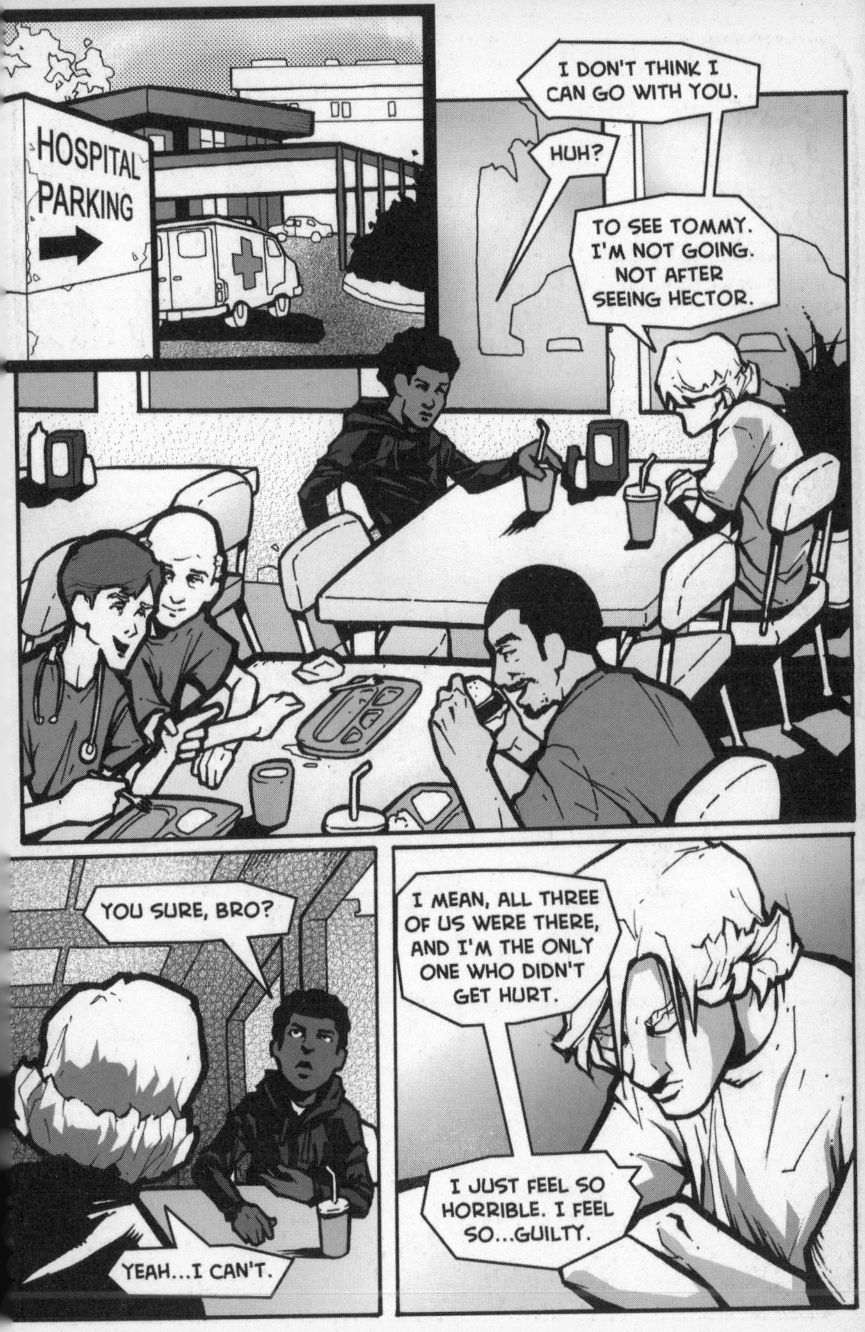
HOSPITAL PARKING
I DON'T THINK I CAN GO WITH YOU.
HUH?
TO SEE TOMMY. I'M NOT GOING. NOT AFTER SEEING HECTOR.
YOU SURE, BRO?
YEAH...I CAN'T.
I MEAN, ALL THREE OF US WERE THERE, AND I'M THE ONLY ONE WHO DIDN'T GET HURT.
I JUST FEEL SO HORRIBLE. I FEEL SO...GUILTY.

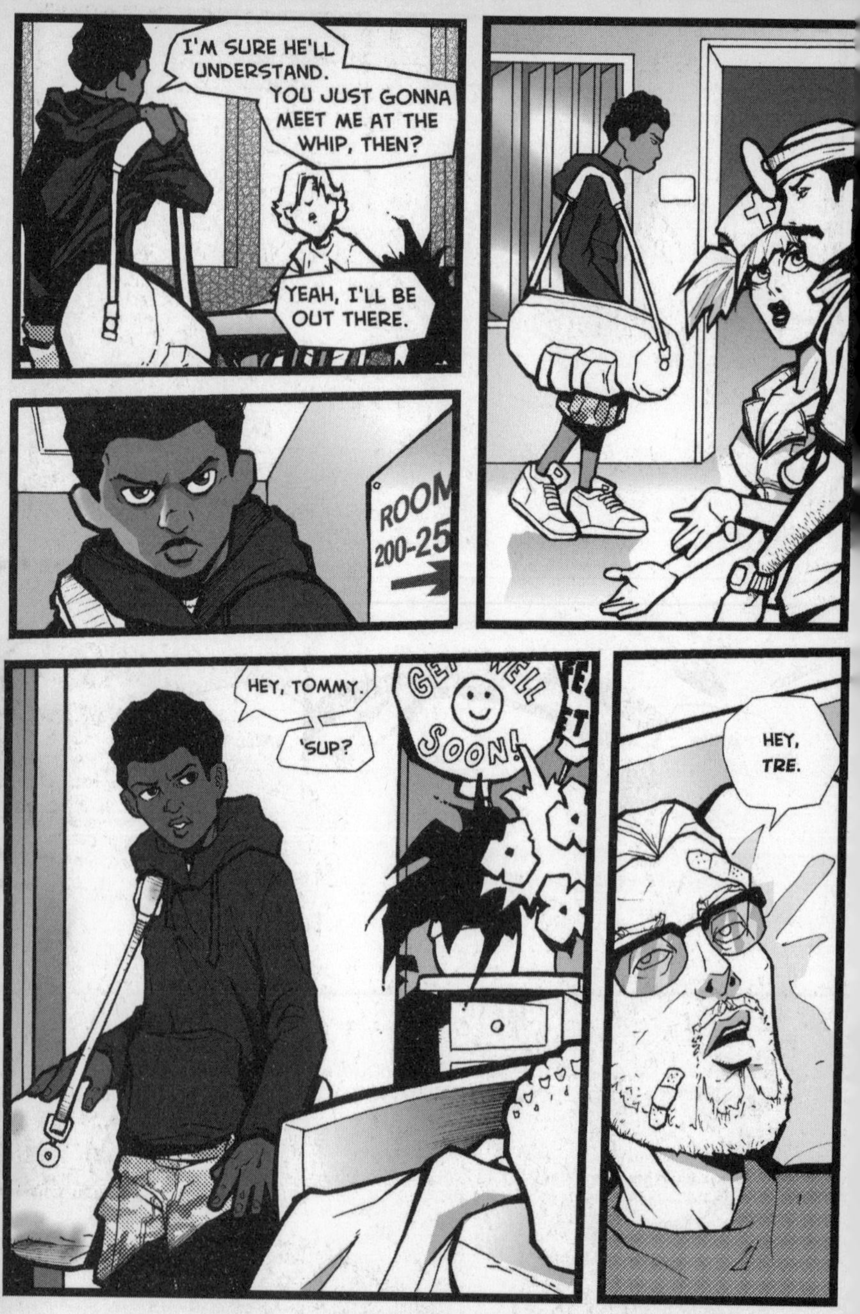
I'M SURE HE'LL UNDERSTAND.
YOU JUST GONNA MEET ME AT THE WHIP, THEN?
YEAH, I'LL BE OUT THERE.
ROOM 200-25
HEY, TOMMY.
'SUP?
GET WELL SOON!
HEY, TRE.

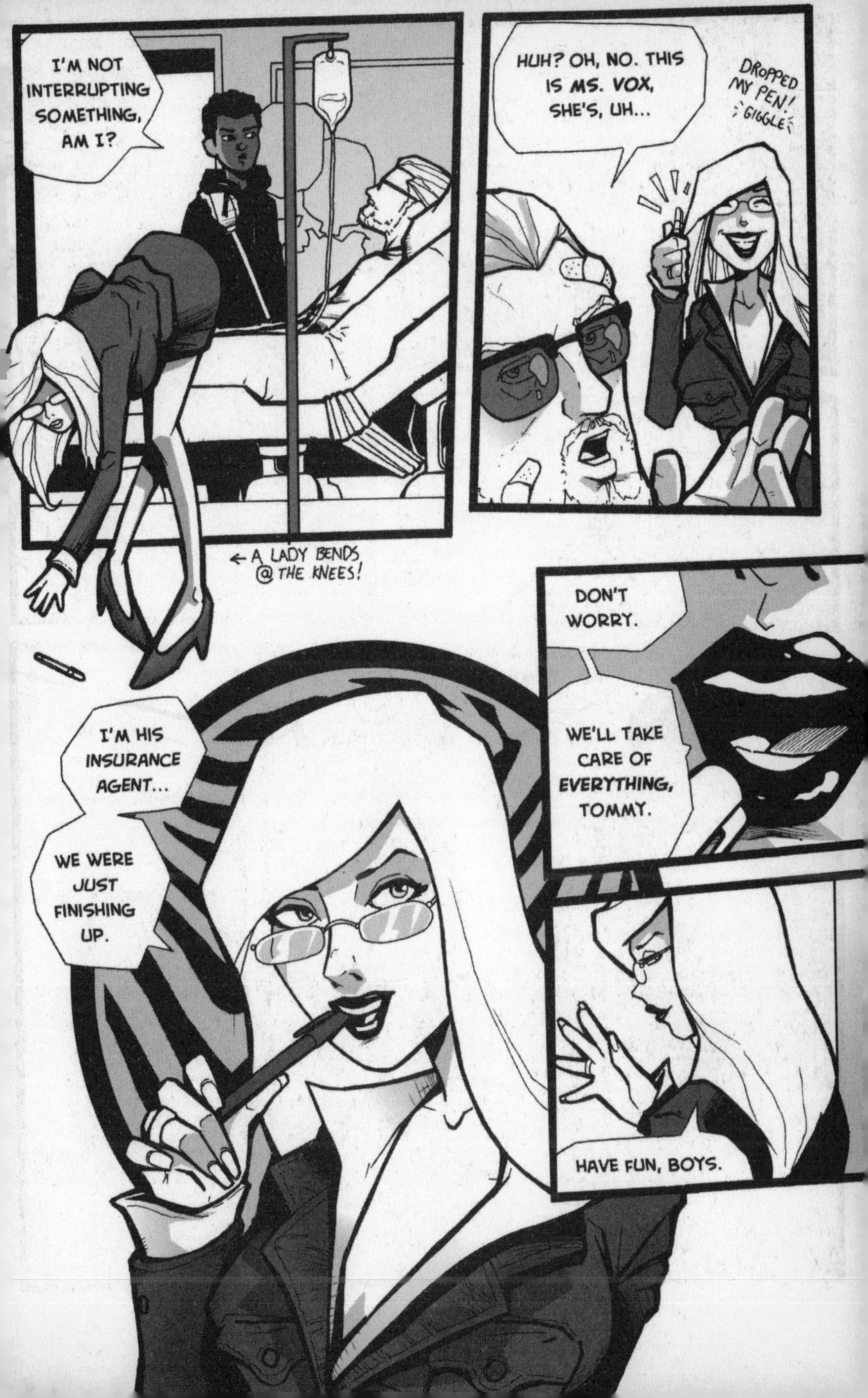
I'M NOT INTERRUPTING SOMETHING, AM I?
HUH? OH, NO. THIS IS MS. VOX, SHE'S, UH...
DROPPED MY PEN! GIGGLE
← A LADY BENDS @ THE KNEES!
DON'T WORRY.
I'M HIS INSURANCE AGENT...
WE WERE JUST FINISHING UP.
WE'LL TAKE CARE OF EVERYTHING, TOMMY.
HAVE FUN, BOYS.

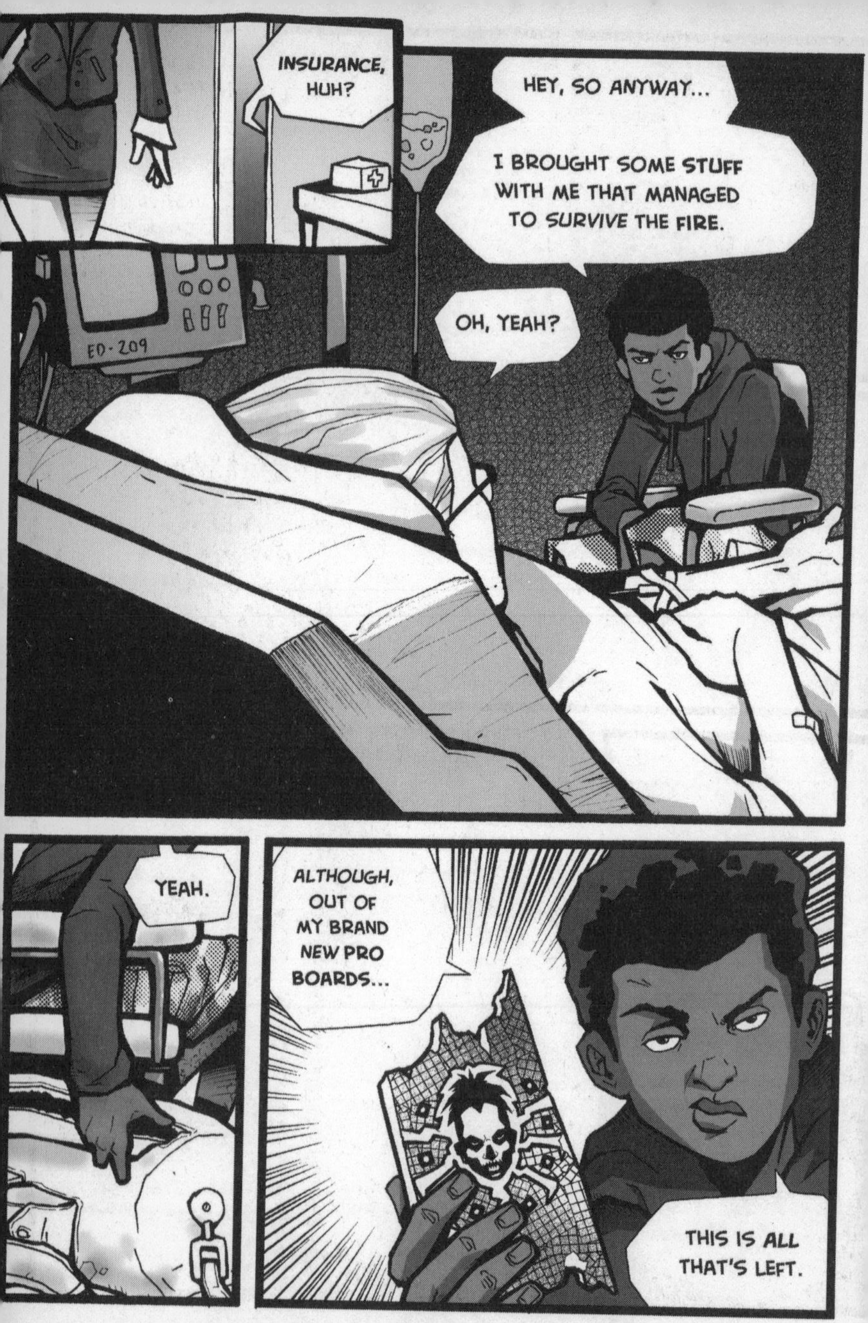
INSURANCE, HUH?
HEY, SO ANYWAY...
I BROUGHT SOME STUFF WITH ME THAT MANAGED TO SURVIVE THE FIRE.
OH, YEAH?
ED-209
YEAH.
ALTHOUGH, OUT OF MY BRAND NEW PRO BOARDS...
THIS IS ALL THAT'S LEFT.

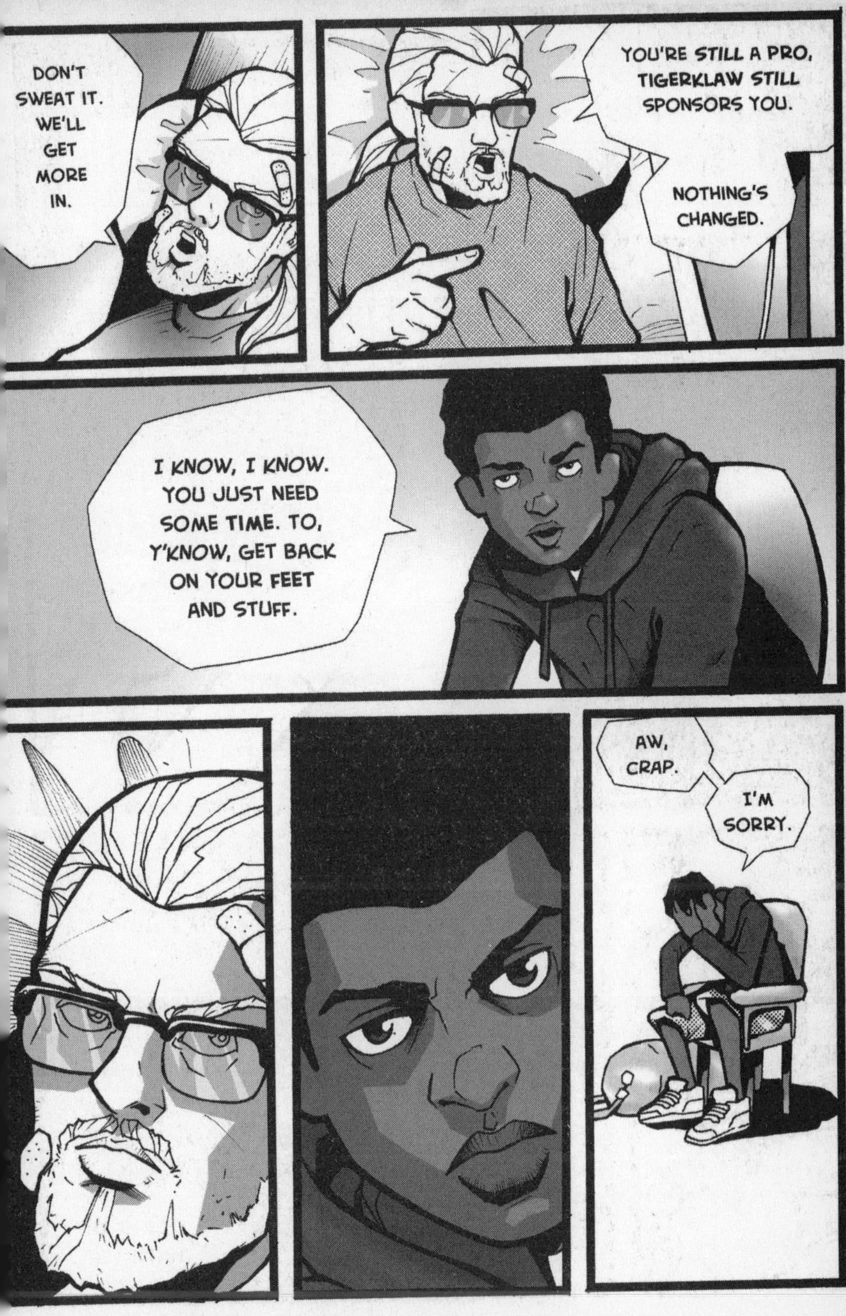
DON'T SWEAT IT. WE'LL GET MORE IN.
YOU'RE STILL A PRO, TIGERKLAW STILL SPONSORS YOU.
NOTHING'S CHANGED.
I KNOW, I KNOW. YOU JUST NEED SOME TIME. TO, Y'KNOW, GET BACK ON YOUR FEET AND STUFF.
AW, CRAP.
I'M SORRY.

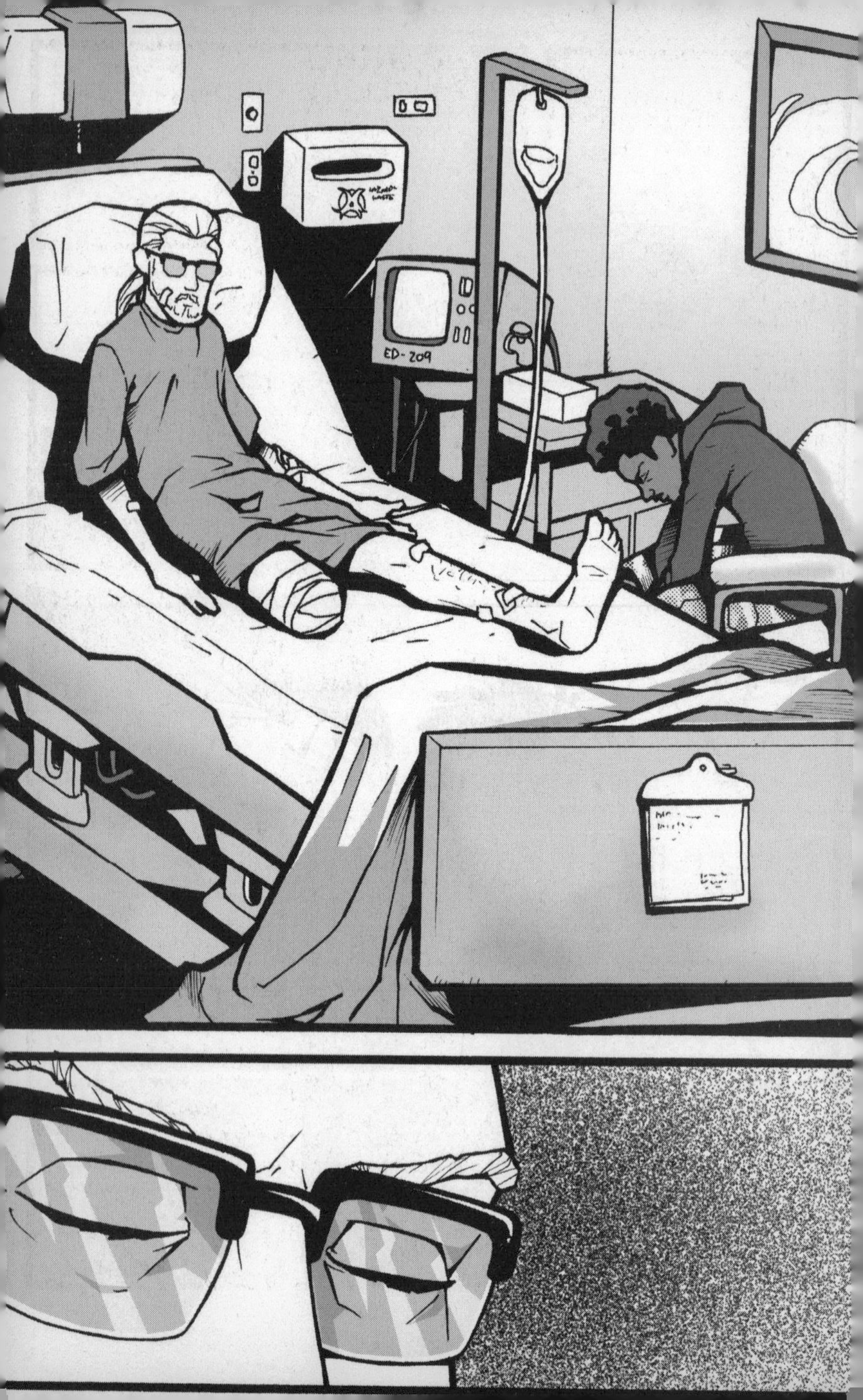
ED-209

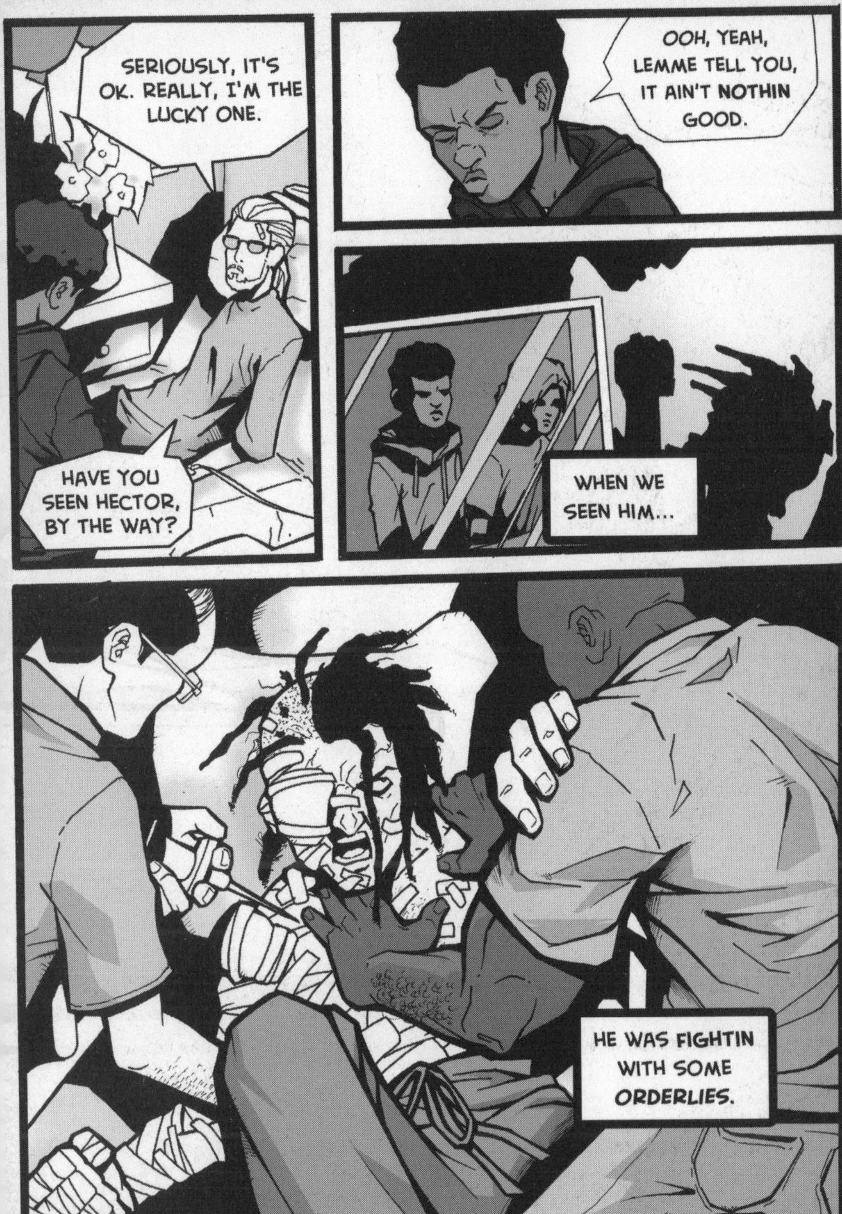
SERIOUSLY, IT'S OK. REALLY, I'M THE LUCKY ONE.
HAVE YOU SEEN HECTOR, BY THE WAY?
OOH, YEAH, LEMME TELL YOU, IT AIN'T NOTHIN GOOD.
WHEN WE SEEN HIM...
HE WAS FIGHTIN WITH SOME ORDERLIES.

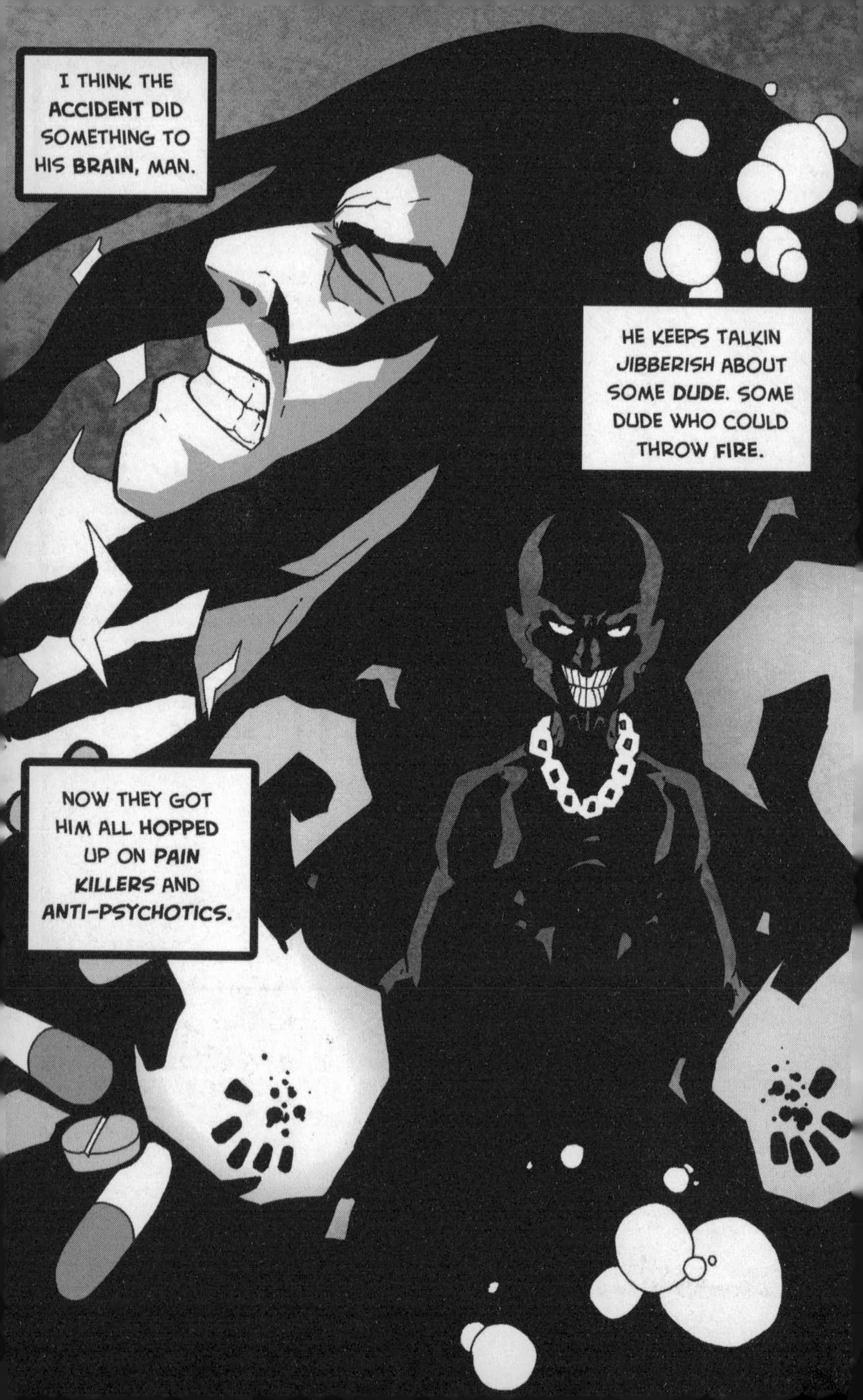
I THINK THE ACCIDENT DID SOMETHING TO HIS BRAIN, MAN.
HE KEEPS TALKIN JIBBERISH ABOUT SOME DUDE. SOME DUDE WHO COULD THROW FIRE.
NOW THEY GOT HIM ALL HOPPED UP ON PAIN KILLERS AND ANTI-PSYCHOTICS.

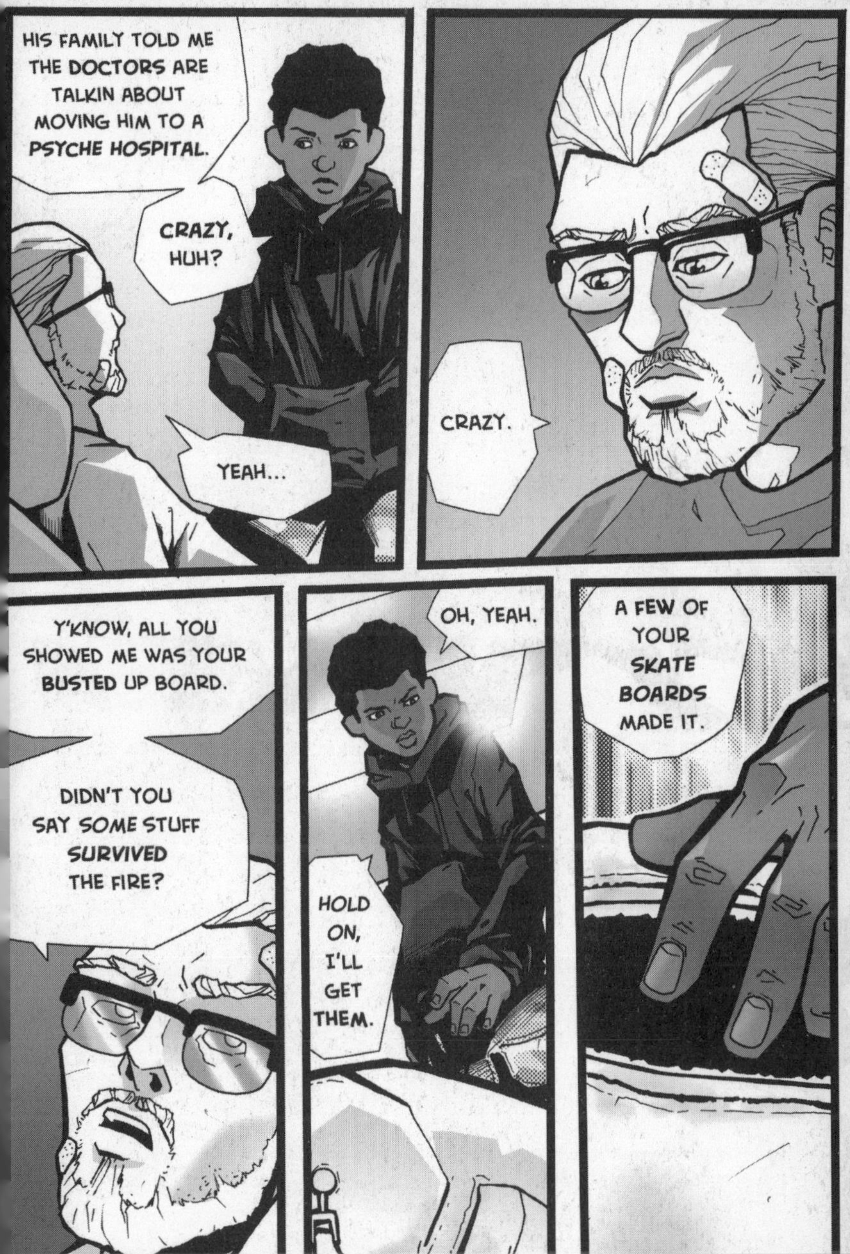
HIS FAMILY TOLD ME THE DOCTORS ARE TALKIN ABOUT MOVING HIM TO A PSYCHE HOSPITAL.
CRAZY, HUH?
YEAH...
CRAZY.
Y'KNOW, ALL YOU SHOWED ME WAS YOUR BUSTED UP BOARD.
DIDN'T YOU SAY SOME STUFF SURVIVED THE FIRE?
OH, YEAH.
HOLD ON, I'LL GET THEM.
A FEW OF YOUR SKATE BOARDS MADE IT.

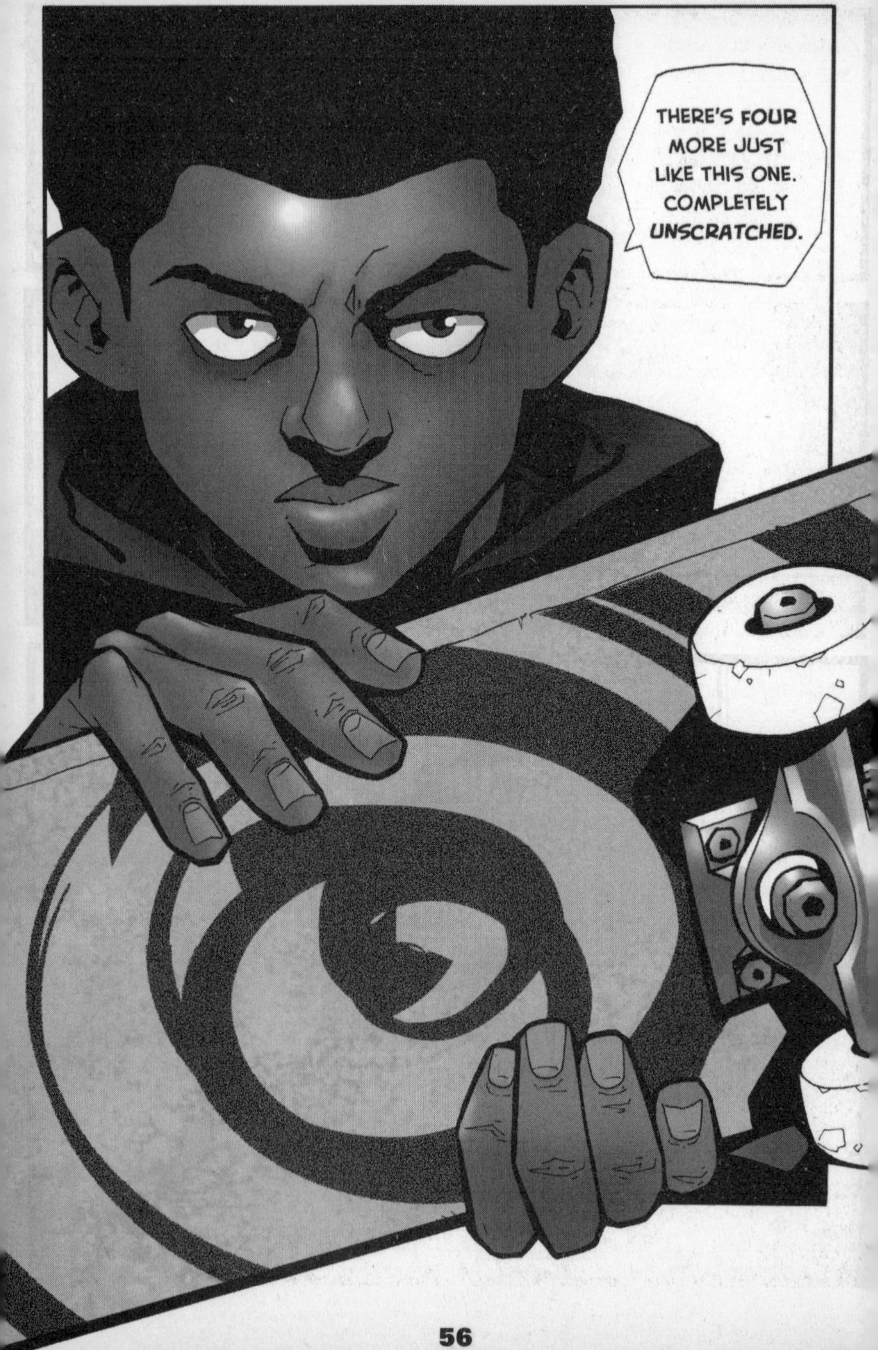
THERE'S FOUR MORE JUST LIKE THIS ONE. COMPLETELY UNSCRATCHED.

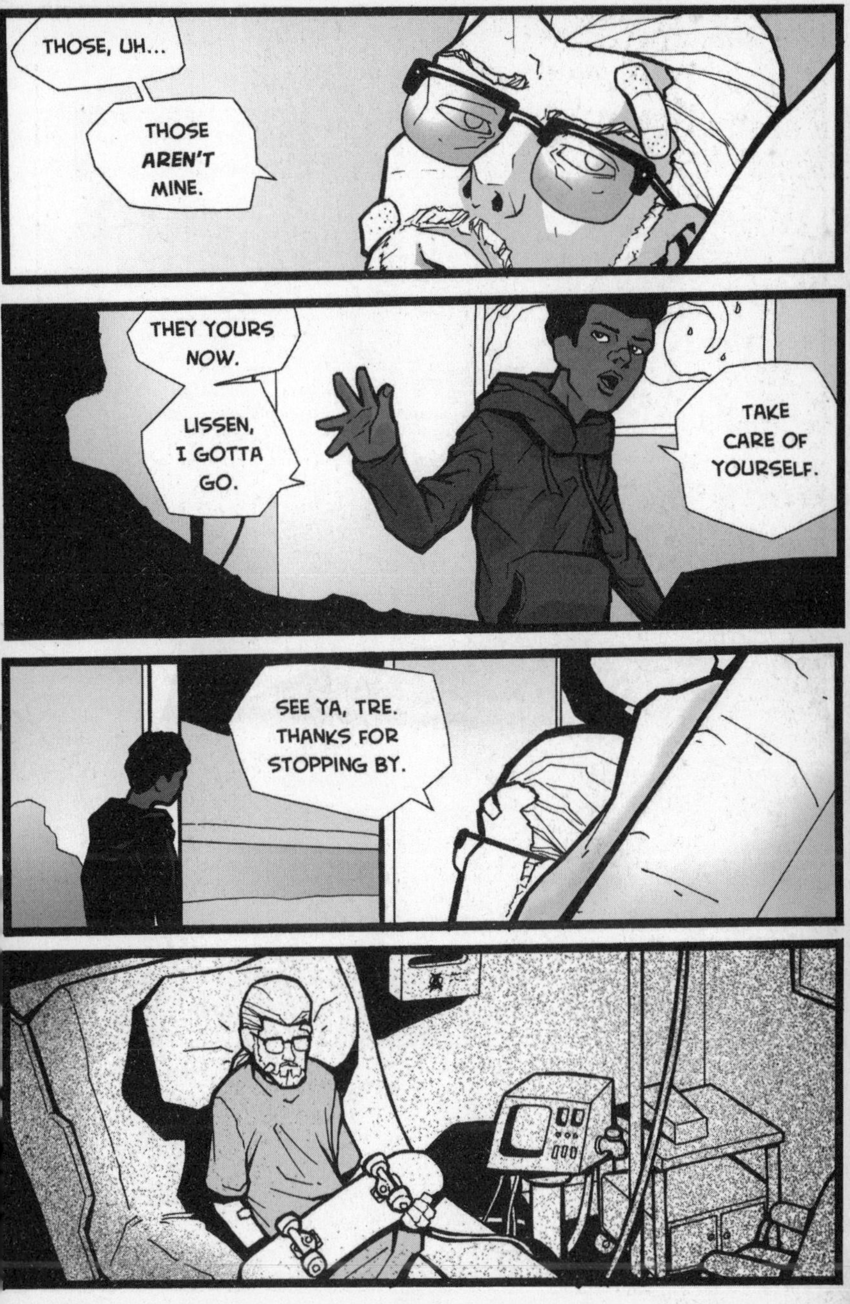
THOSE, UH...
THOSE AREN'T MINE.
THEY YOURS NOW.
LISSEN, I GOTTA GO.
TAKE CARE OF YOURSELF.
SEE YA, TRE. THANKS FOR STOPPING BY.

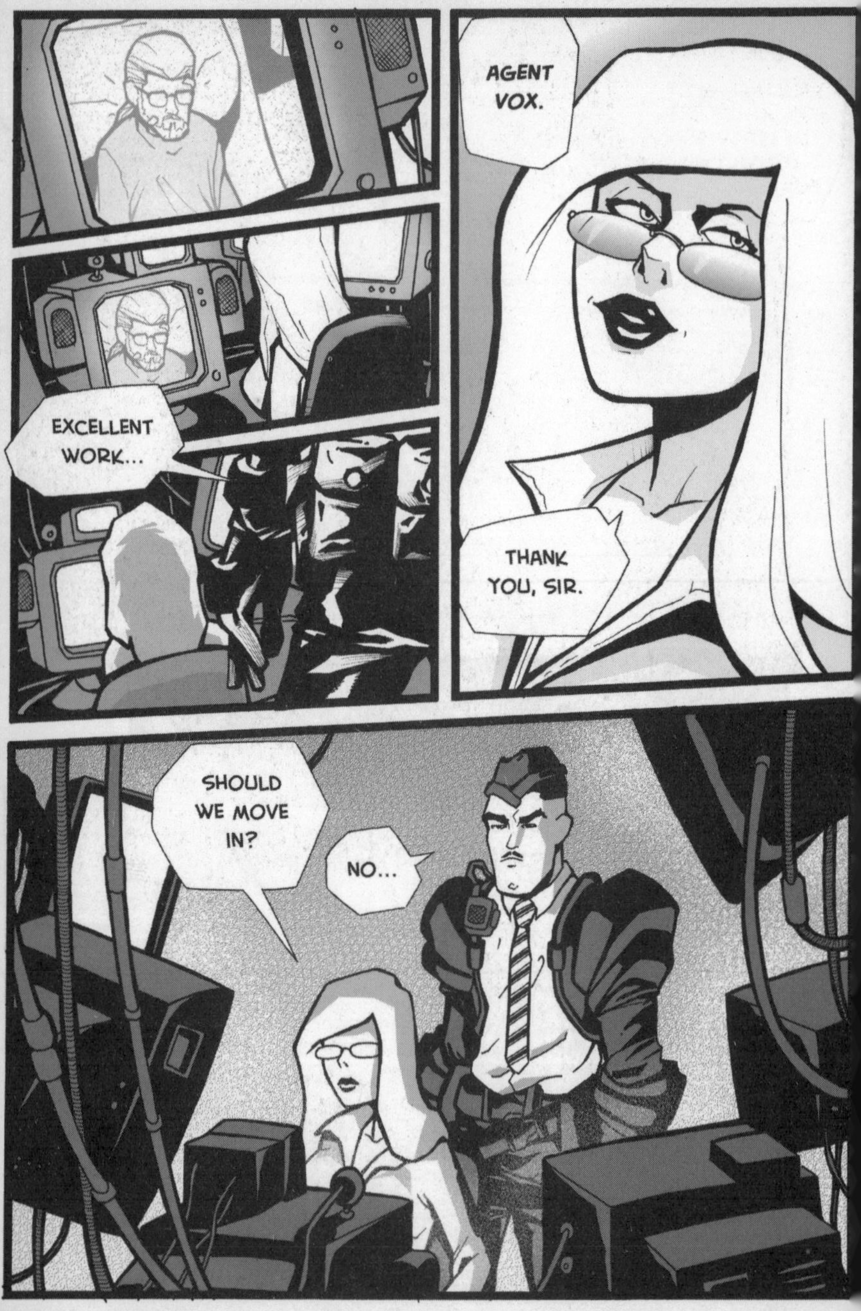
AGENT VOX.
EXCELLENT WORK...
THANK YOU, SIR.
SHOULD WE MOVE IN?
NO...

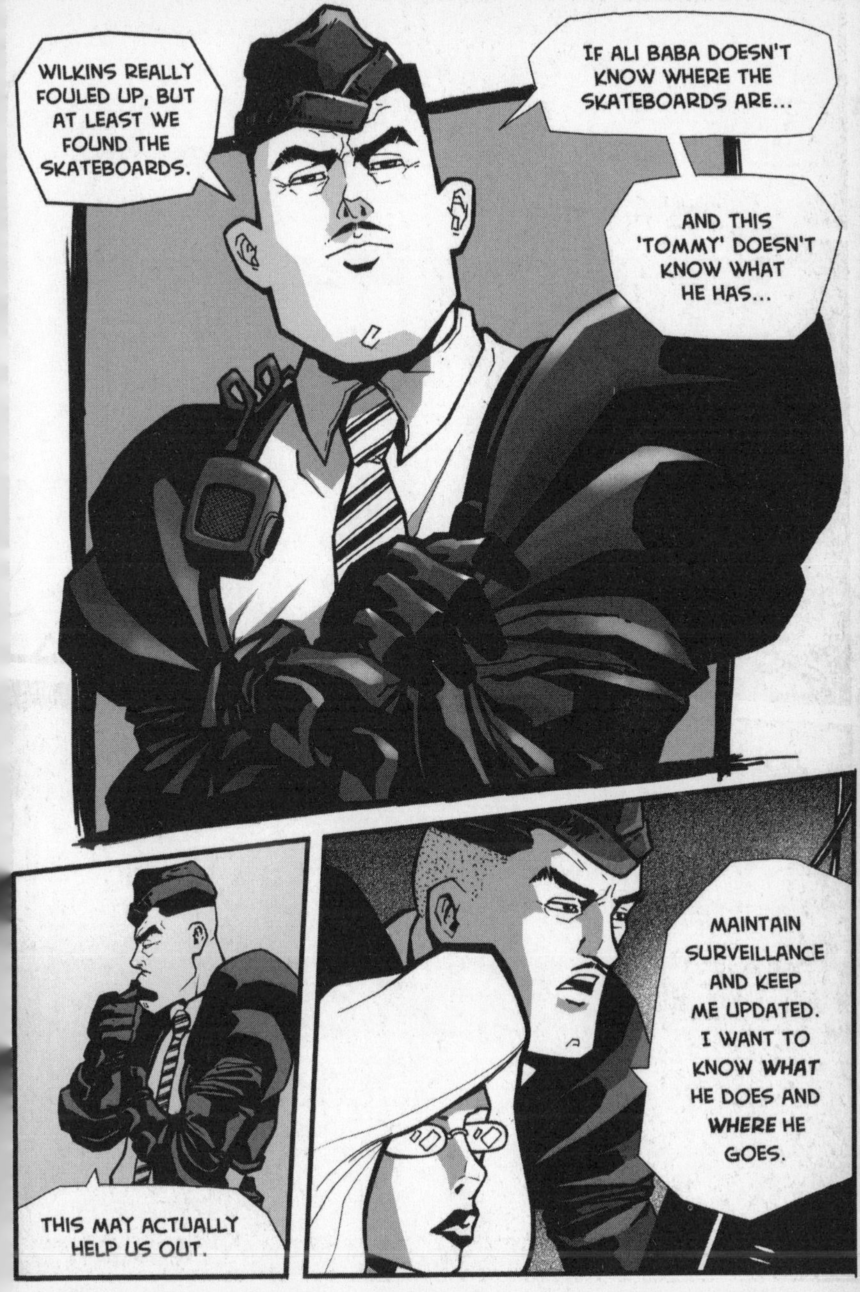
WILKINS REALLY FOULED UP, BUT AT LEAST WE FOUND THE SKATEBOARDS.
IF ALI BABA DOESN'T KNOW WHERE THE SKATEBOARDS ARE...
AND THIS 'TOMMY' DOESN'T KNOW WHAT HE HAS...
THIS MAY ACTUALLY HELP US OUT.
MAINTAIN SURVEILLANCE AND KEEP ME UPDATED. I WANT TO KNOW WHAT HE DOES AND WHERE HE GOES.

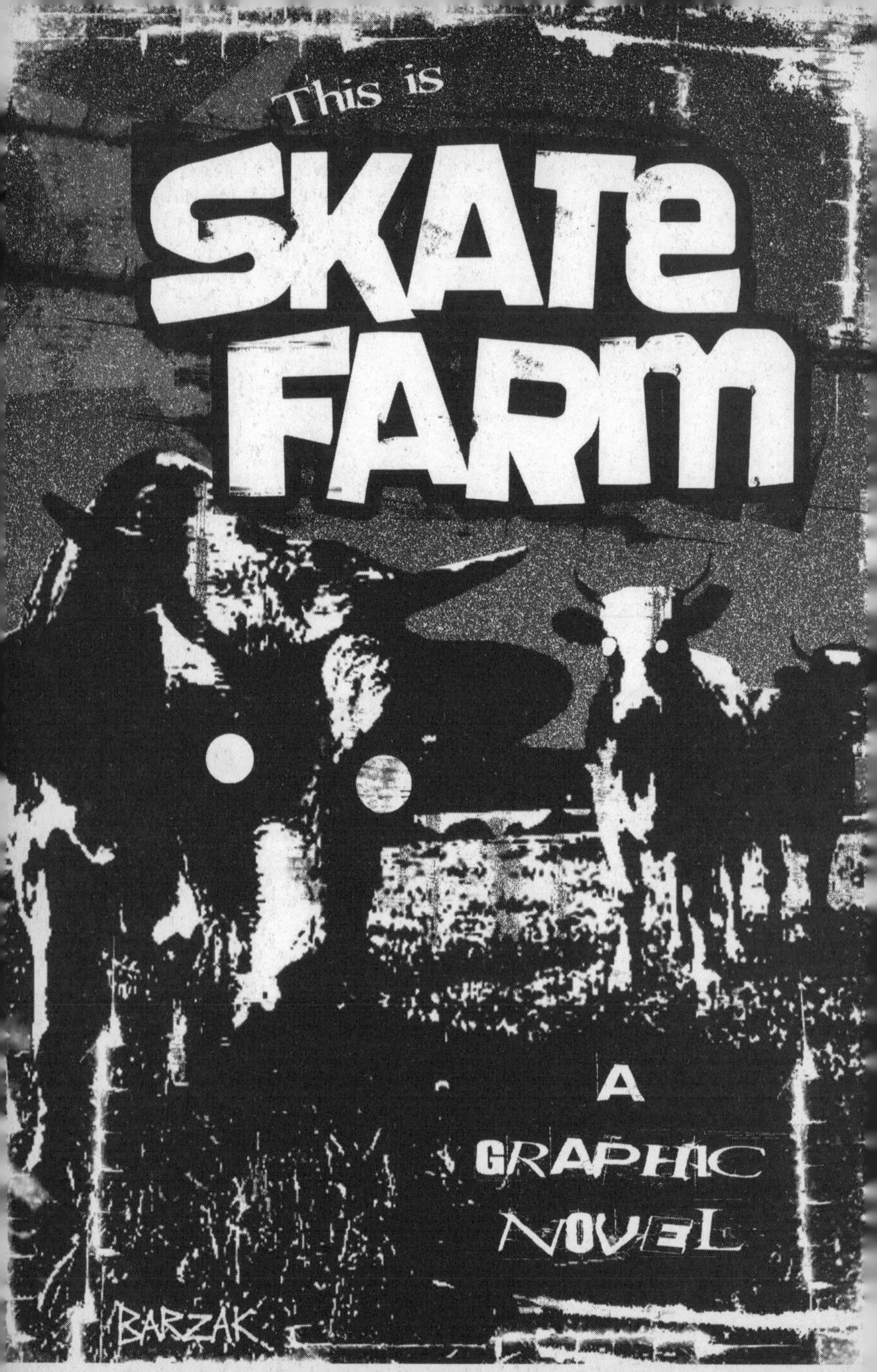
This is
SKATE
FARM
A
GRAPHIC
NOVEL
BARZAK

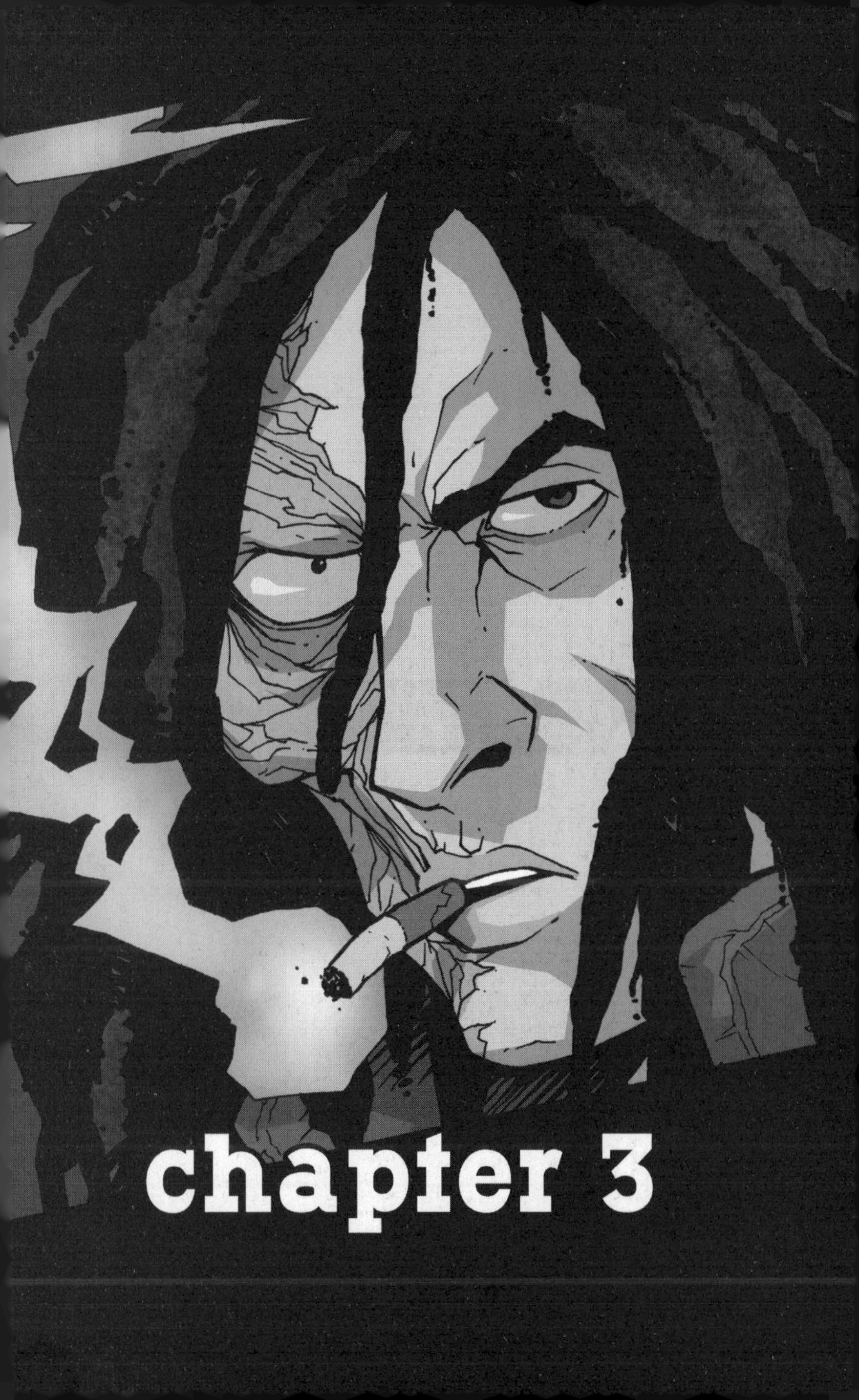
chapter 3

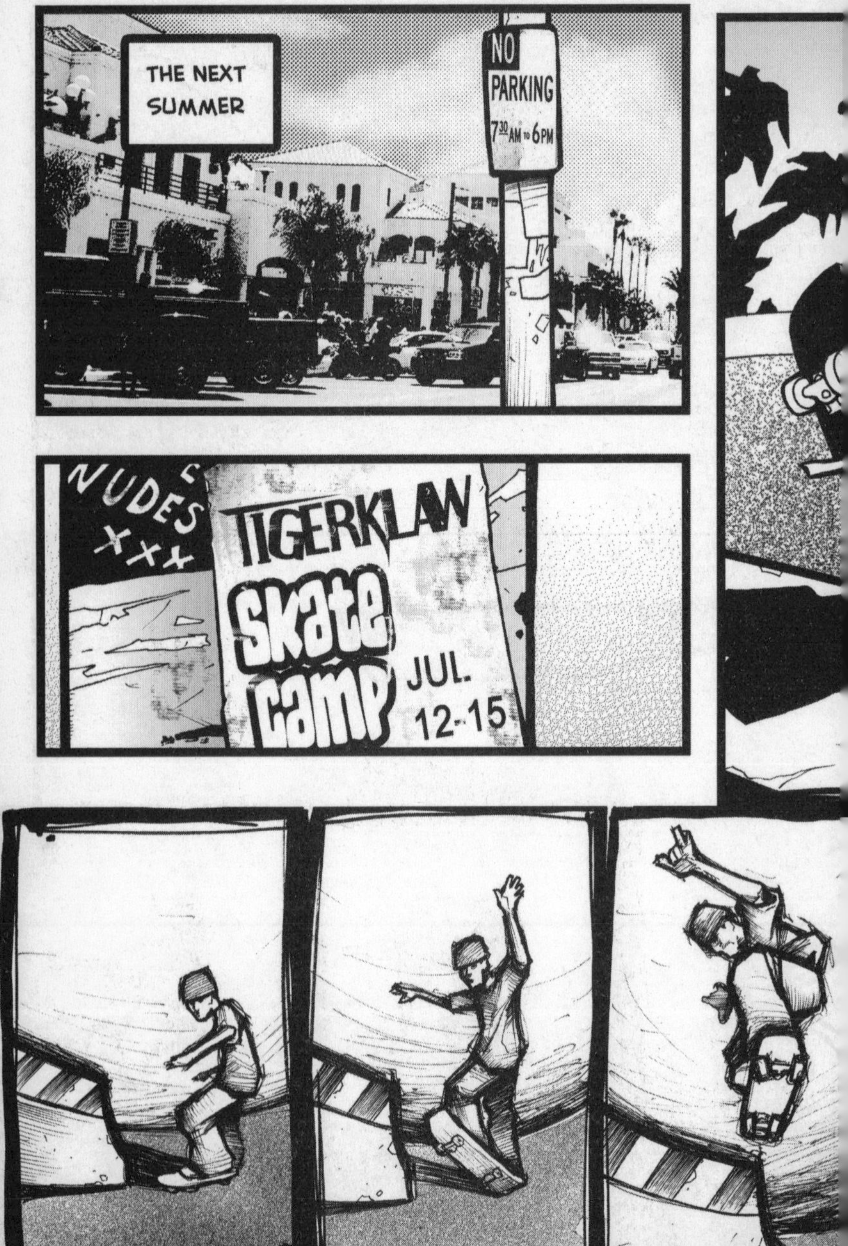
THE NEXT SUMMER
NO PARKING
7^{30} AM TO 6PM
NUDES
XXX
TIGERKLAW
Skate camp
JUL.
12-15

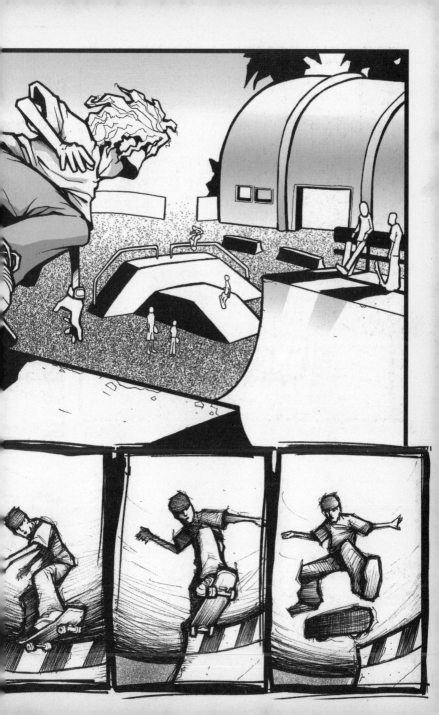

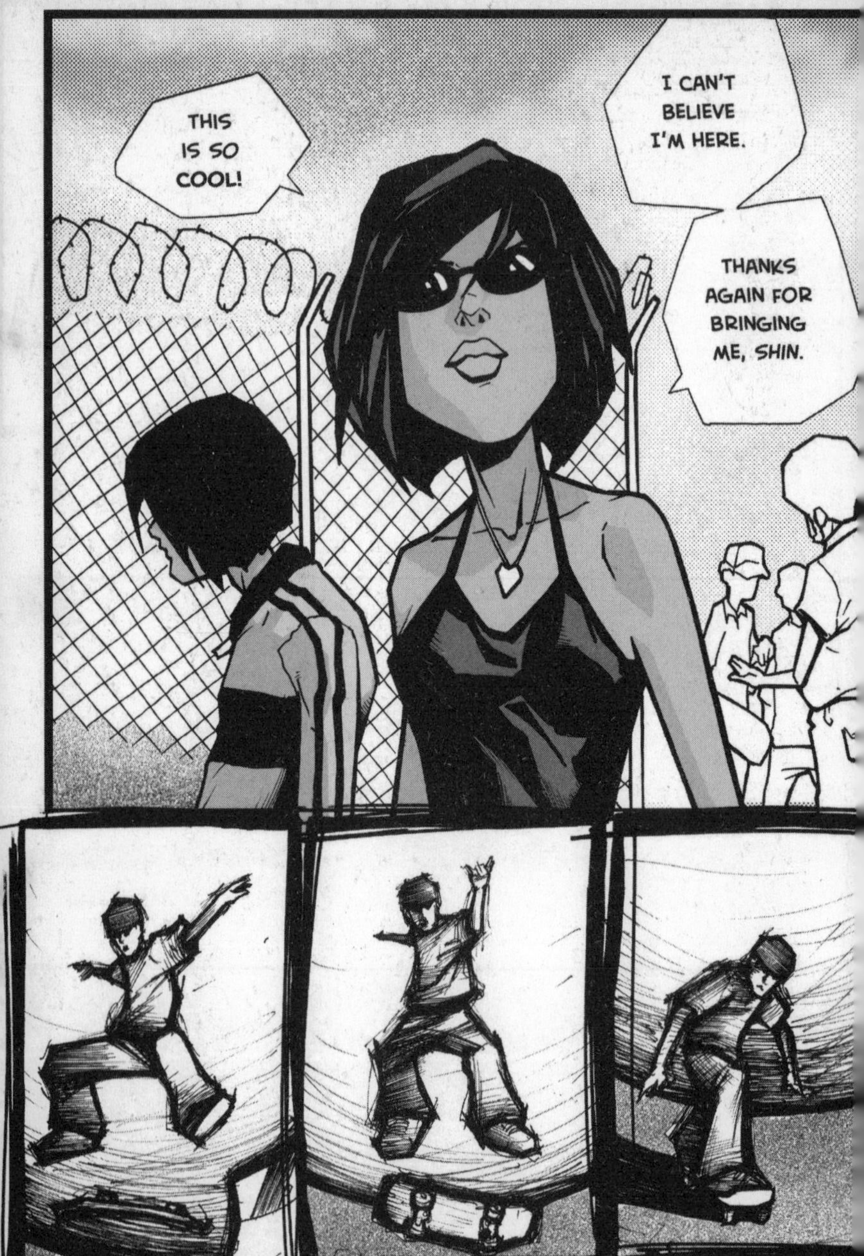
THIS IS SO COOL!
I CAN'T BELIEVE I'M HERE.
THANKS AGAIN FOR BRINGING ME, SHIN.

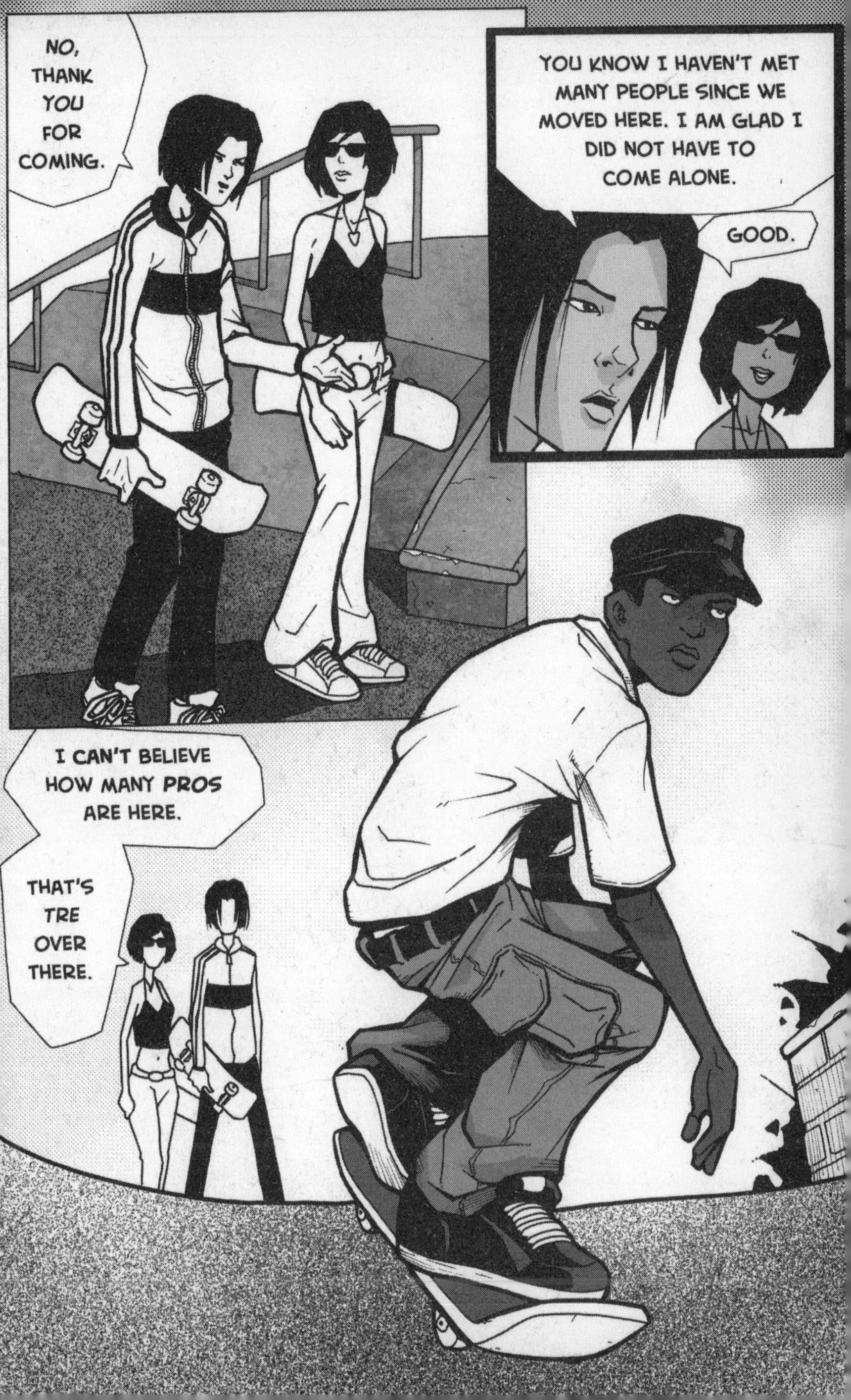
NO, THANK YOU FOR COMING.
YOU KNOW I HAVEN'T MET MANY PEOPLE SINCE WE MOVED HERE. I AM GLAD I DID NOT HAVE TO COME ALONE.
GOOD.
I CAN'T BELIEVE HOW MANY PROS ARE HERE.
THAT'S TRE OVER THERE.

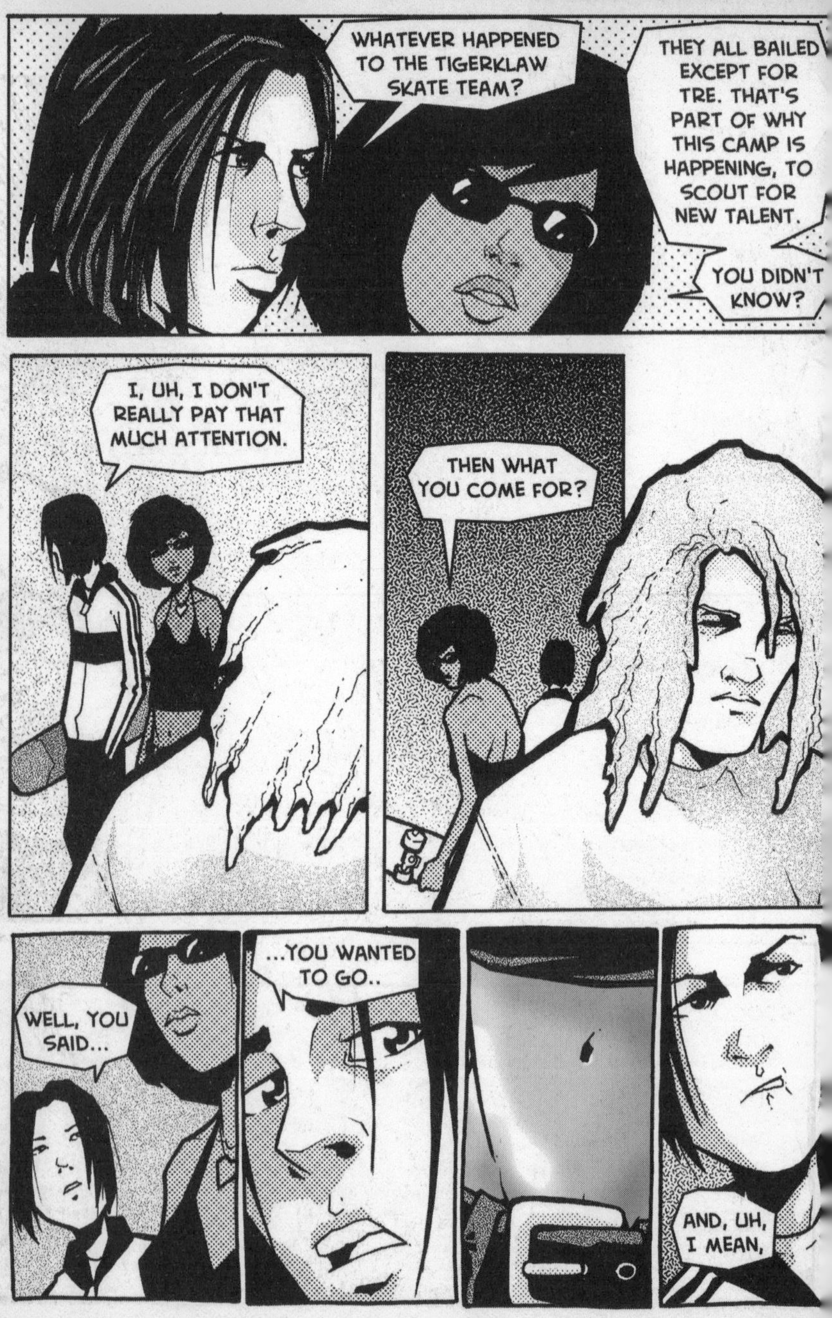
WHATEVER HAPPENED TO THE TIGERKLAW SKATE TEAM?
THEY ALL BAILED EXCEPT FOR TRE. THAT'S PART OF WHY THIS CAMP IS HAPPENING, TO SCOUT FOR NEW TALENT.
YOU DIDN'T KNOW?
I, UH, I DON'T REALLY PAY THAT MUCH ATTENTION.
THEN WHAT YOU COME FOR?
WELL, YOU SAID...
...YOU WANTED TO GO..
AND, UH, I MEAN,

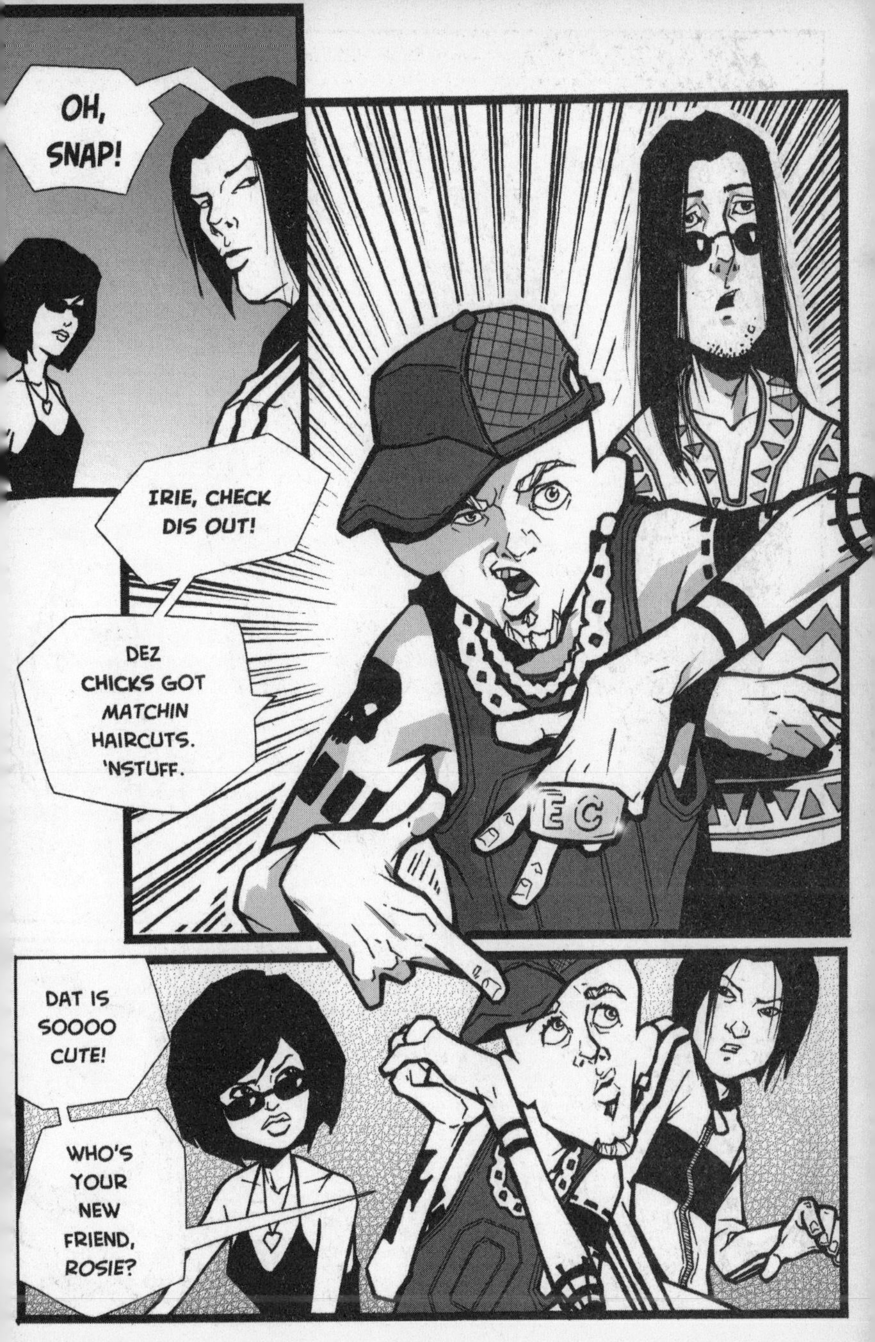
OH, SNAP!
IRIE, CHECK DIS OUT!
DEZ CHICKS GOT MATCHIN HAIRCUTS. 'NSTUFF.
DAT IS SOOOO CUTE!
WHO'S YOUR NEW FRIEND, ROSIE?

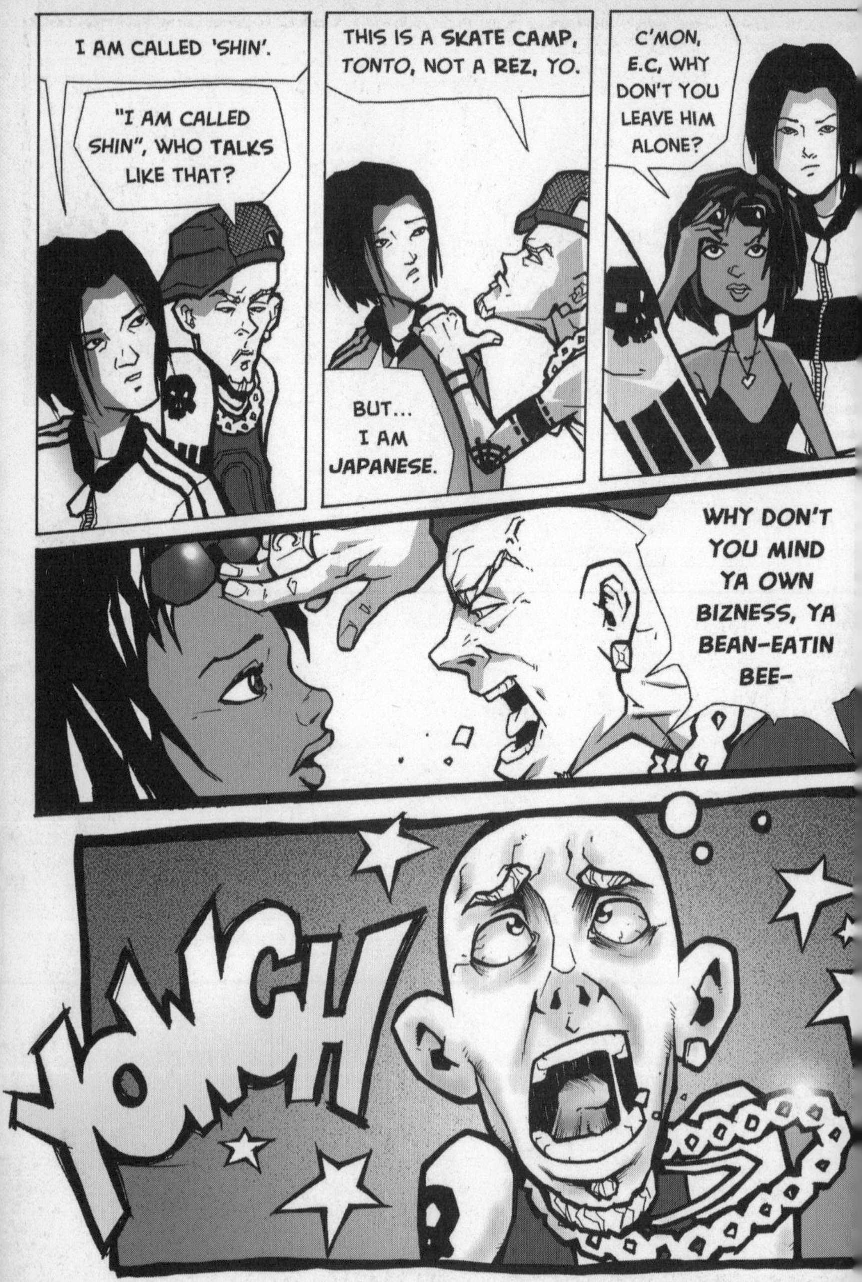
I AM CALLED 'SHIN'.
"I AM CALLED SHIN", WHO TALKS LIKE THAT?
THIS IS A SKATE CAMP, TONTO, NOT A REZ, YO.
BUT... I AM JAPANESE.
C'MON, E.C, WHY DON'T YOU LEAVE HIM ALONE?
WHY DON'T YOU MIND YA OWN BIZNESS, YA BEAN-EATIN BEE-
YOUCH

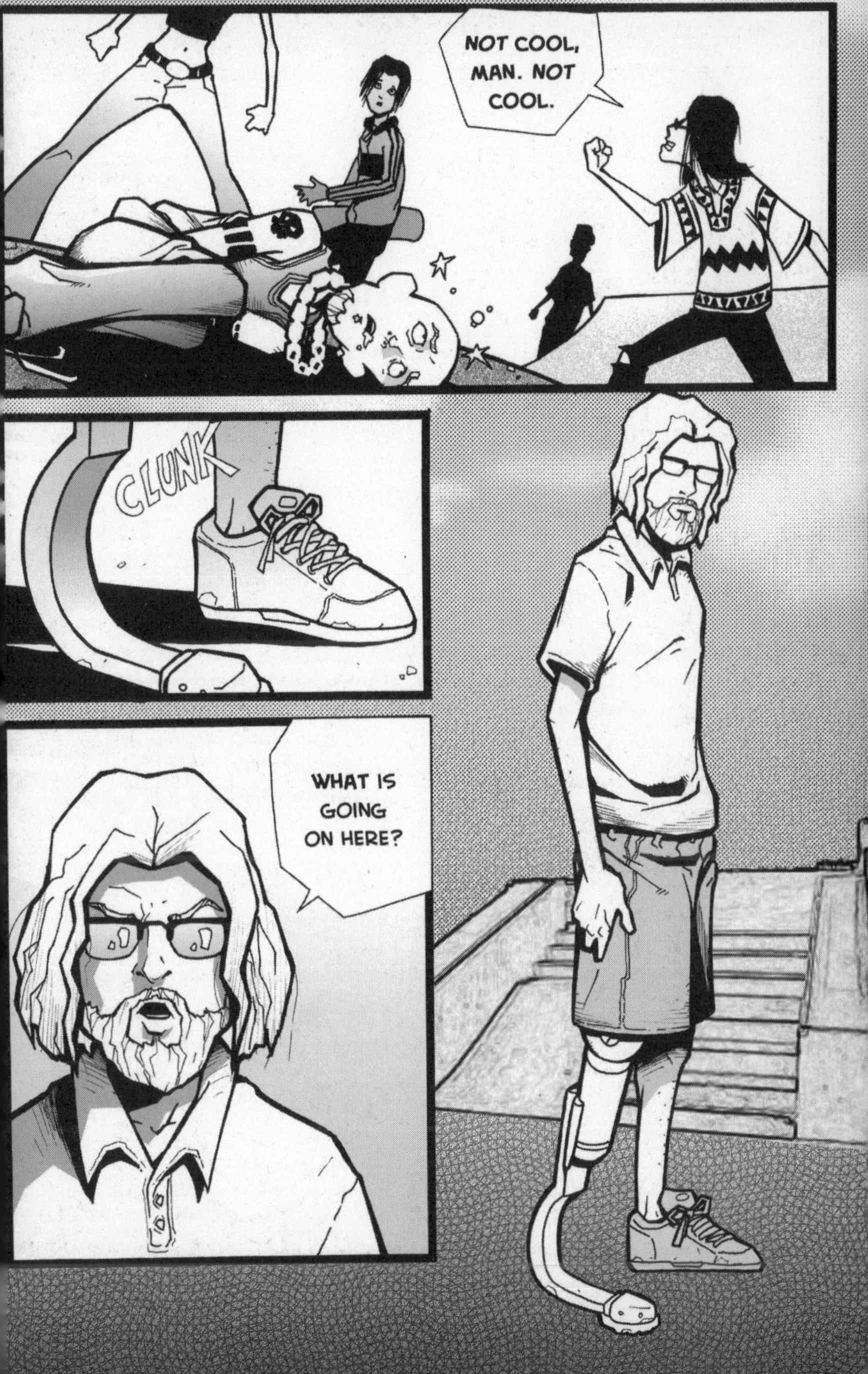
NOT COOL, MAN. NOT COOL.
CLUNK
WHAT IS GOING ON HERE?

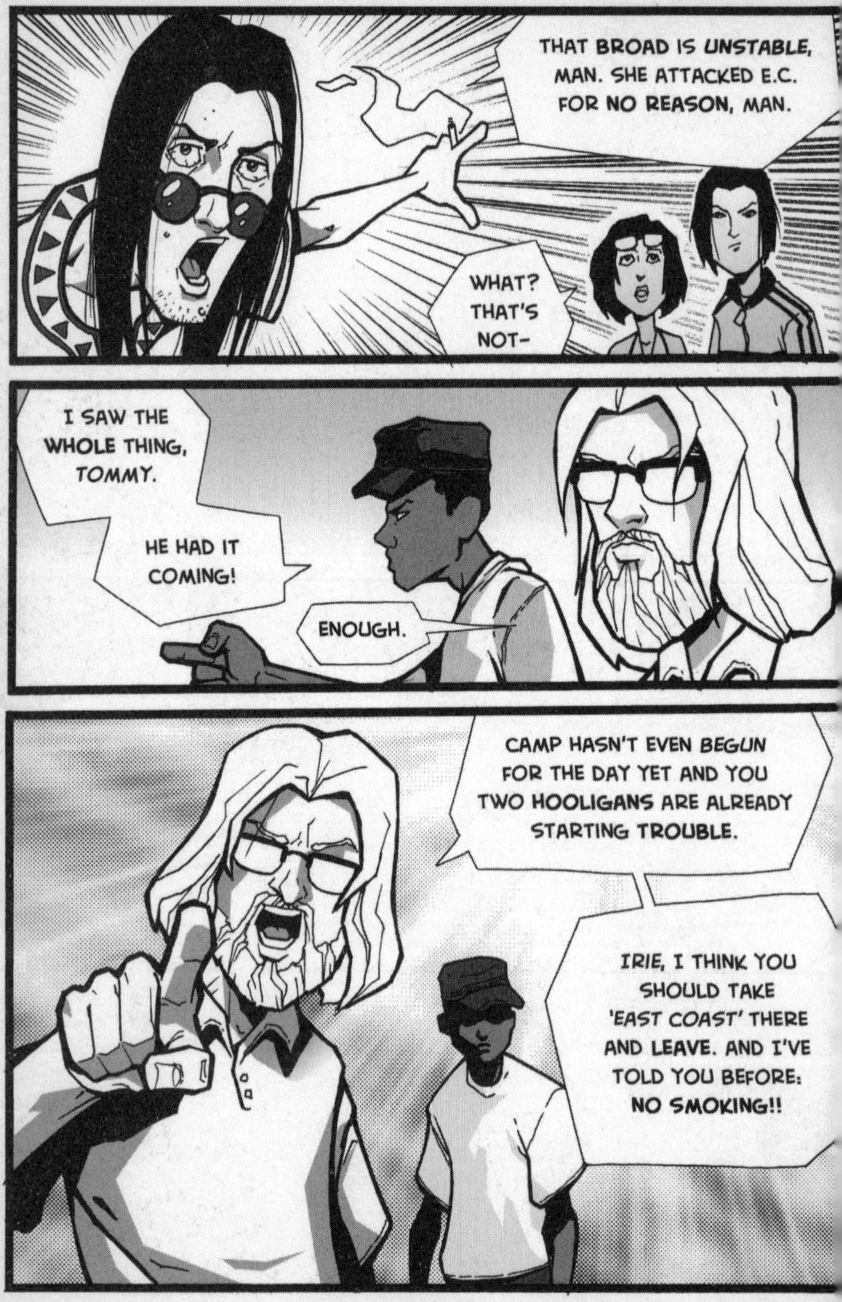
THAT BROAD IS UNSTABLE, MAN. SHE ATTACKED E.C. FOR NO REASON, MAN.
WHAT? THAT'S NOT-
I SAW THE WHOLE THING, TOMMY.
HE HAD IT COMING!
ENOUGH.
CAMP HASN'T EVEN BEGUN FOR THE DAY YET AND YOU TWO HOOLIGANS ARE ALREADY STARTING TROUBLE.
IRIE, I THINK YOU SHOULD TAKE 'EAST COAST' THERE AND LEAVE. AND I'VE TOLD YOU BEFORE: NO SMOKING!!

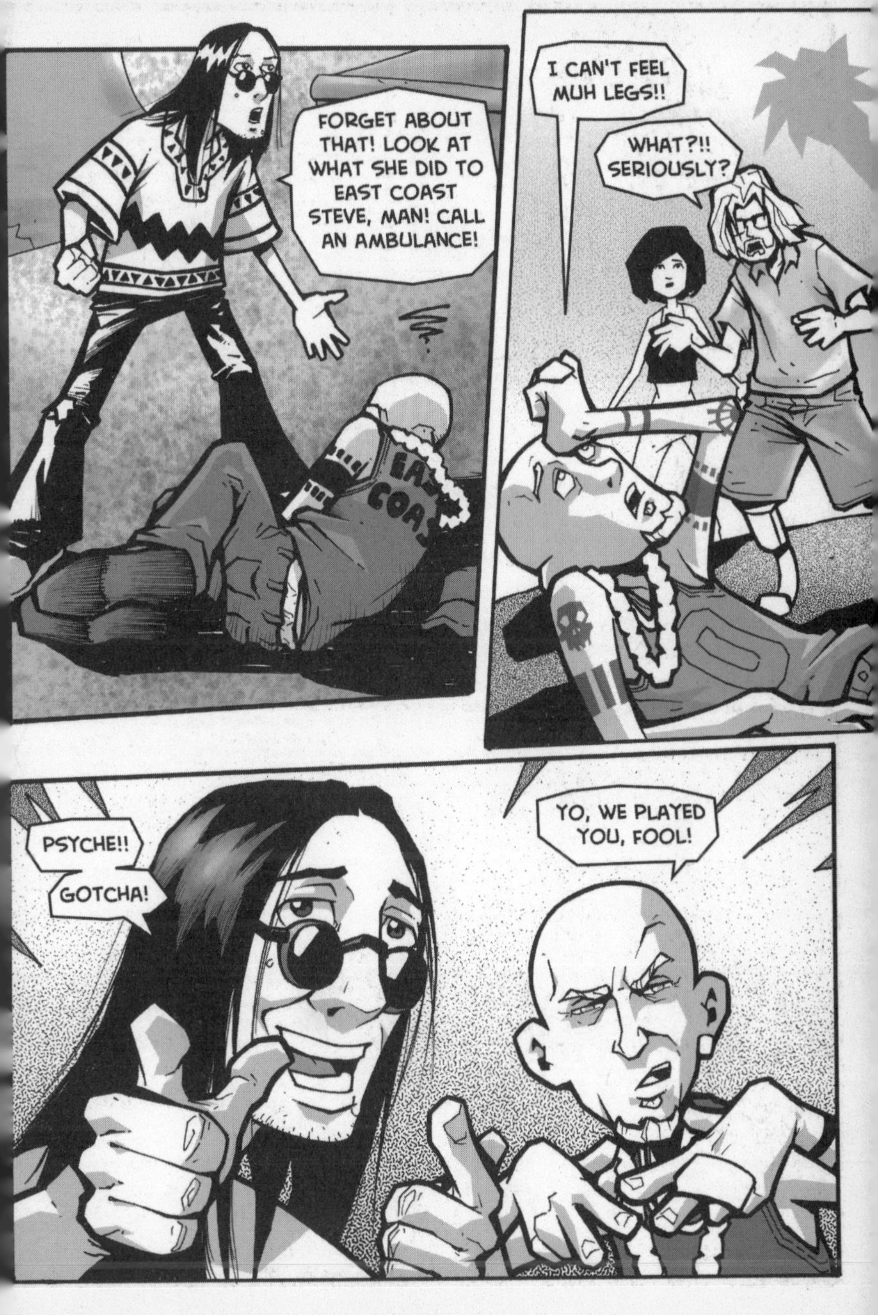
FORGET ABOUT THAT! LOOK AT WHAT SHE DID TO EAST COAST STEVE, MAN! CALL AN AMBULANCE!
I CAN'T FEEL MUH LEGS!!
WHAT?!! SERIOUSLY?
PSYCHE!!
GOTCHA!
YO, WE PLAYED YOU, FOOL!

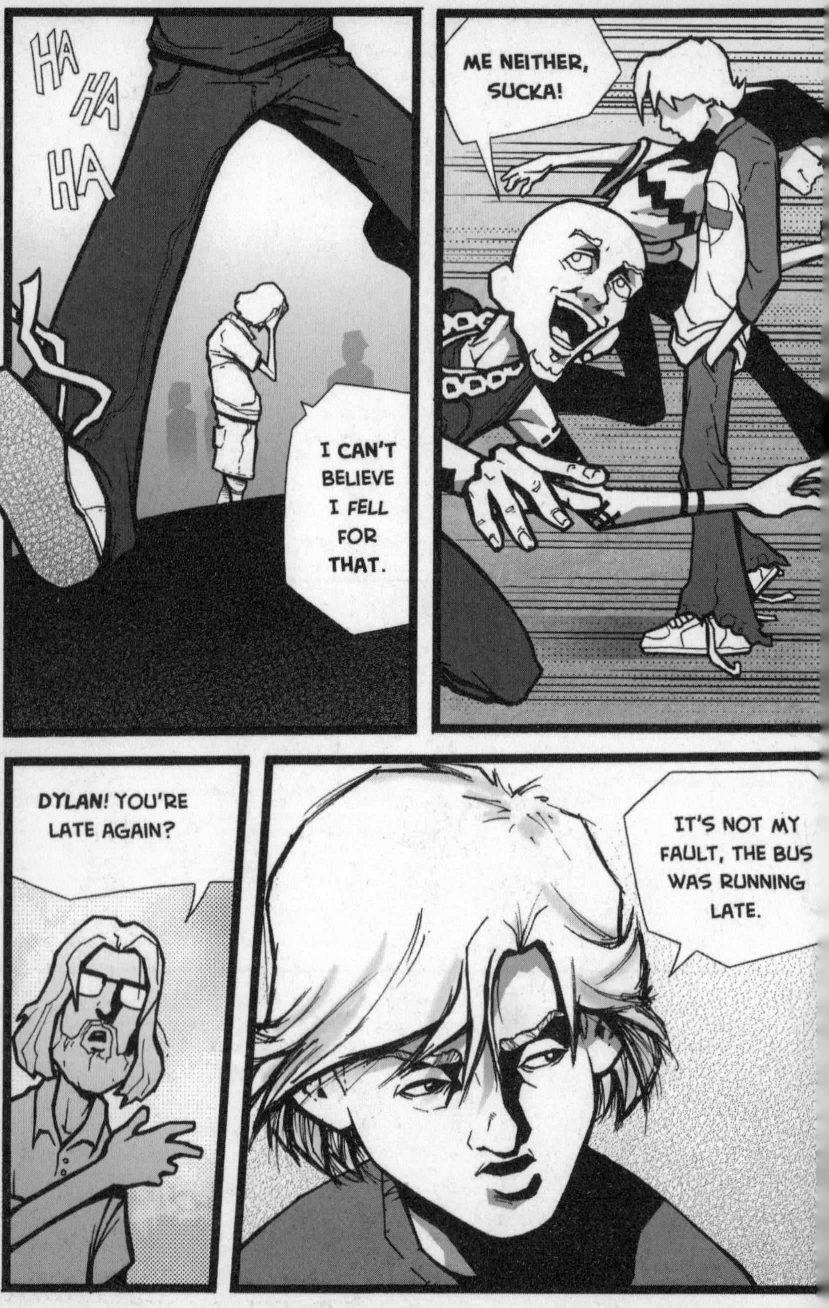
HA HA HA
I CAN'T BELIEVE I FELL FOR THAT.
ME NEITHER, SUCKA!
DYLAN! YOU'RE LATE AGAIN?
IT'S NOT MY FAULT, THE BUS WAS RUNNING LATE.

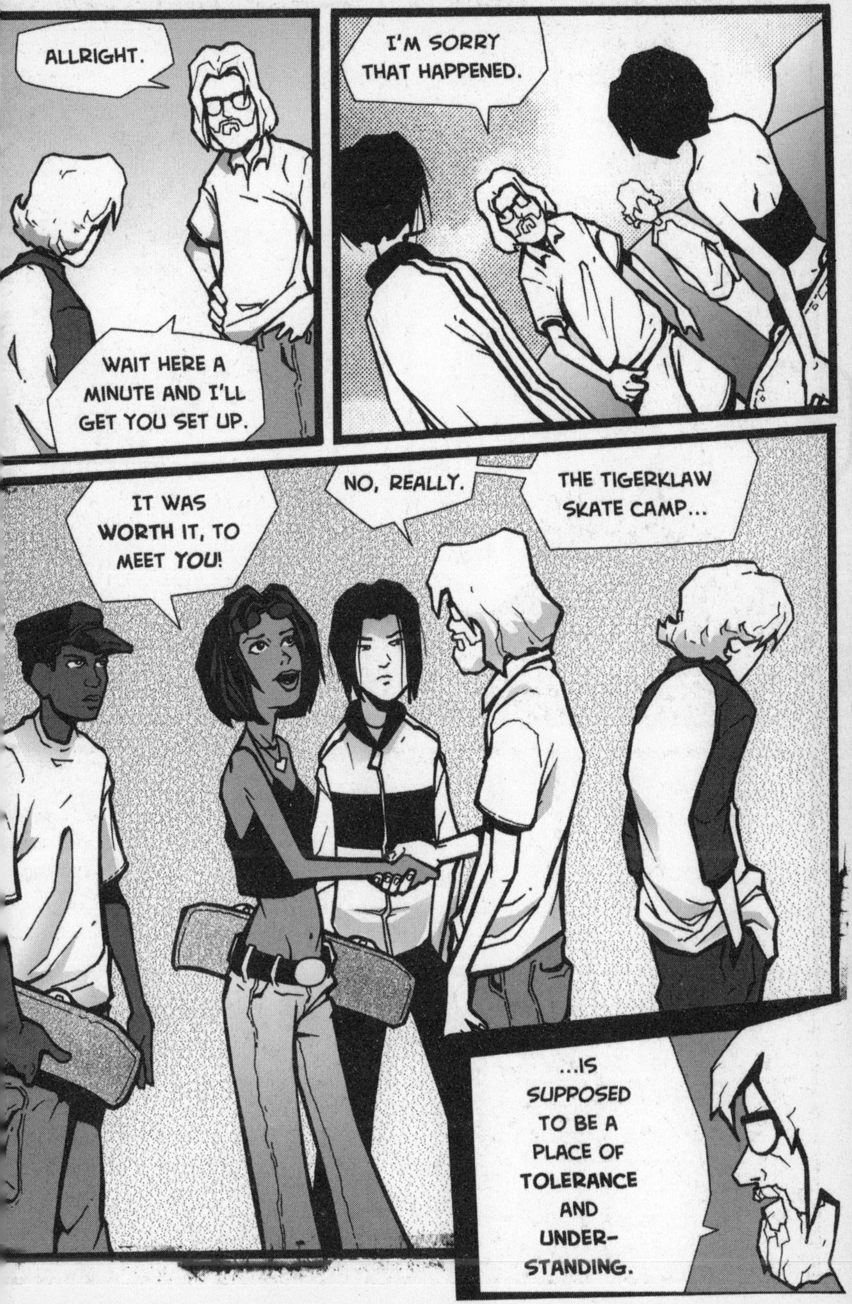
ALLRIGHT.
WAIT HERE A MINUTE AND I'LL GET YOU SET UP.
I'M SORRY THAT HAPPENED.
IT WAS WORTH IT, TO MEET YOU!
NO, REALLY.
THE TIGERKLAW SKATE CAMP...
...IS SUPPOSED TO BE A PLACE OF TOLERANCE AND UNDER-STANDING.

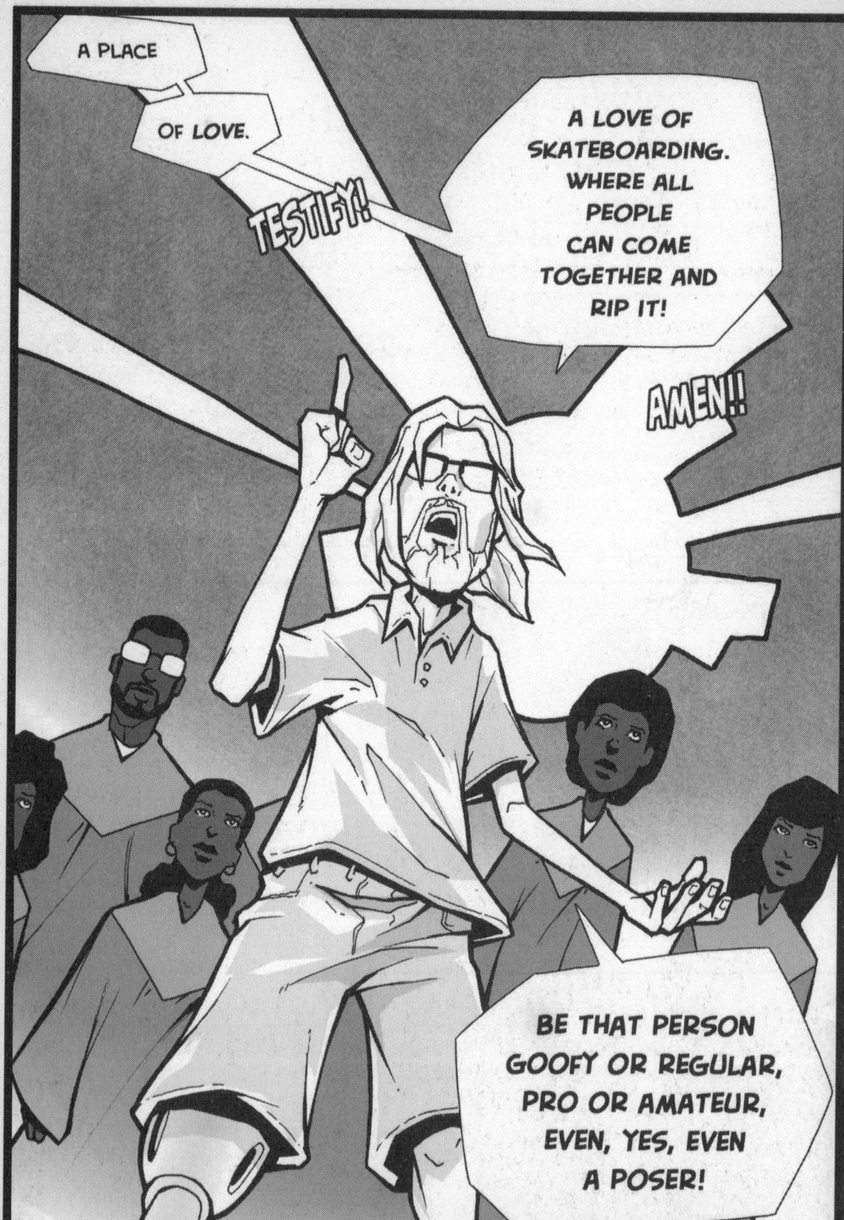
A PLACE
OF LOVE.
A LOVE OF SKATEBOARDING. WHERE ALL PEOPLE CAN COME TOGETHER AND RIP IT!
TESTIFY!
AMEN!!
BE THAT PERSON GOOFY OR REGULAR, PRO OR AMATEUR, EVEN, YES, EVEN A POSER!

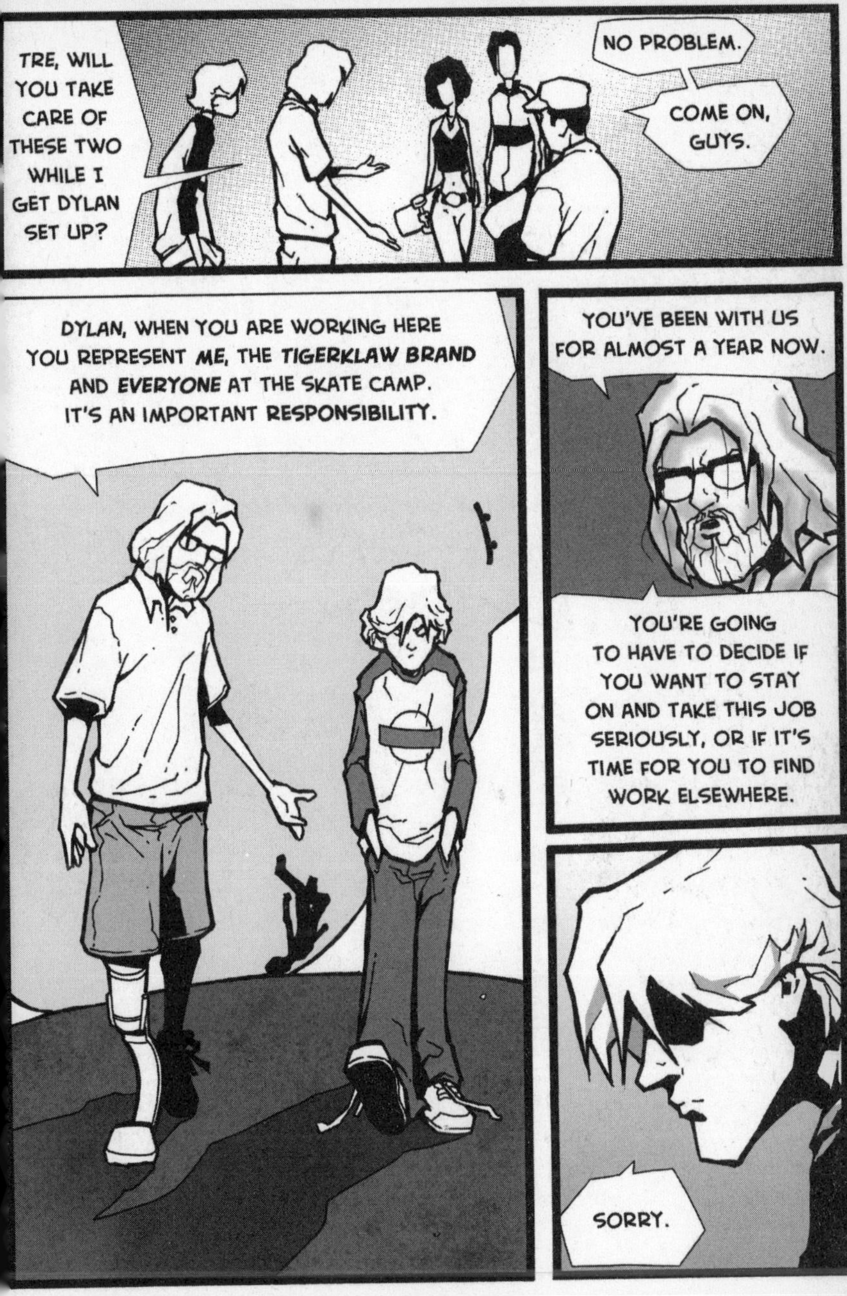
TRE, WILL YOU TAKE CARE OF THESE TWO WHILE I GET DYLAN SET UP?
NO PROBLEM.
COME ON, GUYS.
DYLAN, WHEN YOU ARE WORKING HERE YOU REPRESENT ME, THE TIGERKLAW BRAND AND EVERYONE AT THE SKATE CAMP. IT'S AN IMPORTANT RESPONSIBILITY.
YOU'VE BEEN WITH US FOR ALMOST A YEAR NOW.
YOU'RE GOING TO HAVE TO DECIDE IF YOU WANT TO STAY ON AND TAKE THIS JOB SERIOUSLY, OR IF IT'S TIME FOR YOU TO FIND WORK ELSEWHERE.
SORRY.

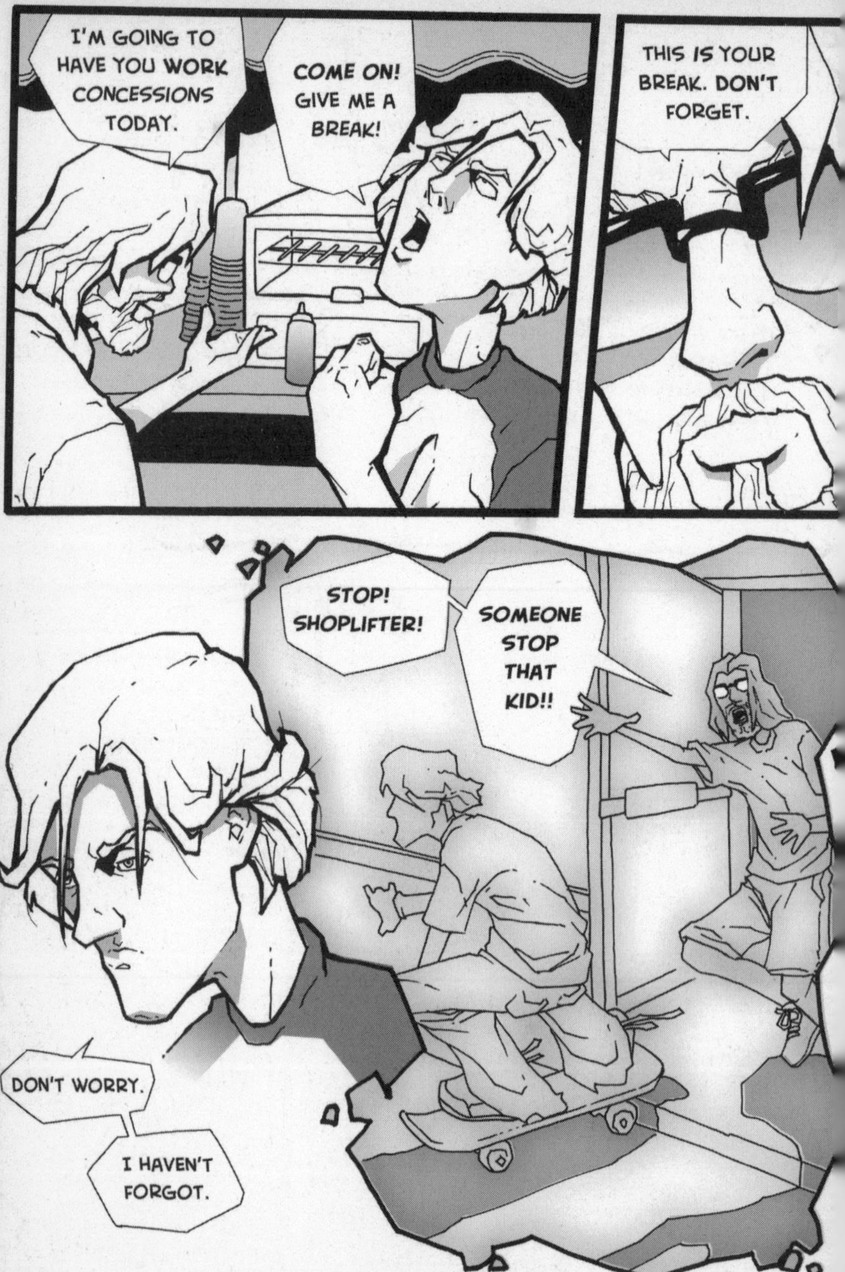

I'M GOING TO HAVE YOU WORK CONCESSIONS TODAY.
COME ON! GIVE ME A BREAK!
THIS IS YOUR BREAK. DON'T FORGET.
STOP! SHOPLIFTER!
SOMEONE STOP THAT KID!!
DON'T WORRY.
I HAVEN'T FORGOT.

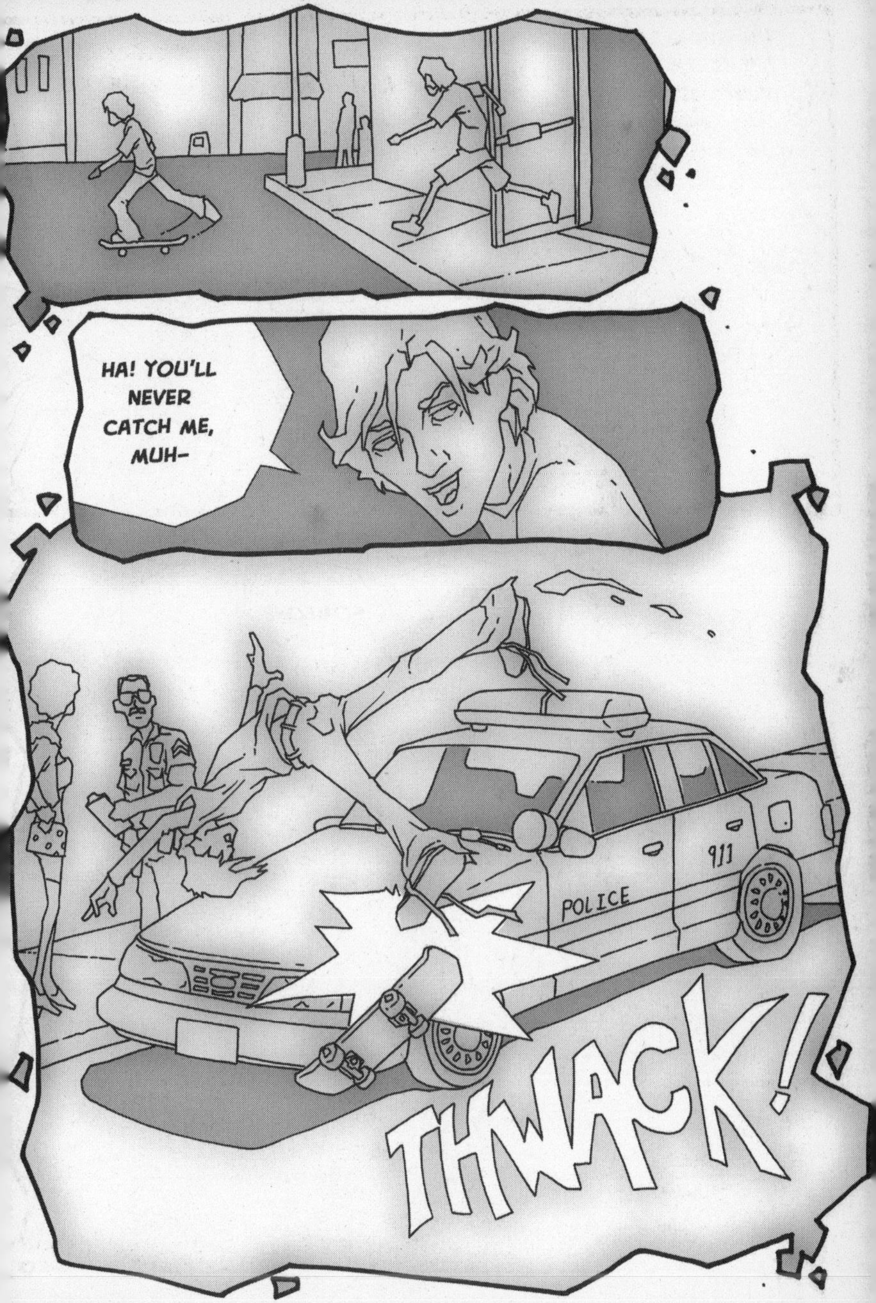
HA! YOU'LL NEVER CATCH ME, MUH-
POLICE
911
THWACK!

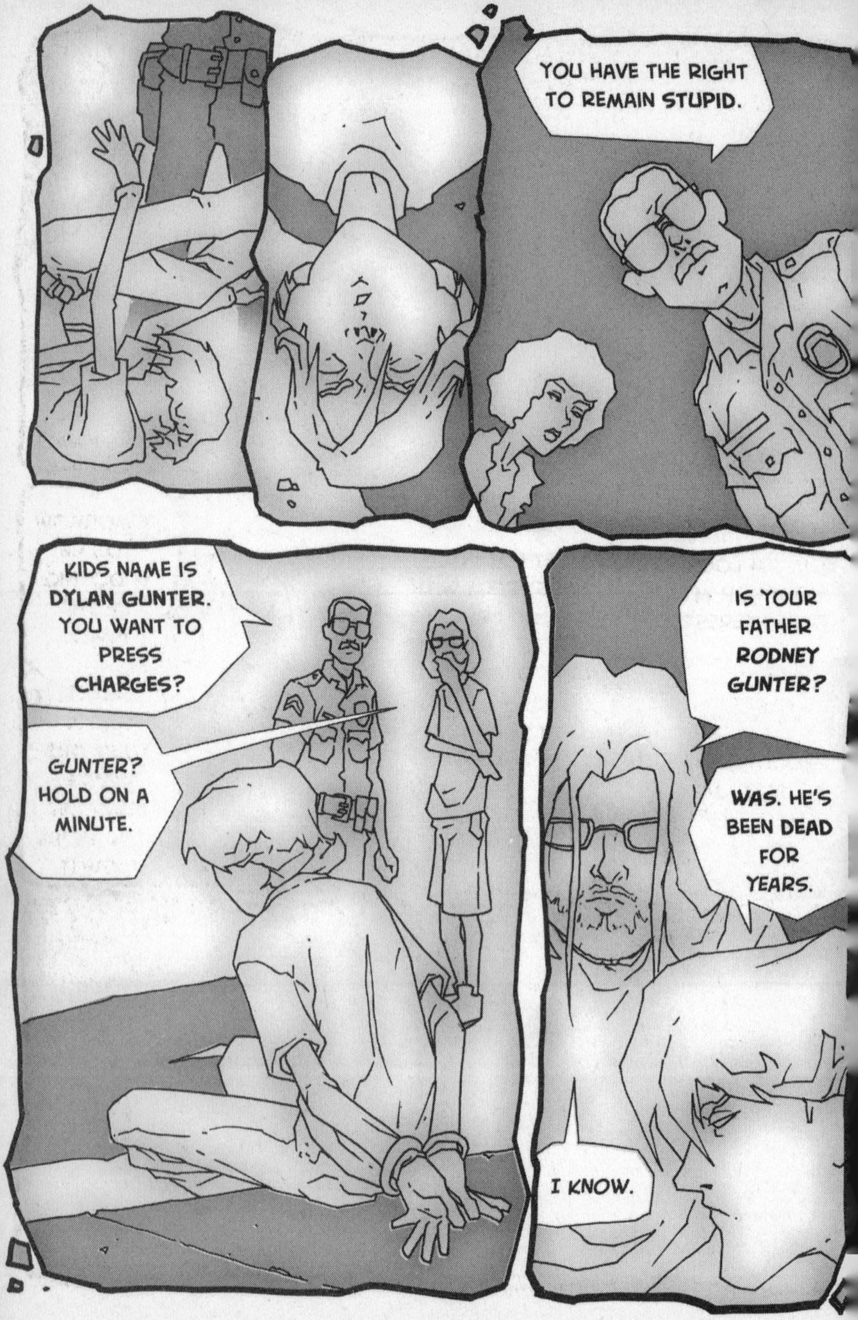
YOU HAVE THE RIGHT TO REMAIN STUPID.
KIDS NAME IS DYLAN GUNTER. YOU WANT TO PRESS CHARGES?
GUNTER? HOLD ON A MINUTE.
IS YOUR FATHER RODNEY GUNTER?
WAS. HE'S BEEN DEAD FOR YEARS.
I KNOW.

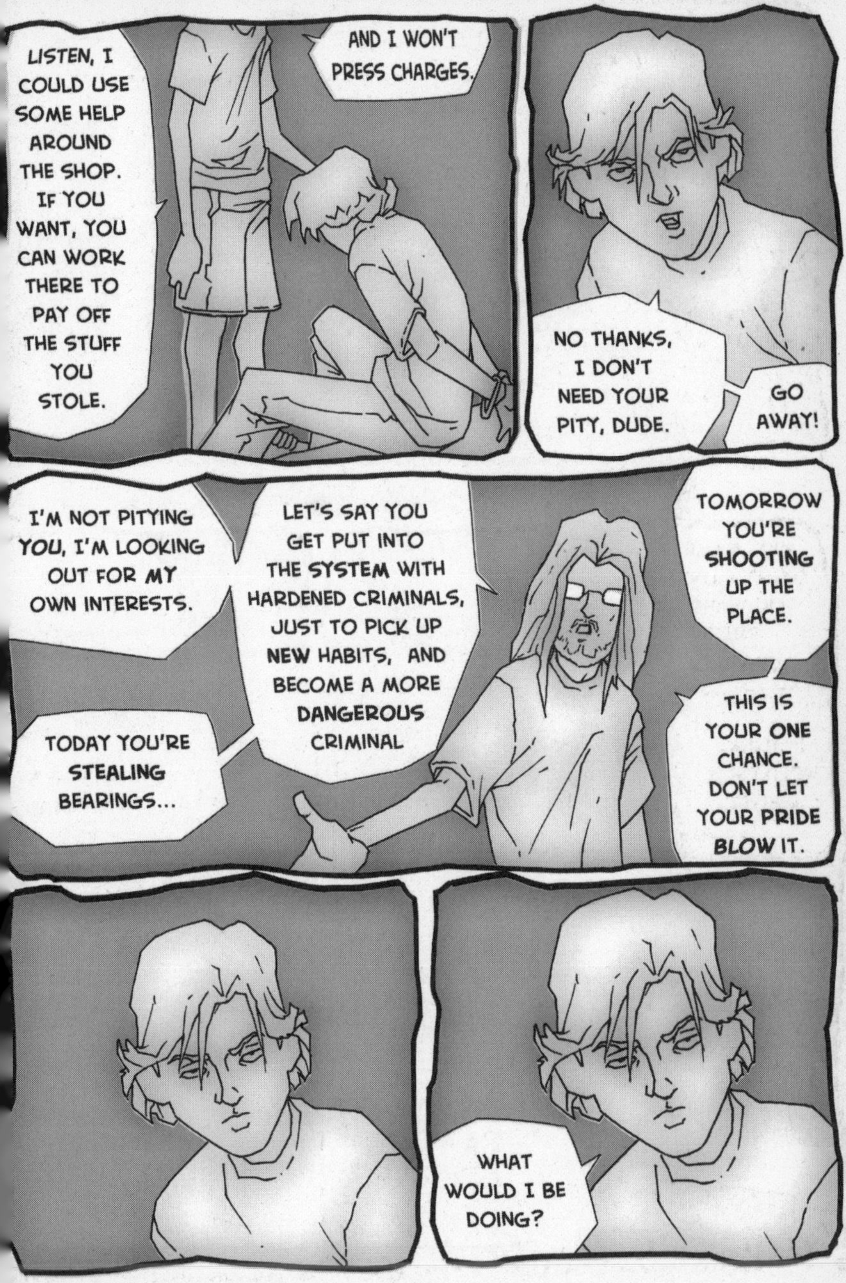
LISTEN, I COULD USE SOME HELP AROUND THE SHOP. IF YOU WANT, YOU CAN WORK THERE TO PAY OFF THE STUFF YOU STOLE.
AND I WON'T PRESS CHARGES.
NO THANKS, I DON'T NEED YOUR PITY, DUDE.
GO AWAY!
I'M NOT PITYING YOU, I'M LOOKING OUT FOR MY OWN INTERESTS.
LET'S SAY YOU GET PUT INTO THE SYSTEM WITH HARDENED CRIMINALS, JUST TO PICK UP NEW HABITS, AND BECOME A MORE DANGEROUS CRIMINAL
TODAY YOU'RE STEALING BEARINGS...
TOMORROW YOU'RE SHOOTING UP THE PLACE.
THIS IS YOUR ONE CHANCE. DON'T LET YOUR PRIDE BLOW IT.
WHAT WOULD I BE DOING?

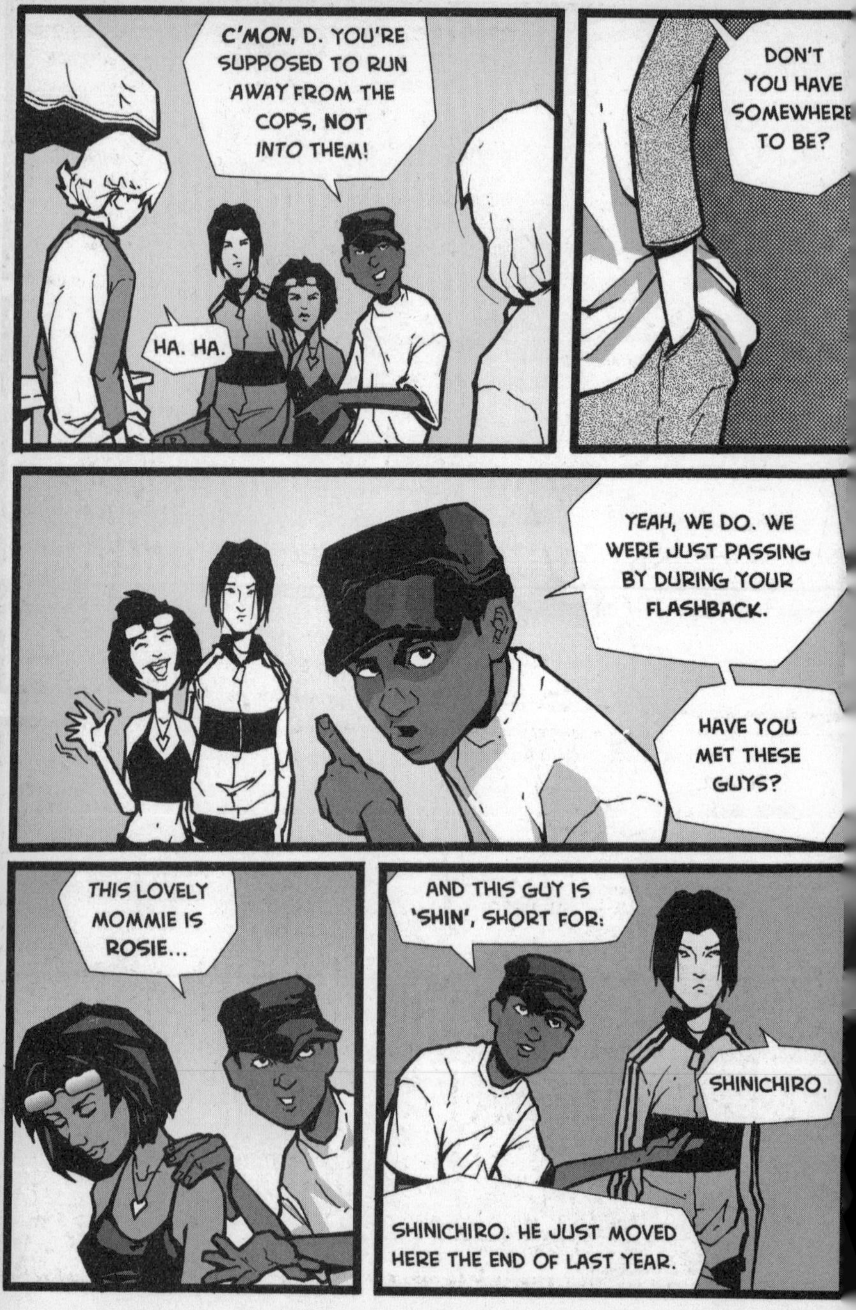
C'MON, D. YOU'RE SUPPOSED TO RUN AWAY FROM THE COPS, NOT INTO THEM!
HA. HA.
DON'T YOU HAVE SOMEWHERE TO BE?
YEAH, WE DO. WE WERE JUST PASSING BY DURING YOUR FLASHBACK.
HAVE YOU MET THESE GUYS?
THIS LOVELY MOMMIE IS ROSIE...
AND THIS GUY IS 'SHIN', SHORT FOR:
SHINICHIRO.
SHINICHIRO. HE JUST MOVED HERE THE END OF LAST YEAR.

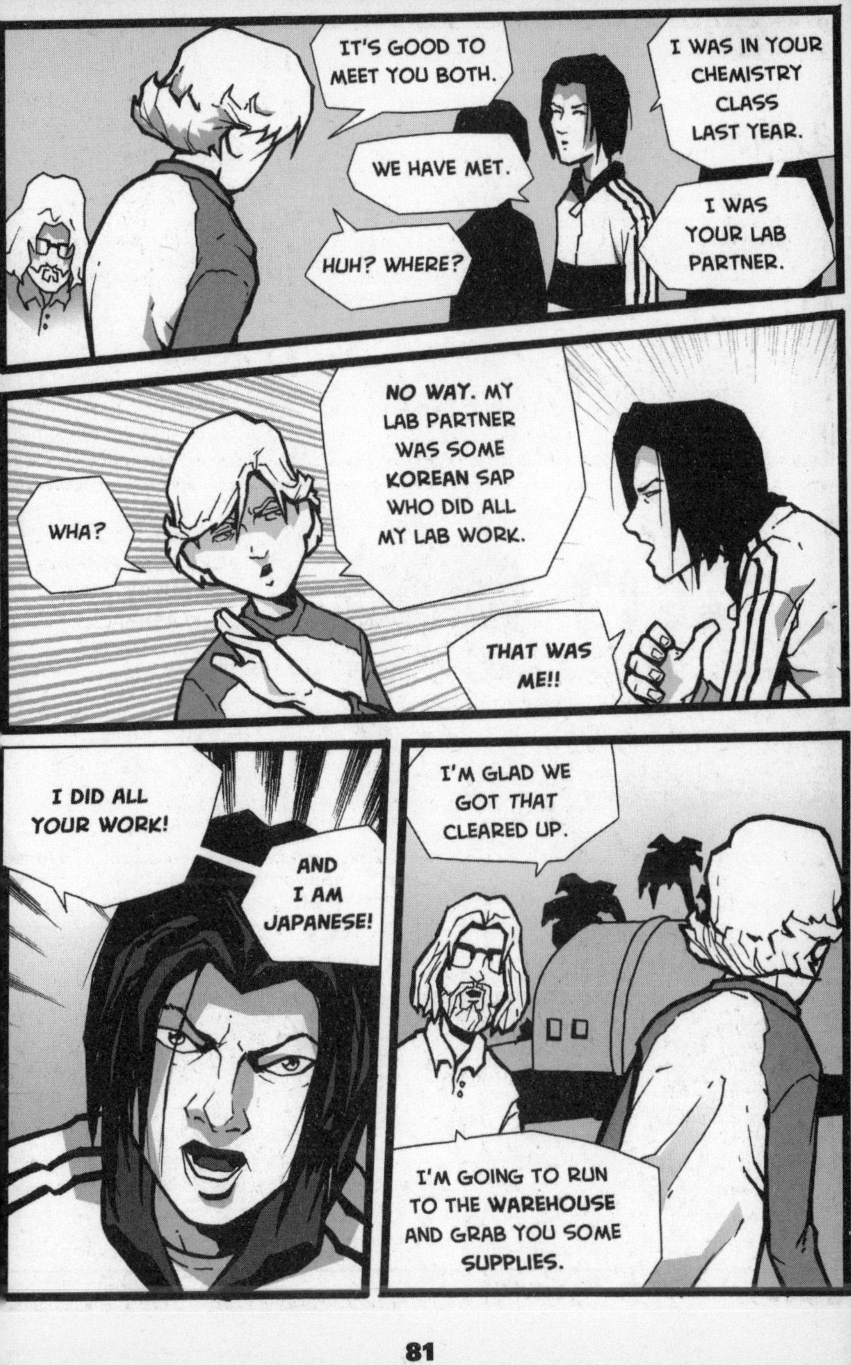
IT'S GOOD TO MEET YOU BOTH.
WE HAVE MET.
HUH? WHERE?
I WAS IN YOUR CHEMISTRY CLASS LAST YEAR.
I WAS YOUR LAB PARTNER.
WHA?
NO WAY. MY LAB PARTNER WAS SOME KOREAN SAP WHO DID ALL MY LAB WORK.
THAT WAS ME!!
I DID ALL YOUR WORK!
AND I AM JAPANESE!
I'M GLAD WE GOT THAT CLEARED UP.
I'M GOING TO RUN TO THE WAREHOUSE AND GRAB YOU SOME SUPPLIES.

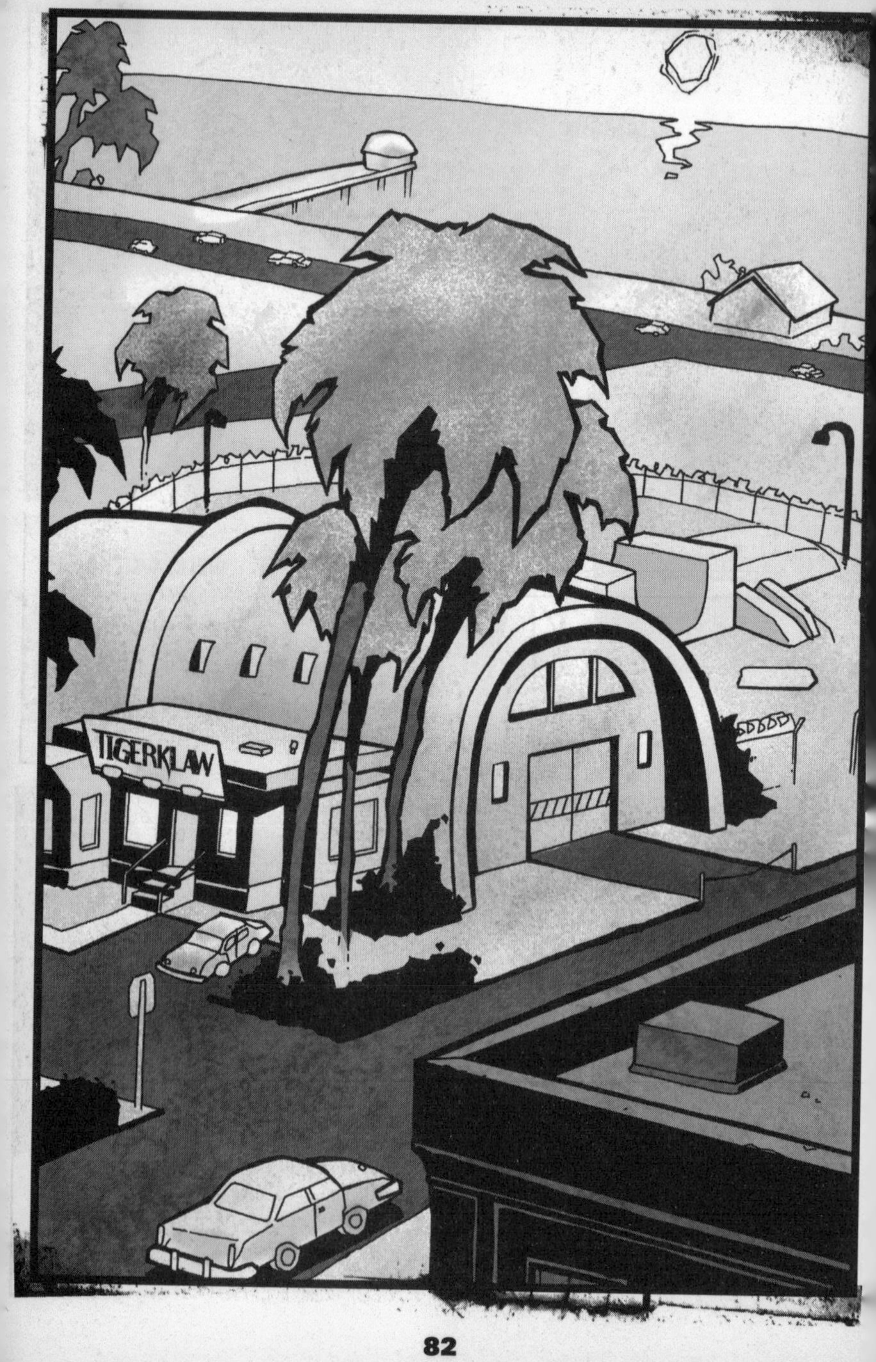
TIGERKLAW

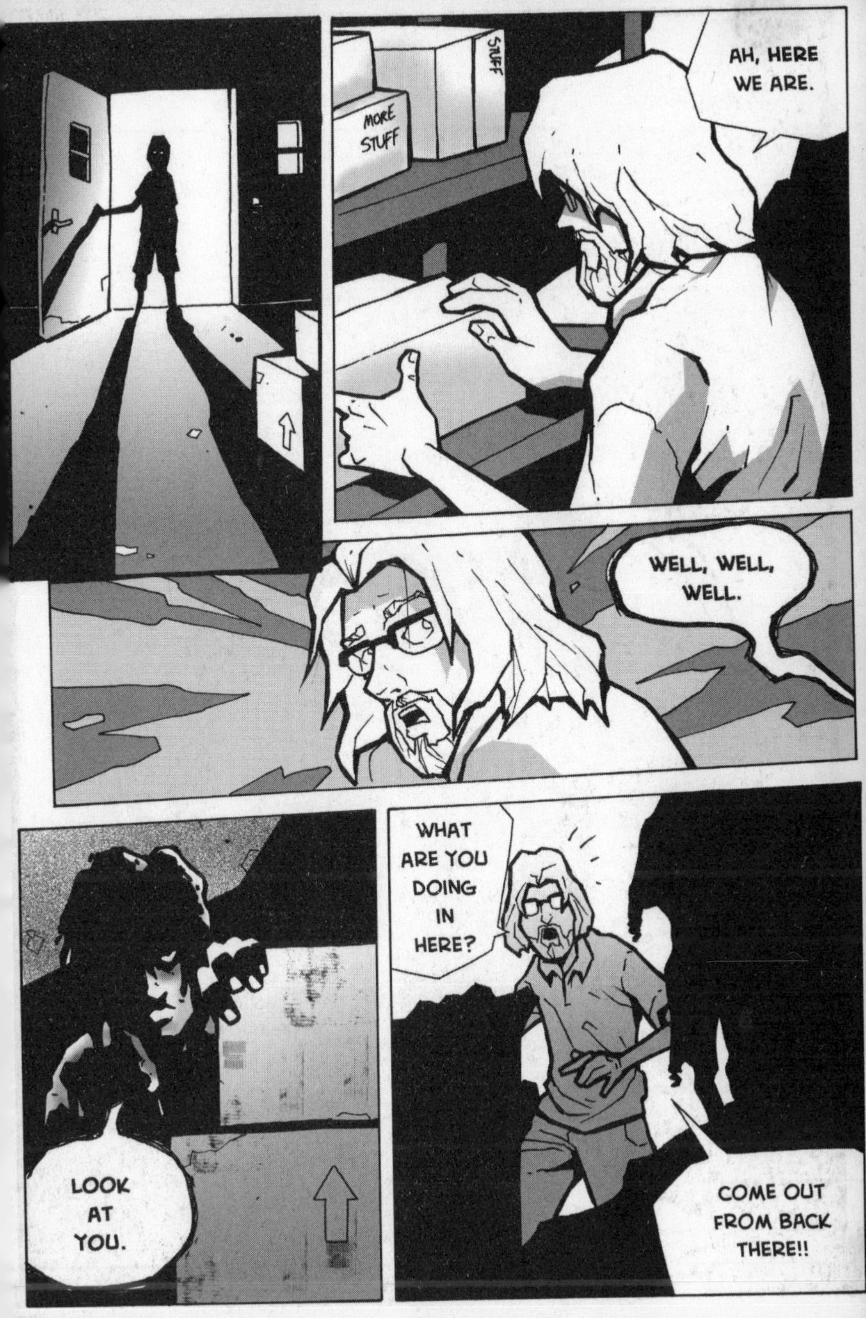
MORE STUFF
STUFF
AH, HERE WE ARE.
WELL, WELL, WELL.
LOOK AT YOU.
WHAT ARE YOU DOING IN HERE?
COME OUT FROM BACK THERE!!

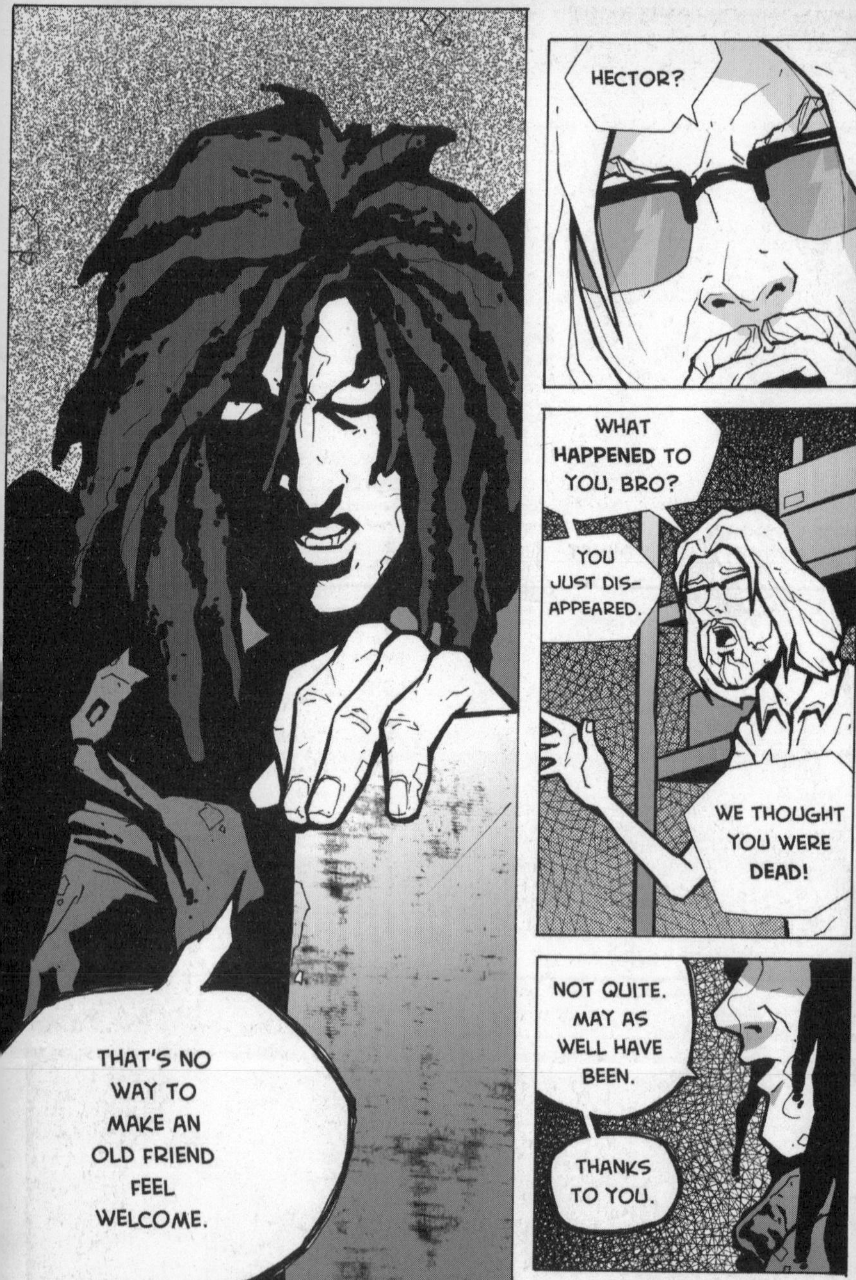
HECTOR?
WHAT HAPPENED TO YOU, BRO?
YOU JUST DIS-APPEARED.
WE THOUGHT YOU WERE DEAD!
THAT'S NO WAY TO MAKE AN OLD FRIEND FEEL WELCOME.
NOT QUITE. MAY AS WELL HAVE BEEN.
THANKS TO YOU.

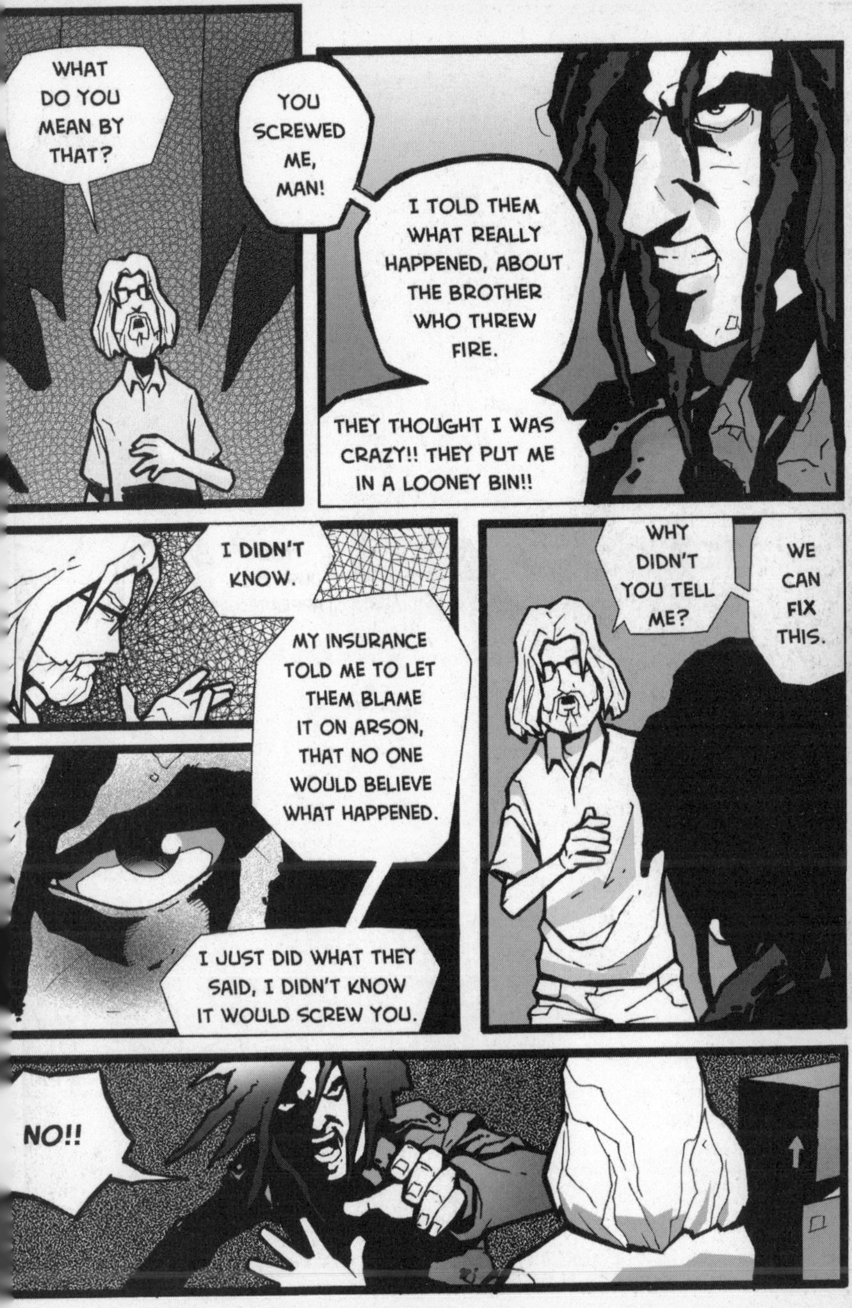
WHAT DO YOU MEAN BY THAT?
YOU SCREWED ME, MAN!
I TOLD THEM WHAT REALLY HAPPENED, ABOUT THE BROTHER WHO THREW FIRE.
THEY THOUGHT I WAS CRAZY!! THEY PUT ME IN A LOONEY BIN!!
I DIDN'T KNOW.
MY INSURANCE TOLD ME TO LET THEM BLAME IT ON ARSON, THAT NO ONE WOULD BELIEVE WHAT HAPPENED.
I JUST DID WHAT THEY SAID, I DIDN'T KNOW IT WOULD SCREW YOU.
WHY DIDN'T YOU TELL ME?
WE CAN FIX THIS.
NO!!

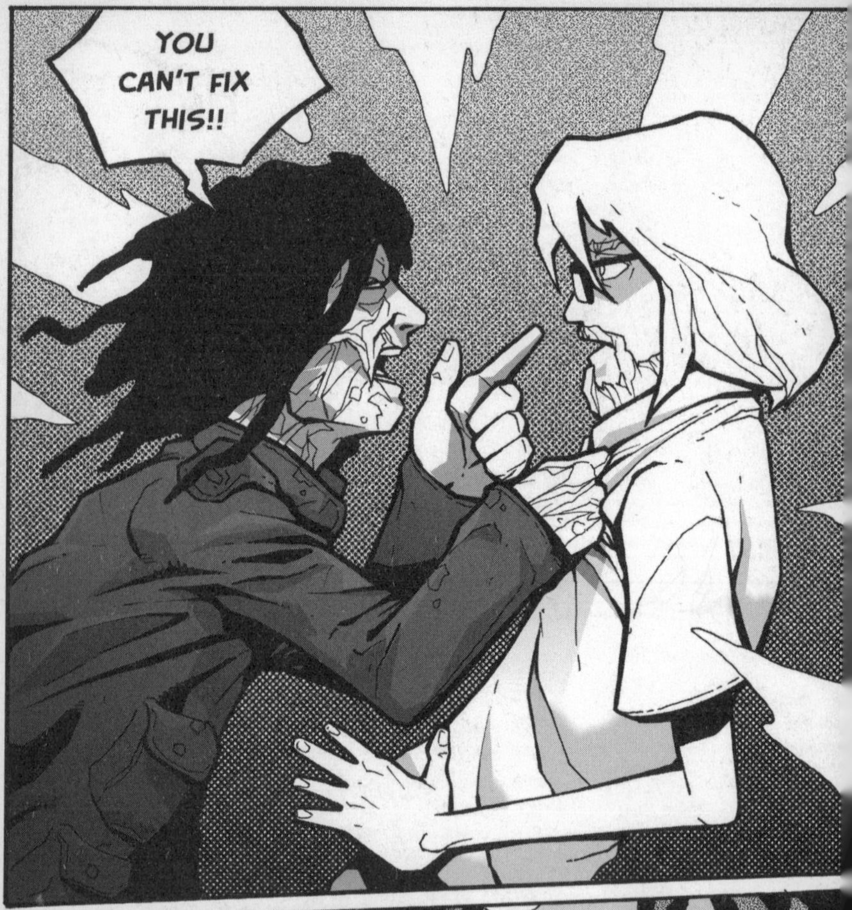
YOU CAN'T FIX THIS!!

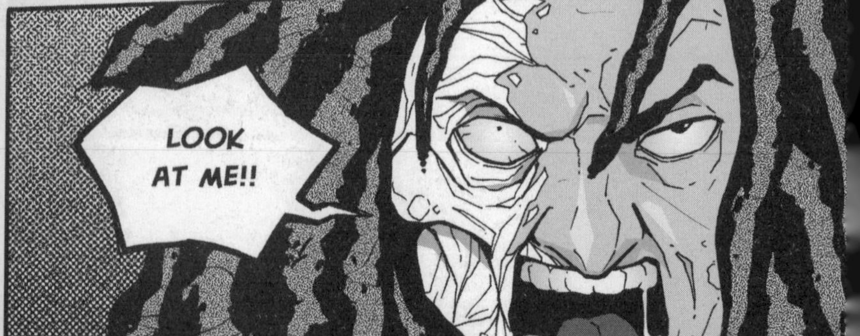
LOOK AT ME!!

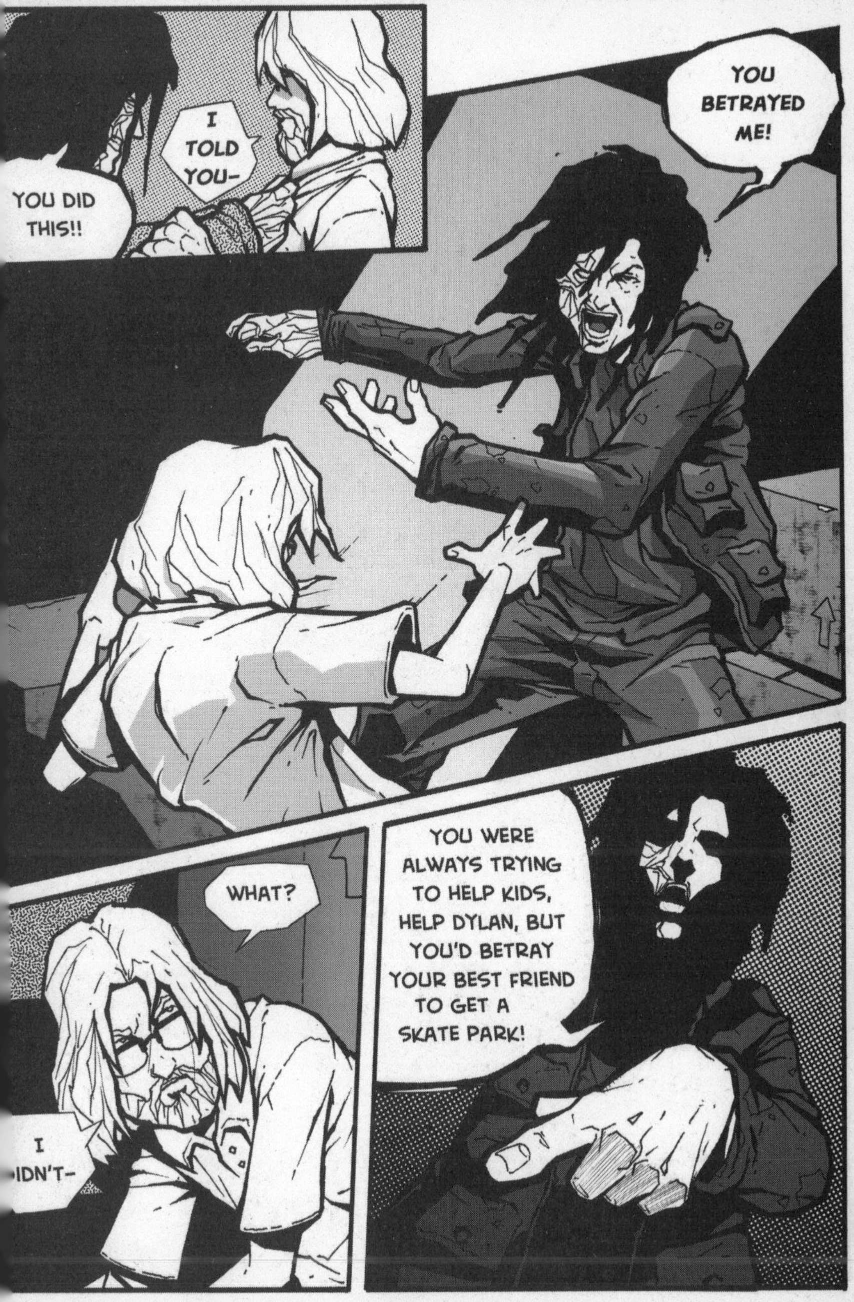
YOU DID THIS!!
I TOLD YOU-
YOU BETRAYED ME!
WHAT?
I DIDN'T-
YOU WERE ALWAYS TRYING TO HELP KIDS, HELP DYLAN, BUT YOU'D BETRAY YOUR BEST FRIEND TO GET A SKATE PARK!

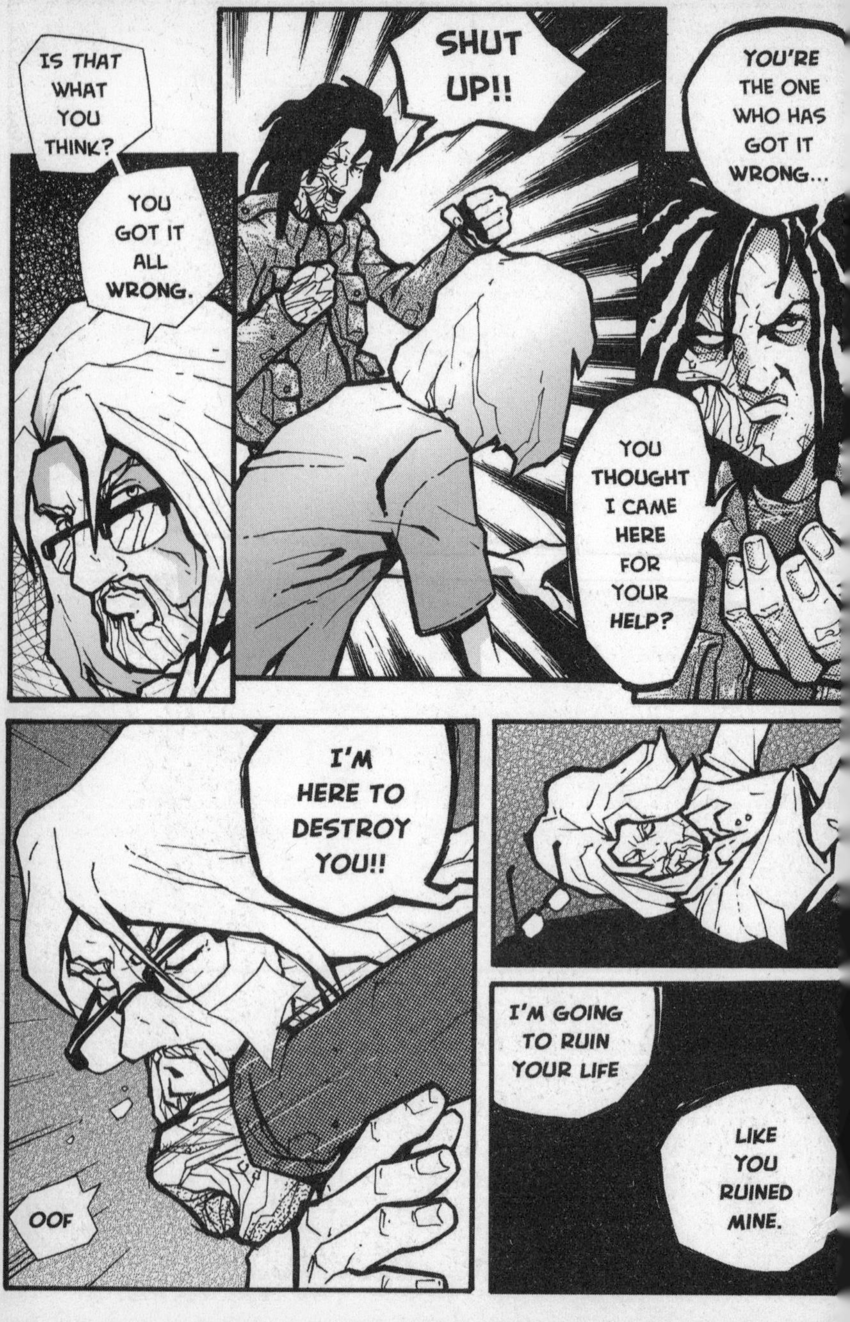
IS THAT WHAT YOU THINK?
YOU GOT IT ALL WRONG.
SHUT UP!!
YOU'RE THE ONE WHO HAS GOT IT WRONG...
YOU THOUGHT I CAME HERE FOR YOUR HELP?
I'M HERE TO DESTROY YOU!!
OOF
I'M GOING TO RUIN YOUR LIFE
LIKE YOU RUINED MINE.

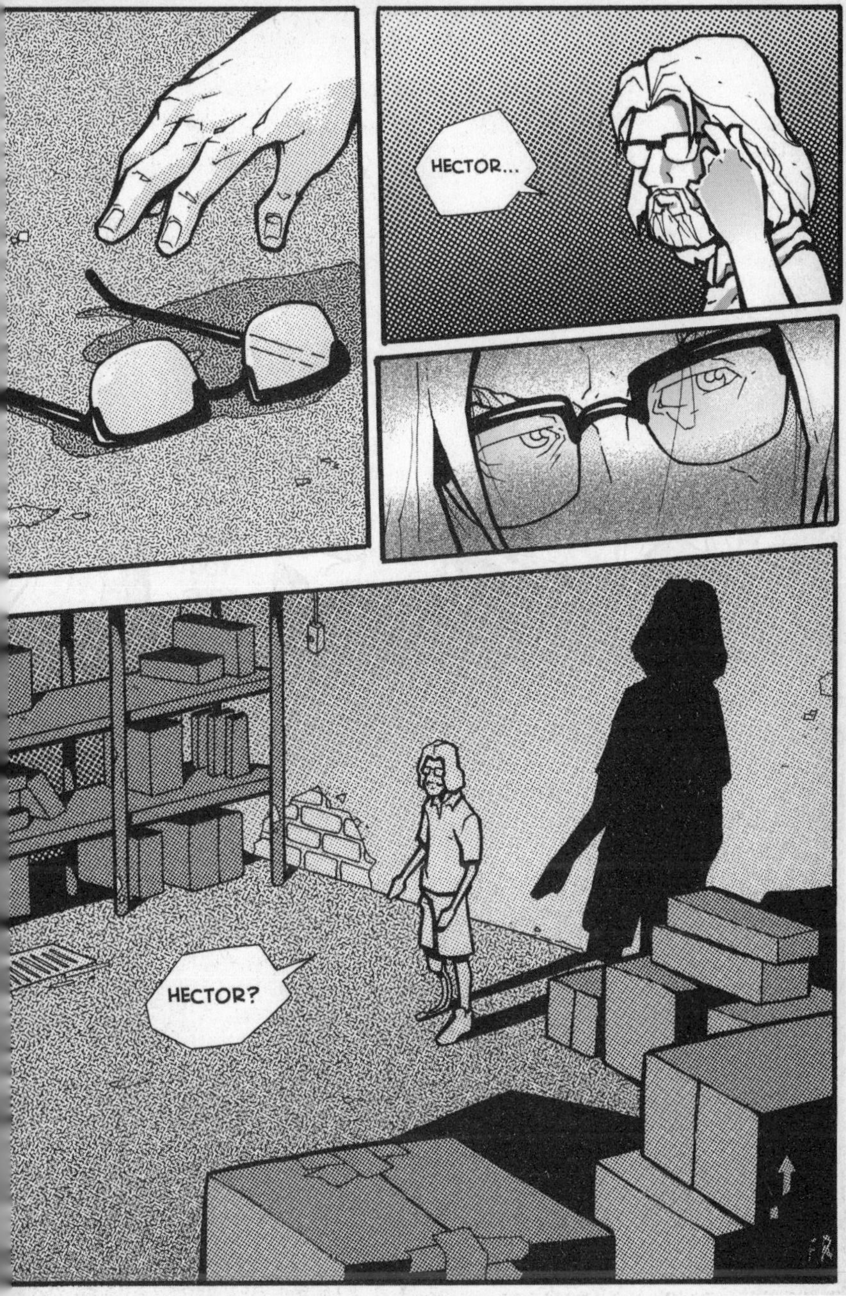
HECTOR...
HECTOR?

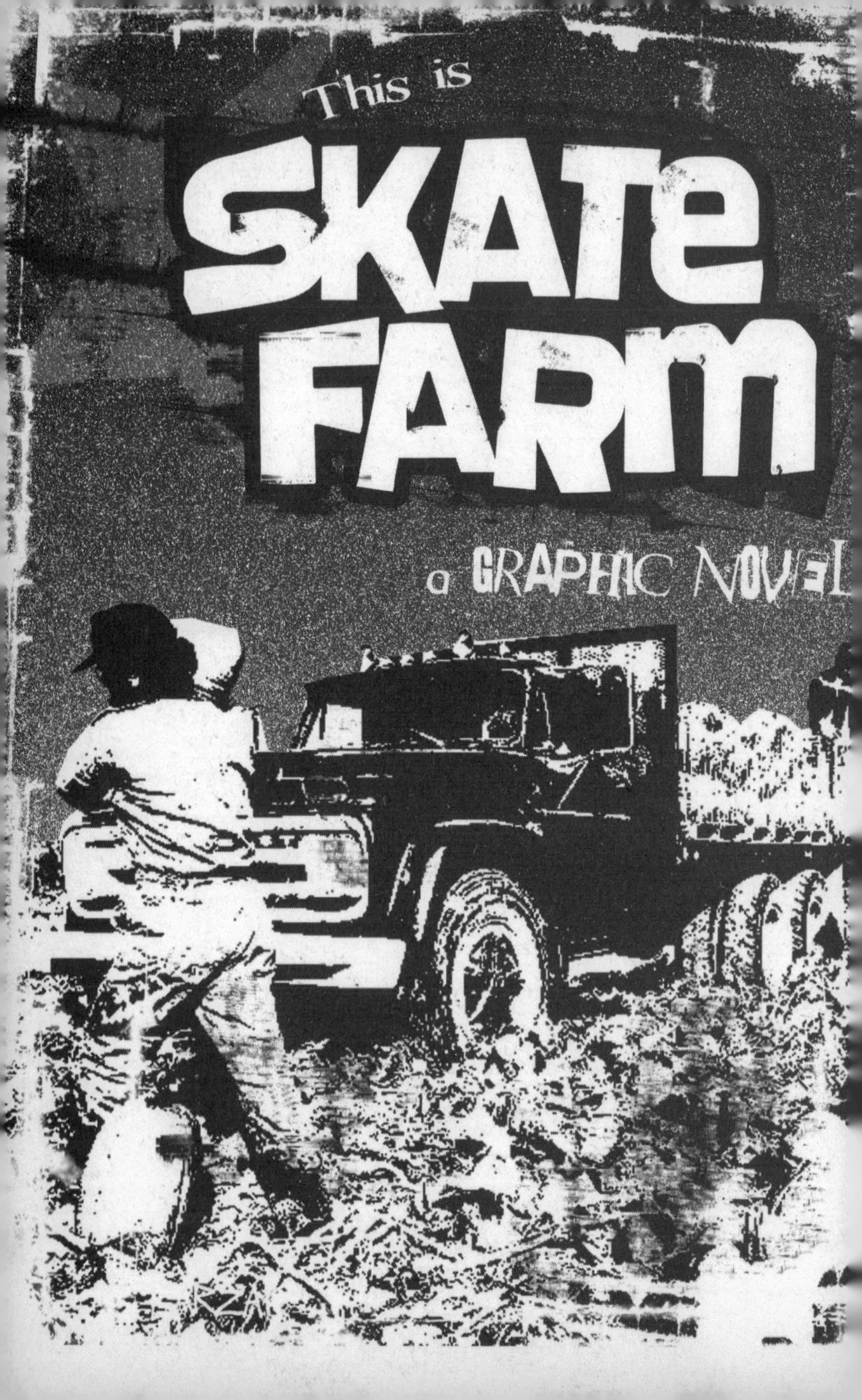
This is
SKATE
FARM
a GRAPHIC NOVEL

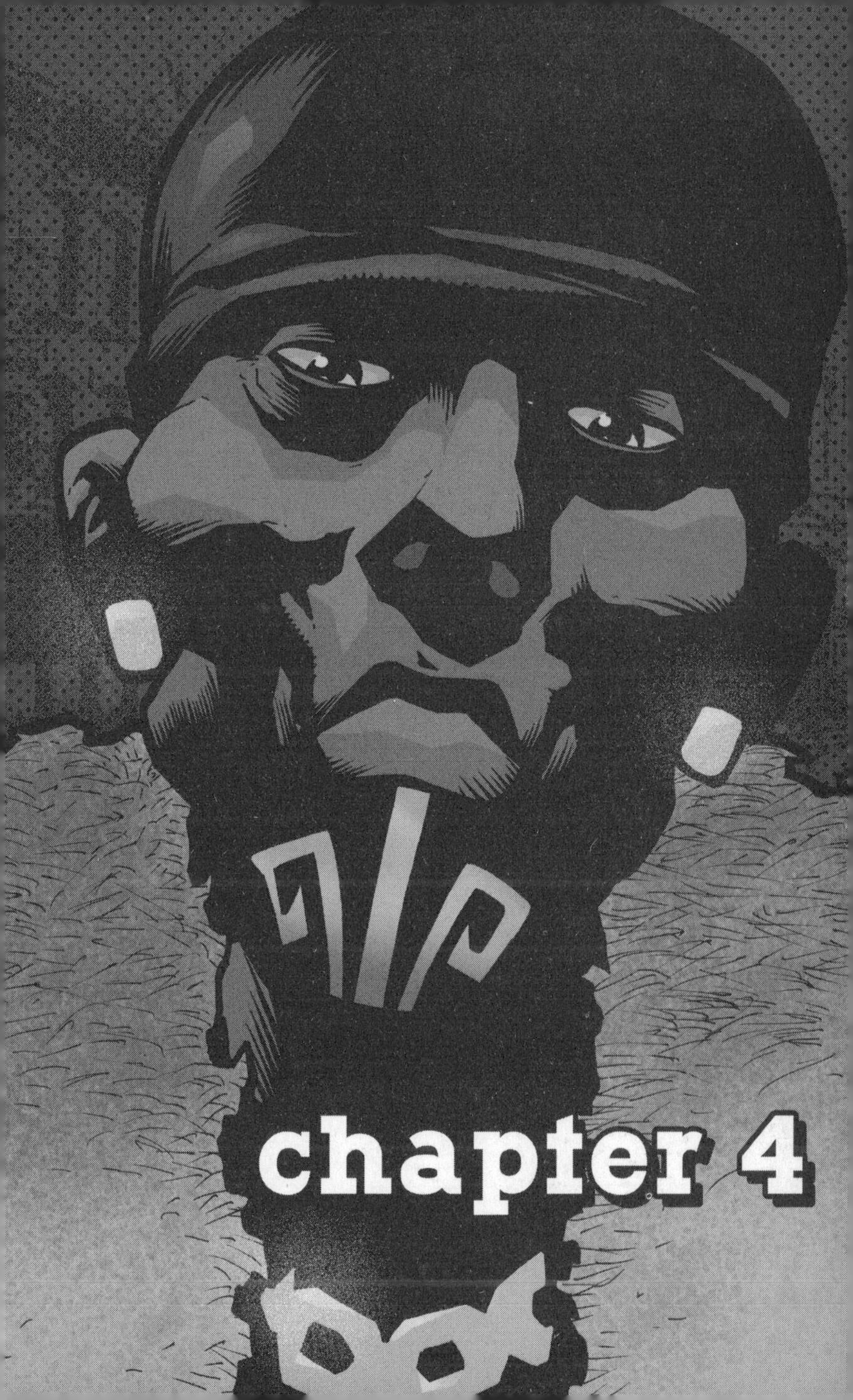
chapter 4

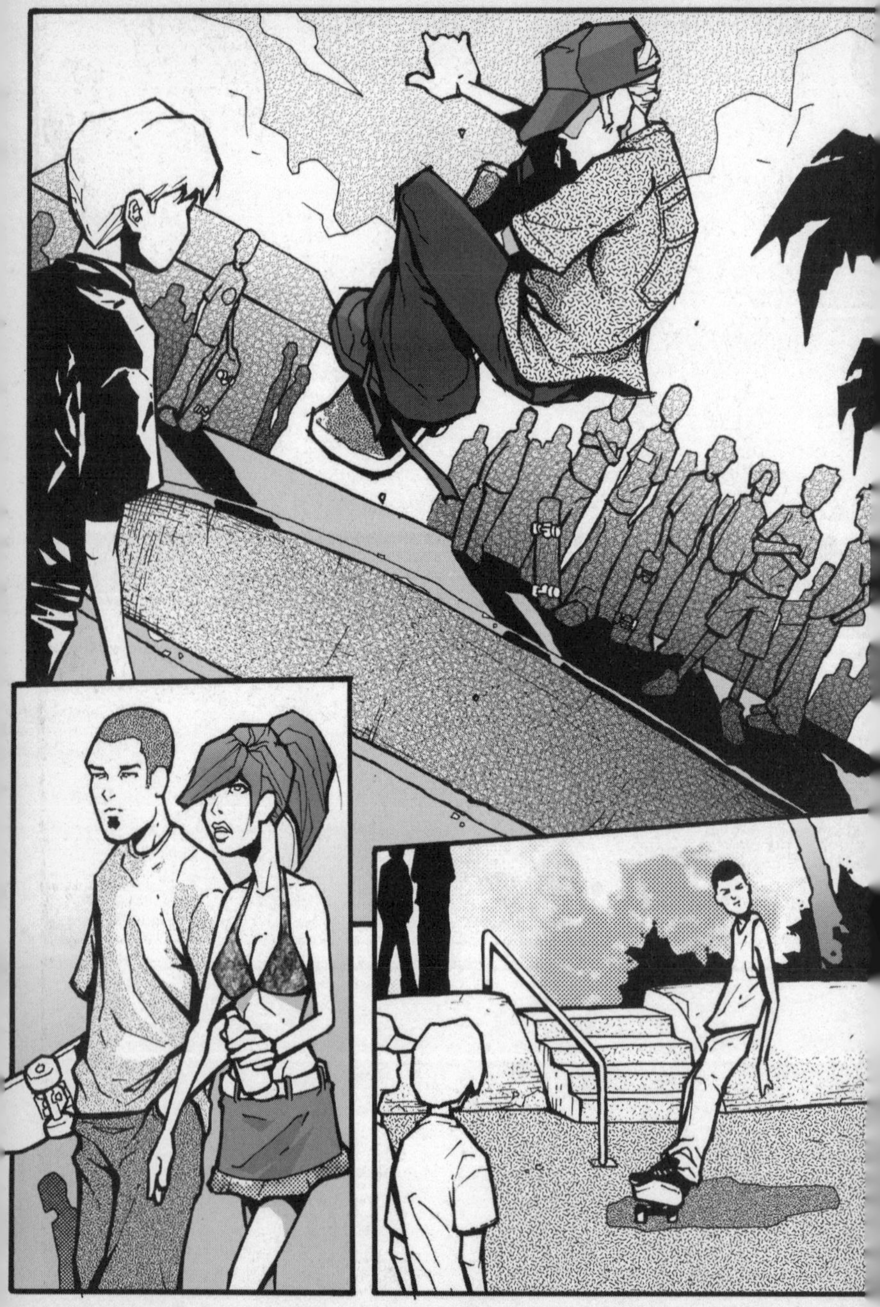

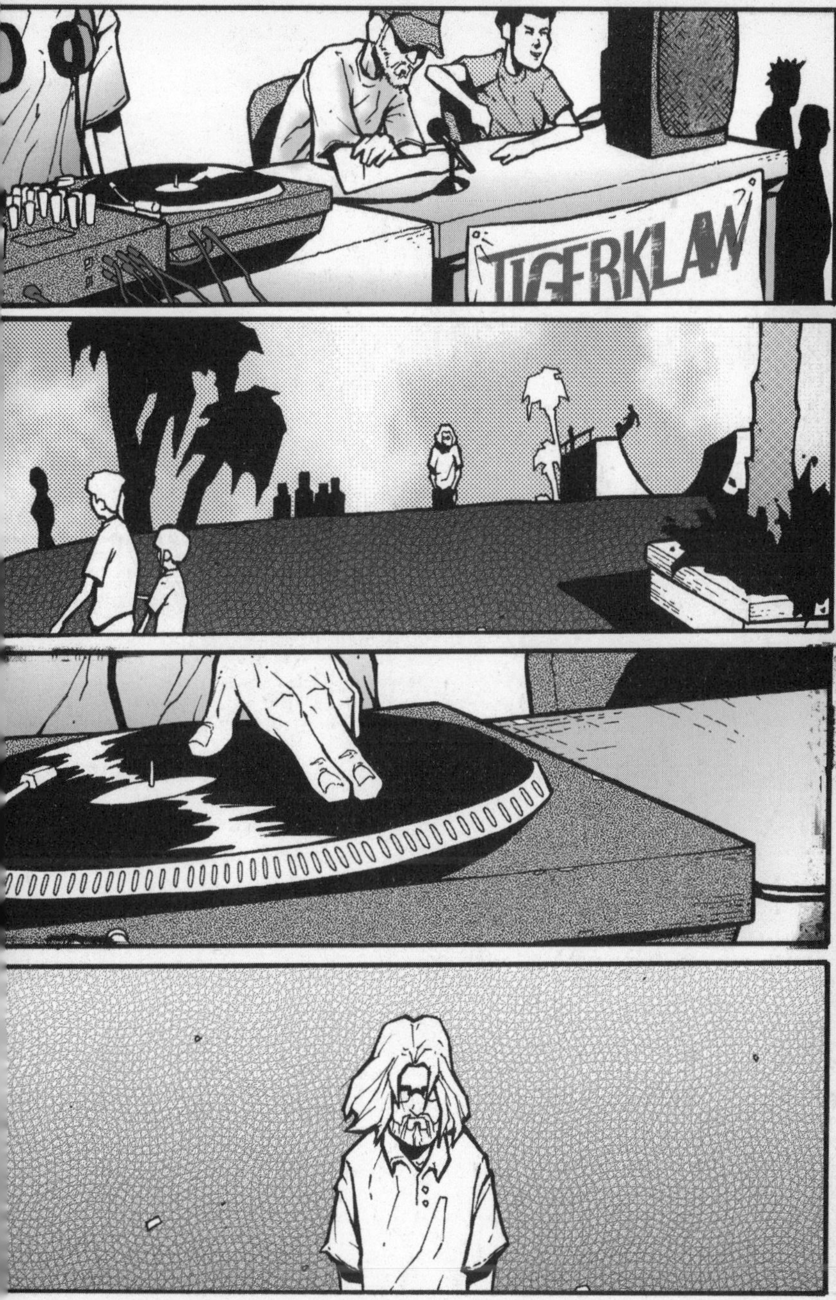
TIGERKLAW

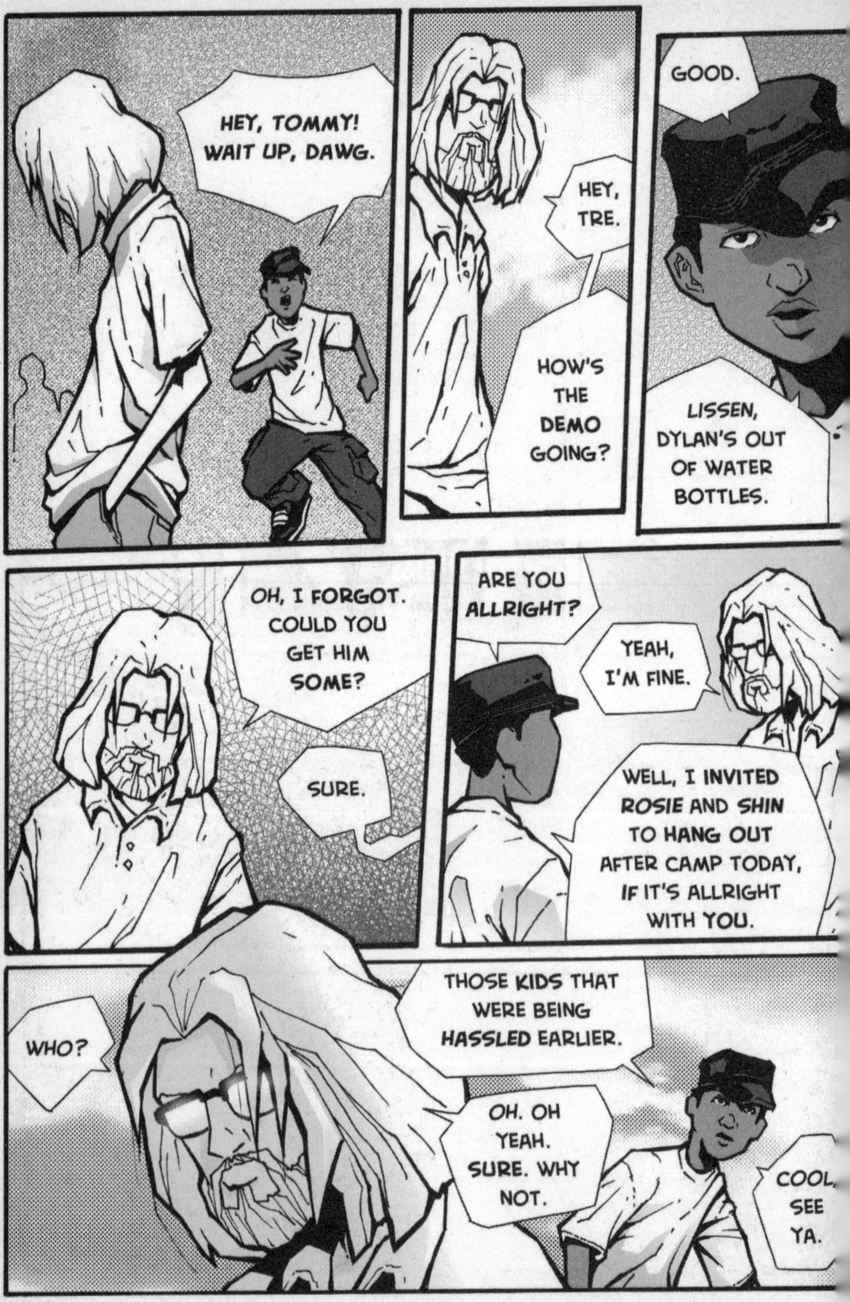
HEY, TOMMY! WAIT UP, DAWG.
HEY, TRE.
HOW'S THE DEMO GOING?
GOOD.
LISSEN, DYLAN'S OUT OF WATER BOTTLES.
OH, I FORGOT. COULD YOU GET HIM SOME?
SURE.
ARE YOU ALLRIGHT?
YEAH, I'M FINE.
WELL, I INVITED ROSIE AND SHIN TO HANG OUT AFTER CAMP TODAY, IF IT'S ALLRIGHT WITH YOU.
WHO?
THOSE KIDS THAT WERE BEING HASSLED EARLIER.
OH. OH YEAH. SURE. WHY NOT.
COOL, SEE YA.

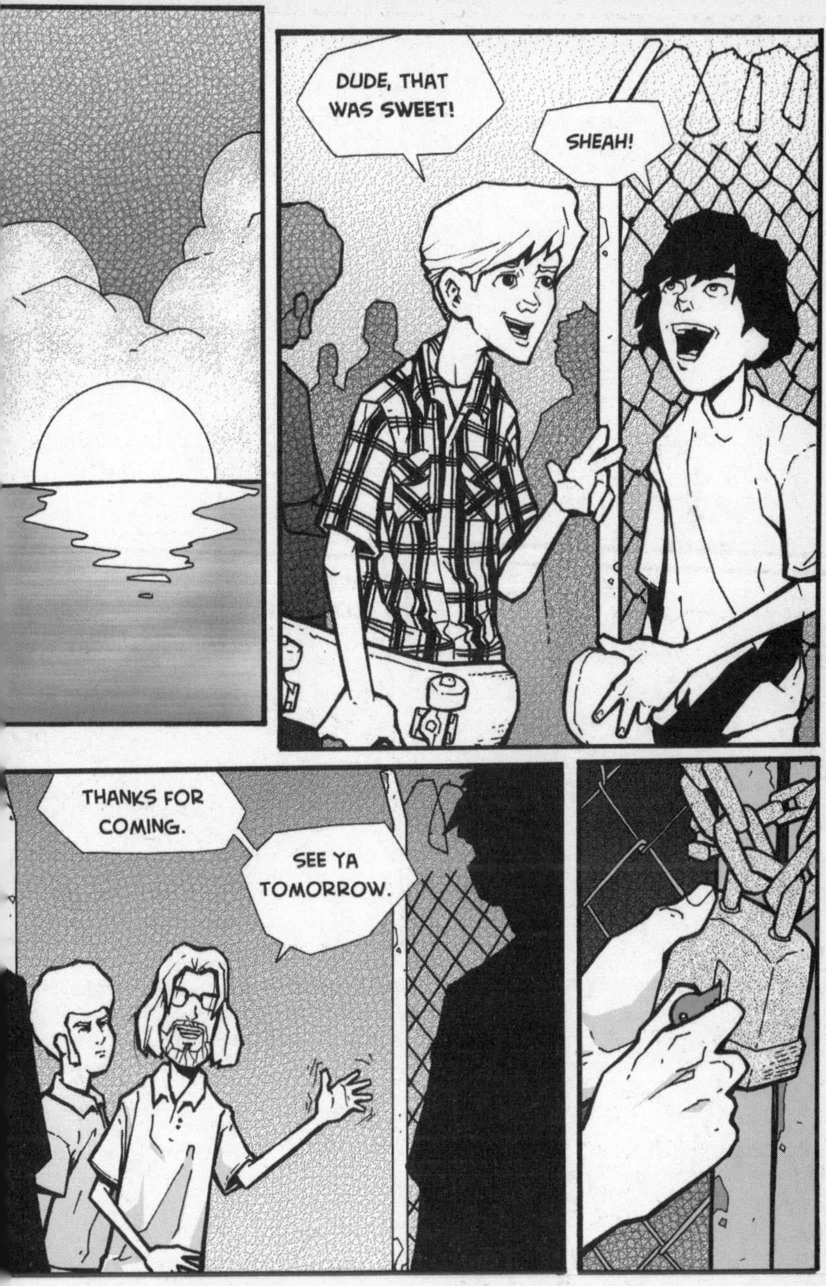
DUDE, THAT WAS SWEET!
SHEAH!
THANKS FOR COMING.
SEE YA TOMORROW.

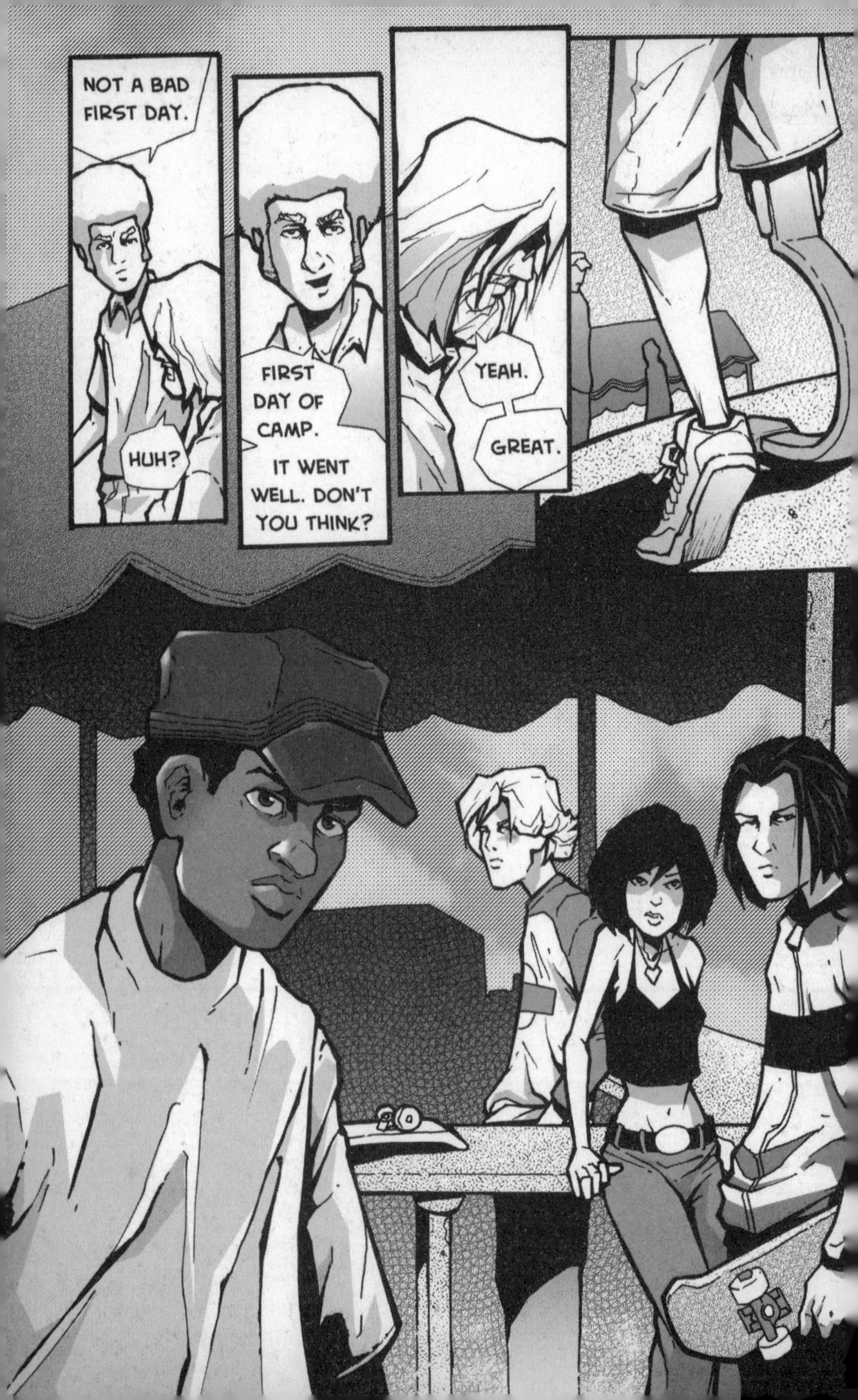
NOT A BAD FIRST DAY.
HUH?
FIRST DAY OF CAMP.
IT WENT WELL. DON'T YOU THINK?
YEAH.
GREAT.

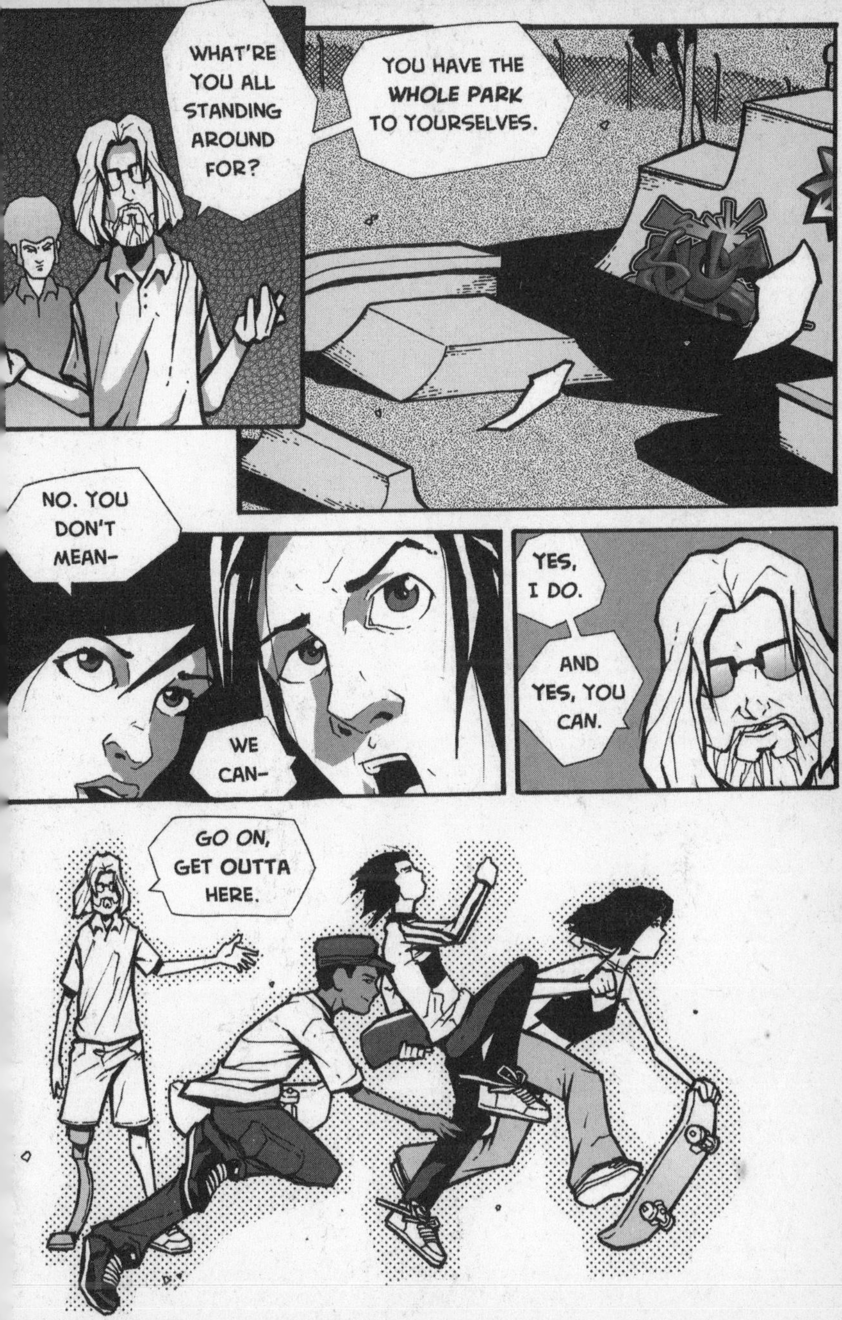
WHAT'RE YOU ALL STANDING AROUND FOR?
YOU HAVE THE WHOLE PARK TO YOURSELVES.
NO. YOU DON'T MEAN-
WE CAN-
YES, I DO.
AND YES, YOU CAN.
GO ON, GET OUTTA HERE.

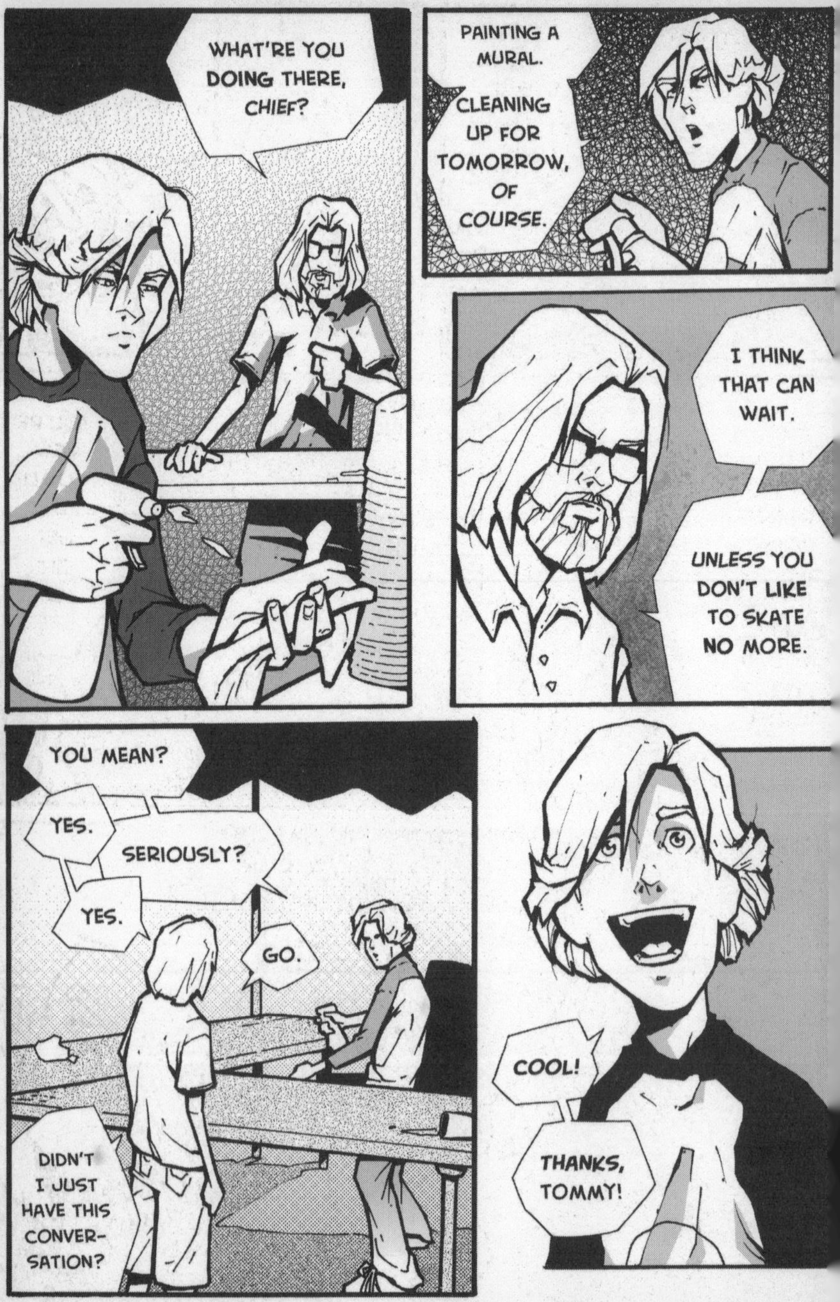

WHAT'RE YOU DOING THERE, CHIEF?
PAINTING A MURAL.
CLEANING UP FOR TOMORROW, OF COURSE.
I THINK THAT CAN WAIT.
UNLESS YOU DON'T LIKE TO SKATE NO MORE.
YOU MEAN?
YES.
SERIOUSLY?
YES.
GO.
DIDN'T I JUST HAVE THIS CONVER-SATION?
COOL!
THANKS, TOMMY!

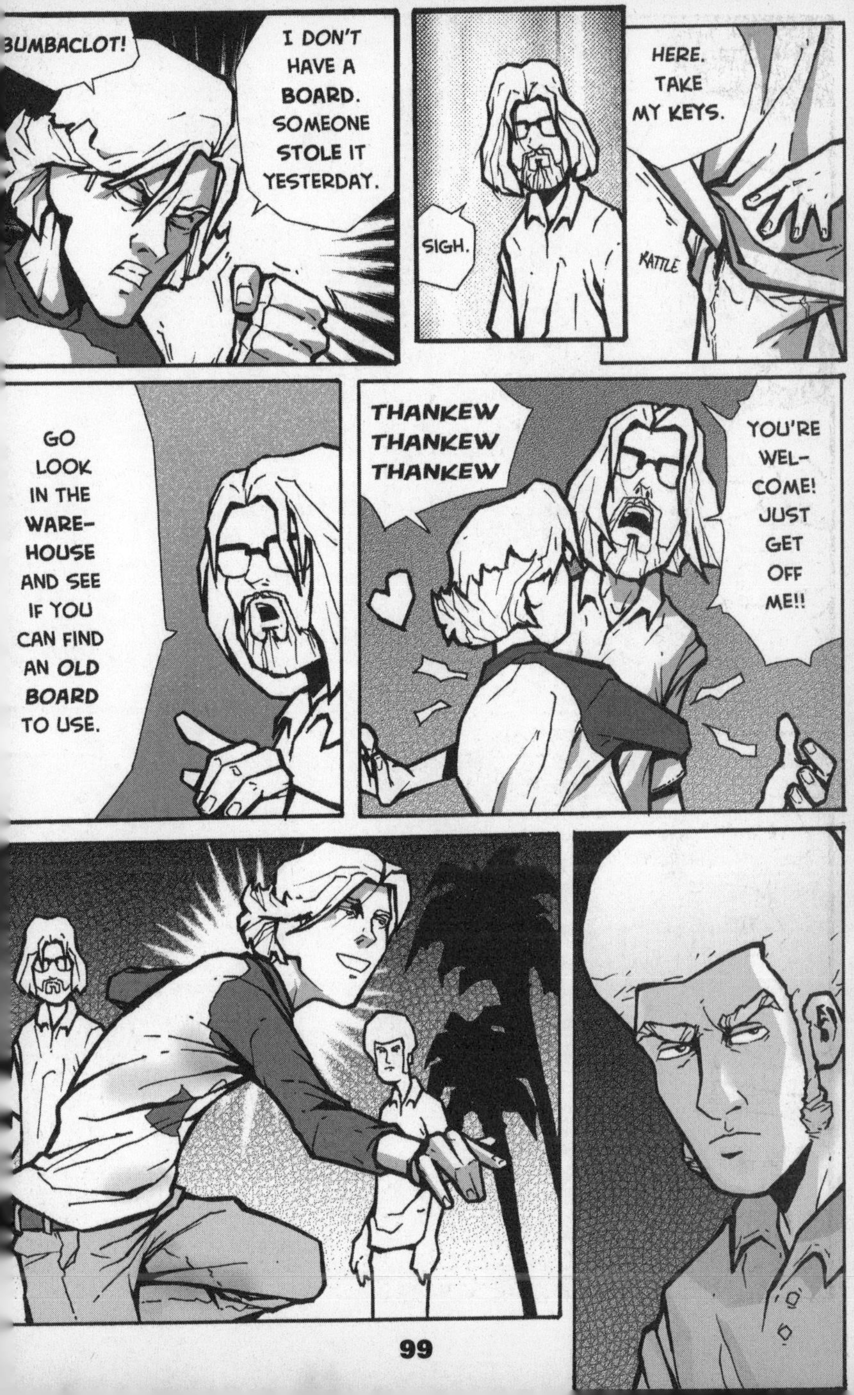
BUMBACLOT!
I DON'T HAVE A BOARD. SOMEONE STOLE IT YESTERDAY.
SIGH.
HERE. TAKE MY KEYS.
KATTLE
GO LOOK IN THE WARE-HOUSE AND SEE IF YOU CAN FIND AN OLD BOARD TO USE.
THANKEW THANKEW THANKEW
YOU'RE WEL-COME! JUST GET OFF ME!!

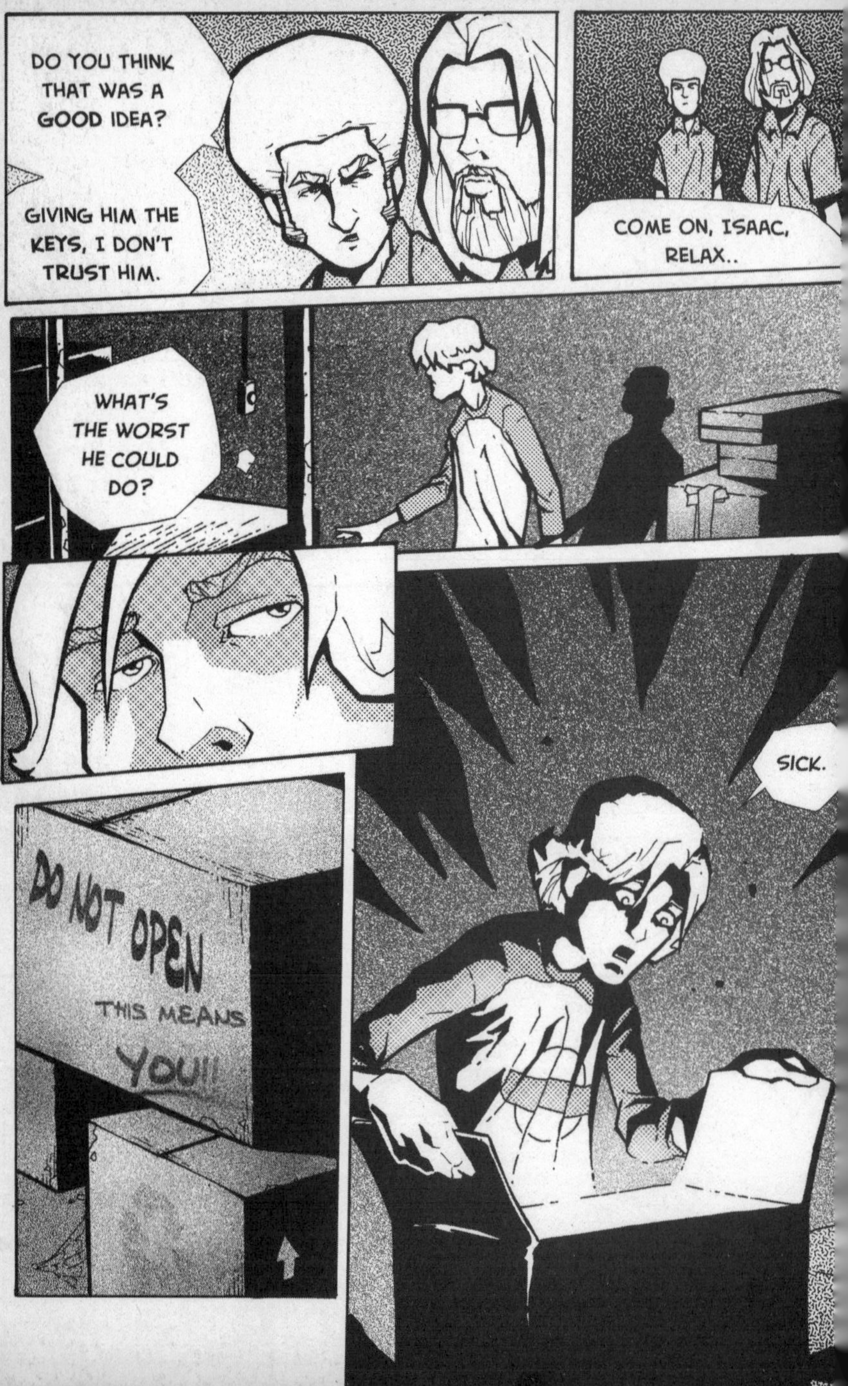
DO YOU THINK THAT WAS A GOOD IDEA?
GIVING HIM THE KEYS, I DON'T TRUST HIM.
COME ON, ISAAC, RELAX..
WHAT'S THE WORST HE COULD DO?
SICK.
DO NOT OPEN
THIS MEANS
YOU!!

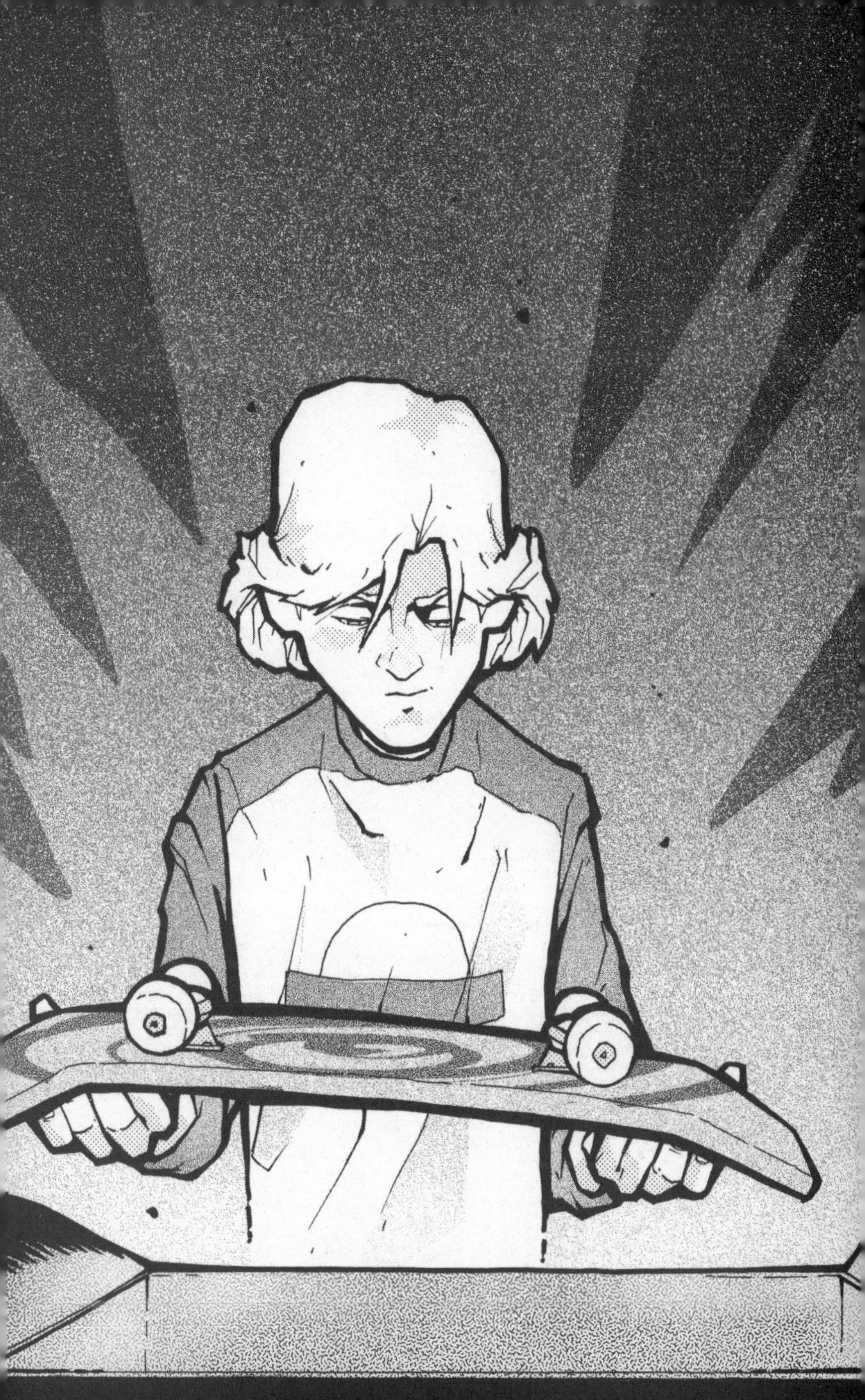

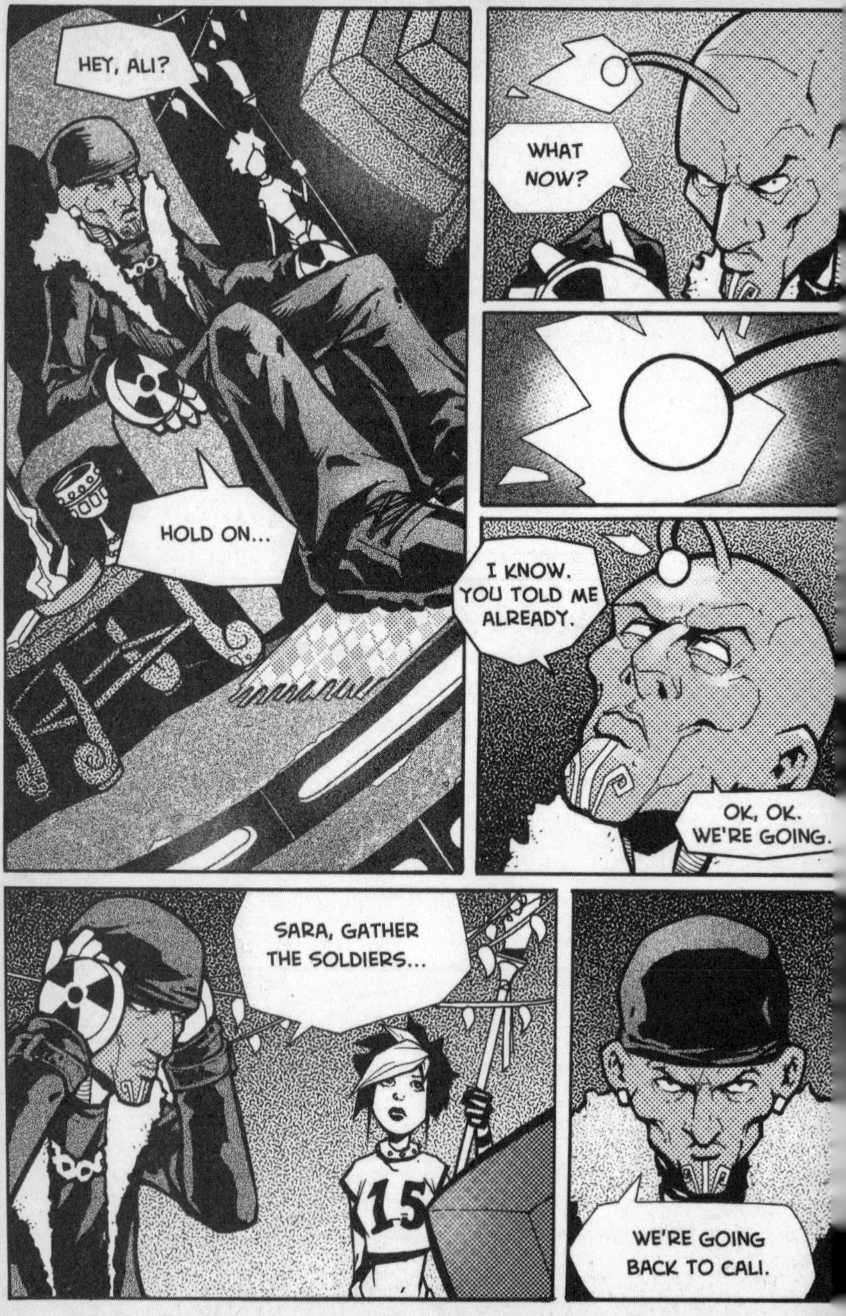
HEY, ALI?
HOLD ON...
WHAT NOW?
I KNOW. YOU TOLD ME ALREADY.
OK, OK. WE'RE GOING.
SARA, GATHER THE SOLDIERS...
WE'RE GOING BACK TO CALI.

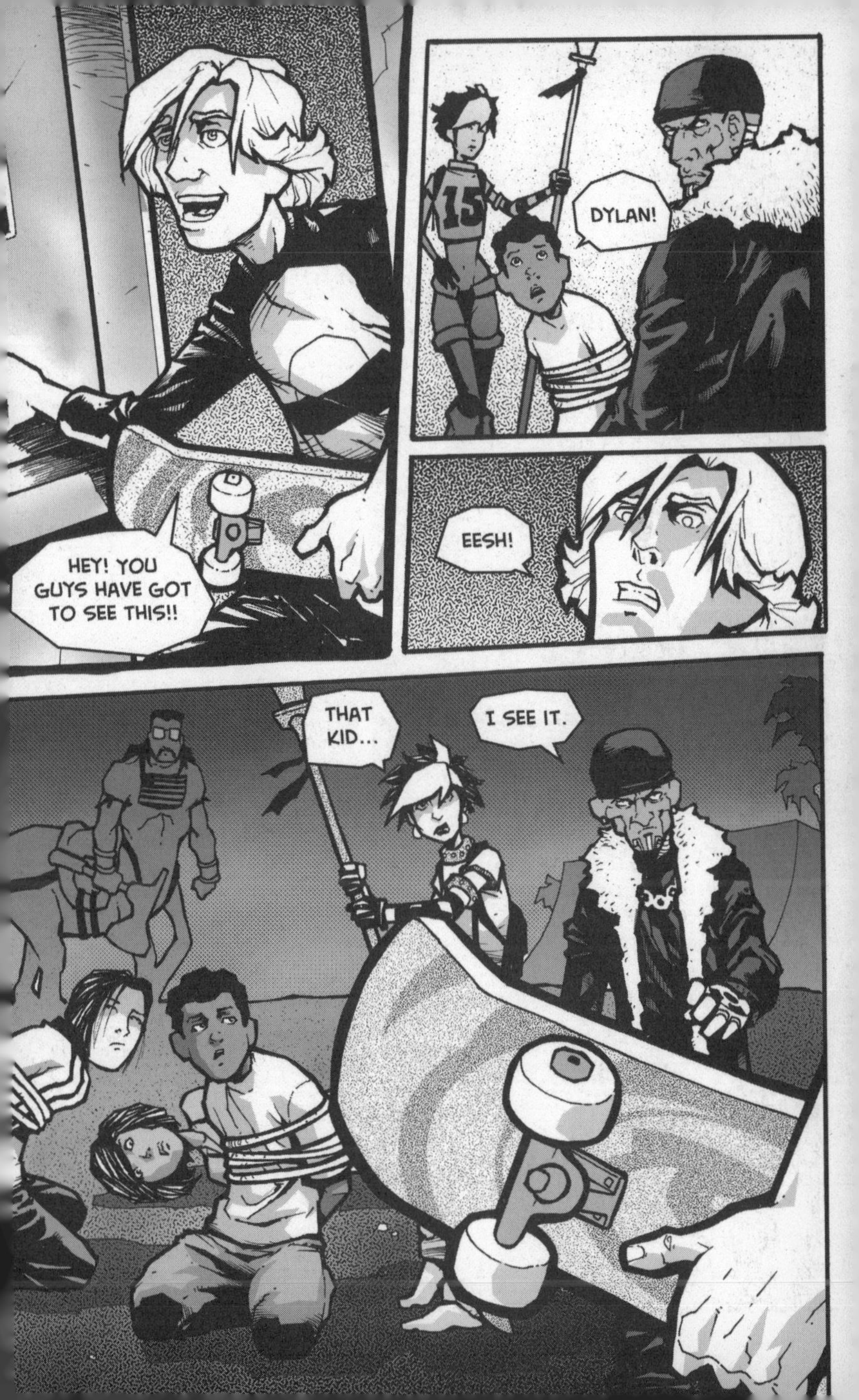
HEY! YOU GUYS HAVE GOT TO SEE THIS!!
DYLAN!
EESH!
THAT KID...
I SEE IT.

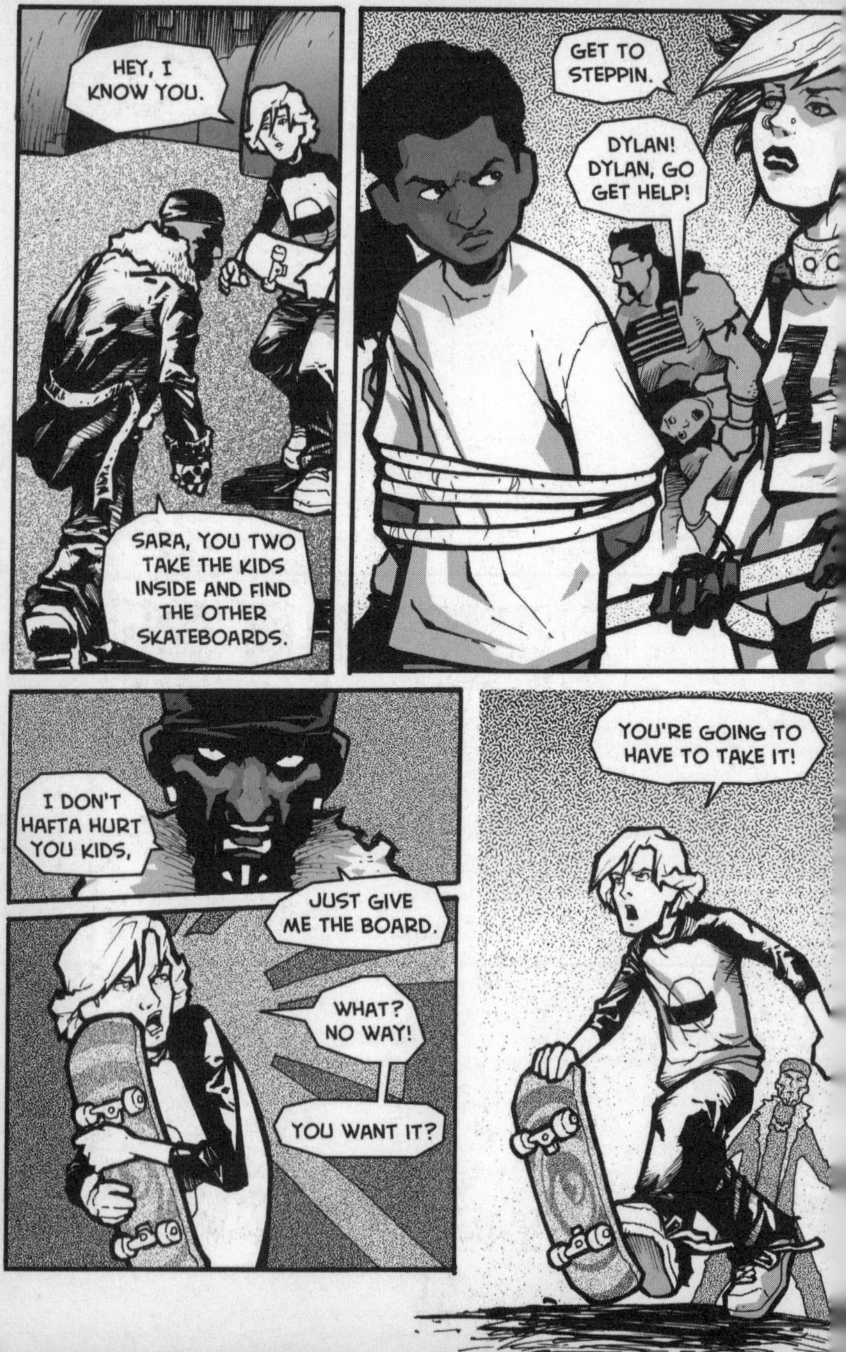
HEY, I KNOW YOU.
SARA, YOU TWO TAKE THE KIDS INSIDE AND FIND THE OTHER SKATEBOARDS.
GET TO STEPPIN.
DYLAN! DYLAN, GO GET HELP!
I DON'T HAFTA HURT YOU KIDS,
JUST GIVE ME THE BOARD.
WHAT? NO WAY!
YOU WANT IT?
YOU'RE GOING TO HAVE TO TAKE IT!

THOSE KIDS ARE STILL OUTSIDE WITH TRE.

DO YOU WANT ME TO HANG AROUND UNTIL THEY LEAVE?

NO, YOU GO AHEAD. I'LL TAKE CARE OF IT.

ALLRIGHT THEN, I'M TAKIN OFF, SEE YOU TOMORROW.

BYE.

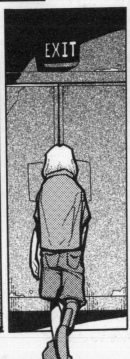

EXIT

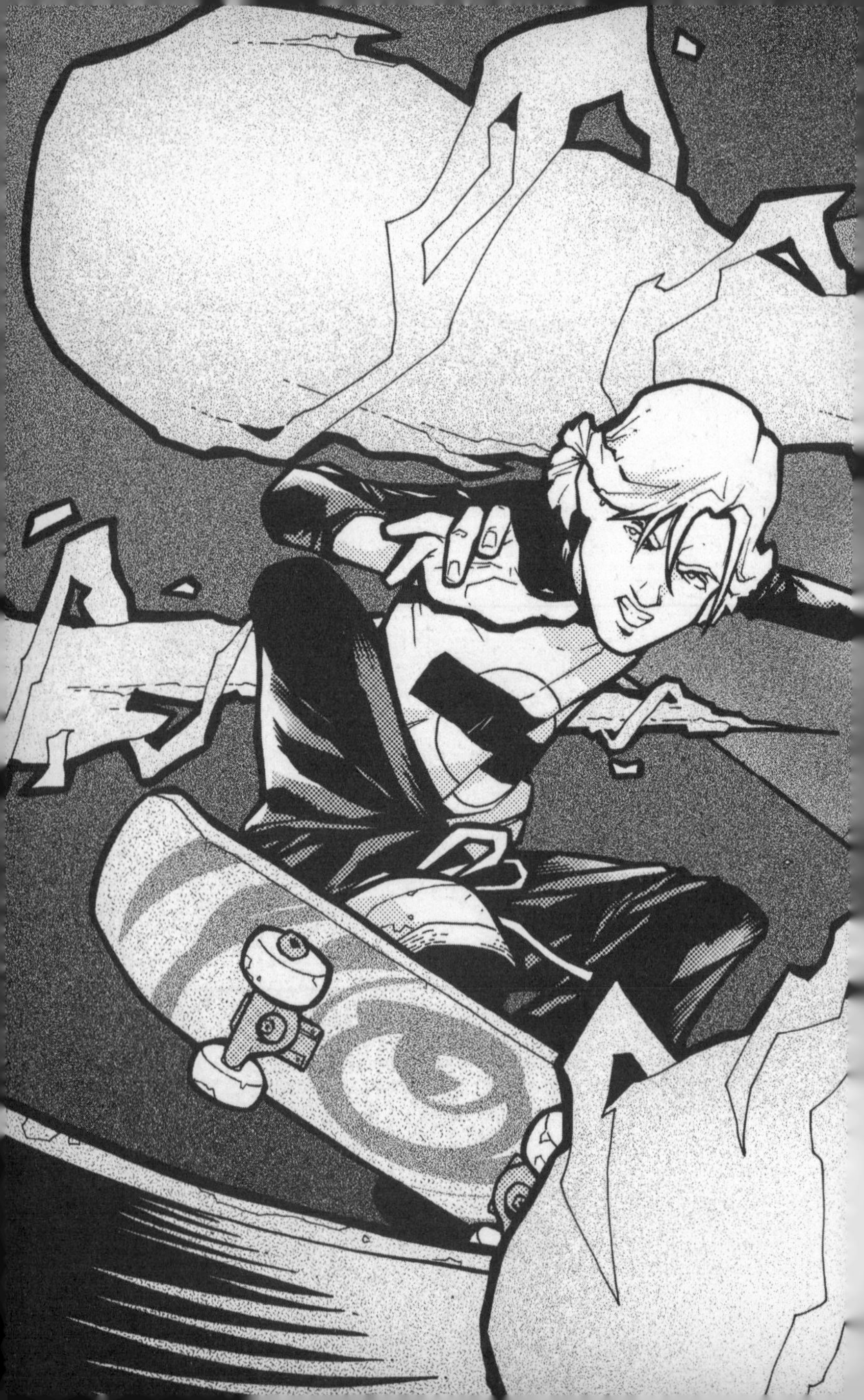

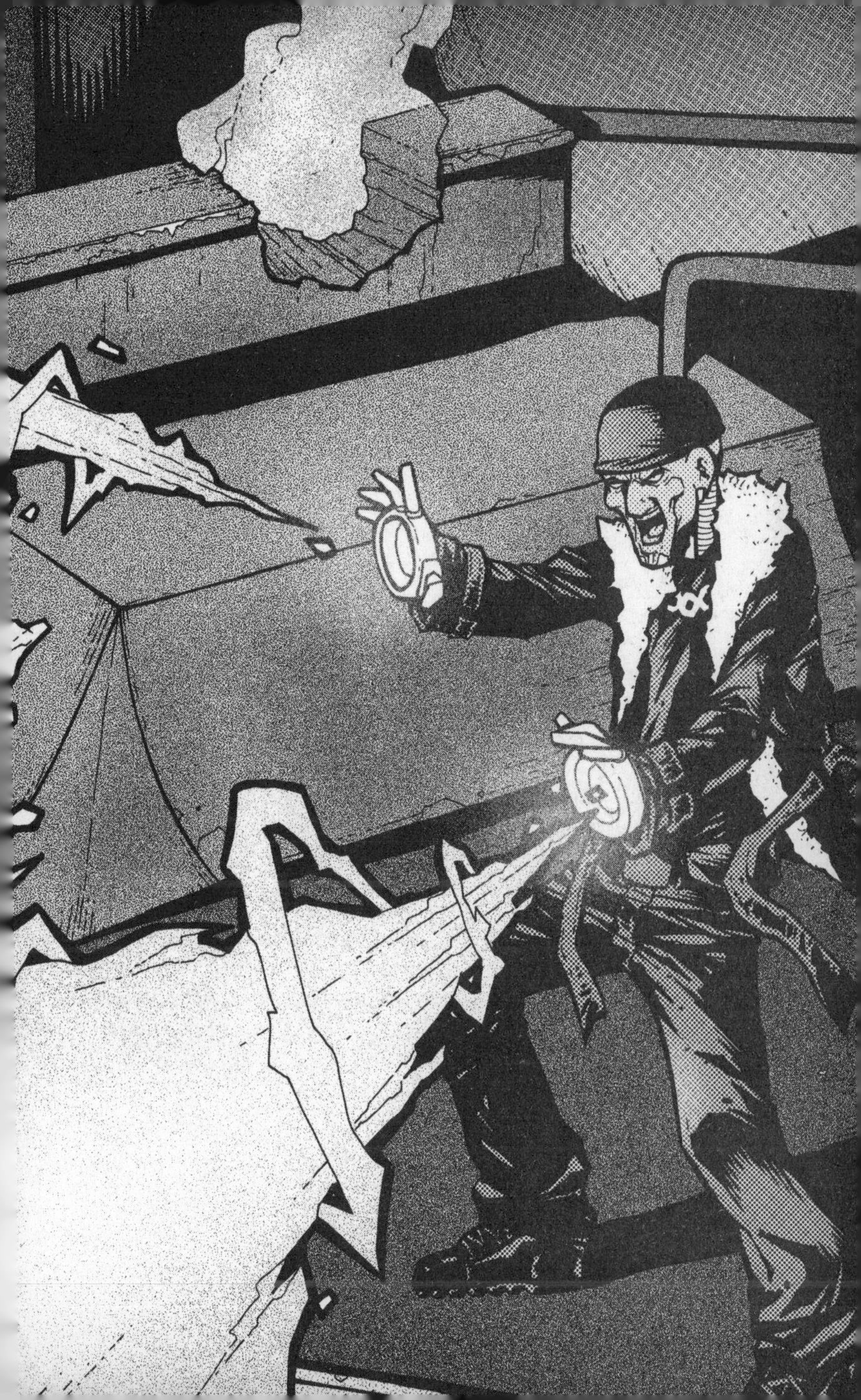

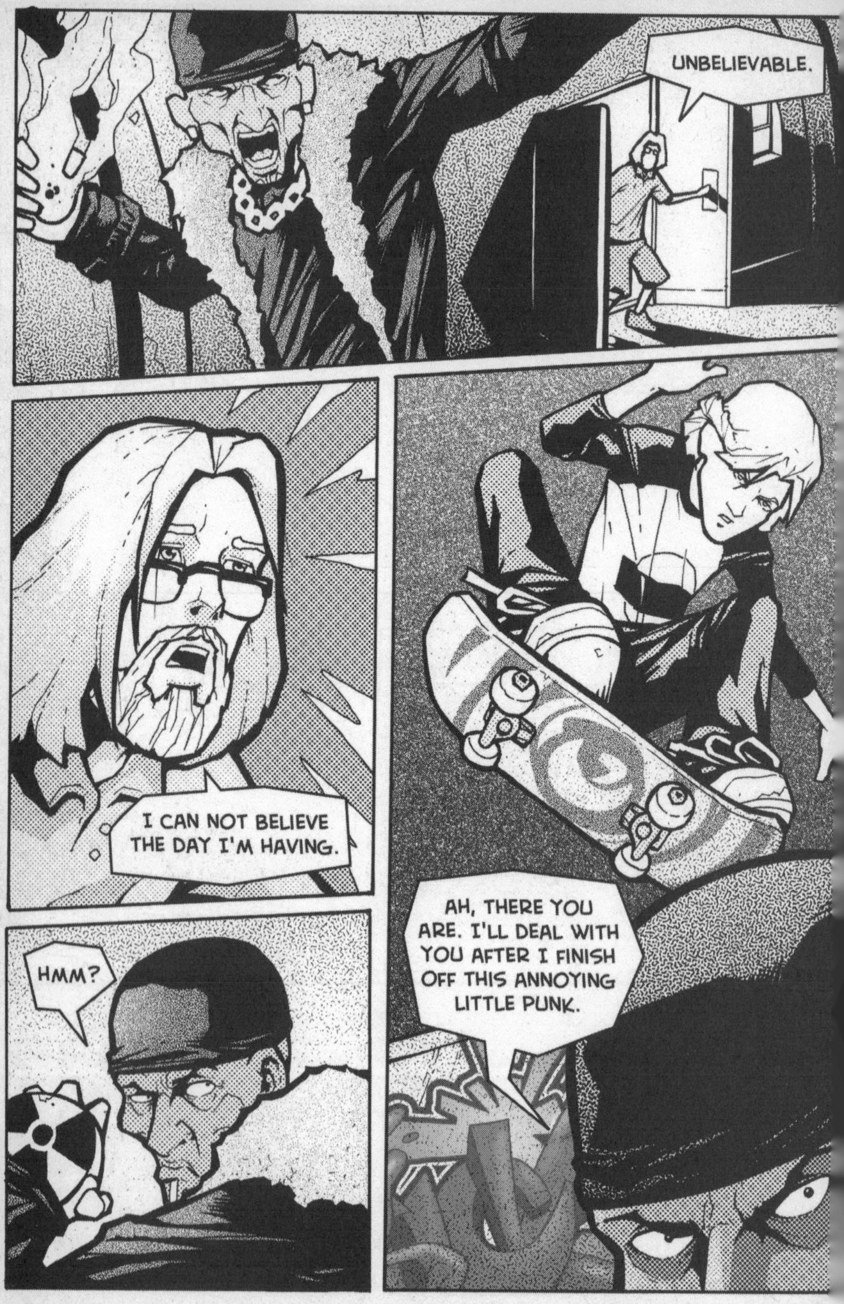
UNBELIEVABLE.
I CAN NOT BELIEVE THE DAY I'M HAVING.
HMM?
AH, THERE YOU ARE. I'LL DEAL WITH YOU AFTER I FINISH OFF THIS ANNOYING LITTLE PUNK.

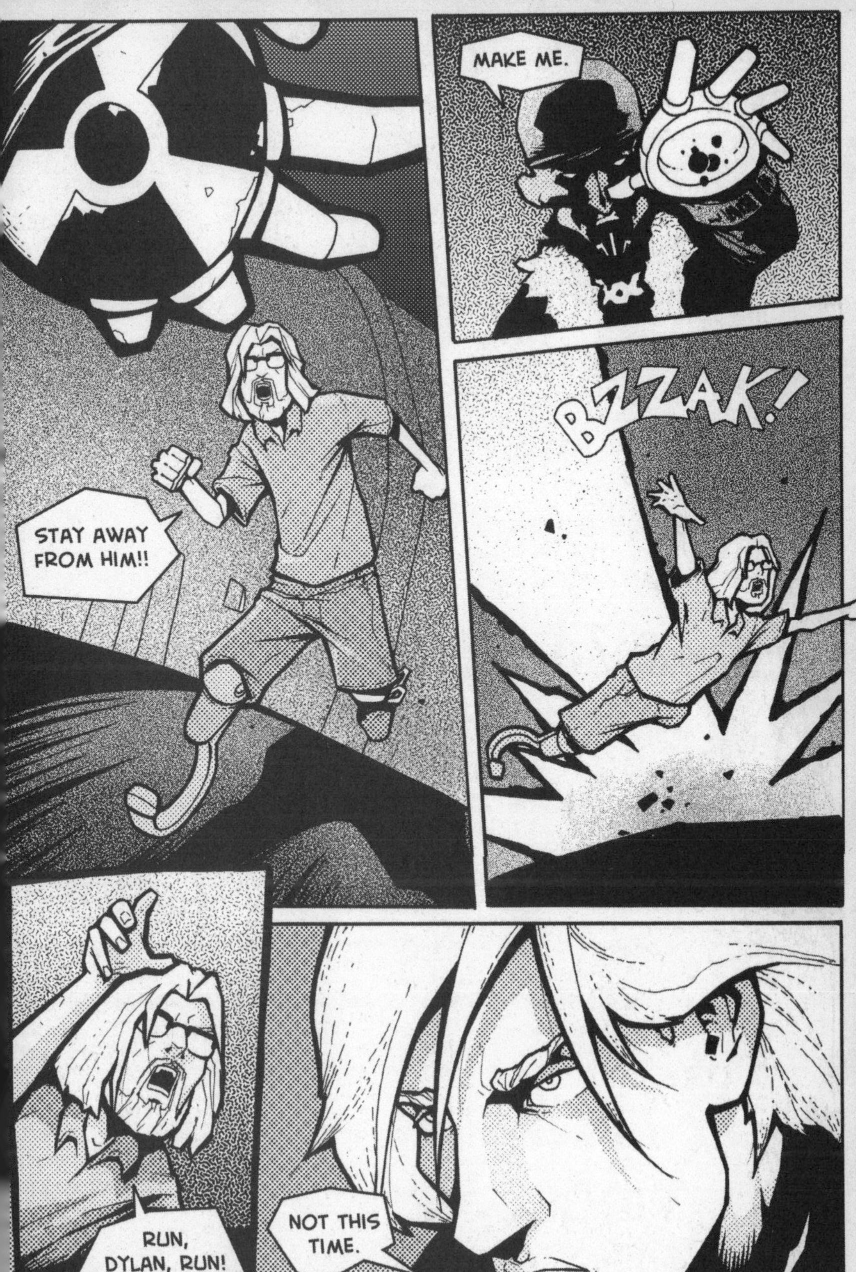
STAY AWAY FROM HIM!!
MAKE ME.
BZZZAK!
RUN, DYLAN, RUN!
NOT THIS TIME.

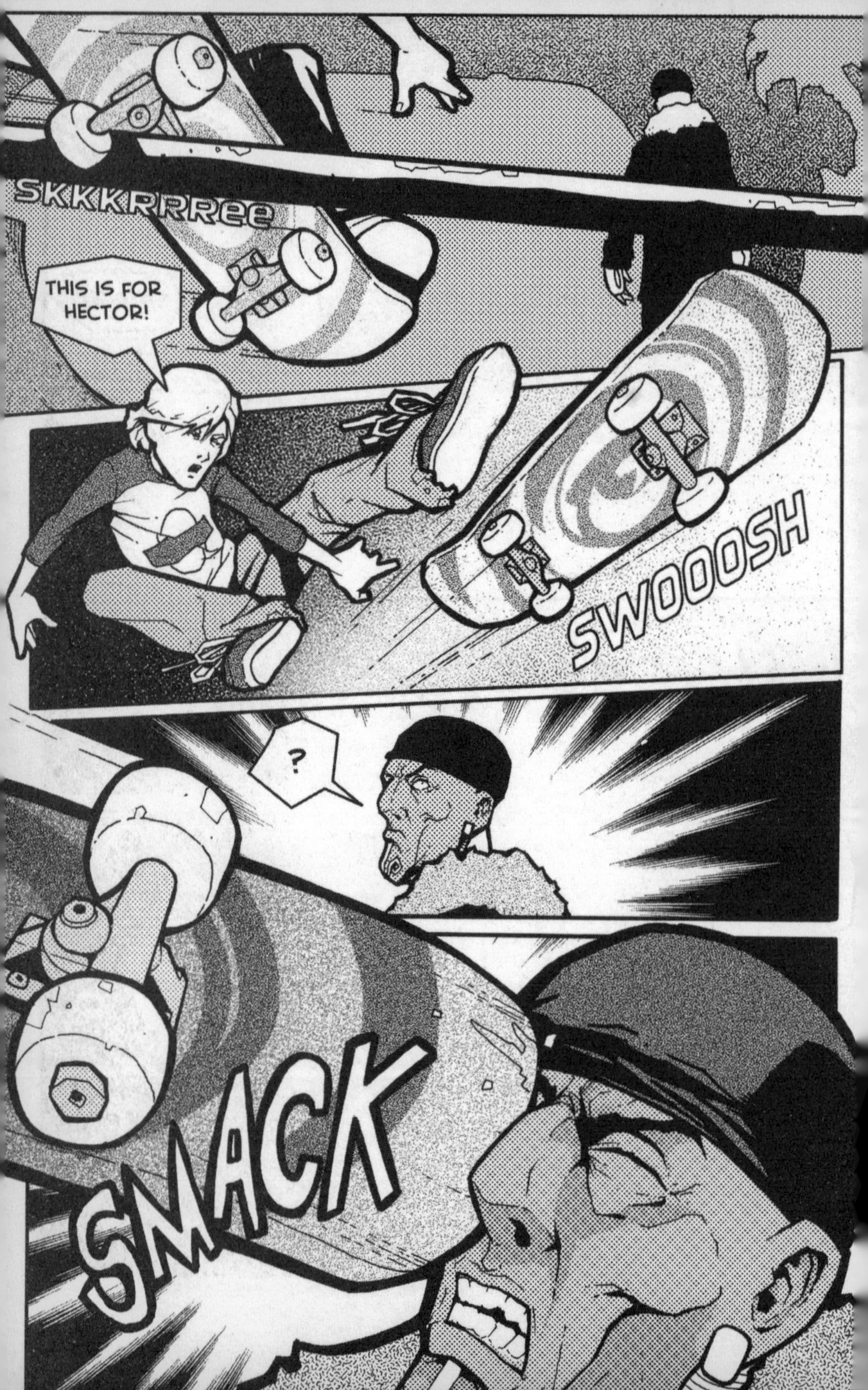
SKKKRRRee
THIS IS FOR HECTOR!
SWOOOSH
?
SMACK

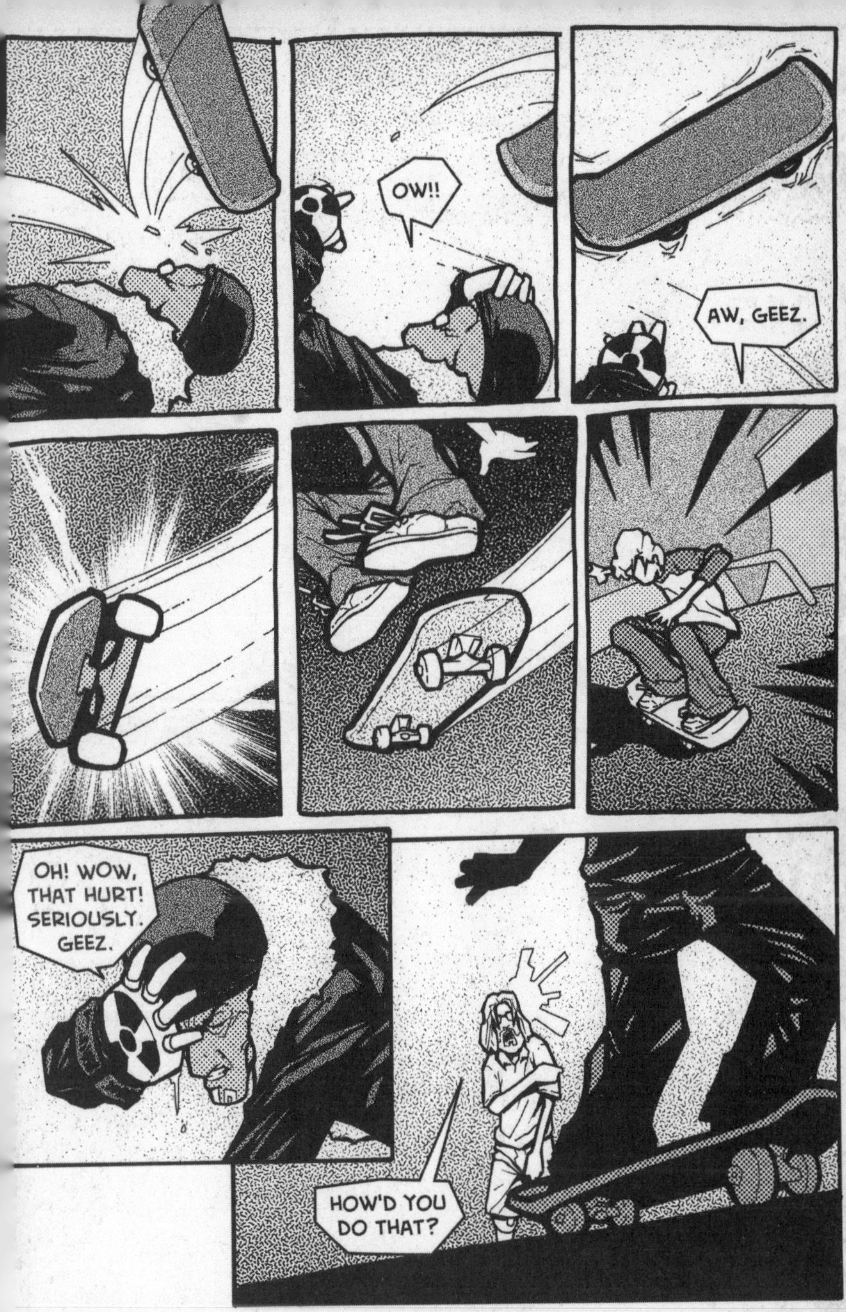
OW!!
AW, GEEZ.
OH! WOW, THAT HURT! SERIOUSLY. GEEZ.
HOW'D YOU DO THAT?

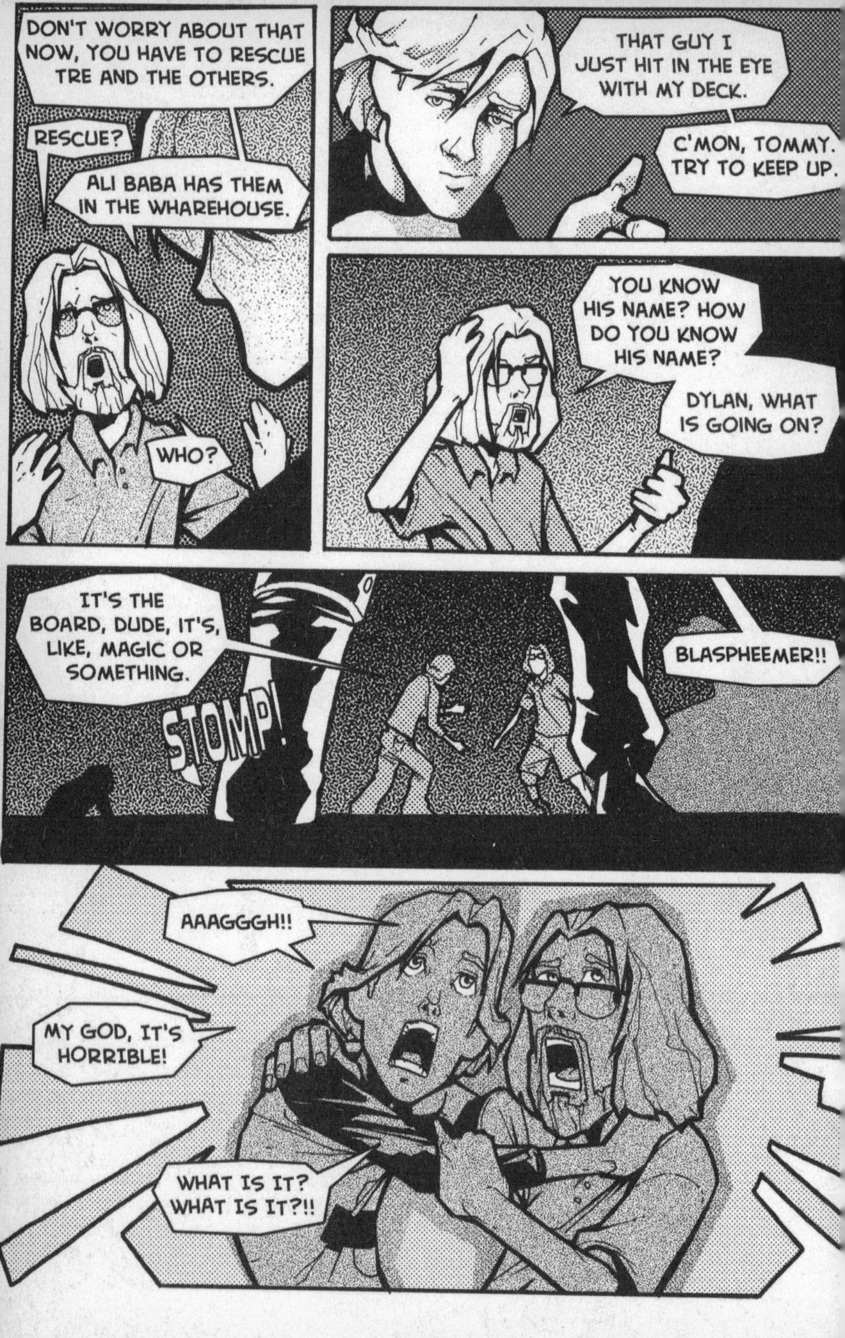

DON'T WORRY ABOUT THAT NOW, YOU HAVE TO RESCUE TRE AND THE OTHERS.
RESCUE?
ALI BABA HAS THEM IN THE WHAREHOUSE.
WHO?
THAT GUY I JUST HIT IN THE EYE WITH MY DECK.
C'MON, TOMMY. TRY TO KEEP UP.
YOU KNOW HIS NAME? HOW DO YOU KNOW HIS NAME?
DYLAN, WHAT IS GOING ON?
IT'S THE BOARD, DUDE, IT'S, LIKE, MAGIC OR SOMETHING.
STOMP!
BLASPHEEMER!!
AAAGGGH!!
MY GOD, IT'S HORRIBLE!
WHAT IS IT? WHAT IS IT?!!

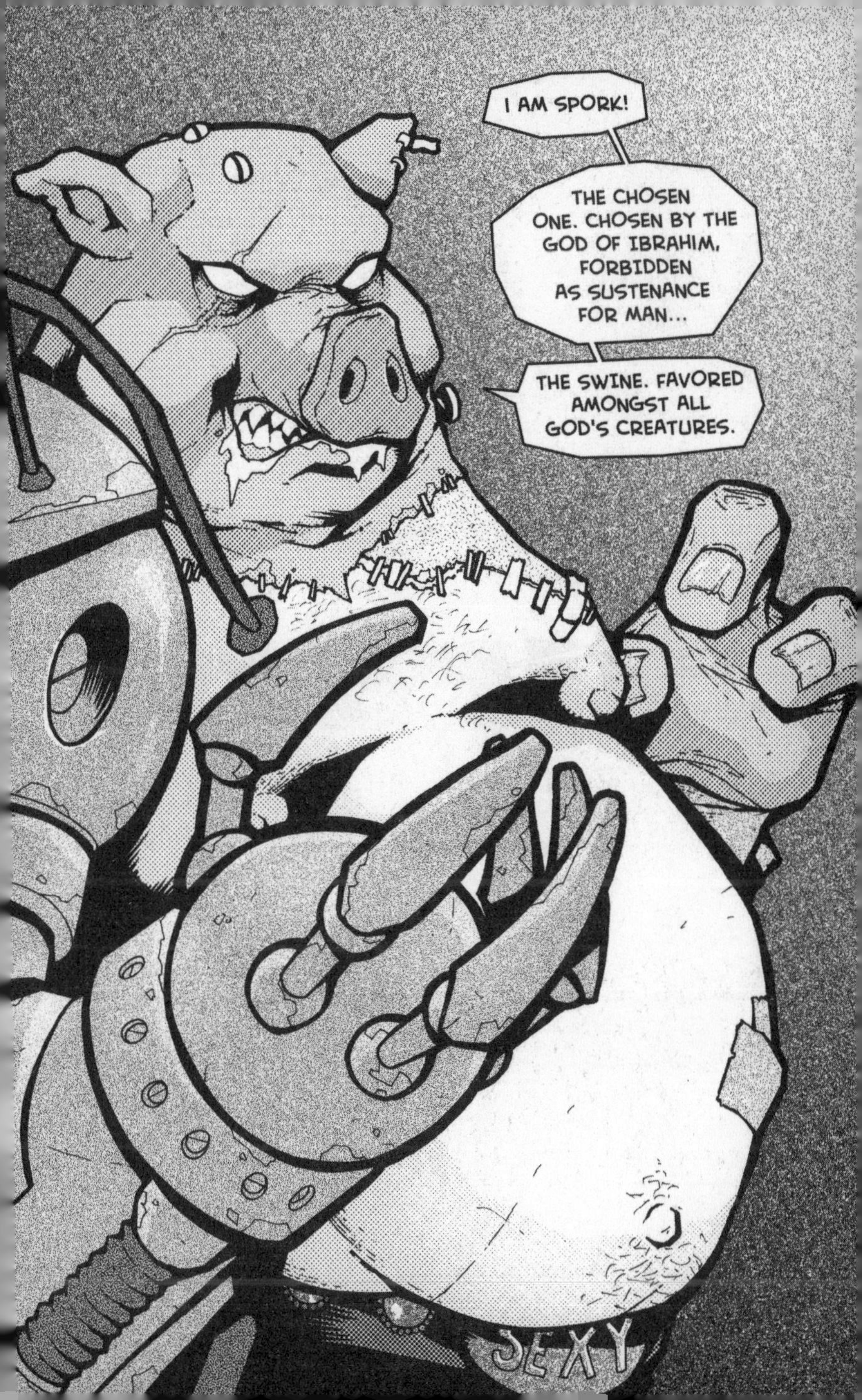
I AM SPORK!
THE CHOSEN ONE. CHOSEN BY THE GOD OF IBRAHIM, FORBIDDEN AS SUSTENANCE FOR MAN...
THE SWINE. FAVORED AMONGST ALL GOD'S CREATURES.
SEXY

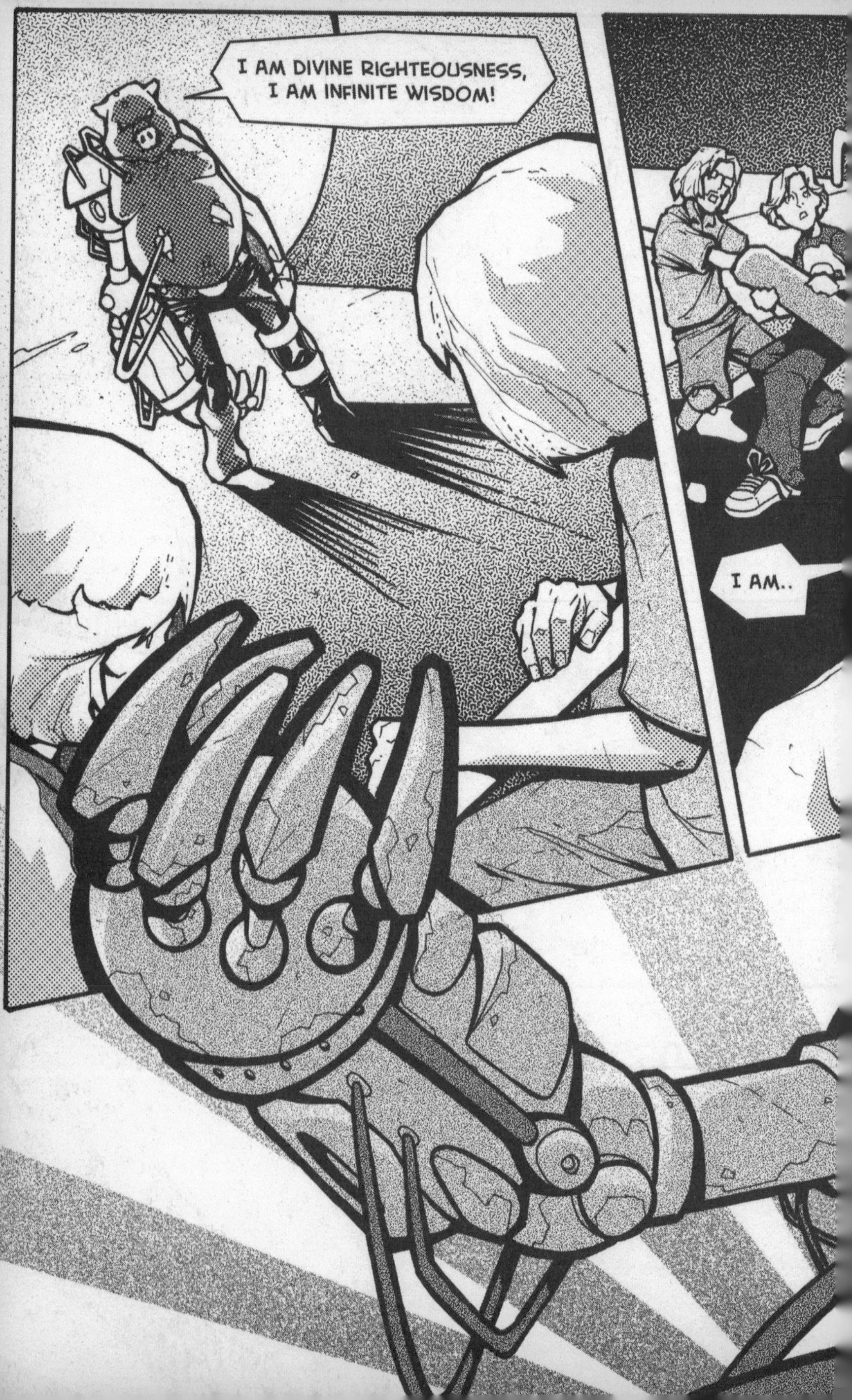
I AM DIVINE RIGHTEOUSNESS,
I AM INFINITE WISDOM!
I AM..

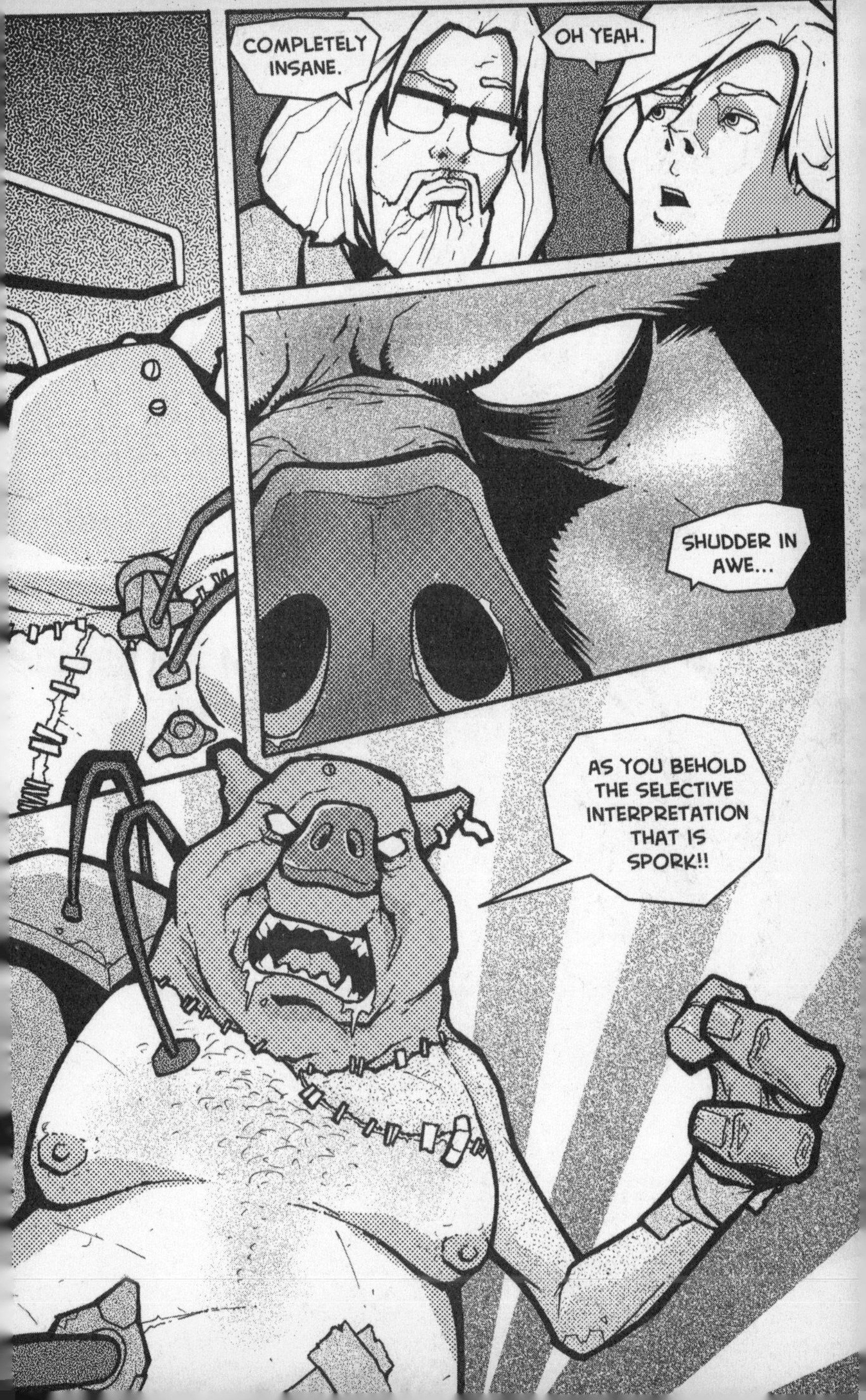
COMPLETELY INSANE.
OH YEAH.
SHUDDER IN AWE...
AS YOU BEHOLD THE SELECTIVE INTERPRETATION THAT IS SPORK!!

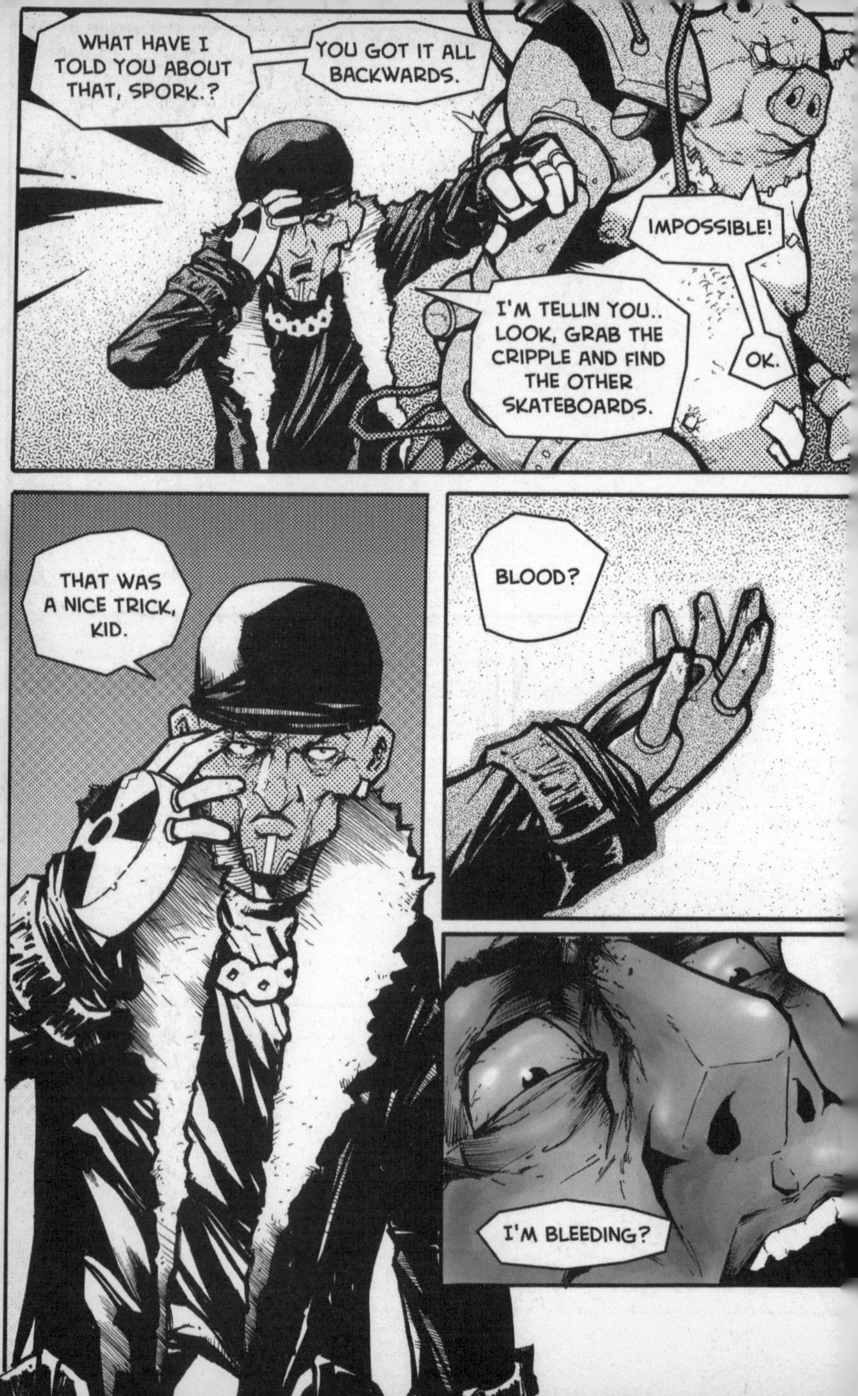
WHAT HAVE I TOLD YOU ABOUT THAT, SPORK.?
YOU GOT IT ALL BACKWARDS.
IMPOSSIBLE!
I'M TELLIN YOU.. LOOK, GRAB THE CRIPPLE AND FIND THE OTHER SKATEBOARDS.
OK.
THAT WAS A NICE TRICK, KID.
BLOOD?
I'M BLEEDING?

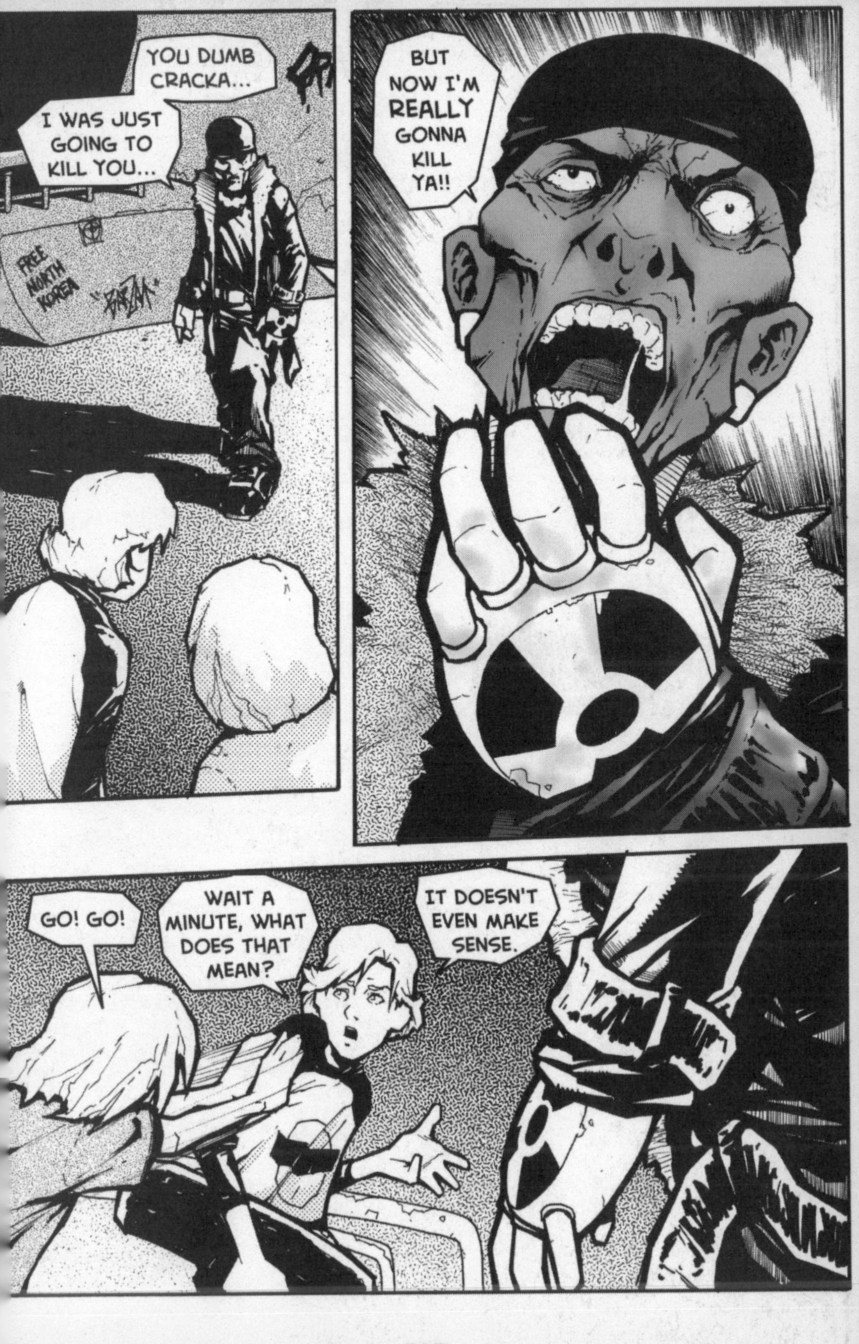
YOU DUMB CRACKA...
I WAS JUST GOING TO KILL YOU...
FREE NORTH KOREA
BUT NOW I'M REALLY GONNA KILL YA!!
GO! GO!
WAIT A MINUTE, WHAT DOES THAT MEAN?
IT DOESN'T EVEN MAKE SENSE.

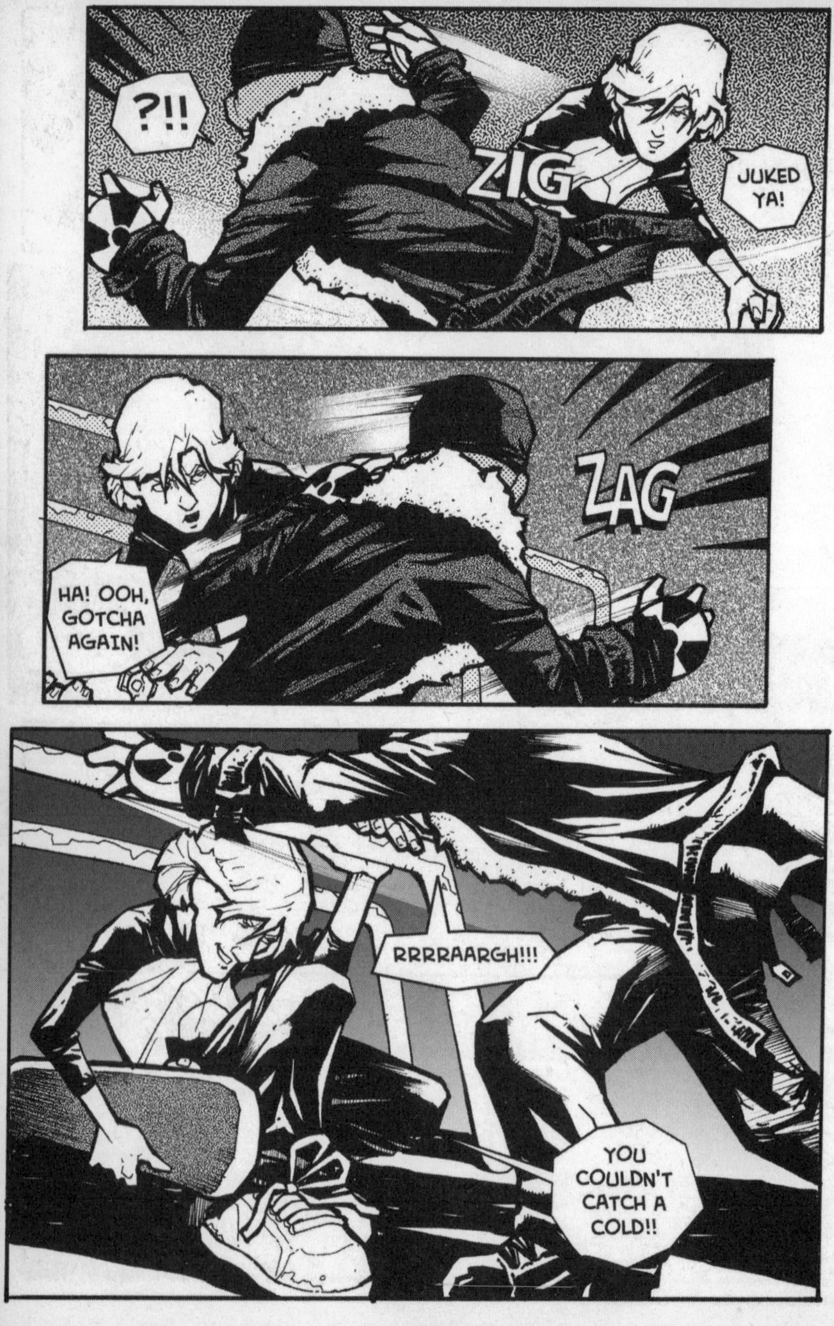
?!!
ZIG
JUKED YA!
ZAG
HA! OOH, GOTCHA AGAIN!
RRRRAARGH!!!
YOU COULDN'T CATCH A COLD!!

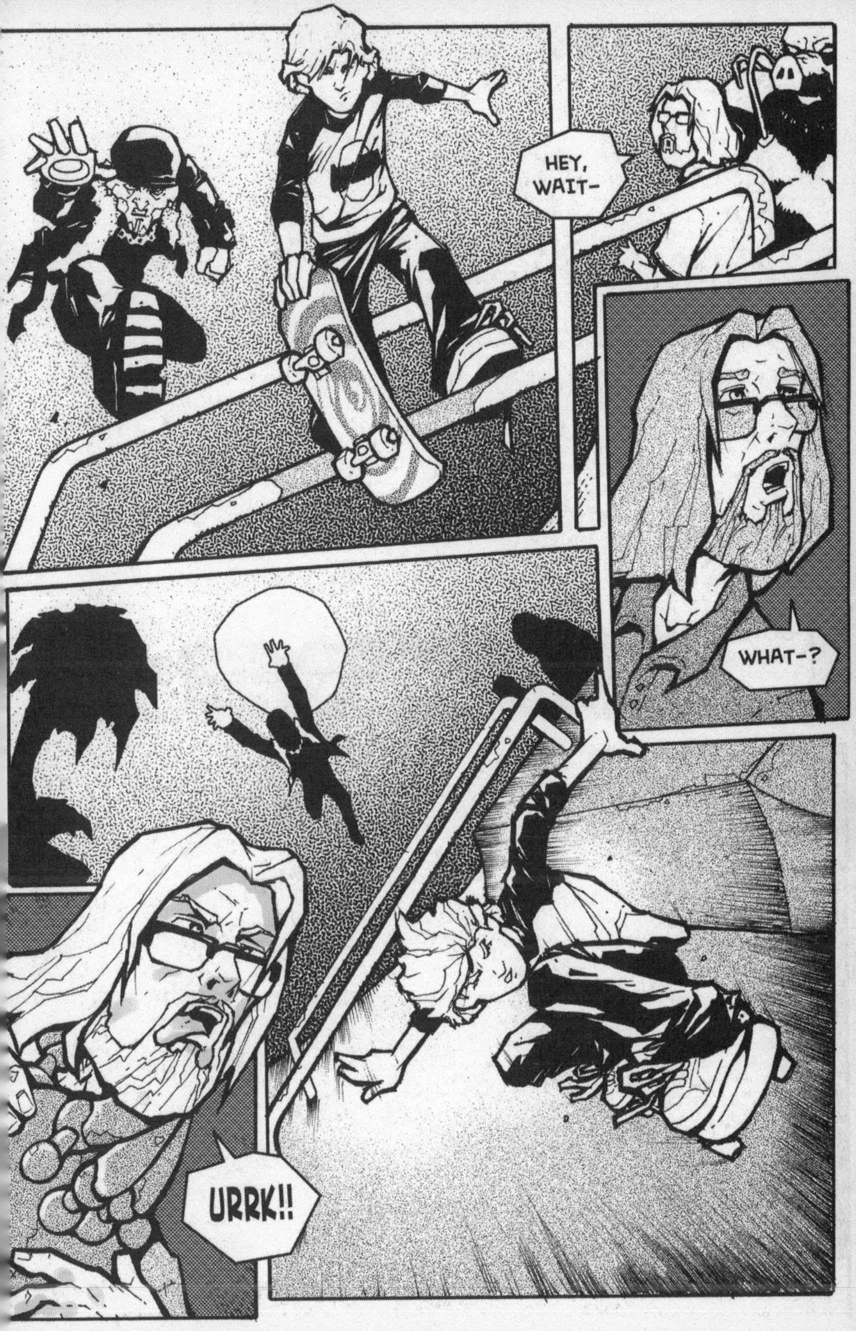
HEY, WAIT-
WHAT-?
URRK!!

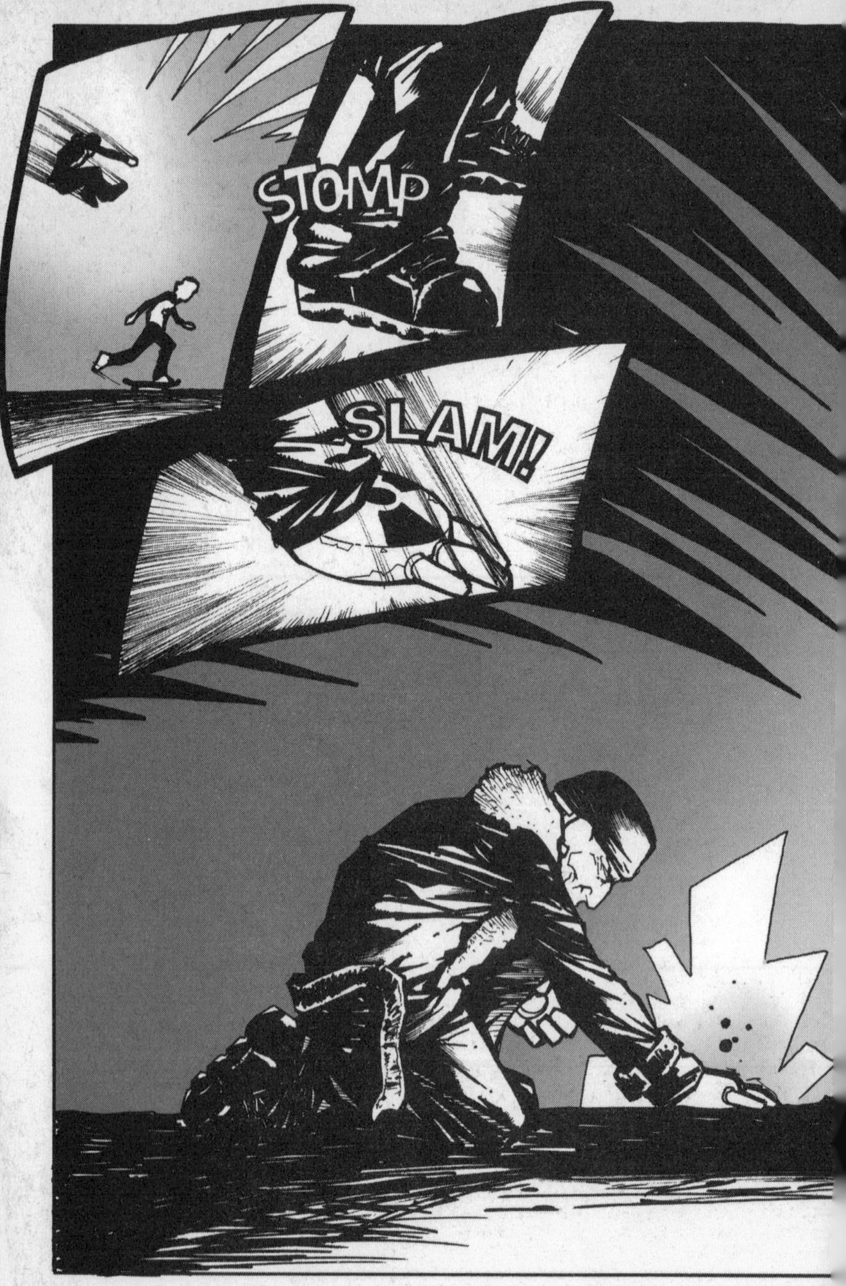
STOMP
SLAM!

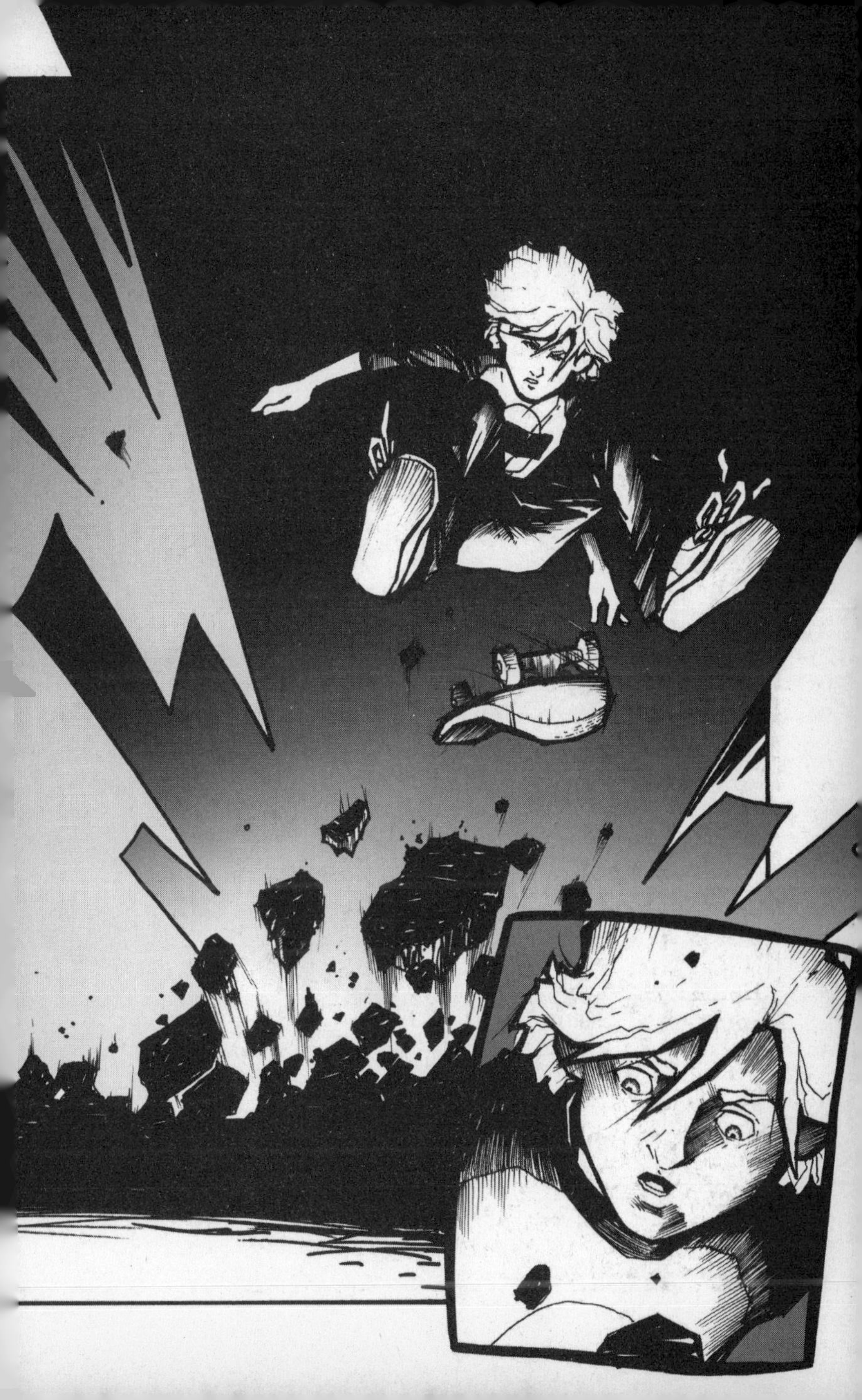

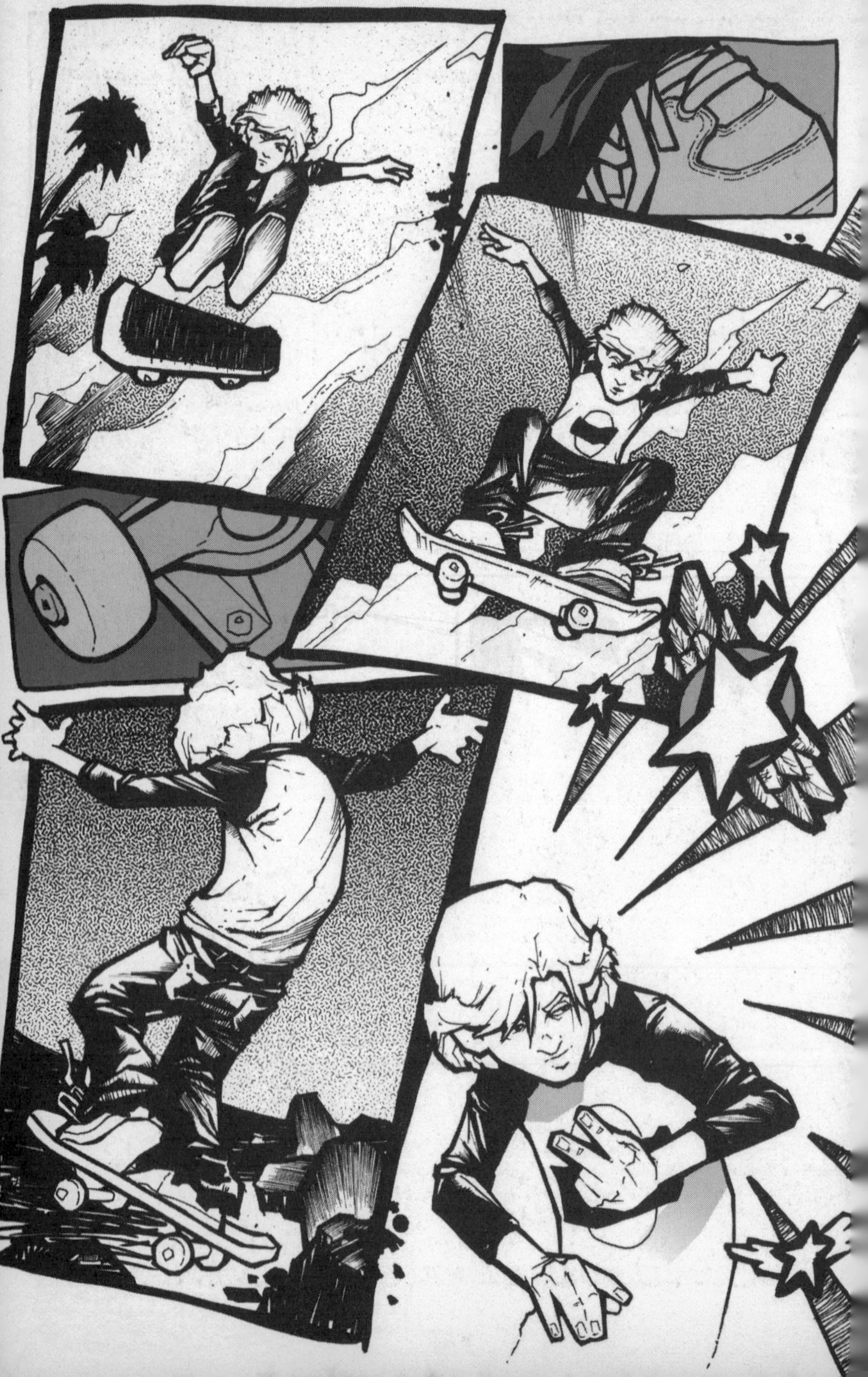

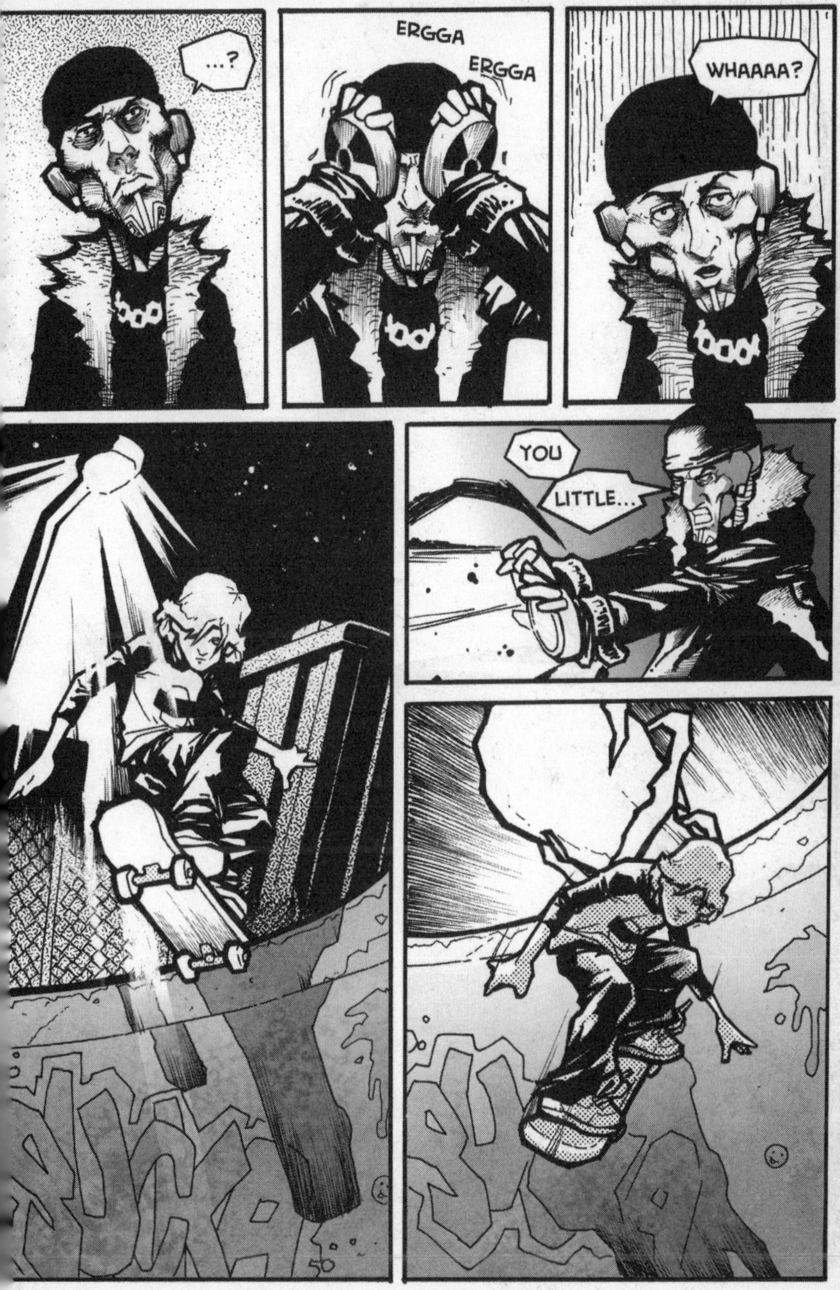
...?
ERGGA
ERGGA
WHAAAA?
YOU
LITTLE...

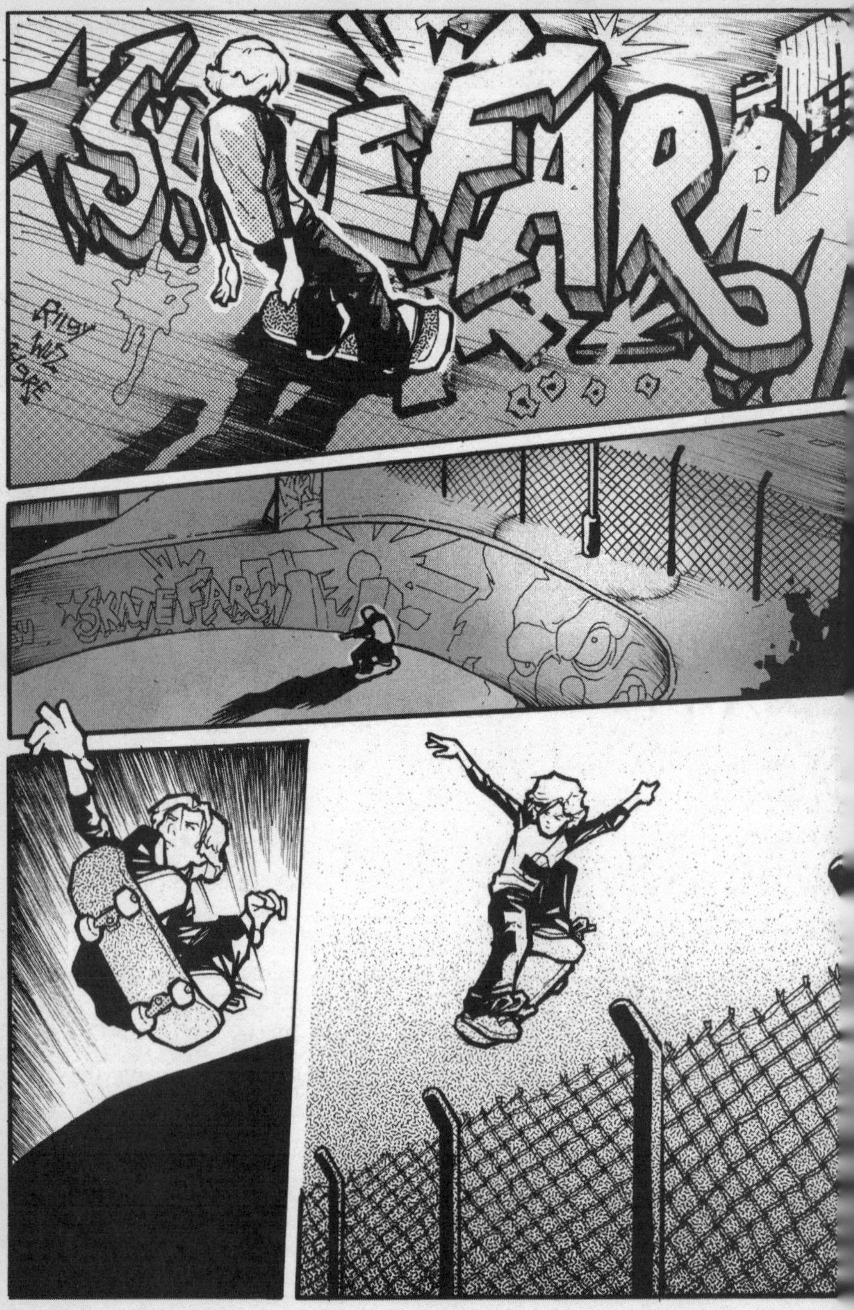
SKATE FARM

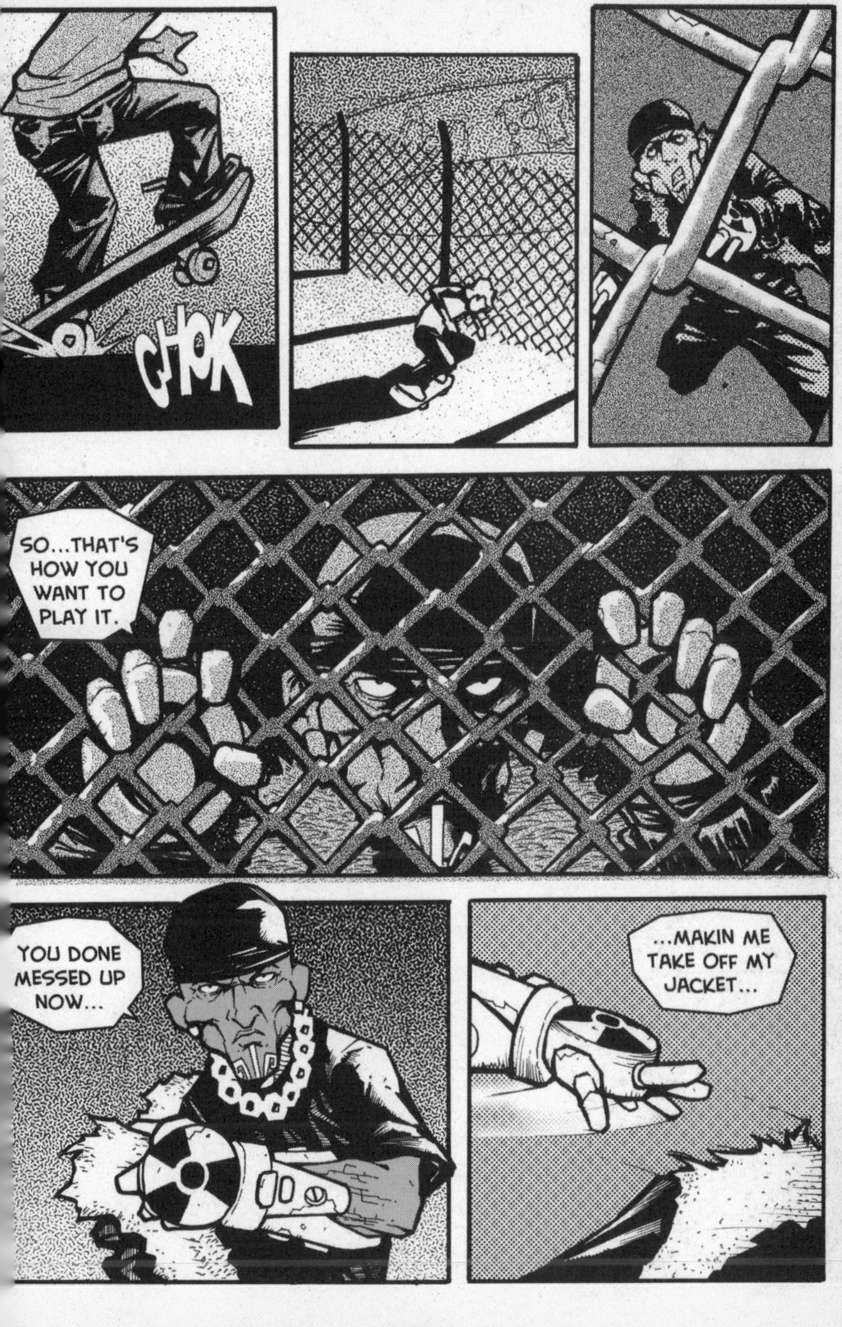
CHOK
SO...THAT'S HOW YOU WANT TO PLAY IT.
YOU DONE MESSED UP NOW...
...MAKIN ME TAKE OFF MY JACKET...

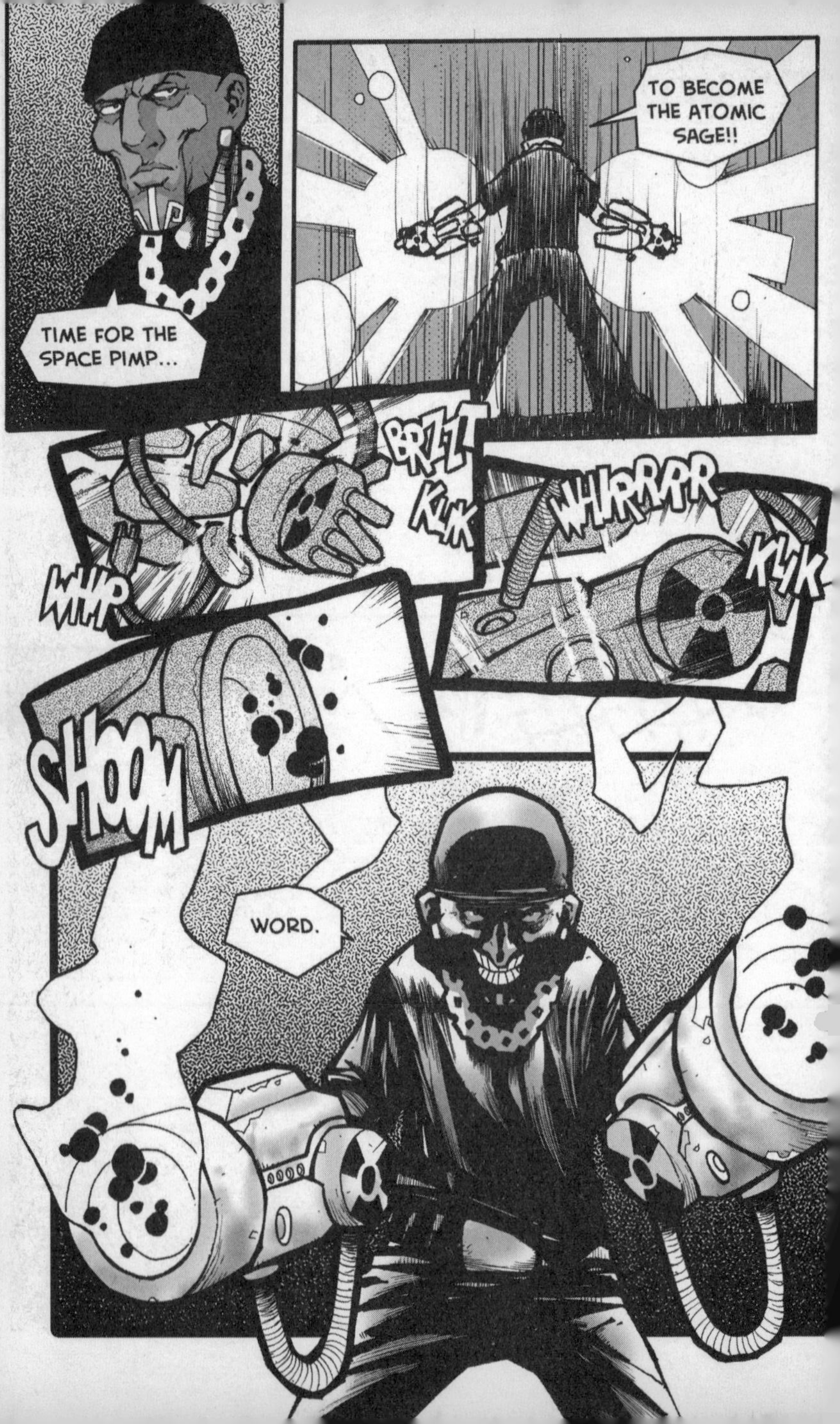
TO BECOME THE ATOMIC SAGE!!
TIME FOR THE SPACE PIMP...
BRZZZT
KLYK
WHIP
WHIRRRR
KLYK
SHOOM
WORD.

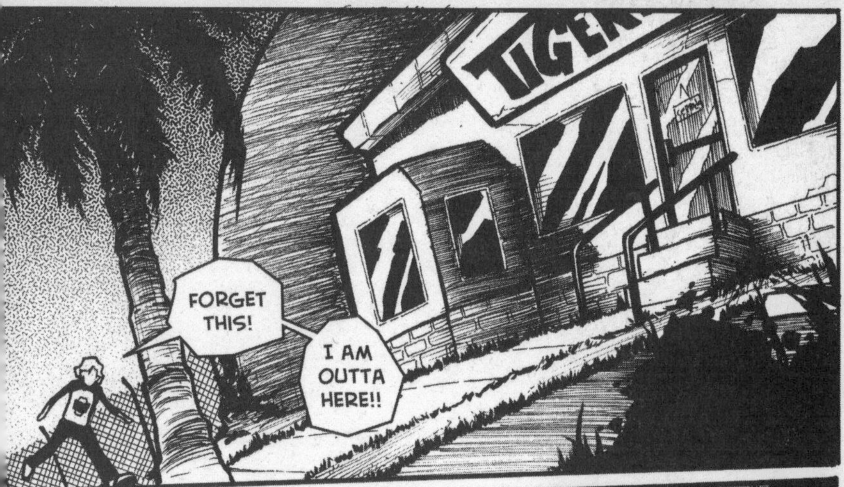
TIGER
FORGET THIS!
I AM OUTTA HERE!!

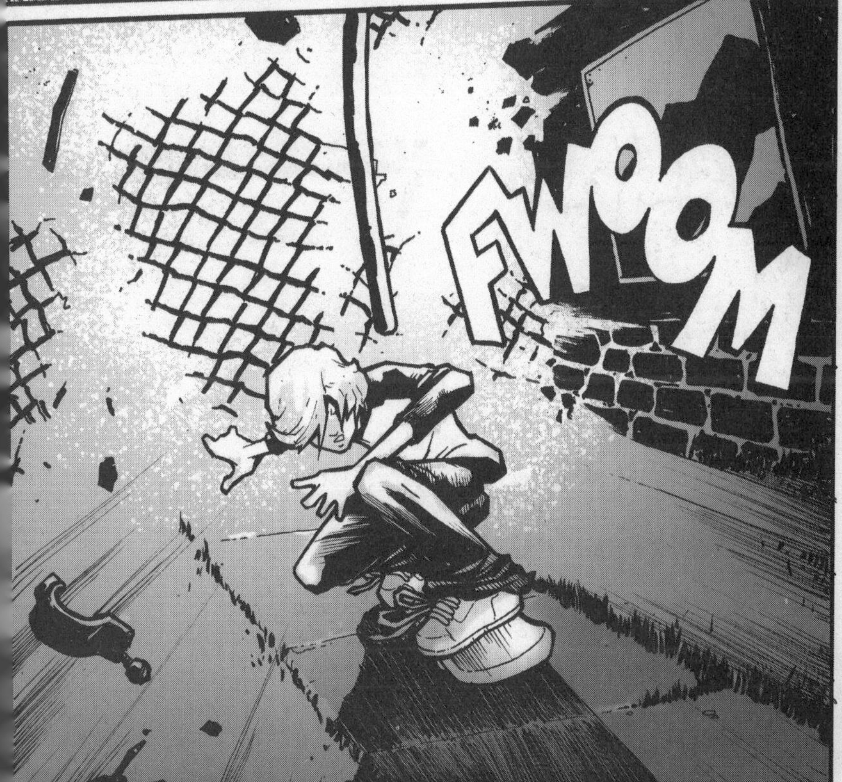
FWOOM

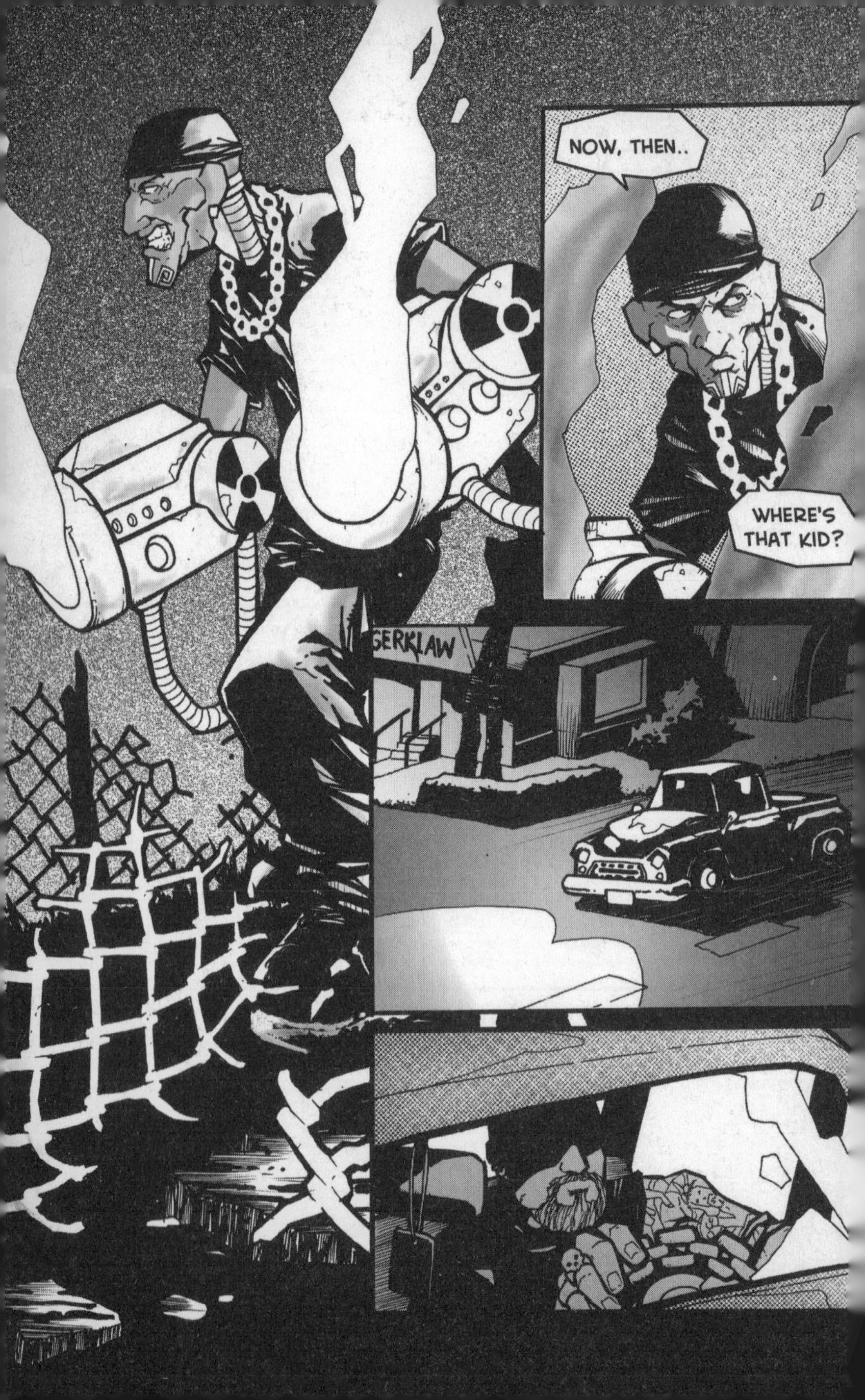
NOW, THEN..
WHERE'S THAT KID?
GERKLAW

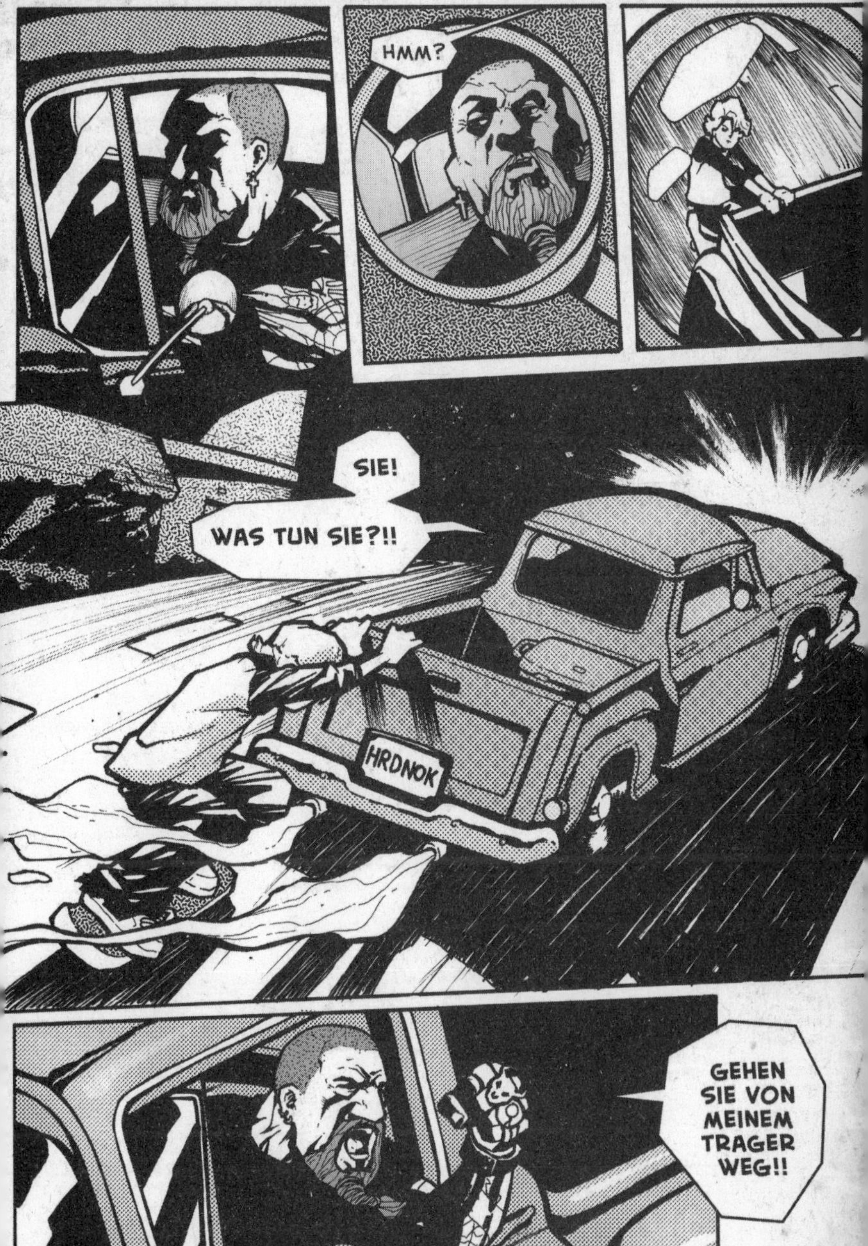
HMM?
SIE!
WAS TUN SIE?!!
HRDNOK
GEHEN SIE VON MEINEM TRAGER WEG!!

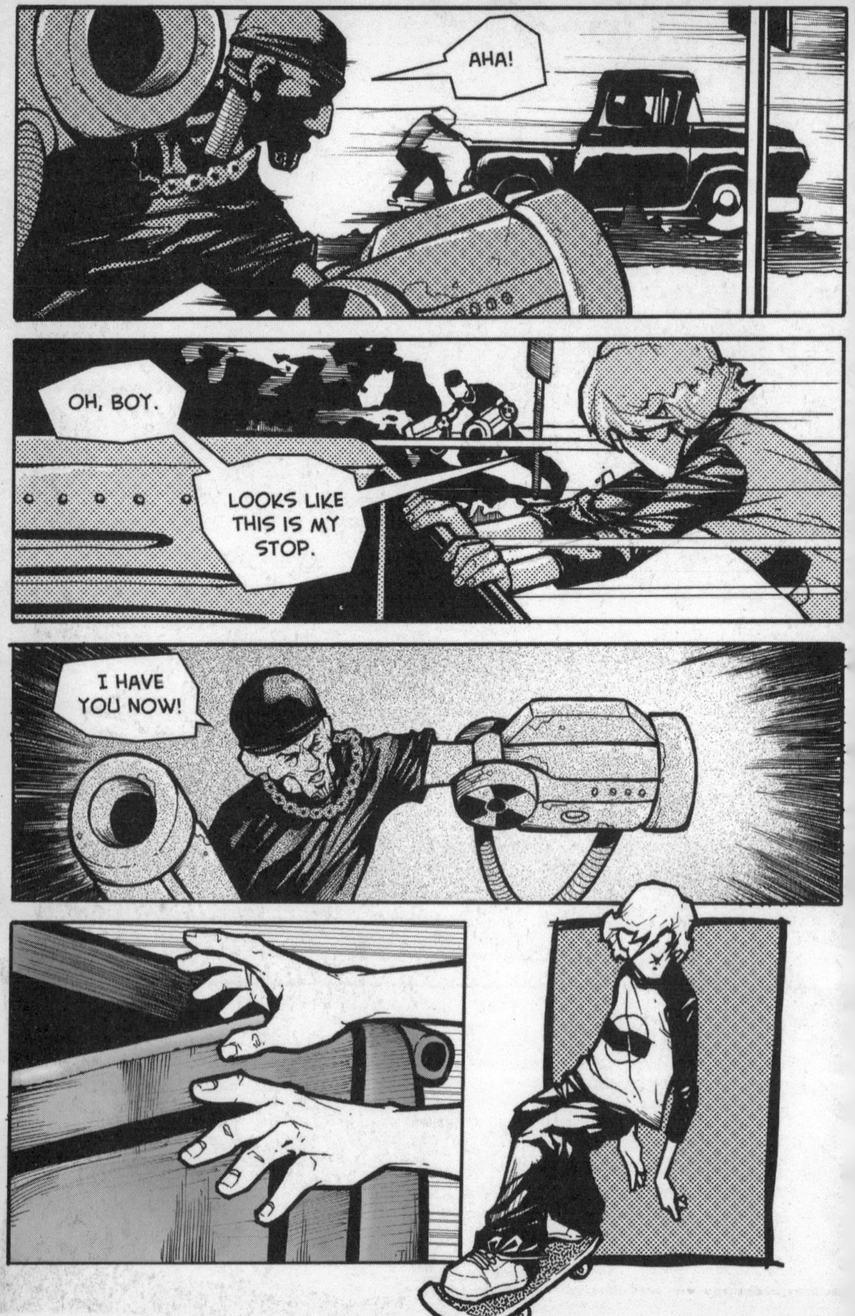
AHA!
OH, BOY.
LOOKS LIKE THIS IS MY STOP.
I HAVE YOU NOW!

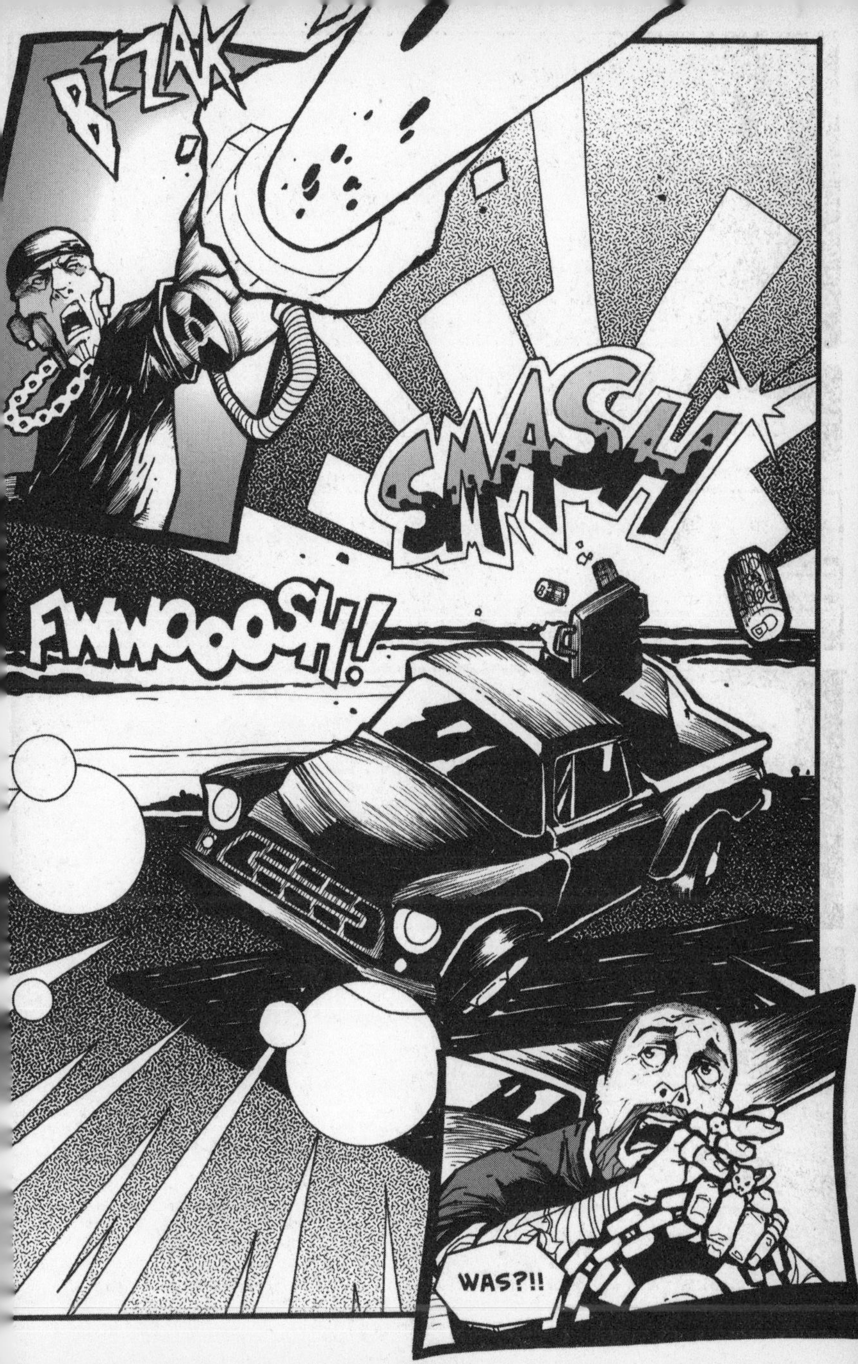
BZZAK
SMASH
FWWOOOSH!
WAS?!!

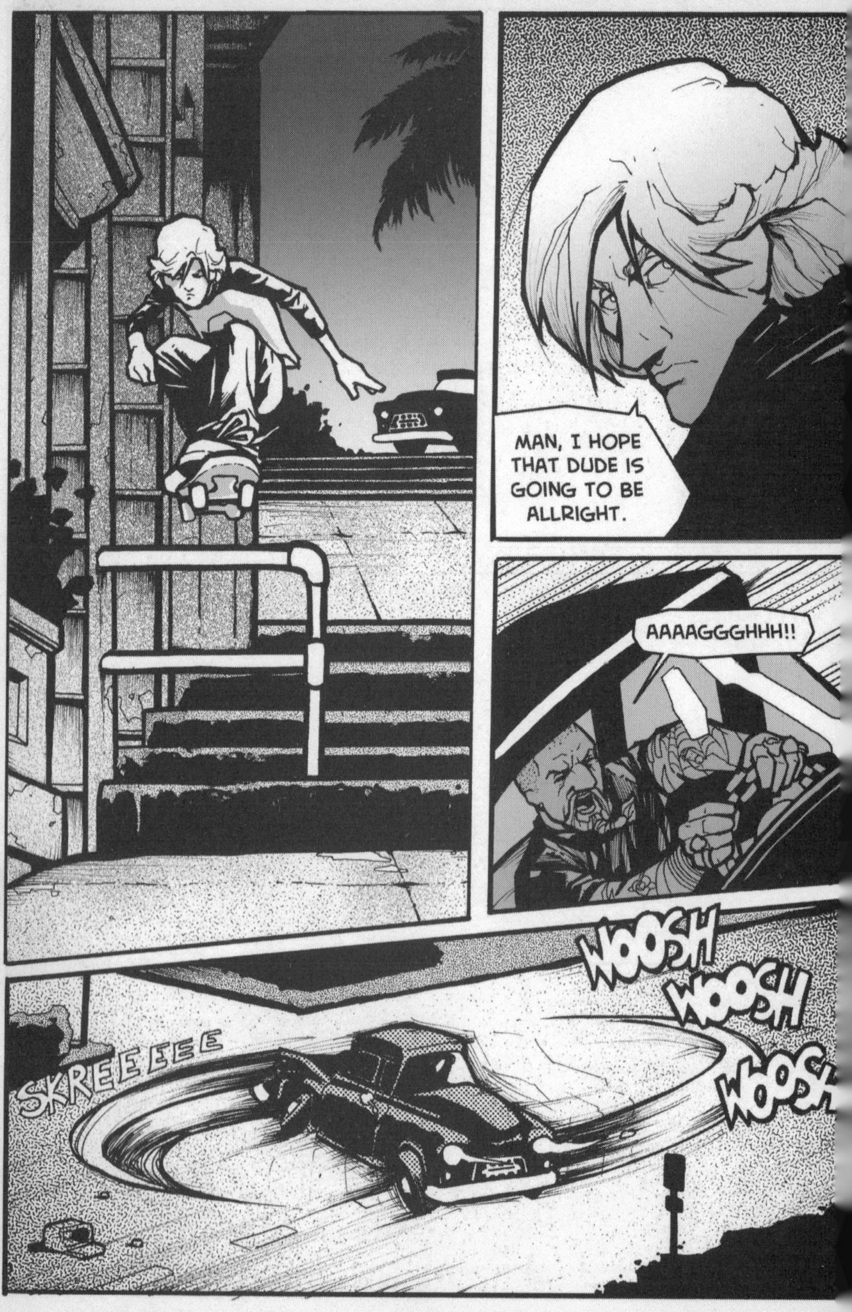
MAN, I HOPE THAT DUDE IS GOING TO BE ALLRIGHT.
AAAAGGGHHH!!
SKREEEEEE
WOOSH
WOOSH
WOOSH

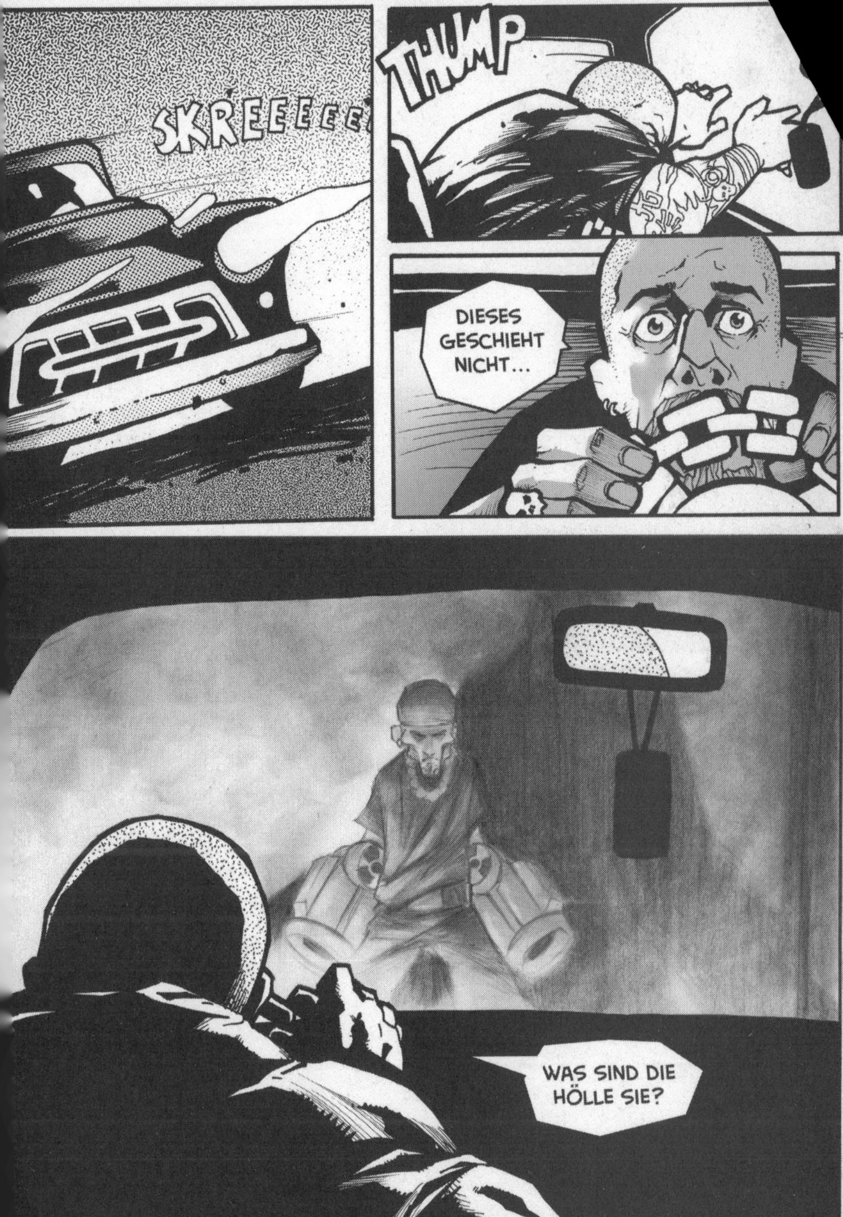
SKREEEEEE
THUMP
DIESES GESCHIEHT NICHT...
WAS SIND DIE HÖLLE SIE?

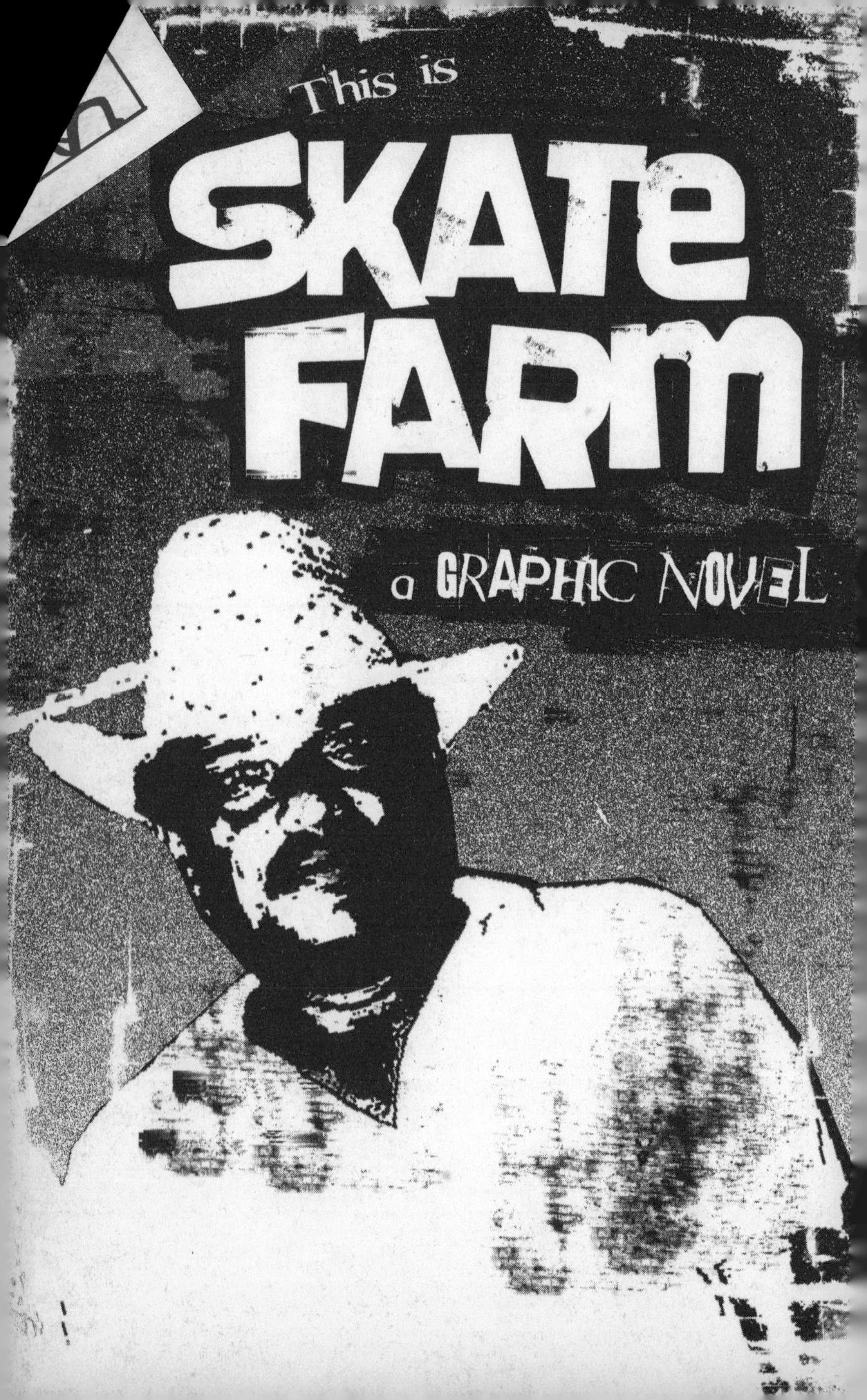

This is
SKATE
FARM
a GRAPHIC NOVEL

chapter 5

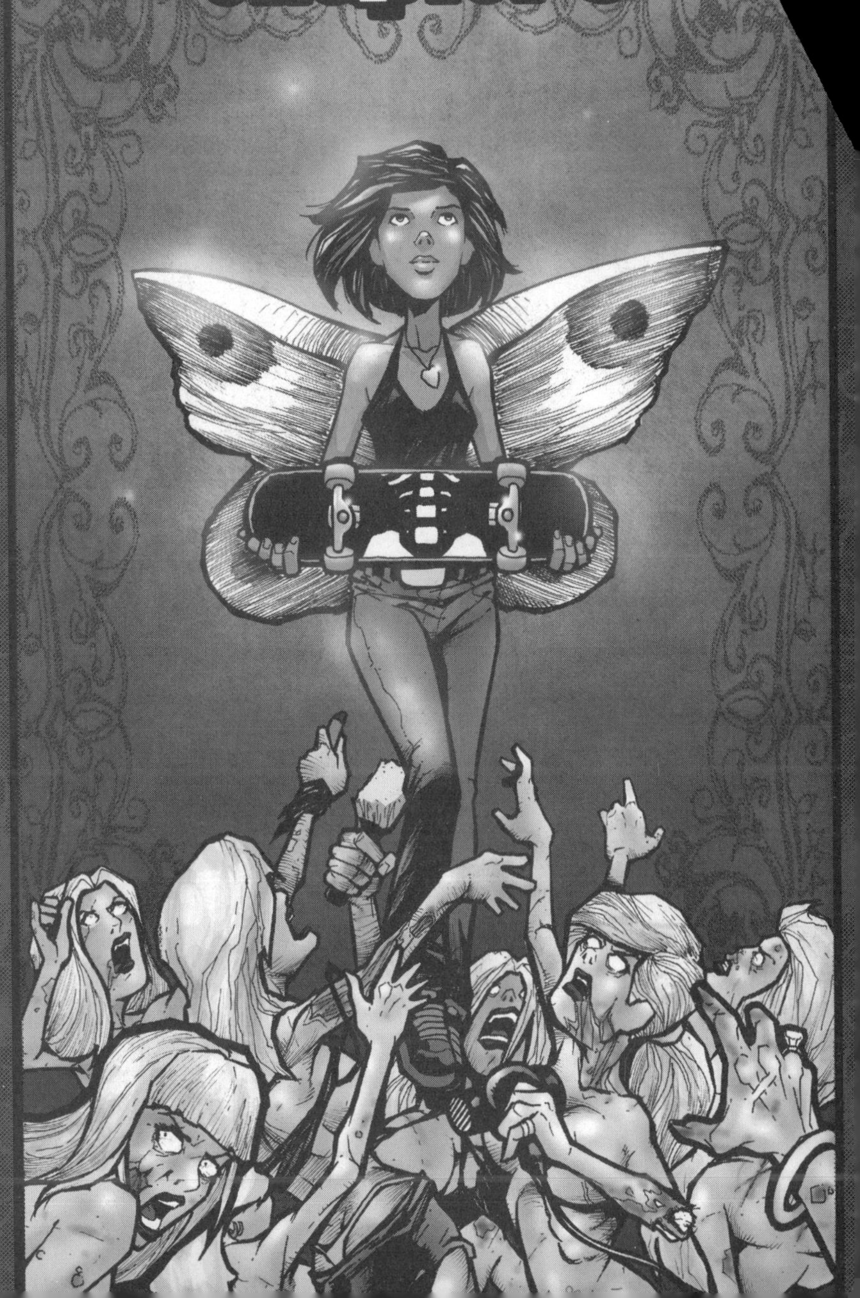

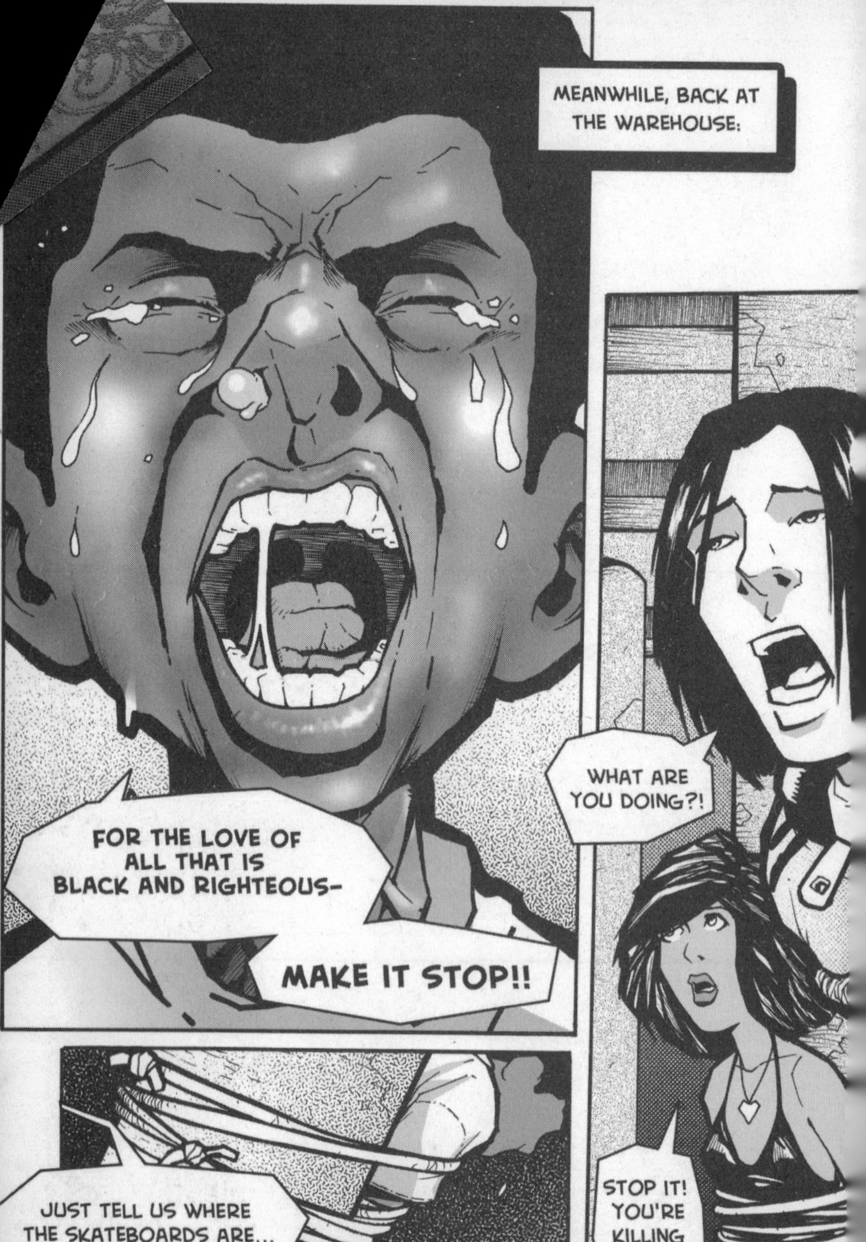
MEANWHILE, BACK AT THE WAREHOUSE:
FOR THE LOVE OF ALL THAT IS BLACK AND RIGHTEOUS-
MAKE IT STOP!!
WHAT ARE YOU DOING?!
JUST TELL US WHERE THE SKATEBOARDS ARE...
STOP IT! YOU'RE KILLING HIM!!

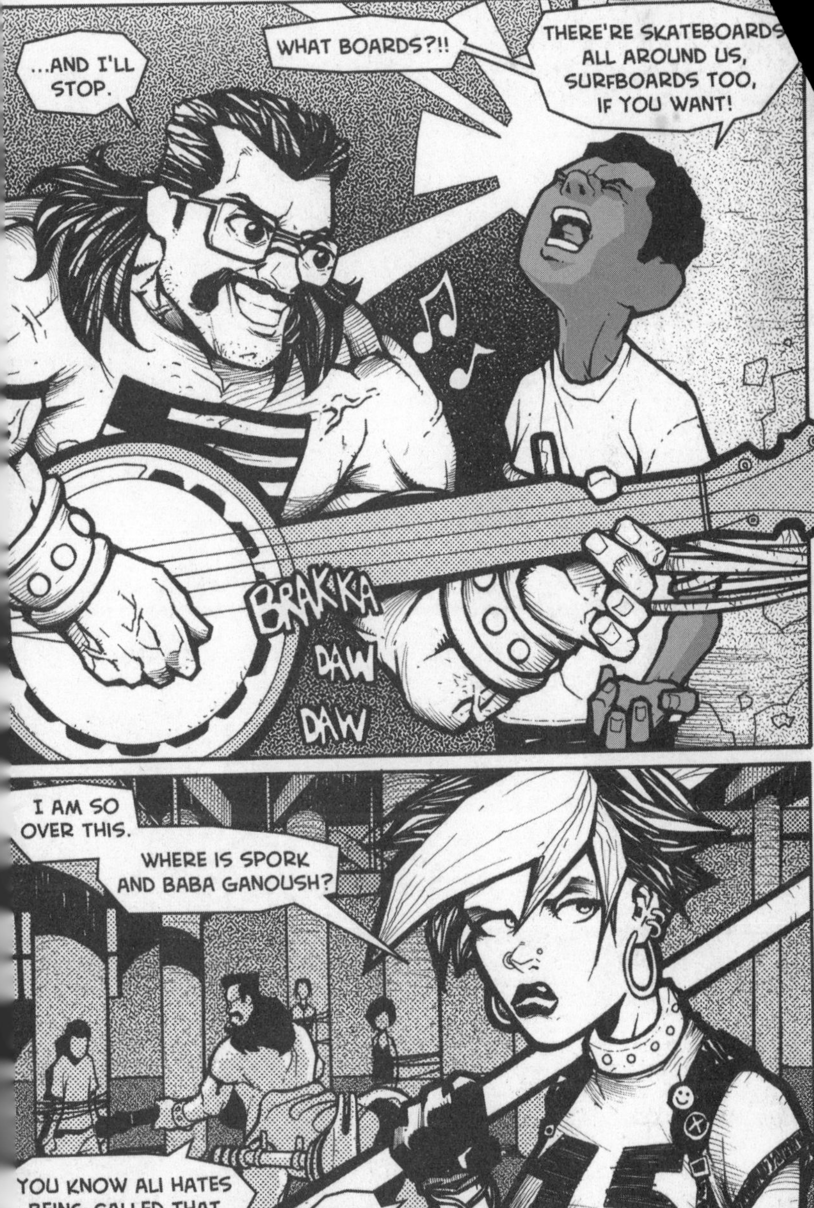
...AND I'LL STOP.
WHAT BOARDS?!!
THERE'RE SKATEBOARDS ALL AROUND US, SURFBOARDS TOO, IF YOU WANT!
BRAKKA
DAW
DAW
I AM SO OVER THIS.
WHERE IS SPORK AND BABA GANOUSH?
YOU KNOW ALI HATES BEING CALLED THAT.
LIKE I CARE.

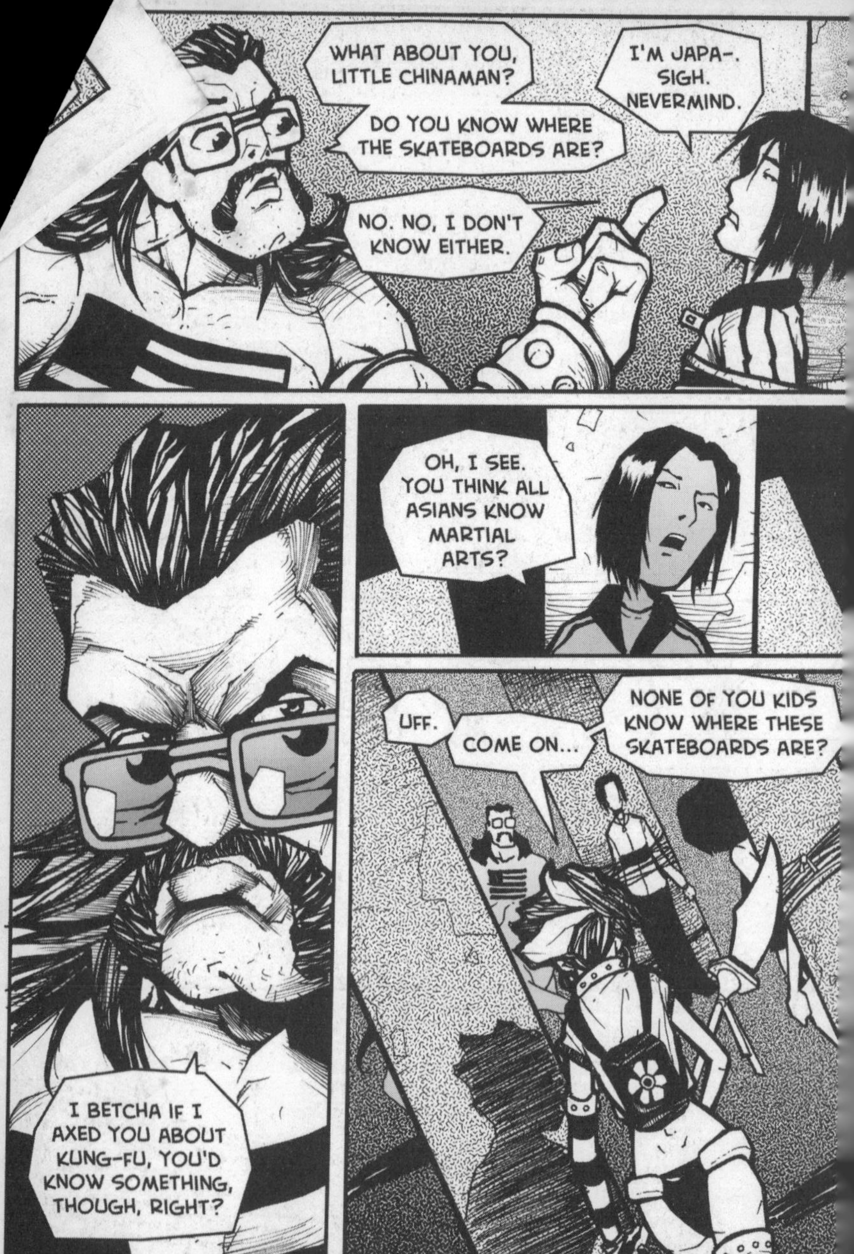
WHAT ABOUT YOU, LITTLE CHINAMAN?
DO YOU KNOW WHERE THE SKATEBOARDS ARE?
I'M JAPA-. SIGH. NEVERMIND.
NO. NO, I DON'T KNOW EITHER.
I BETCHA IF I AXED YOU ABOUT KUNG-FU, YOU'D KNOW SOMETHING, THOUGH, RIGHT?
OH, I SEE. YOU THINK ALL ASIANS KNOW MARTIAL ARTS?
UFF.
COME ON...
NONE OF YOU KIDS KNOW WHERE THESE SKATEBOARDS ARE?

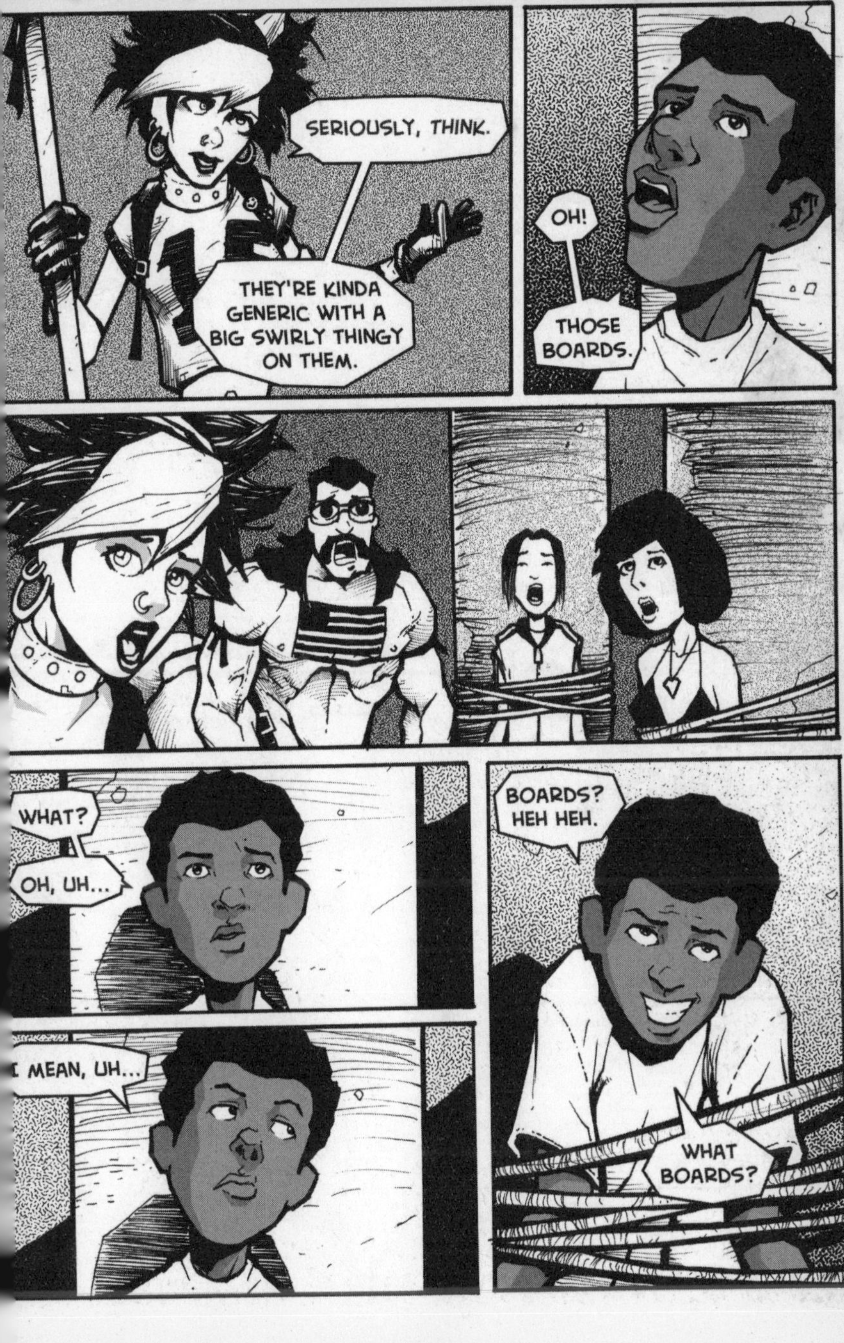
SERIOUSLY, THINK.
THEY'RE KINDA GENERIC WITH A BIG SWIRLY THINGY ON THEM.
OH!
THOSE BOARDS.
WHAT?
OH, UH...
I MEAN, UH...
BOARDS? HEH HEH.
WHAT BOARDS?

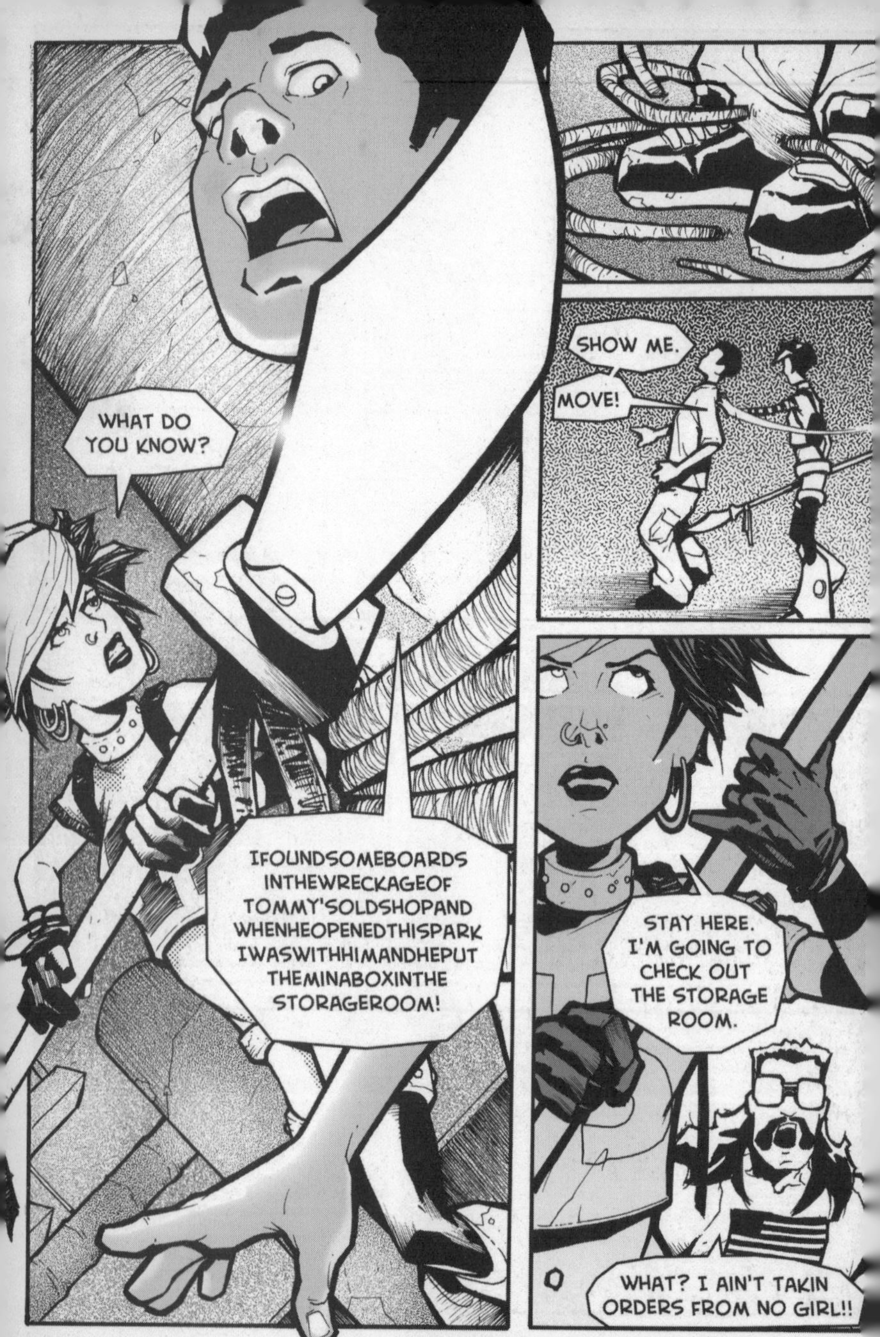
WHAT DO YOU KNOW?
IFOUNDSOMEBOARDS INTHEWRECKAGEOF TOMMY'SOLDSHOPAND WHENHEOPENEDTHISPARK IWASWITHHIMANDHEPUT THEMINABOXINTHE STORAGEROOM!
SHOW ME.
MOVE!
STAY HERE. I'M GOING TO CHECK OUT THE STORAGE ROOM.
WHAT? I AIN'T TAKIN ORDERS FROM NO GIRL!!

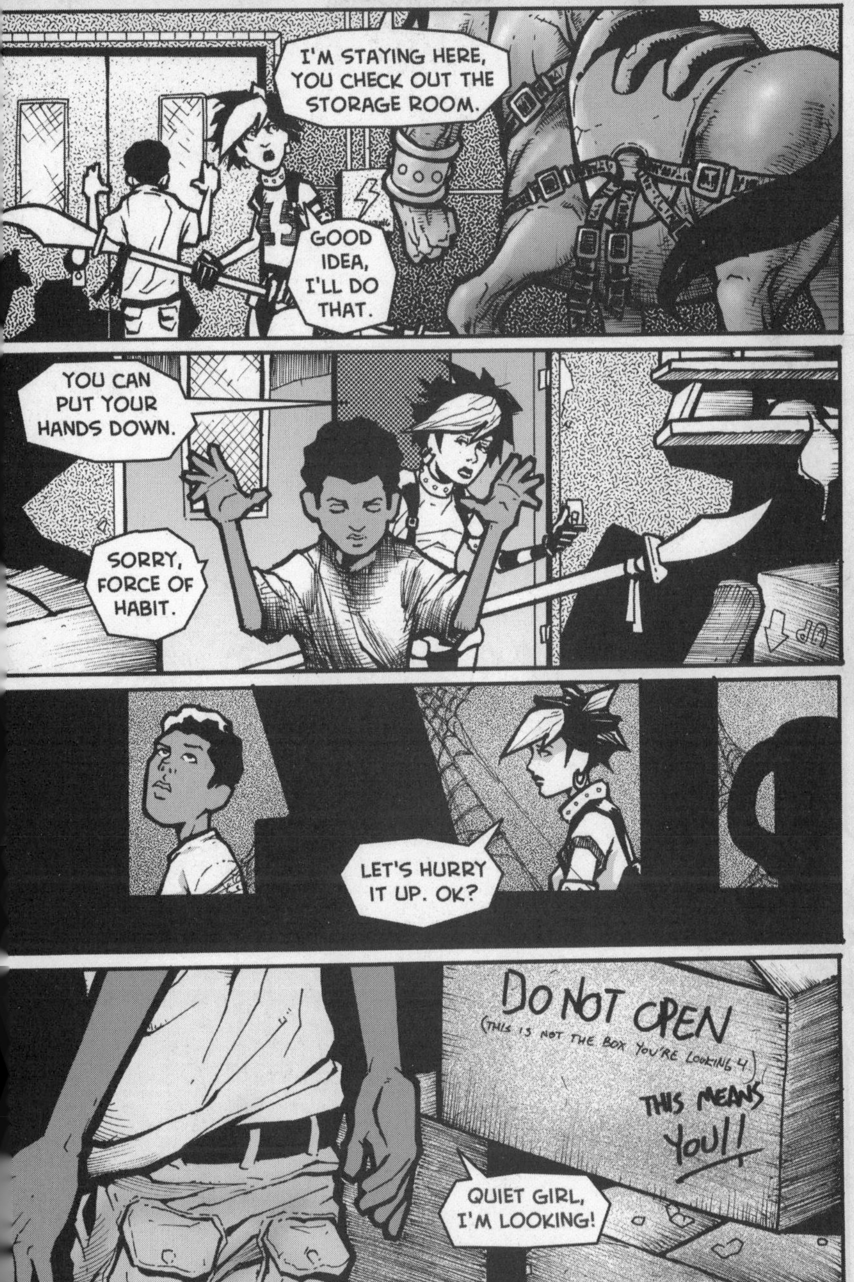
I'M STAYING HERE, YOU CHECK OUT THE STORAGE ROOM.
GOOD IDEA, I'LL DO THAT.
YOU CAN PUT YOUR HANDS DOWN.
SORRY, FORCE OF HABIT.
UP
LET'S HURRY IT UP. OK?
DO NOT OPEN
(THIS IS NOT THE BOX YOU'RE LOOKING 4)
THIS MEANS YOU!!
QUIET GIRL, I'M LOOKING!

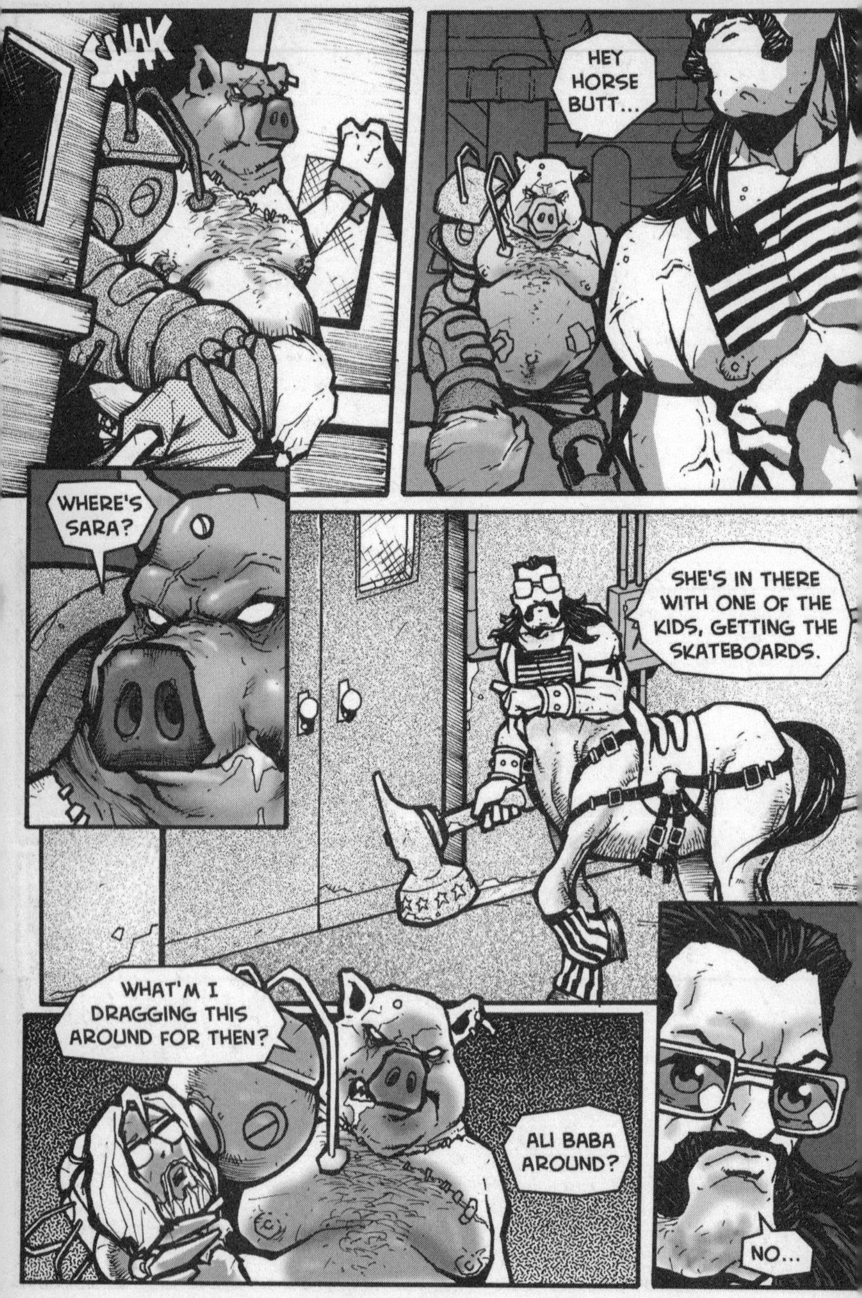
SWAK
HEY HORSE BUTT...
WHERE'S SARA?
SHE'S IN THERE WITH ONE OF THE KIDS, GETTING THE SKATEBOARDS.
WHAT'M I DRAGGING THIS AROUND FOR THEN?
ALI BABA AROUND?
NO...

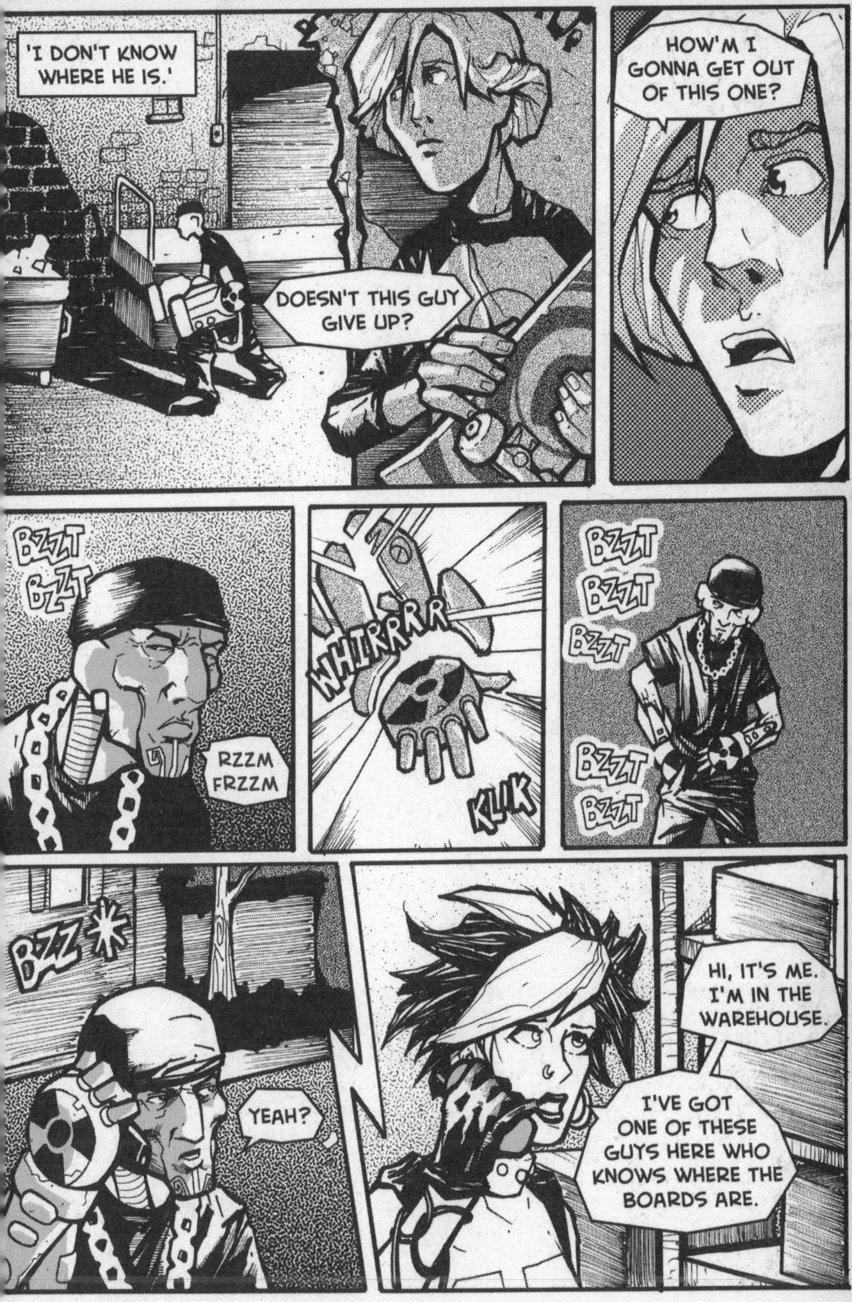
'I DON'T KNOW WHERE HE IS.'
DOESN'T THIS GUY GIVE UP?
HOW'M I GONNA GET OUT OF THIS ONE?
BZZT
BZZT
RZZM FRZZM
WHIRRRR
KLIK
BZZT
BZZT
BZZT
BZZT
BZZT
BZZ
YEAH?
HI, IT'S ME. I'M IN THE WAREHOUSE.
I'VE GOT ONE OF THESE GUYS HERE WHO KNOWS WHERE THE BOARDS ARE.

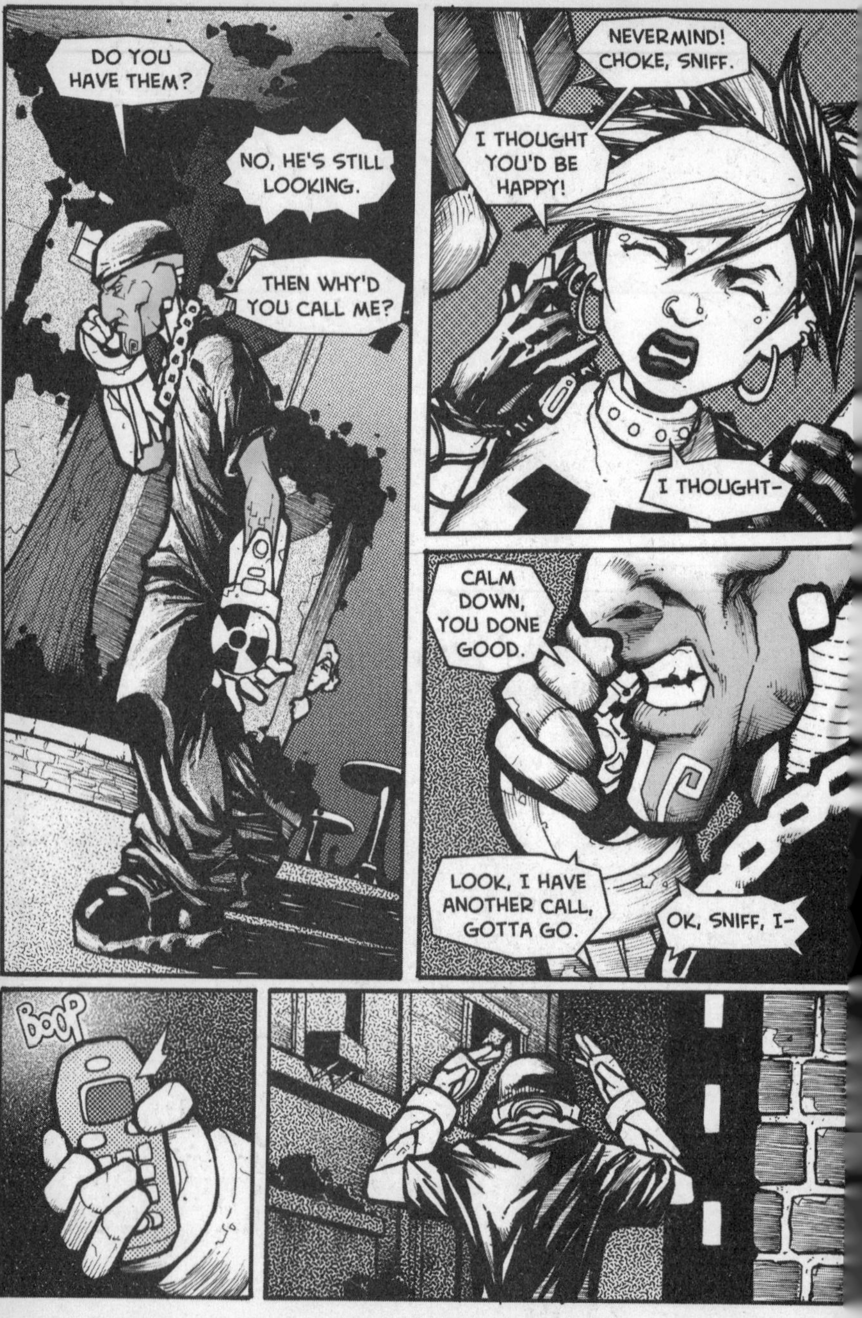
DO YOU HAVE THEM?
NO, HE'S STILL LOOKING.
THEN WHY'D YOU CALL ME?
NEVERMIND! CHOKE, SNIFF.
I THOUGHT YOU'D BE HAPPY!
I THOUGHT-
CALM DOWN, YOU DONE GOOD.
LOOK, I HAVE ANOTHER CALL, GOTTA GO.
OK, SNIFF, I-
BOOP

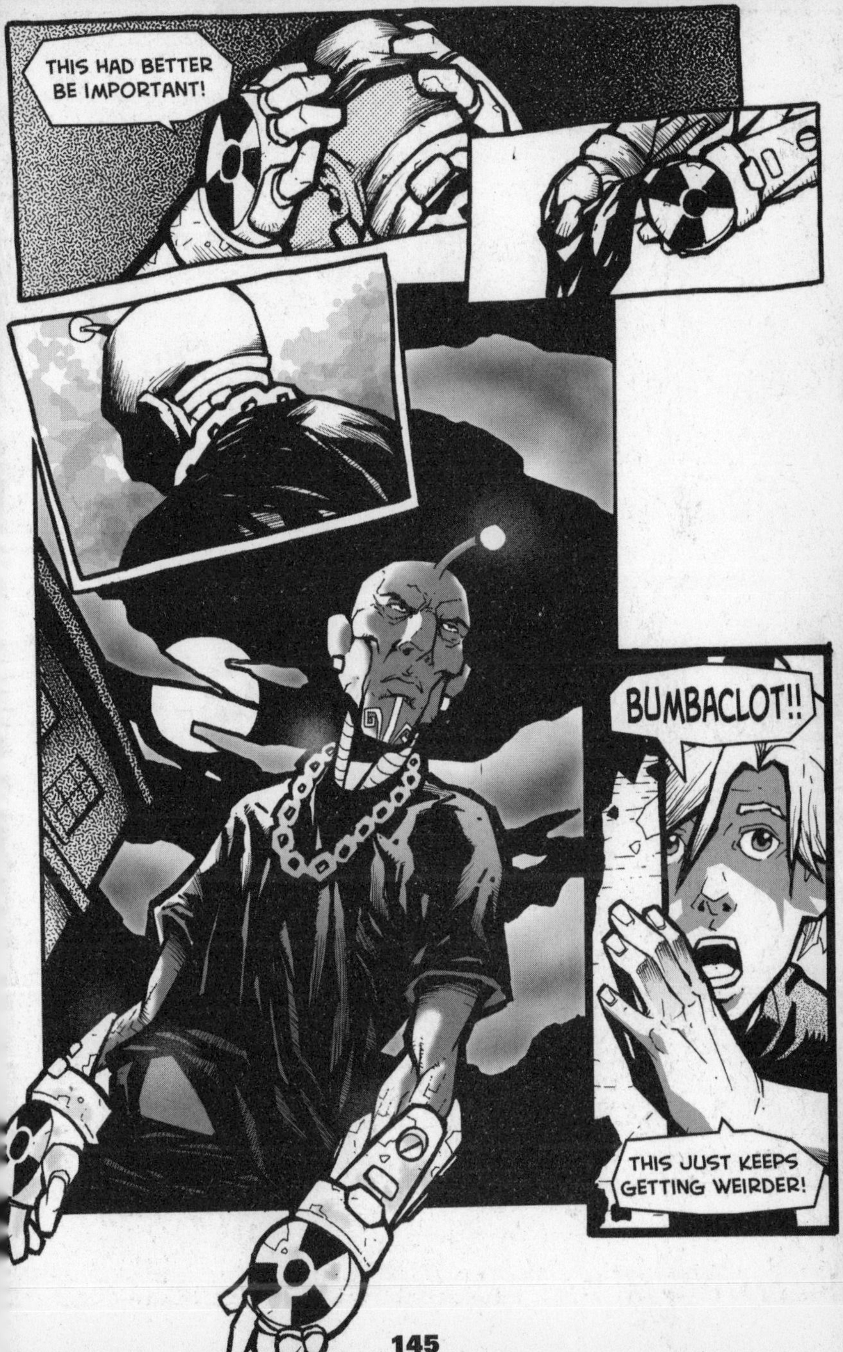
THIS HAD BETTER BE IMPORTANT!
BUMBACLOT!!
THIS JUST KEEPS GETTING WEIRDER!

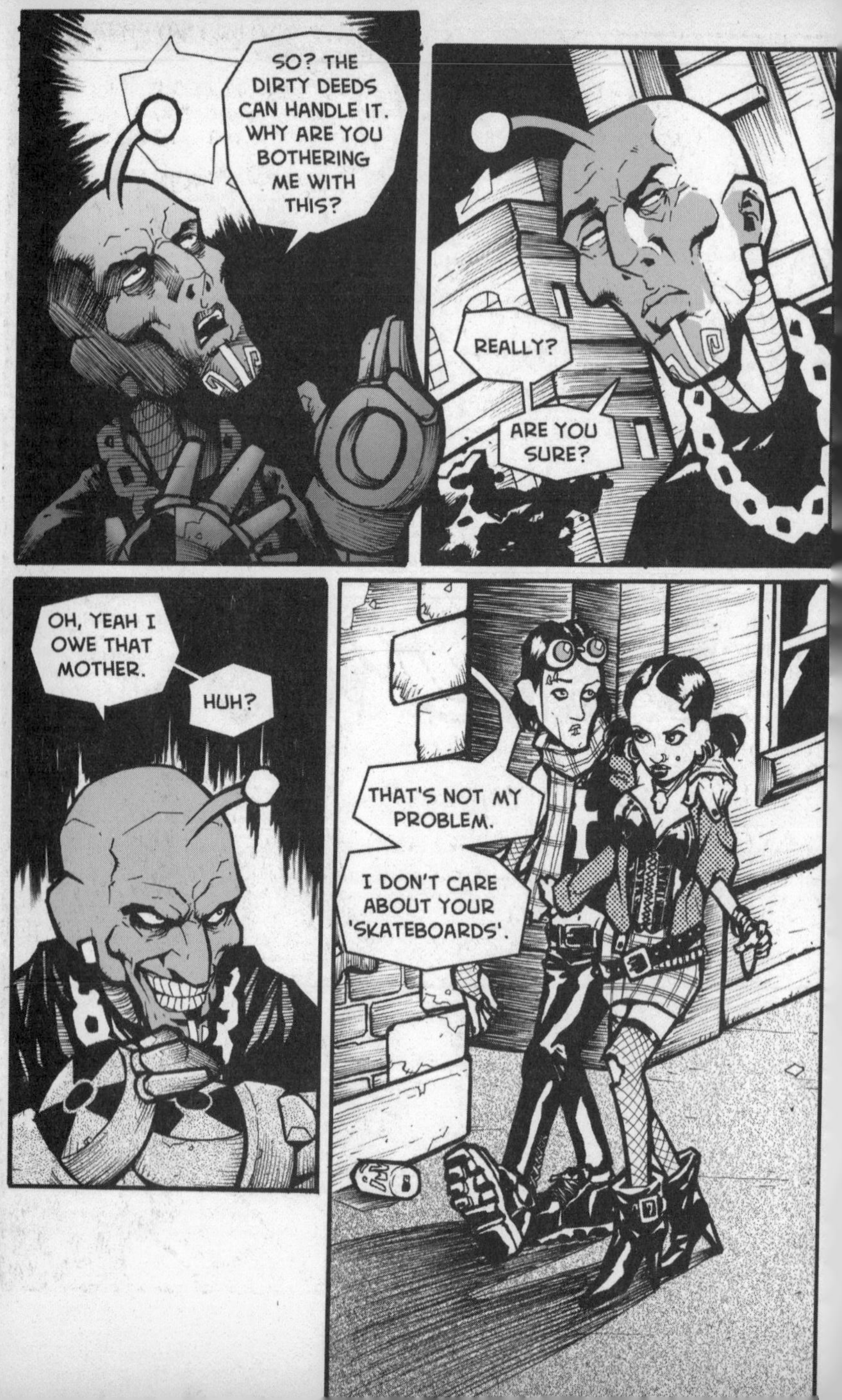
SO? THE DIRTY DEEDS CAN HANDLE IT. WHY ARE YOU BOTHERING ME WITH THIS?
REALLY?
ARE YOU SURE?
OH, YEAH I OWE THAT MOTHER.
HUH?
THAT'S NOT MY PROBLEM.
I DON'T CARE ABOUT YOUR 'SKATEBOARDS'.

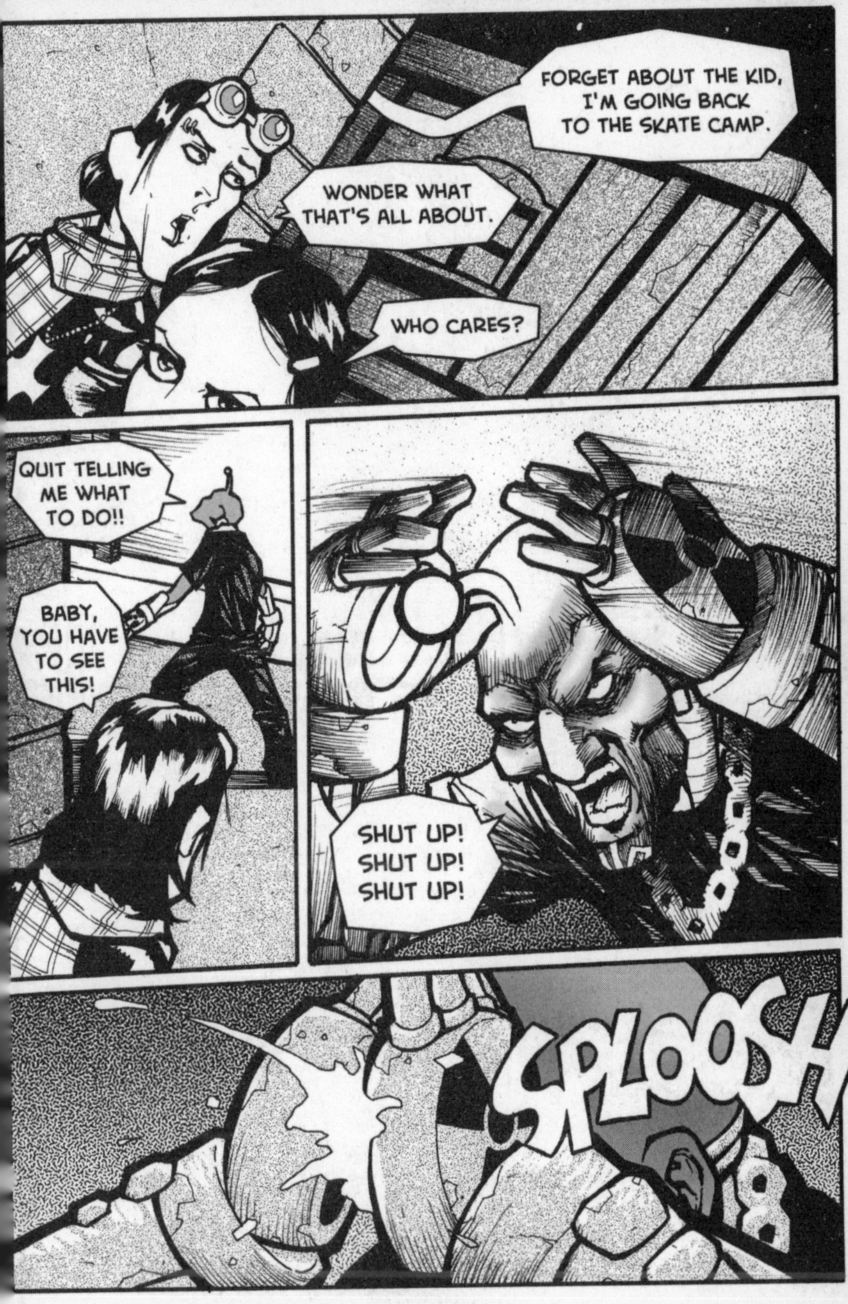
FORGET ABOUT THE KID, I'M GOING BACK TO THE SKATE CAMP.
WONDER WHAT THAT'S ALL ABOUT.
WHO CARES?
QUIT TELLING ME WHAT TO DO!!
BABY, YOU HAVE TO SEE THIS!
SHUT UP! SHUT UP! SHUT UP!
SPLOOSH

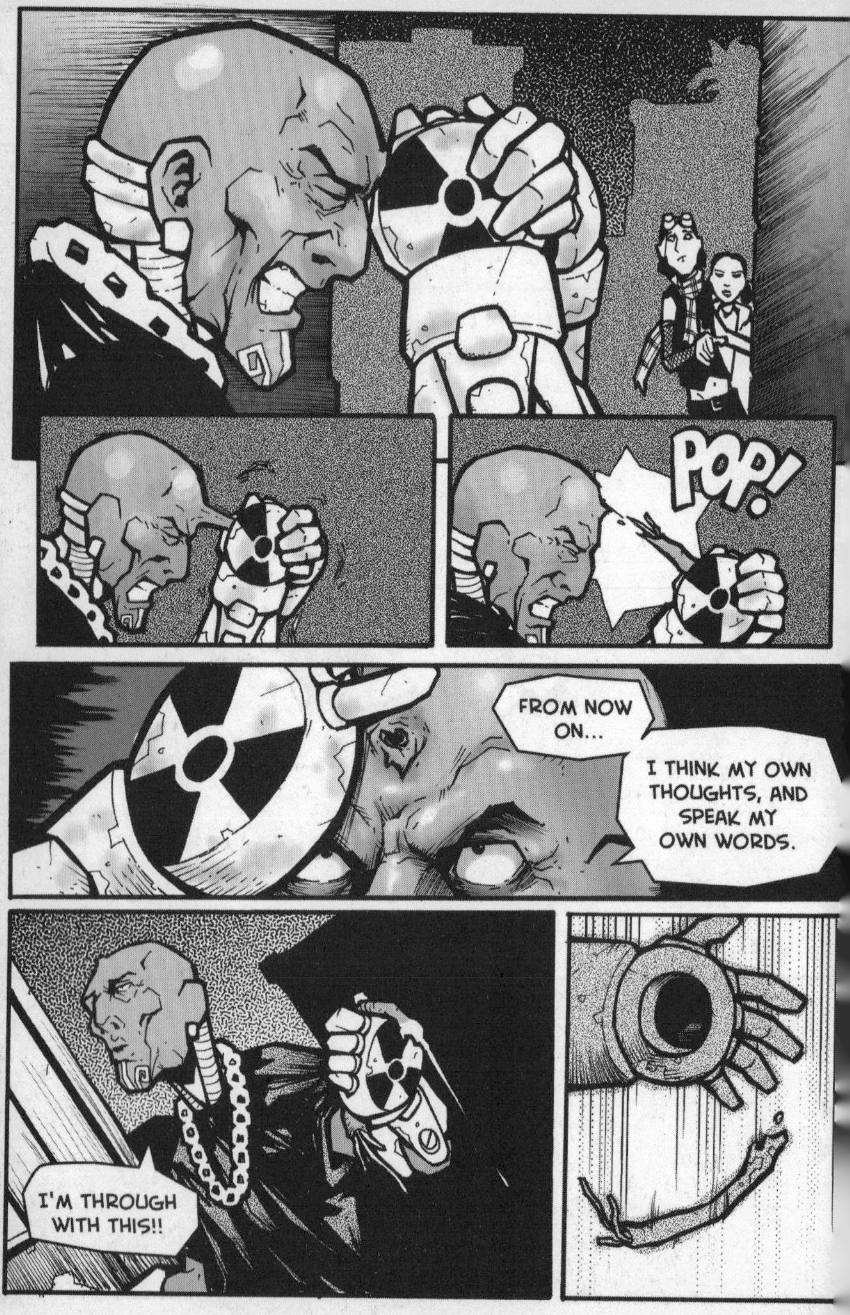
POP!
FROM NOW ON...
I THINK MY OWN THOUGHTS, AND SPEAK MY OWN WORDS.
I'M THROUGH WITH THIS!!

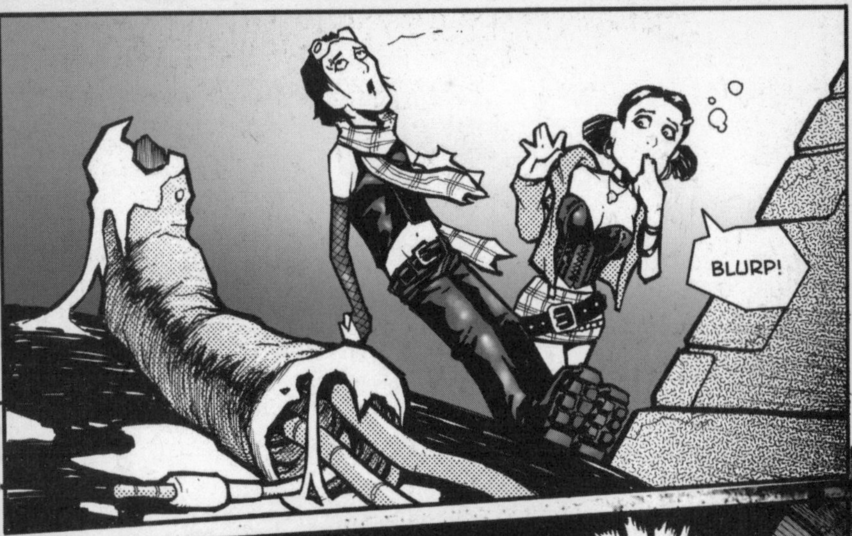
BLURP!

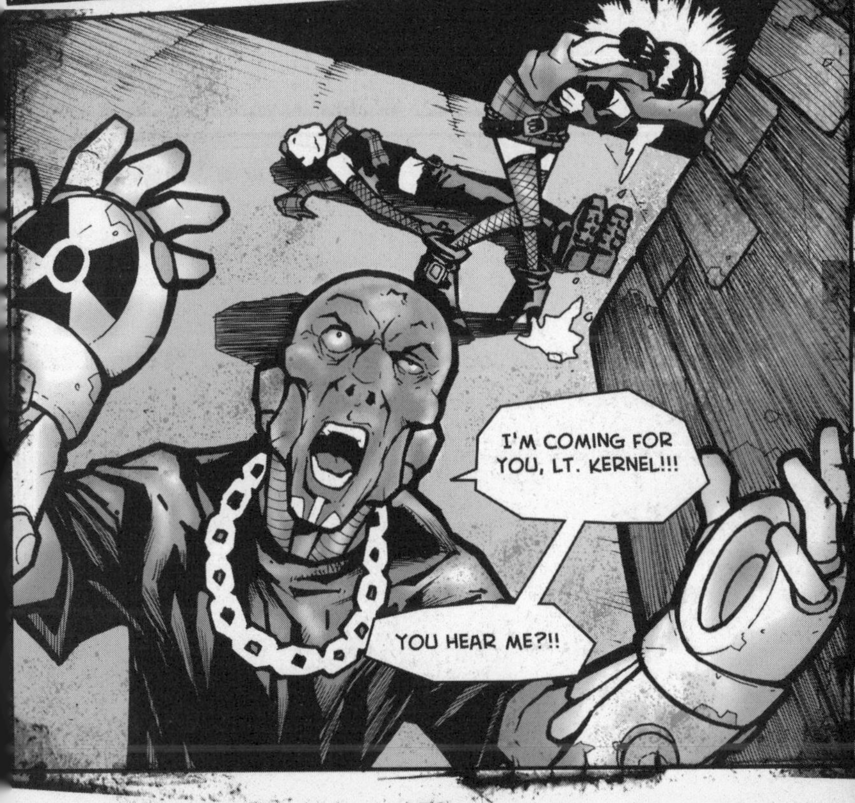
I'M COMING FOR YOU, LT. KERNEL!!!
YOU HEAR ME?!!

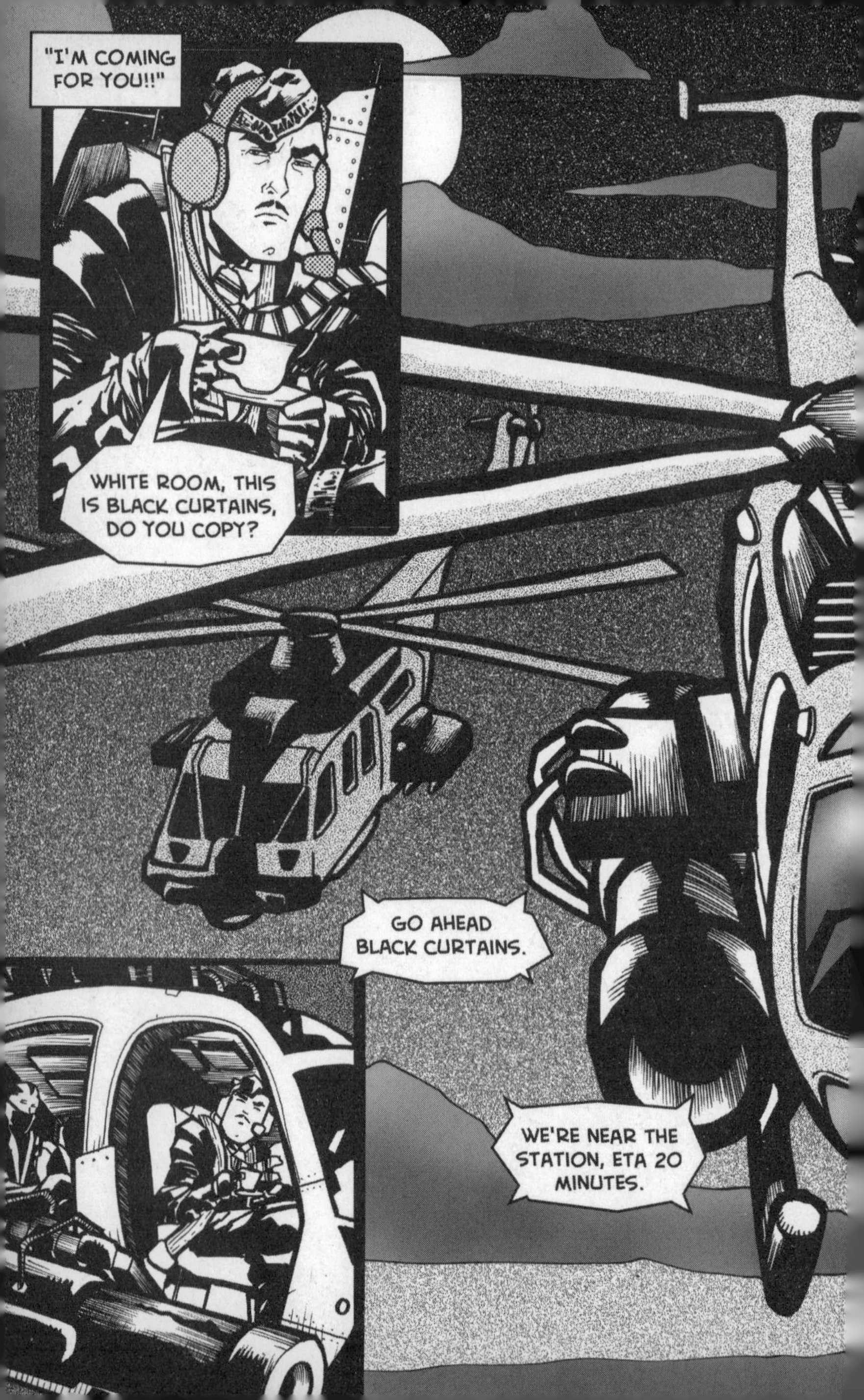
"I'M COMING FOR YOU!!"
WHITE ROOM, THIS IS BLACK CURTAINS, DO YOU COPY?
GO AHEAD BLACK CURTAINS.
WE'RE NEAR THE STATION, ETA 20 MINUTES.

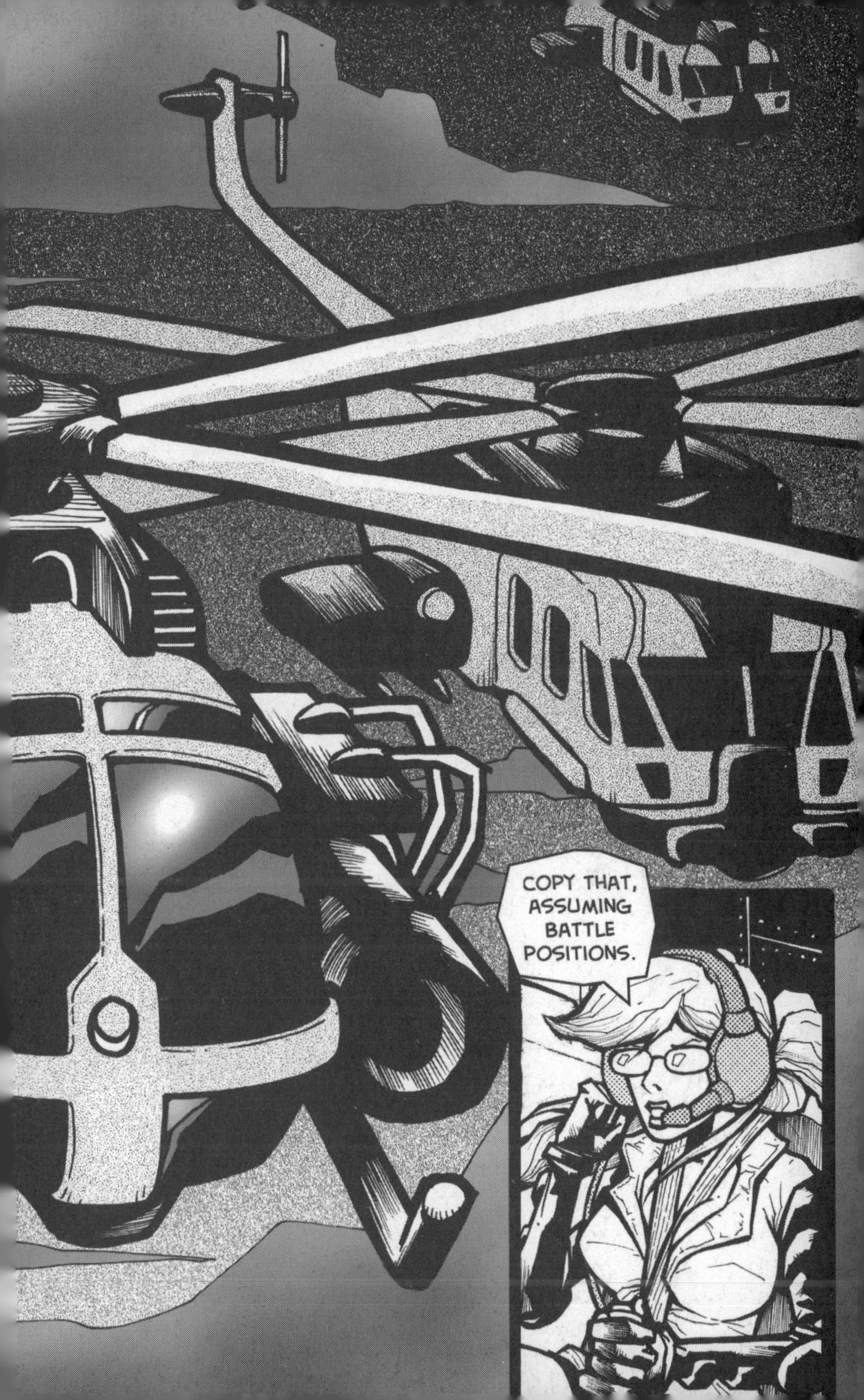
COPY THAT, ASSUMING BATTLE POSITIONS.

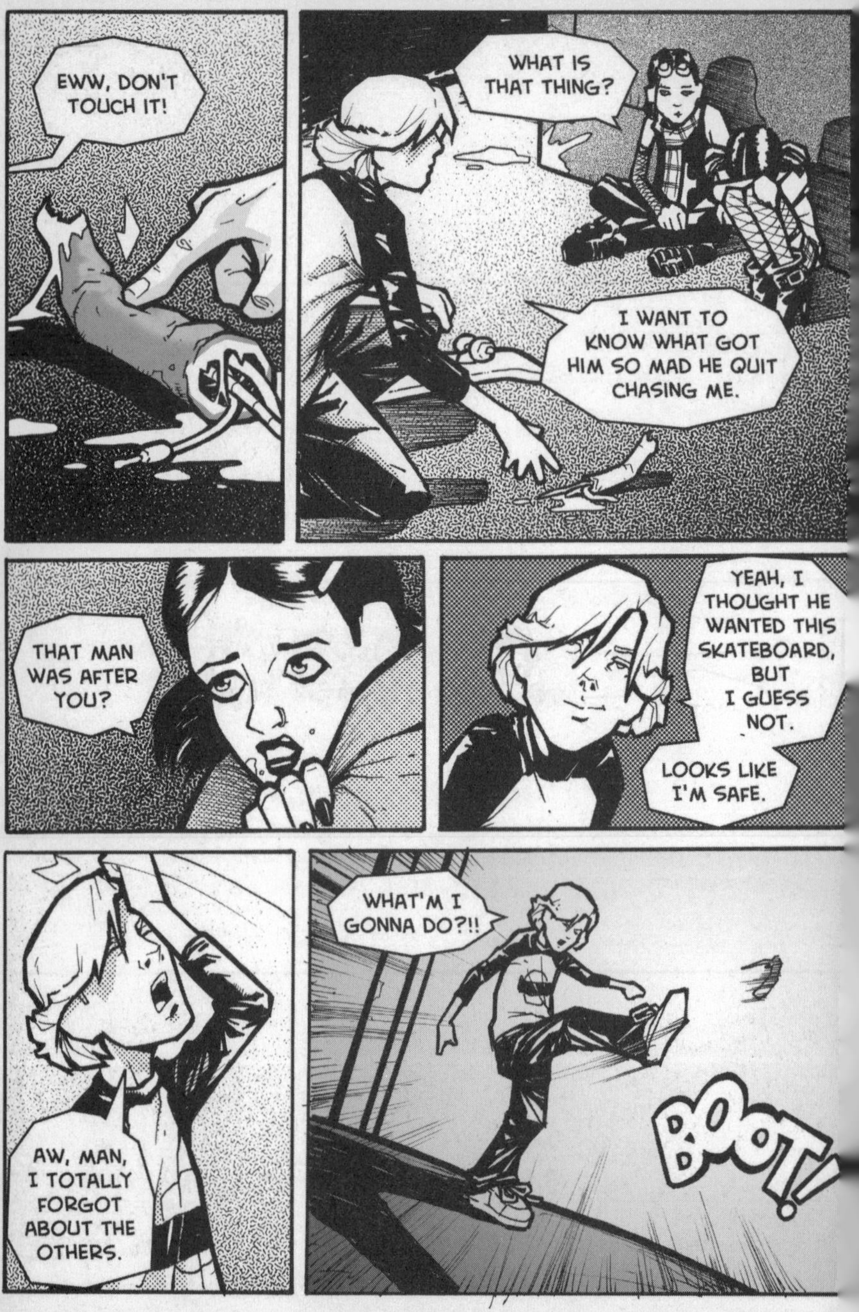
EWW, DON'T TOUCH IT!
WHAT IS THAT THING?
I WANT TO KNOW WHAT GOT HIM SO MAD HE QUIT CHASING ME.
THAT MAN WAS AFTER YOU?
YEAH, I THOUGHT HE WANTED THIS SKATEBOARD, BUT I GUESS NOT.
LOOKS LIKE I'M SAFE.
AW, MAN, I TOTALLY FORGOT ABOUT THE OTHERS.
WHAT'M I GONNA DO?!!
BOOT!

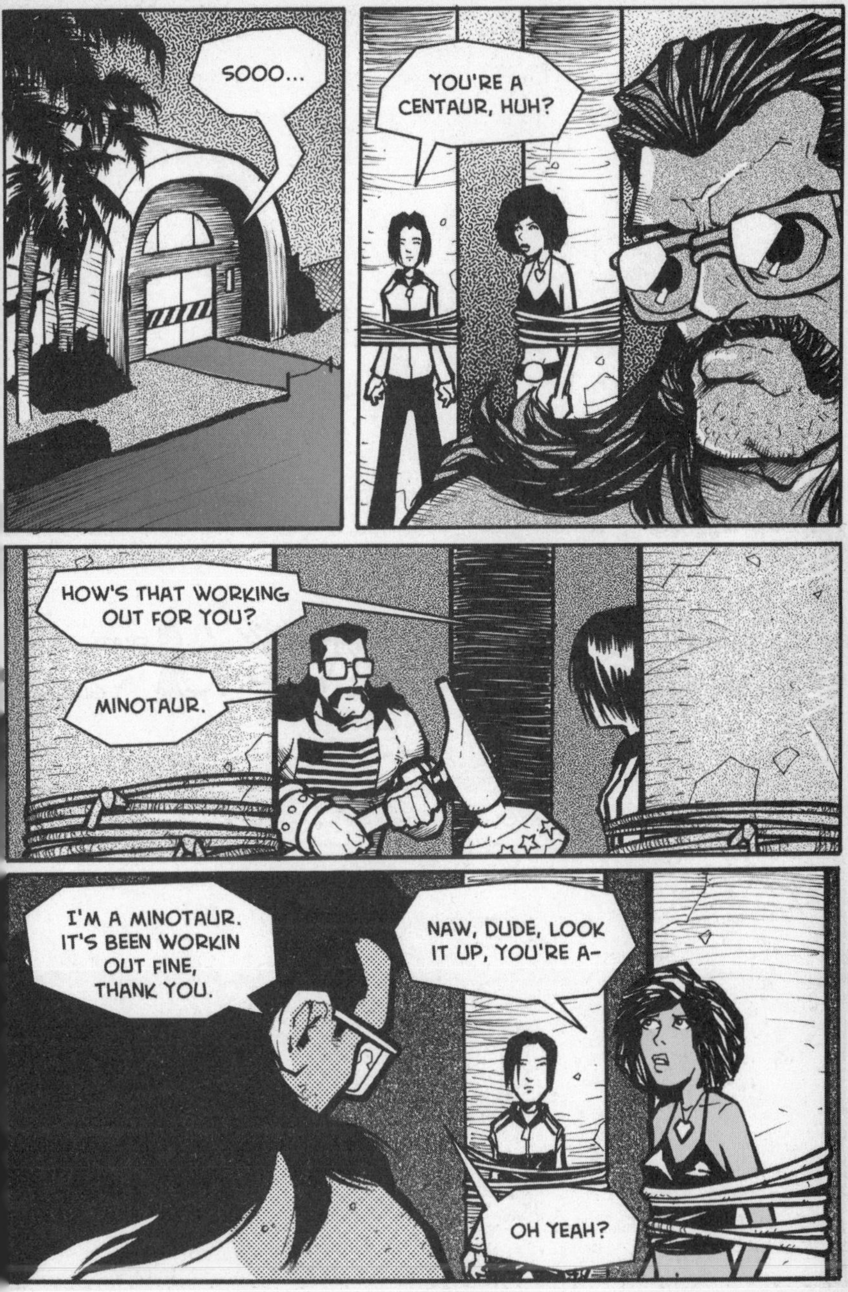
SOOO...
YOU'RE A CENTAUR, HUH?
HOW'S THAT WORKING OUT FOR YOU?
MINOTAUR.
I'M A MINOTAUR. IT'S BEEN WORKIN OUT FINE, THANK YOU.
NAW, DUDE, LOOK IT UP, YOU'RE A-
OH YEAH?

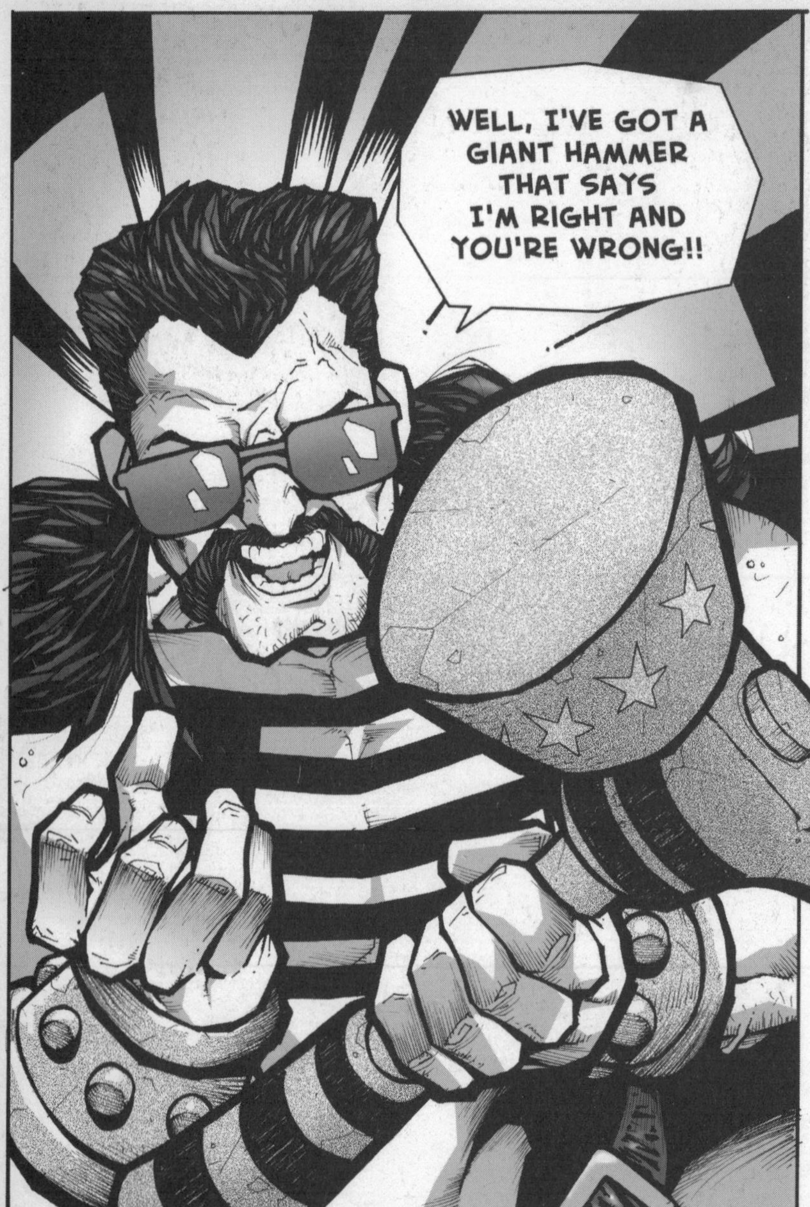
WELL, I'VE GOT A GIANT HAMMER THAT SAYS I'M RIGHT AND YOU'RE WRONG!!

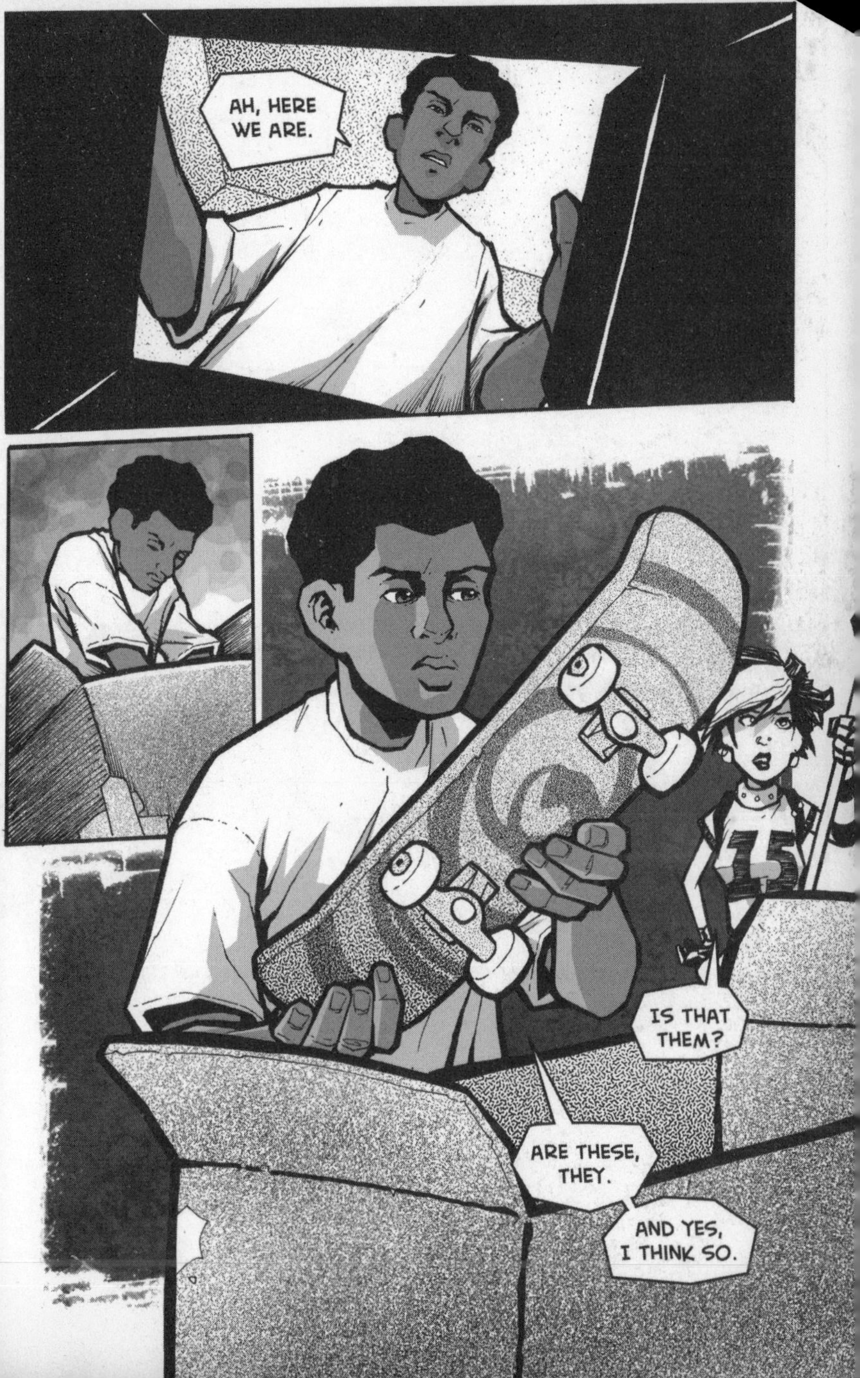
AH, HERE WE ARE.
IS THAT THEM?
ARE THESE, THEY.
AND YES, I THINK SO.

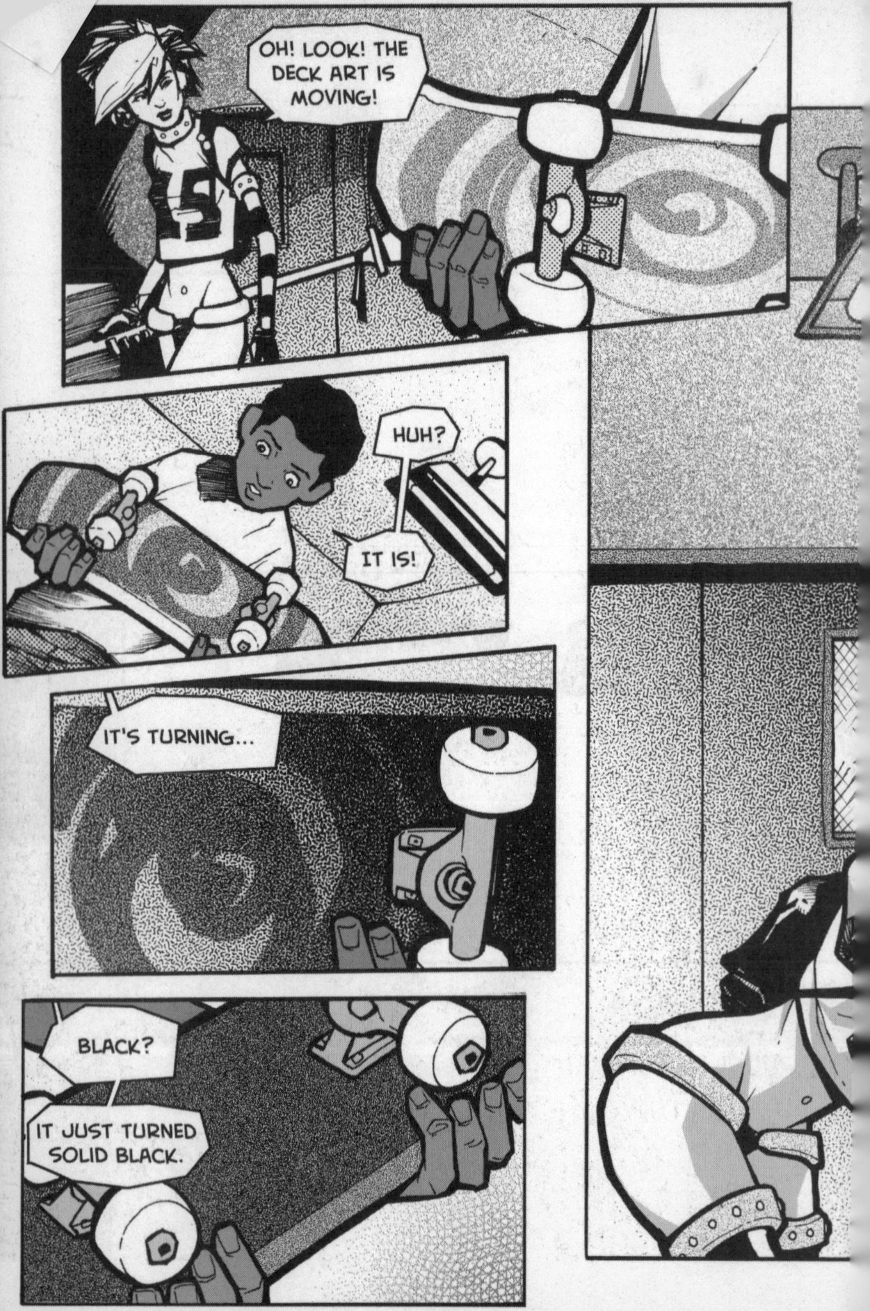
OH! LOOK! THE DECK ART IS MOVING!
HUH?
IT IS!
IT'S TURNING...
BLACK?
IT JUST TURNED SOLID BLACK.

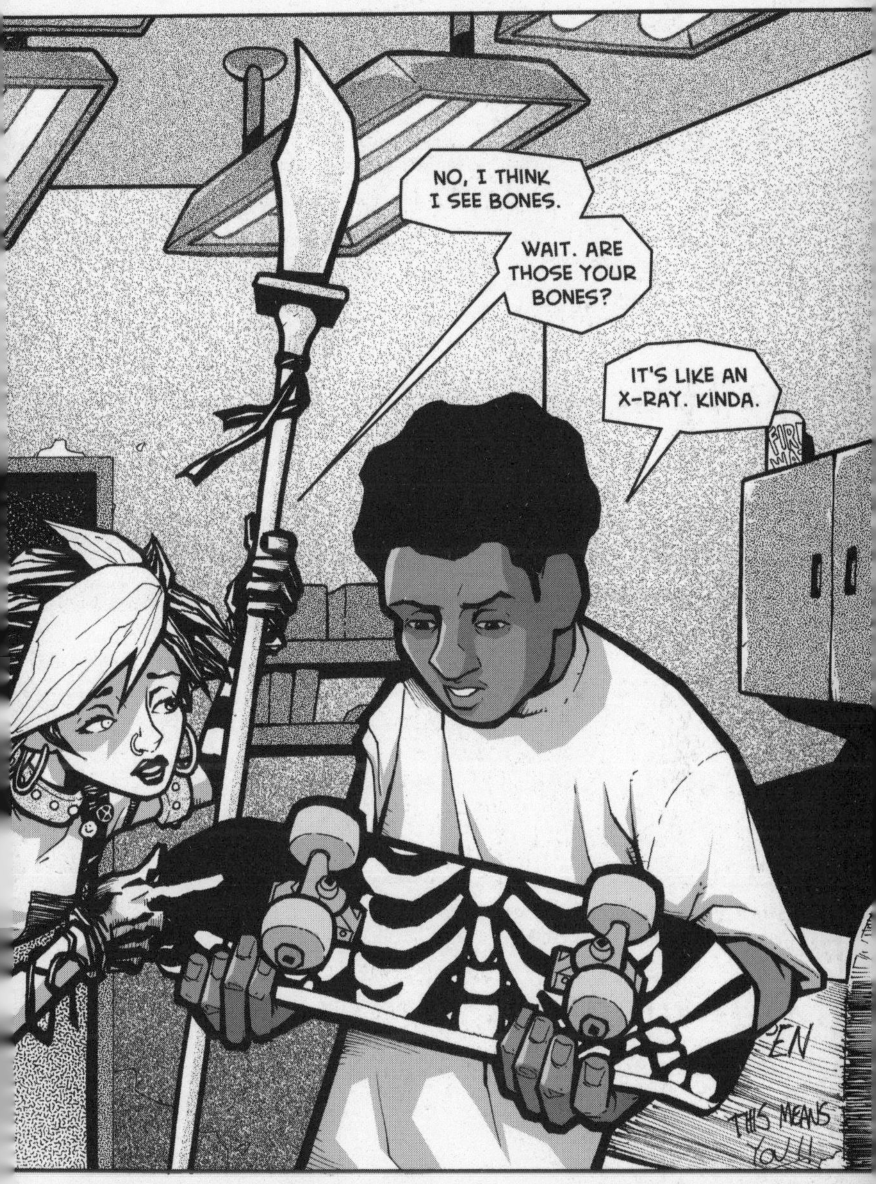
NO, I THINK I SEE BONES.
WAIT. ARE THOSE YOUR BONES?
IT'S LIKE AN X-RAY. KINDA.
THIS MEANS YOU!!

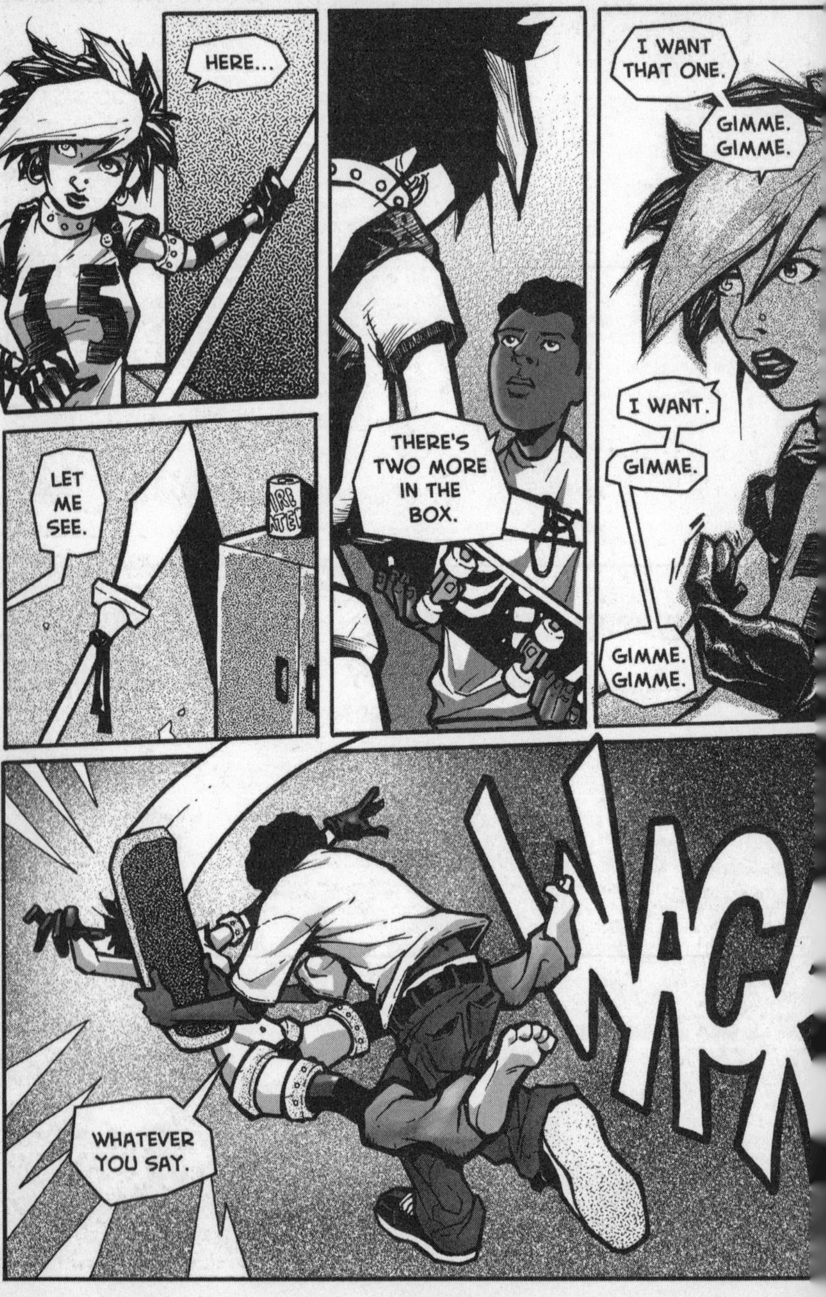
HERE...
LET ME SEE.
THERE'S TWO MORE IN THE BOX.
I WANT THAT ONE.
GIMME. GIMME.
I WANT.
GIMME.
GIMME. GIMME.
WHATEVER YOU SAY.
WAC

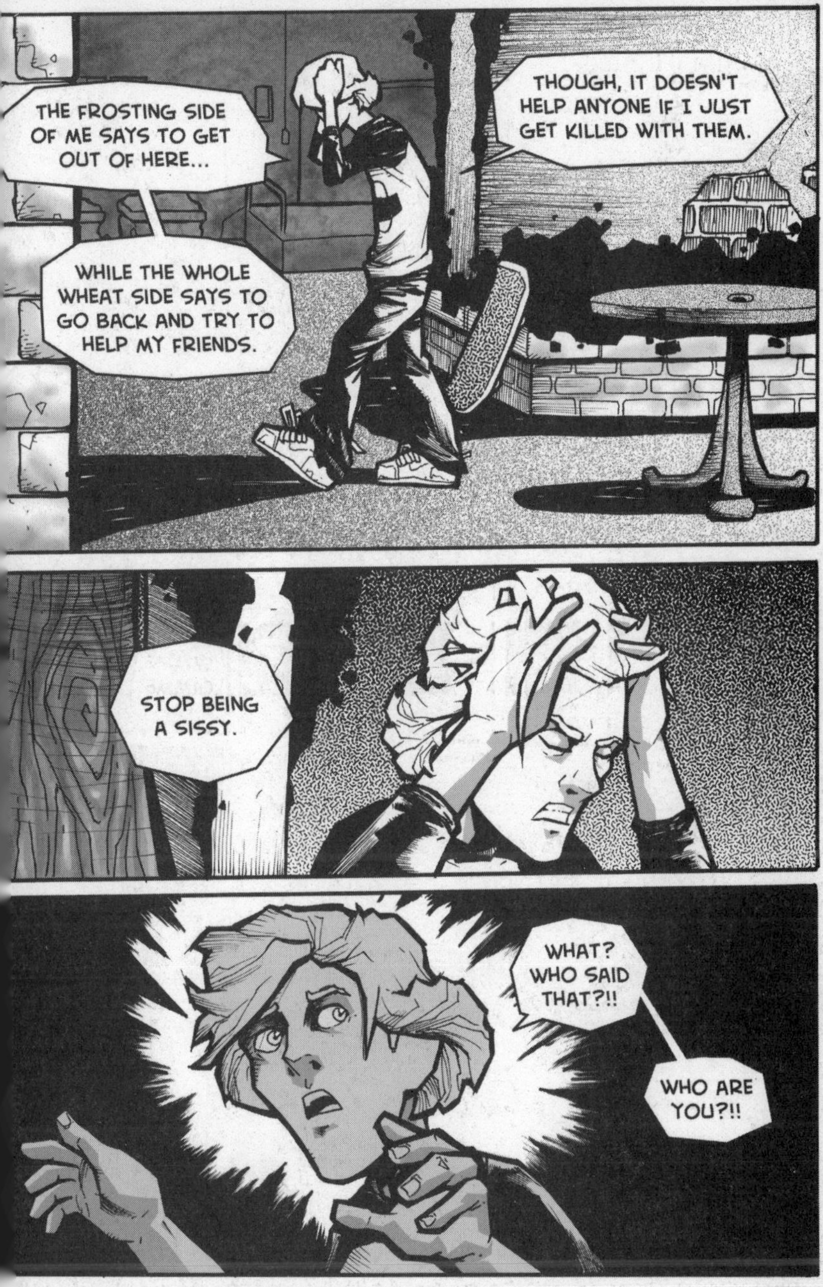
THE FROSTING SIDE OF ME SAYS TO GET OUT OF HERE...
WHILE THE WHOLE WHEAT SIDE SAYS TO GO BACK AND TRY TO HELP MY FRIENDS.
THOUGH, IT DOESN'T HELP ANYONE IF I JUST GET KILLED WITH THEM.
STOP BEING A SISSY.
WHAT? WHO SAID THAT?!!
WHO ARE YOU?!!

WHO AM I? ARE YOU THAT STUPID?

I'M YOU, DUDE.

THE YOU THAT DOESN'T SUCK

HUH?

Dylan's MONSTER

GEEZ, DYLAN. YOU REALLY DON'T GET IT?

I'M A PHYSICAL MANIFESTATION OF A METAPHORICAL REPRESENTATION OF YOUR INTERNAL STRUGGLE BETWEEN YOUR OWN SELF PRESERVATION AND YOUR OBLIGATION TO ASSIST YOUR FRIENDS.

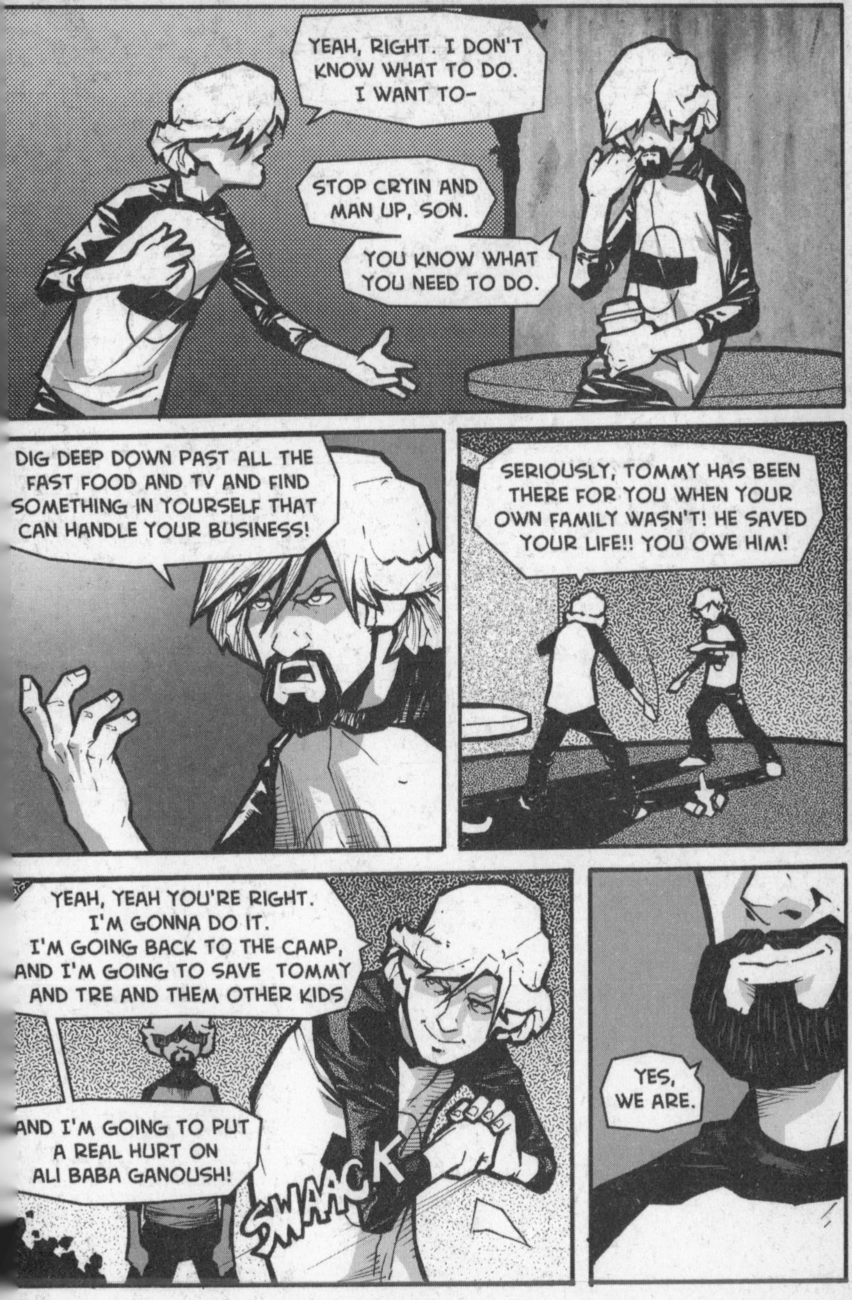
YEAH, RIGHT. I DON'T KNOW WHAT TO DO. I WANT TO-
STOP CRYIN AND MAN UP, SON.
YOU KNOW WHAT YOU NEED TO DO.
DIG DEEP DOWN PAST ALL THE FAST FOOD AND TV AND FIND SOMETHING IN YOURSELF THAT CAN HANDLE YOUR BUSINESS!
SERIOUSLY, TOMMY HAS BEEN THERE FOR YOU WHEN YOUR OWN FAMILY WASN'T! HE SAVED YOUR LIFE!! YOU OWE HIM!
YEAH, YEAH YOU'RE RIGHT. I'M GONNA DO IT. I'M GOING BACK TO THE CAMP, AND I'M GOING TO SAVE TOMMY AND TRE AND THEM OTHER KIDS
AND I'M GOING TO PUT A REAL HURT ON ALI BABA GANOUSH!
SWAACK
YES, WE ARE.

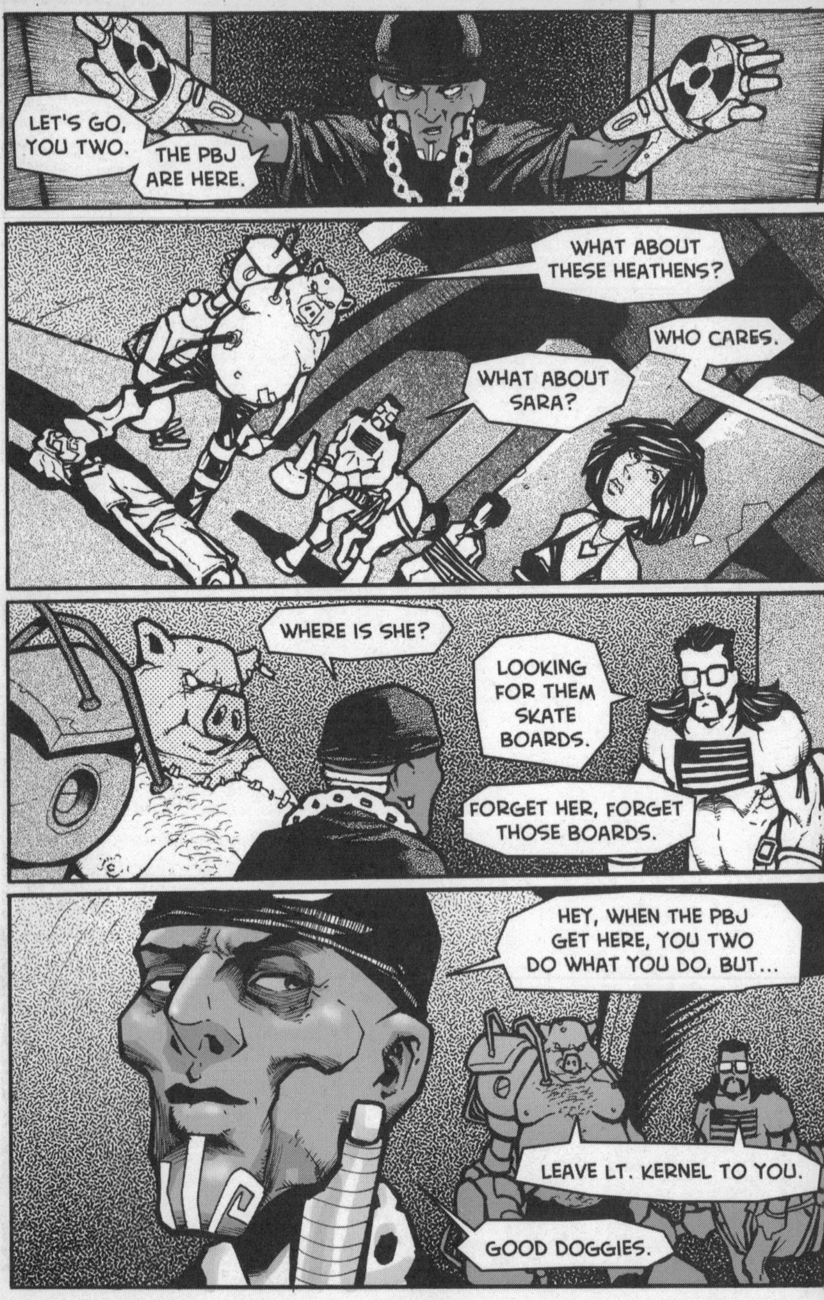
LET'S GO, YOU TWO.
THE PBJ ARE HERE.
WHAT ABOUT THESE HEATHENS?
WHO CARES.
WHAT ABOUT SARA?
WHERE IS SHE?
LOOKING FOR THEM SKATE BOARDS.
FORGET HER, FORGET THOSE BOARDS.
HEY, WHEN THE PBJ GET HERE, YOU TWO DO WHAT YOU DO, BUT...
LEAVE LT. KERNEL TO YOU.
GOOD DOGGIES.

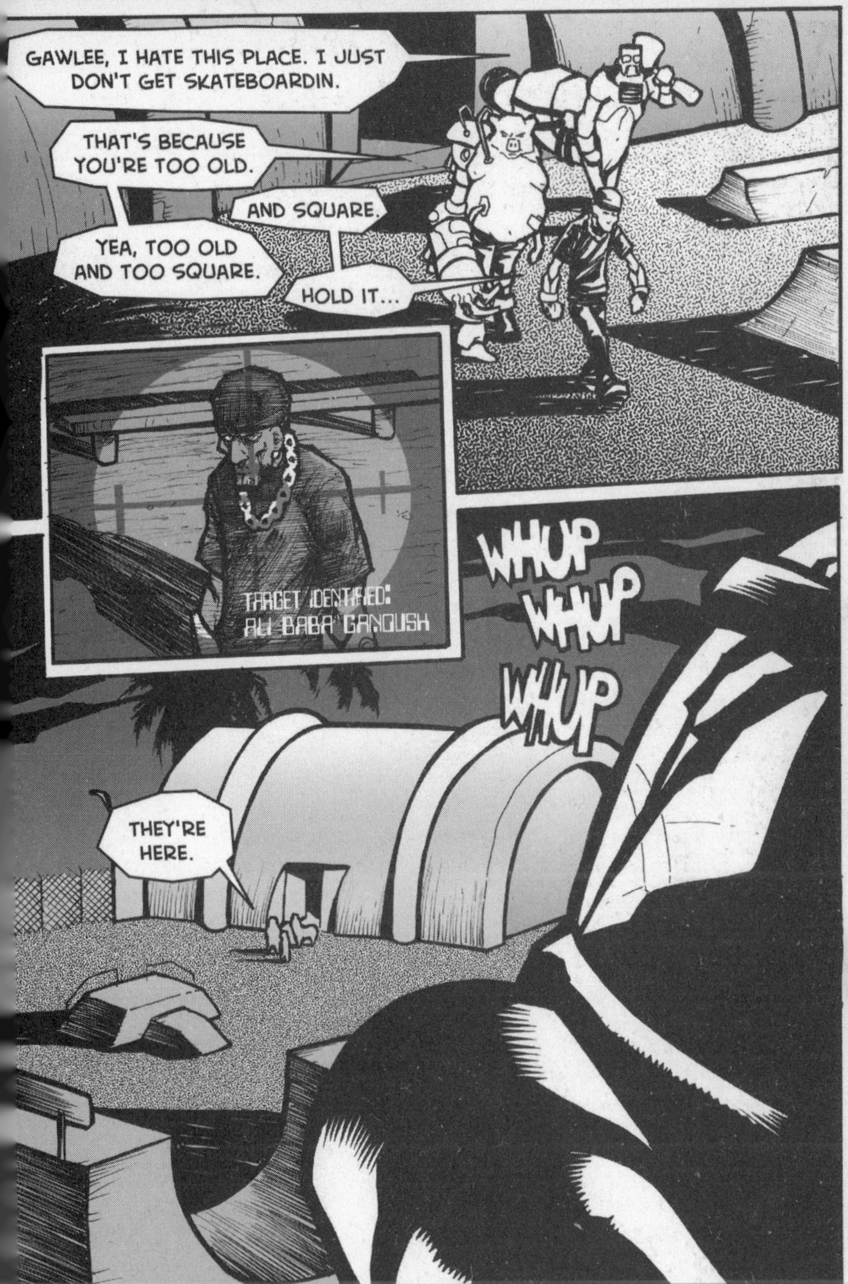
GAWLEE, I HATE THIS PLACE. I JUST DON'T GET SKATEBOARDIN.
THAT'S BECAUSE YOU'RE TOO OLD.
AND SQUARE.
YEA, TOO OLD AND TOO SQUARE.
HOLD IT...
TARGET IDENTIFIED:
ALI BABA GANOUSH
WHUP
WHUP
WHUP
THEY'RE HERE.

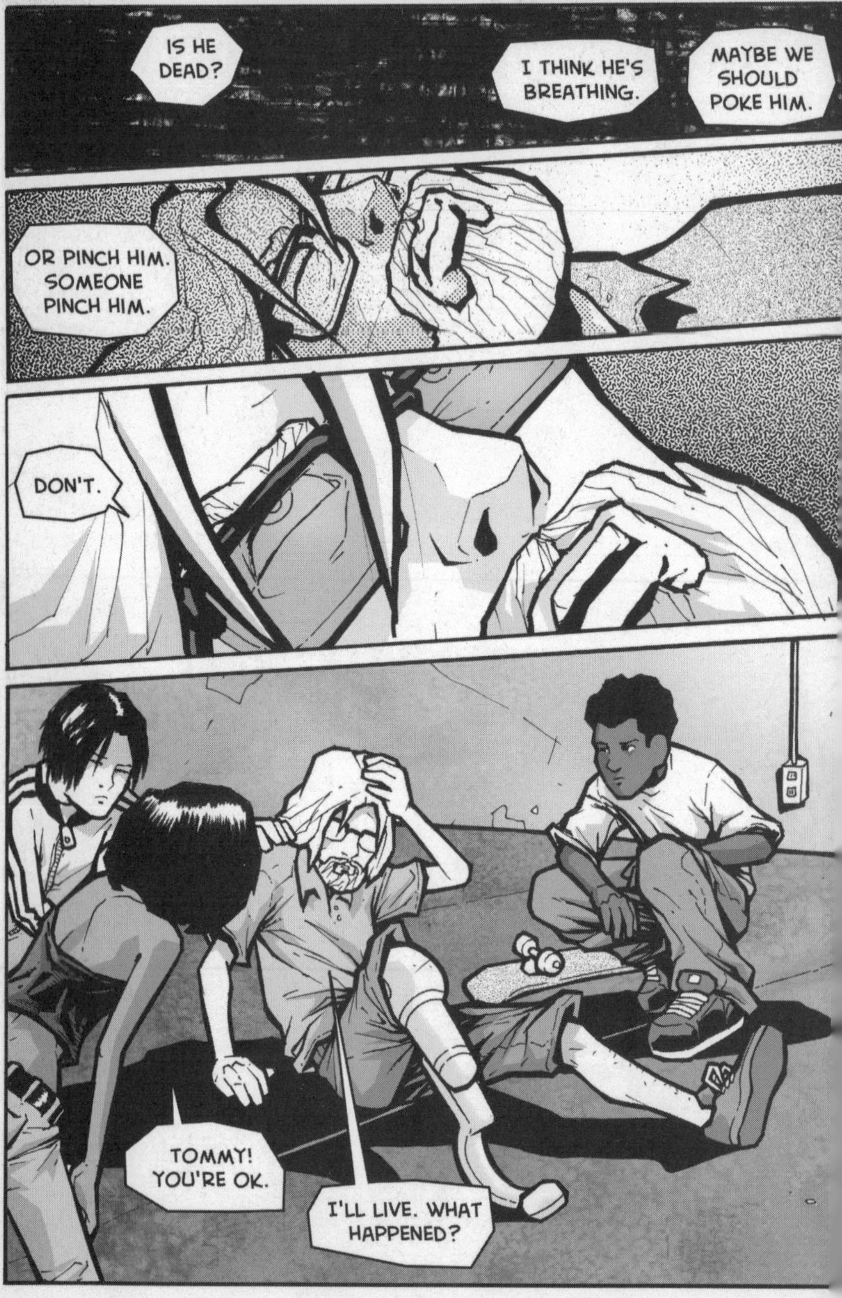
IS HE DEAD?
I THINK HE'S BREATHING.
MAYBE WE SHOULD POKE HIM.
OR PINCH HIM. SOMEONE PINCH HIM.
DON'T.
TOMMY! YOU'RE OK.
I'LL LIVE. WHAT HAPPENED?

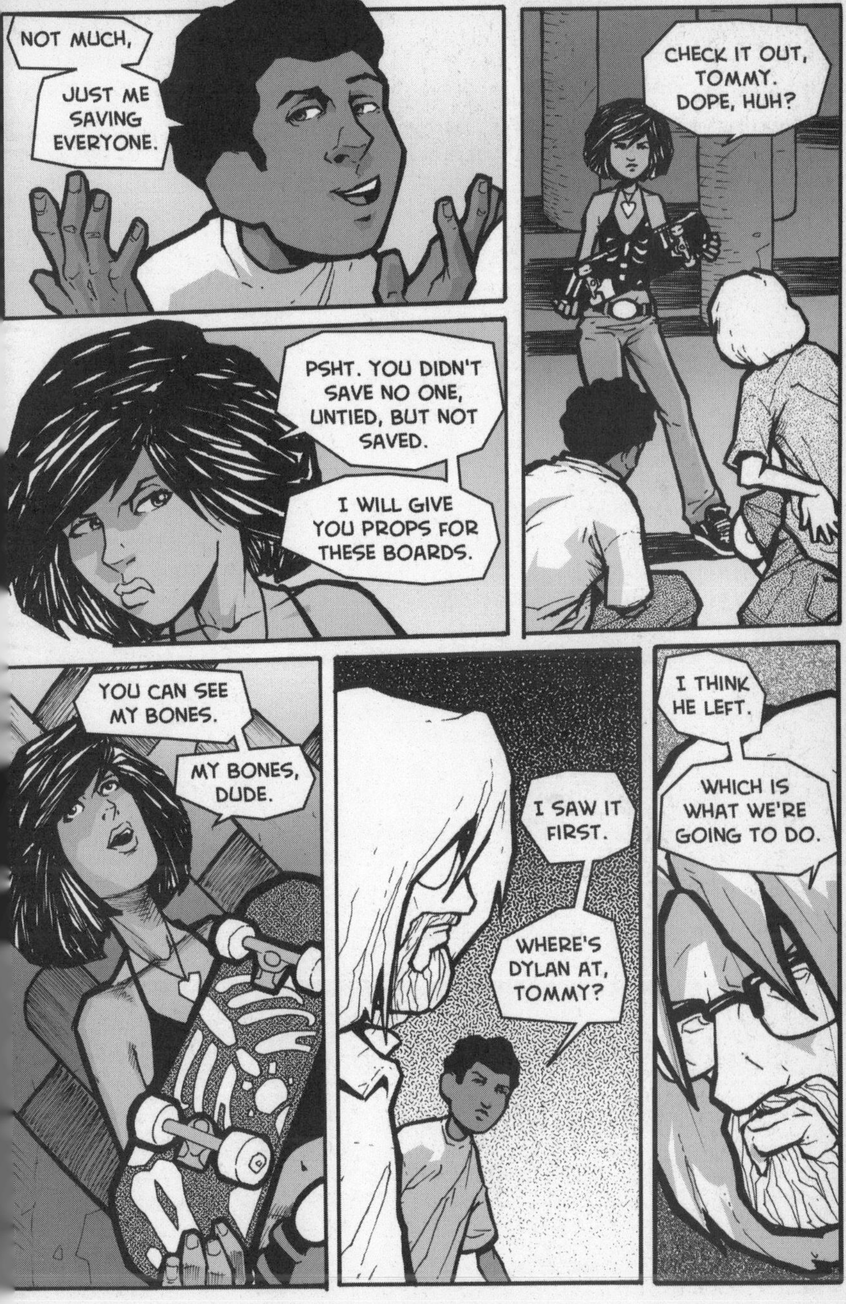
NOT MUCH,
JUST ME SAVING EVERYONE.
CHECK IT OUT, TOMMY. DOPE, HUH?
PSHT. YOU DIDN'T SAVE NO ONE, UNTIED, BUT NOT SAVED.
I WILL GIVE YOU PROPS FOR THESE BOARDS.
YOU CAN SEE MY BONES.
MY BONES, DUDE.
I SAW IT FIRST.
WHERE'S DYLAN AT, TOMMY?
I THINK HE LEFT.
WHICH IS WHAT WE'RE GOING TO DO.

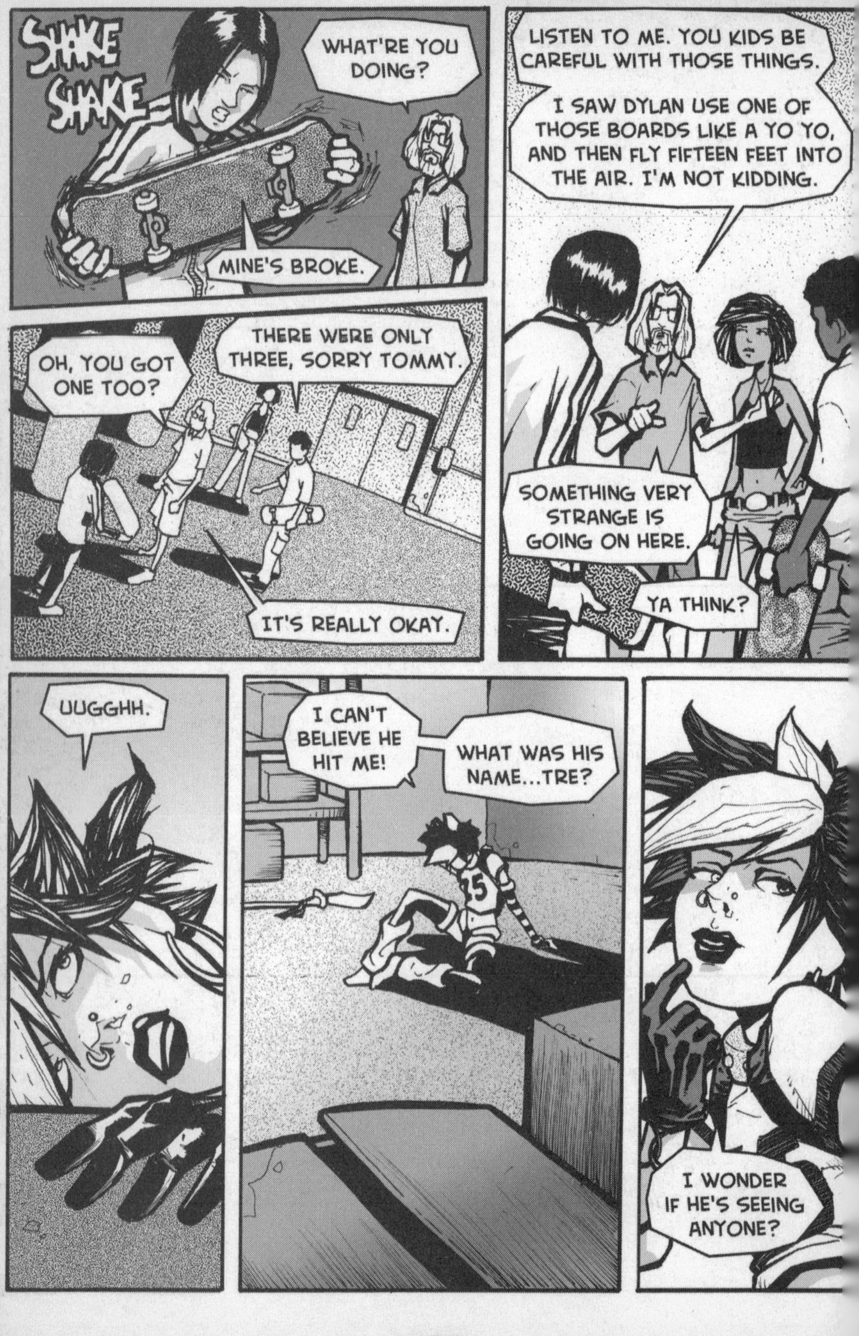
SHAKE SHAKE
WHAT'RE YOU DOING?
MINE'S BROKE.
LISTEN TO ME. YOU KIDS BE CAREFUL WITH THOSE THINGS.
I SAW DYLAN USE ONE OF THOSE BOARDS LIKE A YO YO, AND THEN FLY FIFTEEN FEET INTO THE AIR. I'M NOT KIDDING.
OH, YOU GOT ONE TOO?
THERE WERE ONLY THREE, SORRY TOMMY.
IT'S REALLY OKAY.
SOMETHING VERY STRANGE IS GOING ON HERE.
YA THINK?
UUGGHH.
I CAN'T BELIEVE HE HIT ME!
WHAT WAS HIS NAME...TRE?
I WONDER IF HE'S SEEING ANYONE?

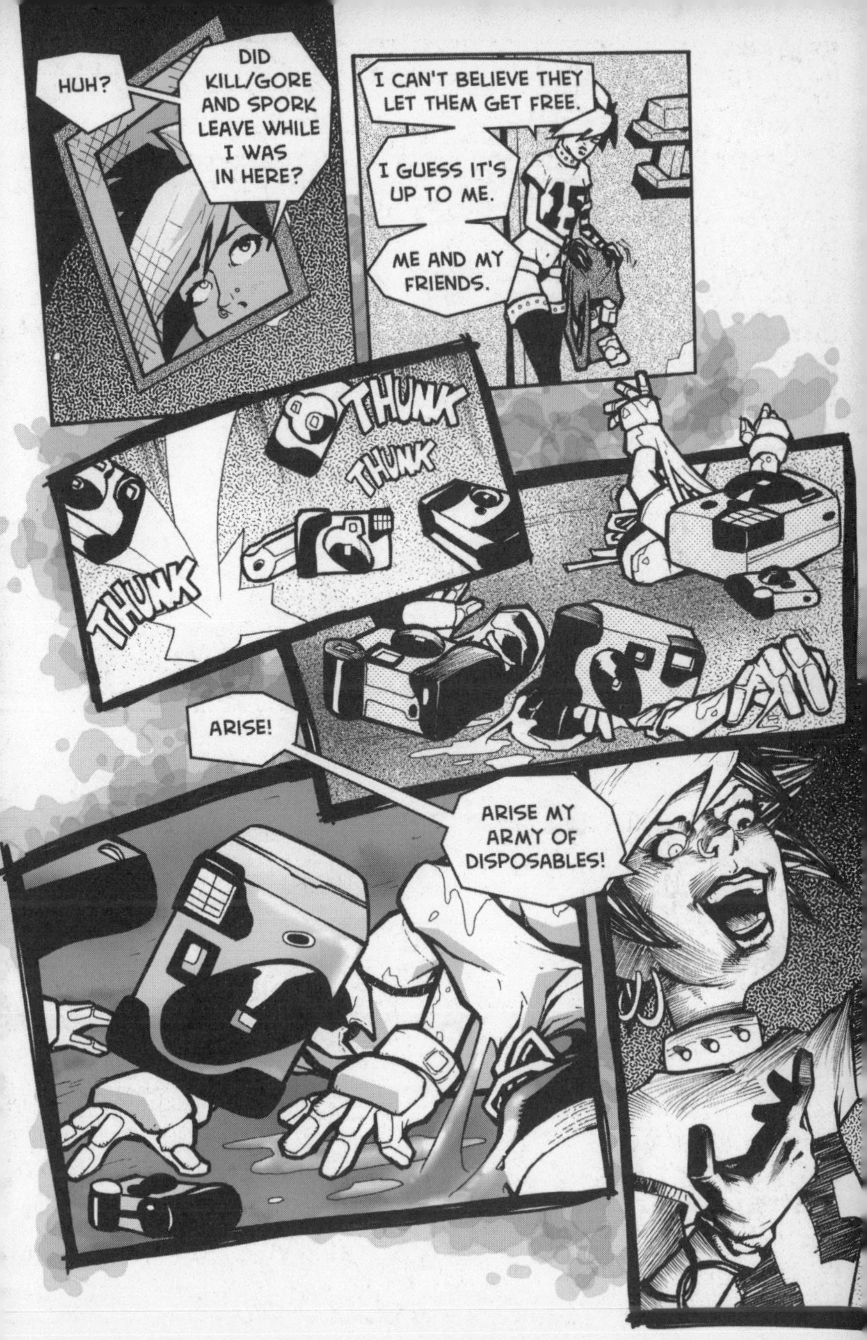
HUH?
DID KILL/GORE AND SPORK LEAVE WHILE I WAS IN HERE?
I CAN'T BELIEVE THEY LET THEM GET FREE.
I GUESS IT'S UP TO ME.
ME AND MY FRIENDS.
THUNK
THUNK
THUNK
ARISE!
ARISE MY ARMY OF DISPOSABLES!

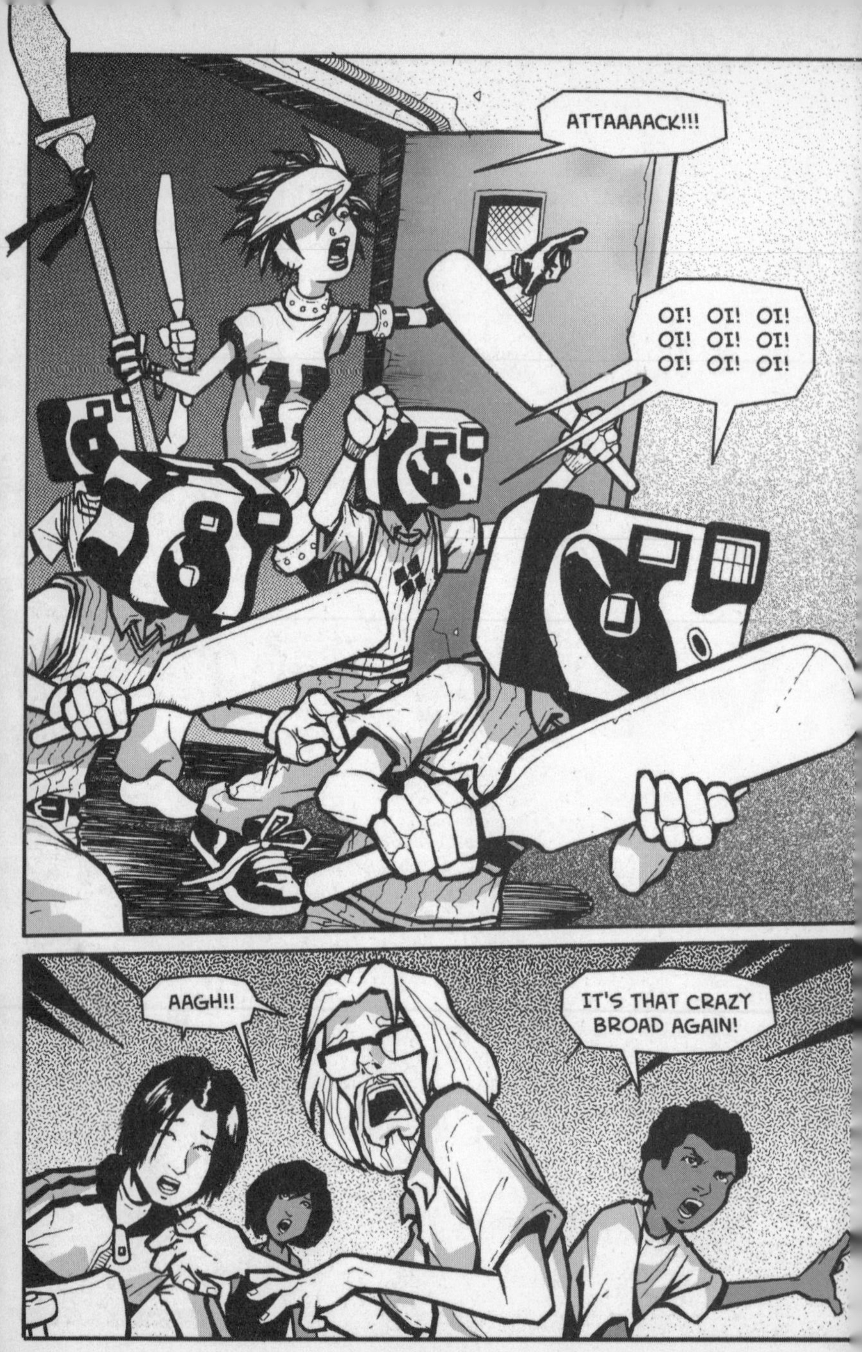
ATTAAAACK!!!
OI! OI! OI! OI! OI! OI! OI! OI! OI!
AAGH!!
IT'S THAT CRAZY BROAD AGAIN!

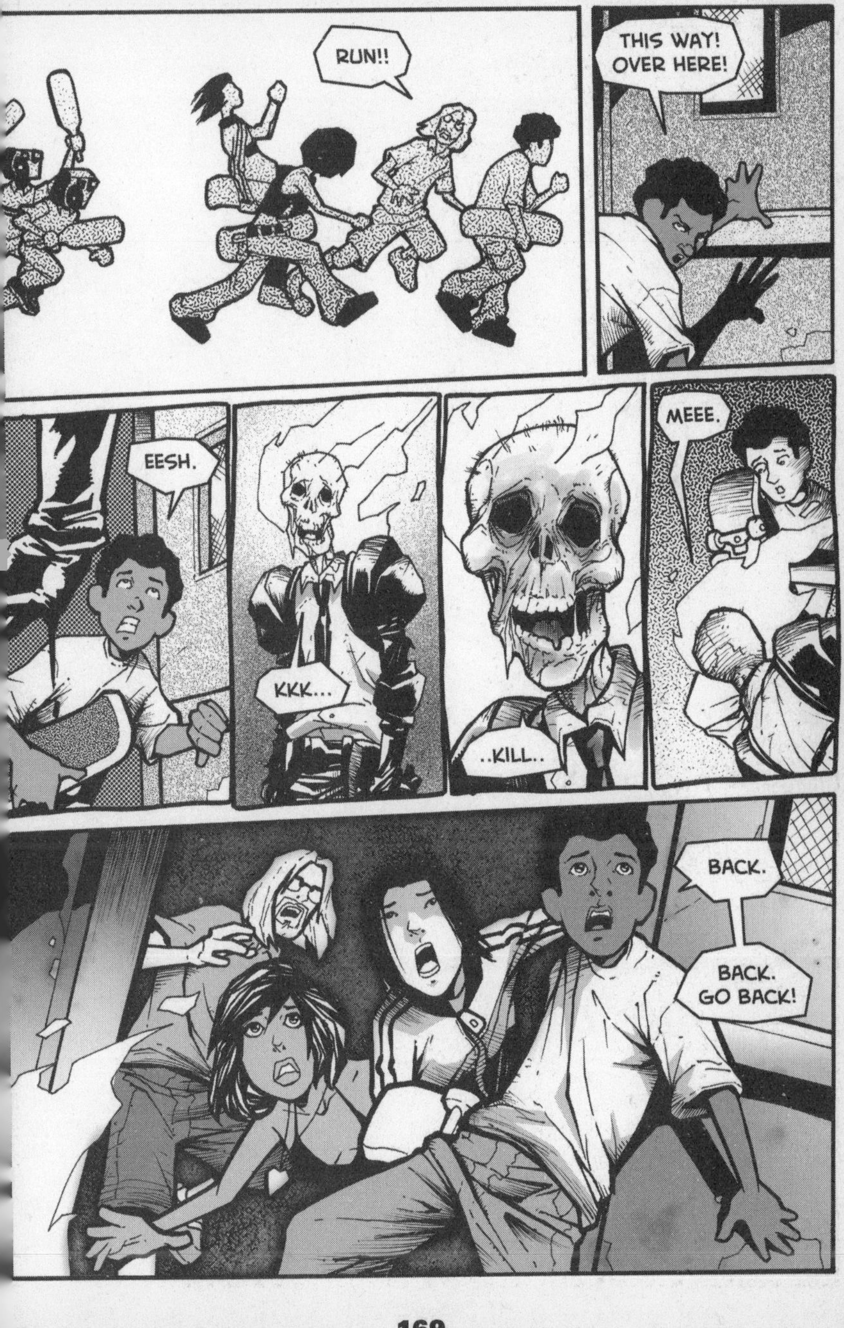
RUN!!
THIS WAY! OVER HERE!
EESH.
KKK...
..KILL..
MEEE.
BACK.
BACK. GO BACK!

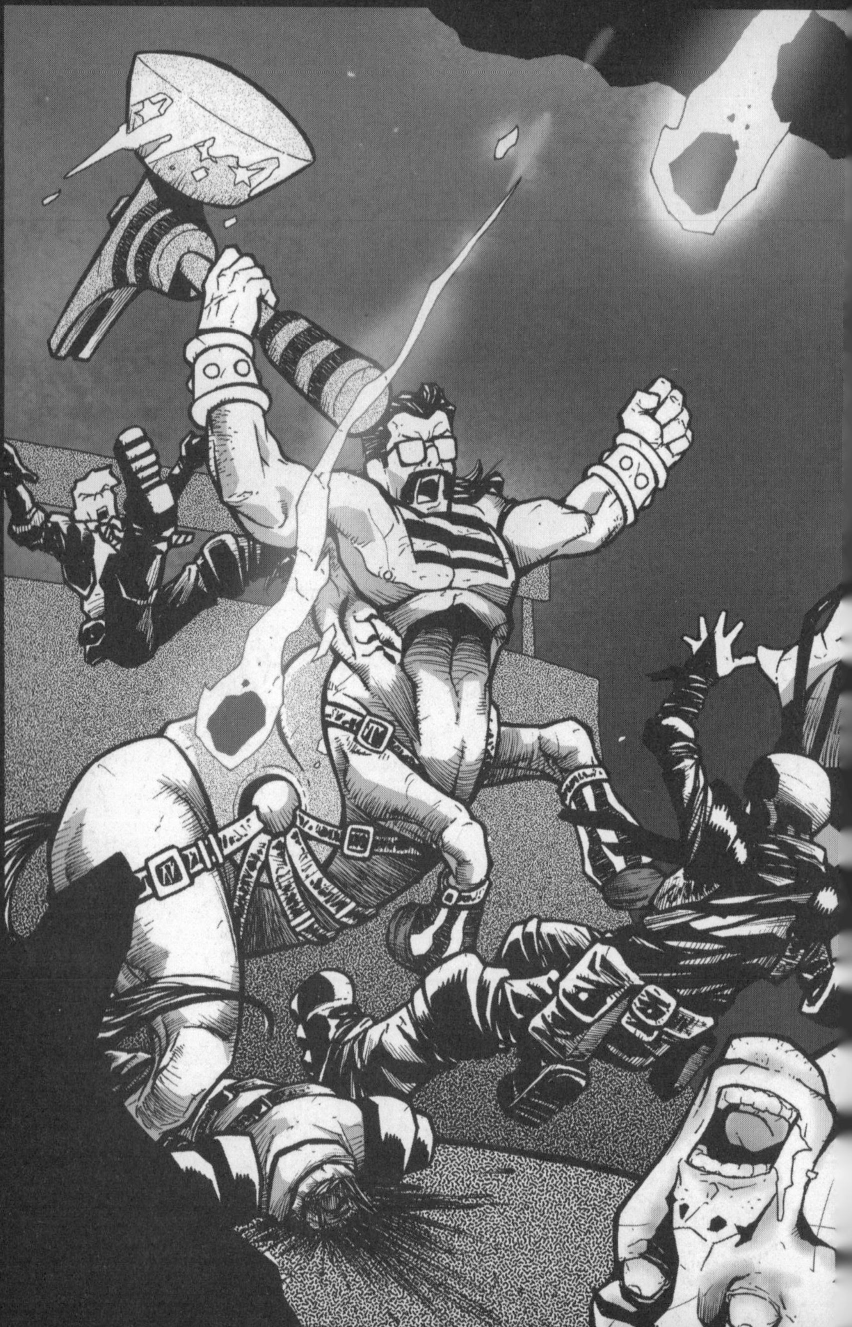

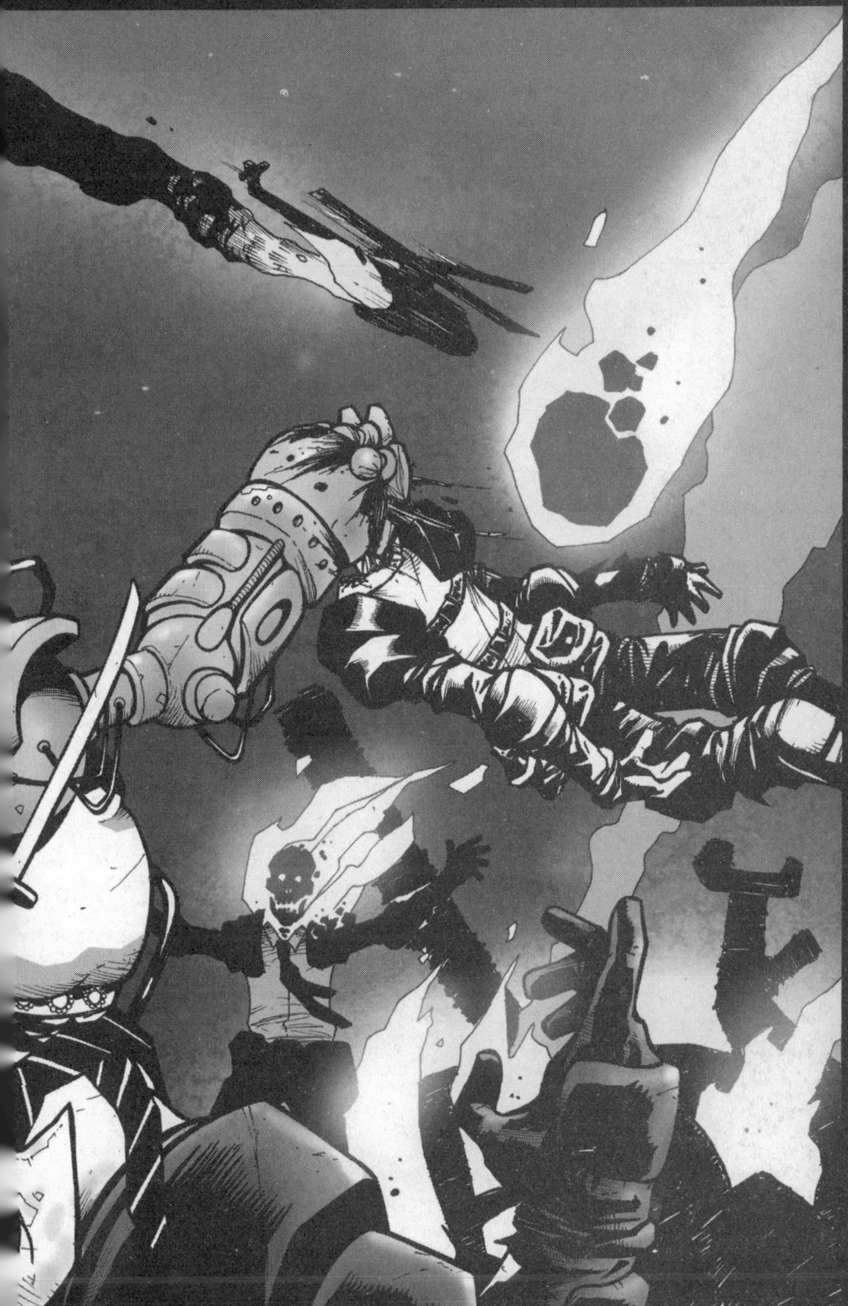

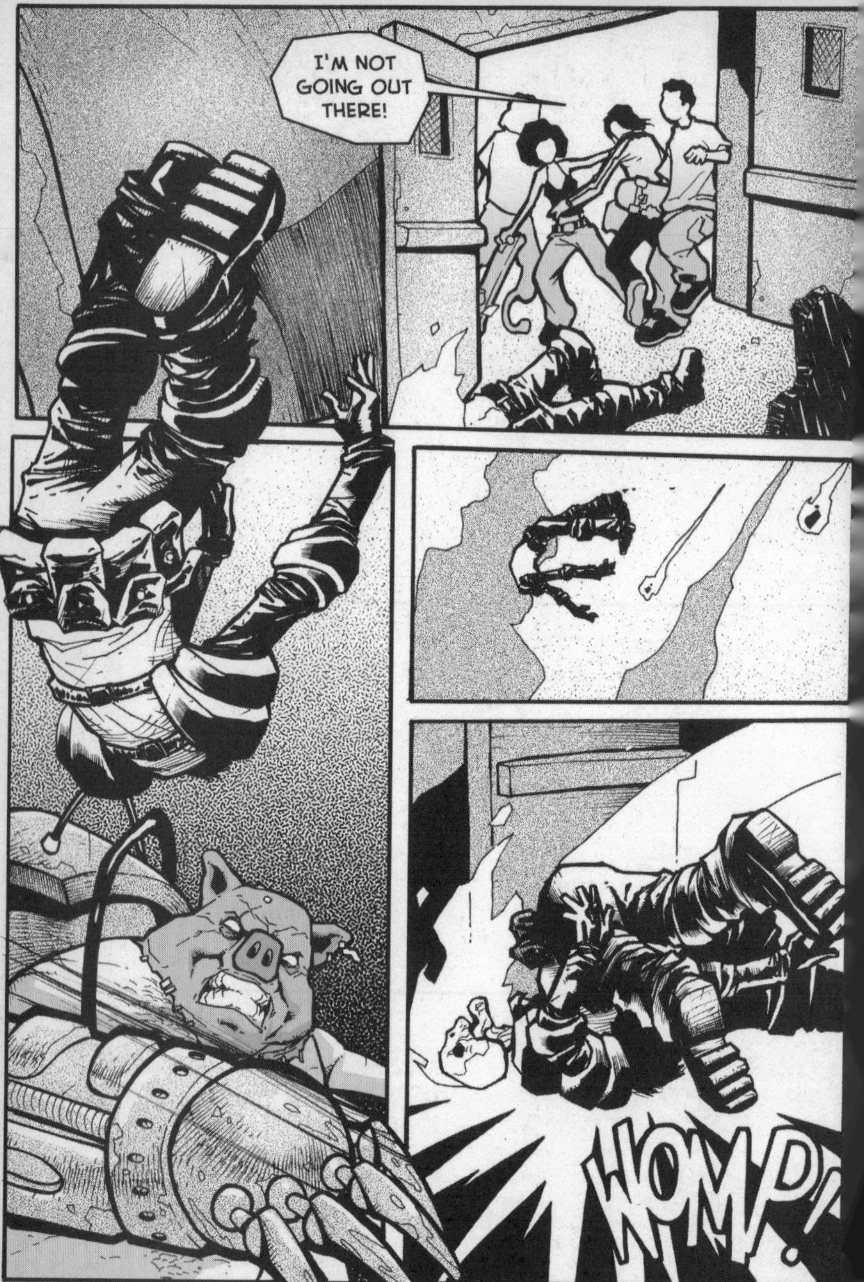
I'M NOT GOING OUT THERE!
WOMP!

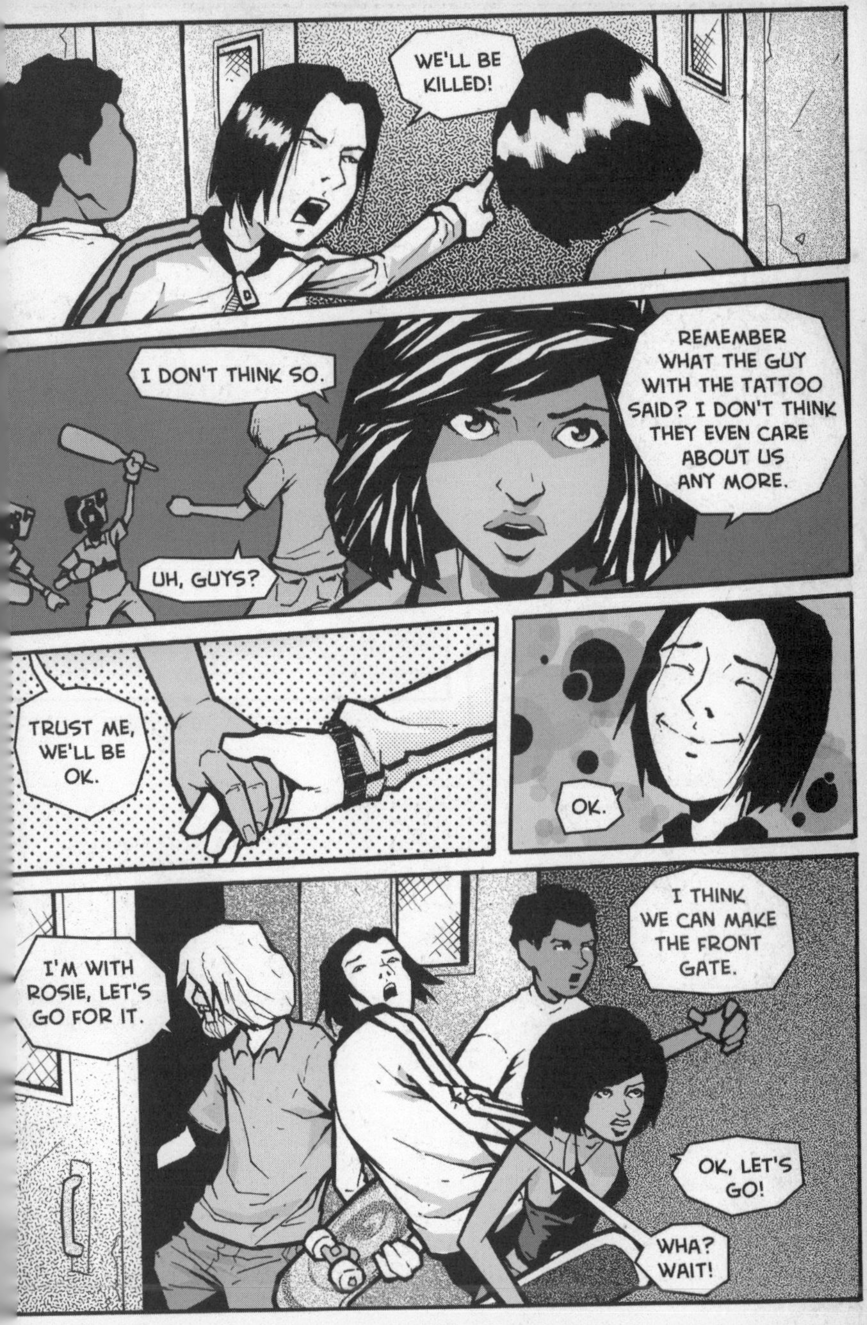
WE'LL BE KILLED!
I DON'T THINK SO.
REMEMBER WHAT THE GUY WITH THE TATTOO SAID? I DON'T THINK THEY EVEN CARE ABOUT US ANY MORE.
UH, GUYS?
TRUST ME, WE'LL BE OK.
OK.
I'M WITH ROSIE, LET'S GO FOR IT.
I THINK WE CAN MAKE THE FRONT GATE.
OK, LET'S GO!
WHA? WAIT!

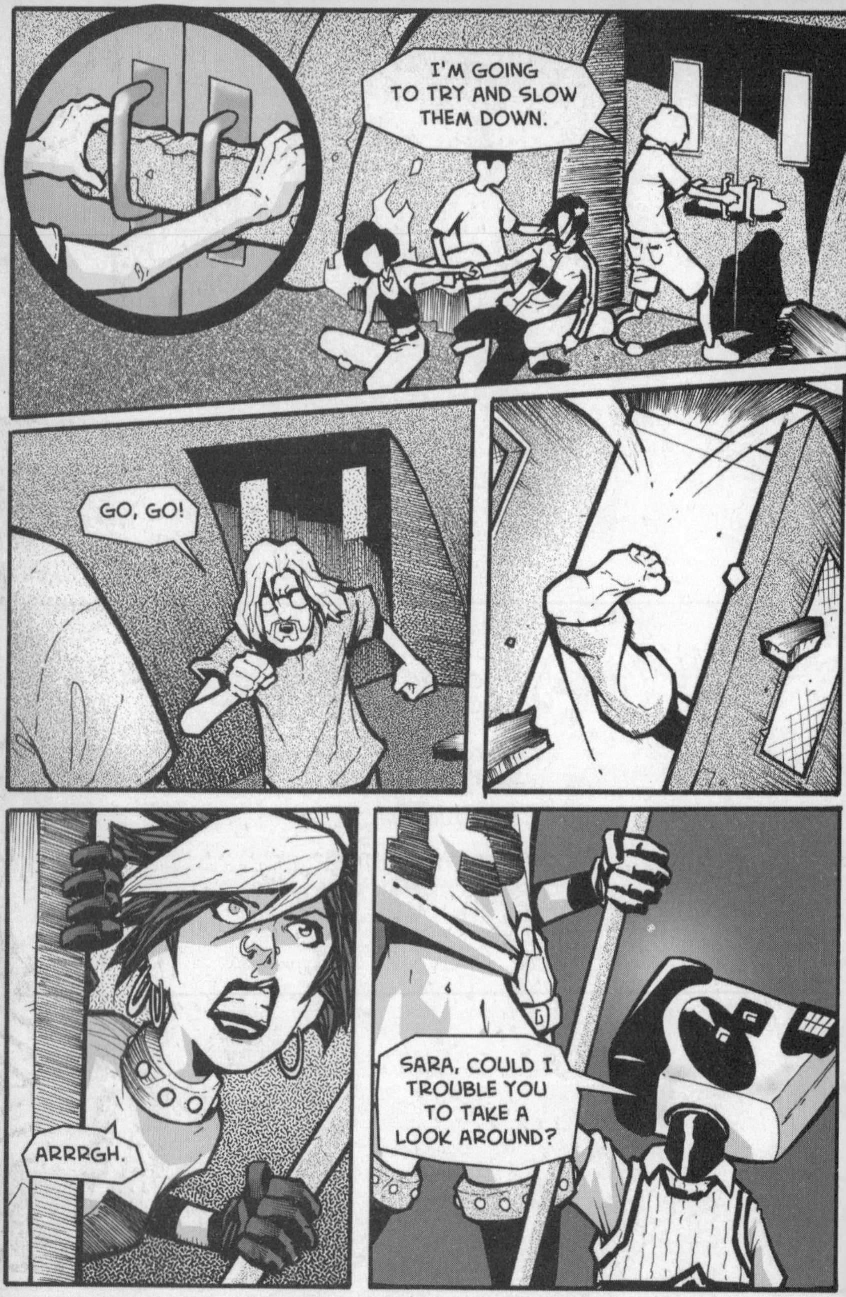
I'M GOING TO TRY AND SLOW THEM DOWN.
GO, GO!
ARRRGH.
SARA, COULD I TROUBLE YOU TO TAKE A LOOK AROUND?

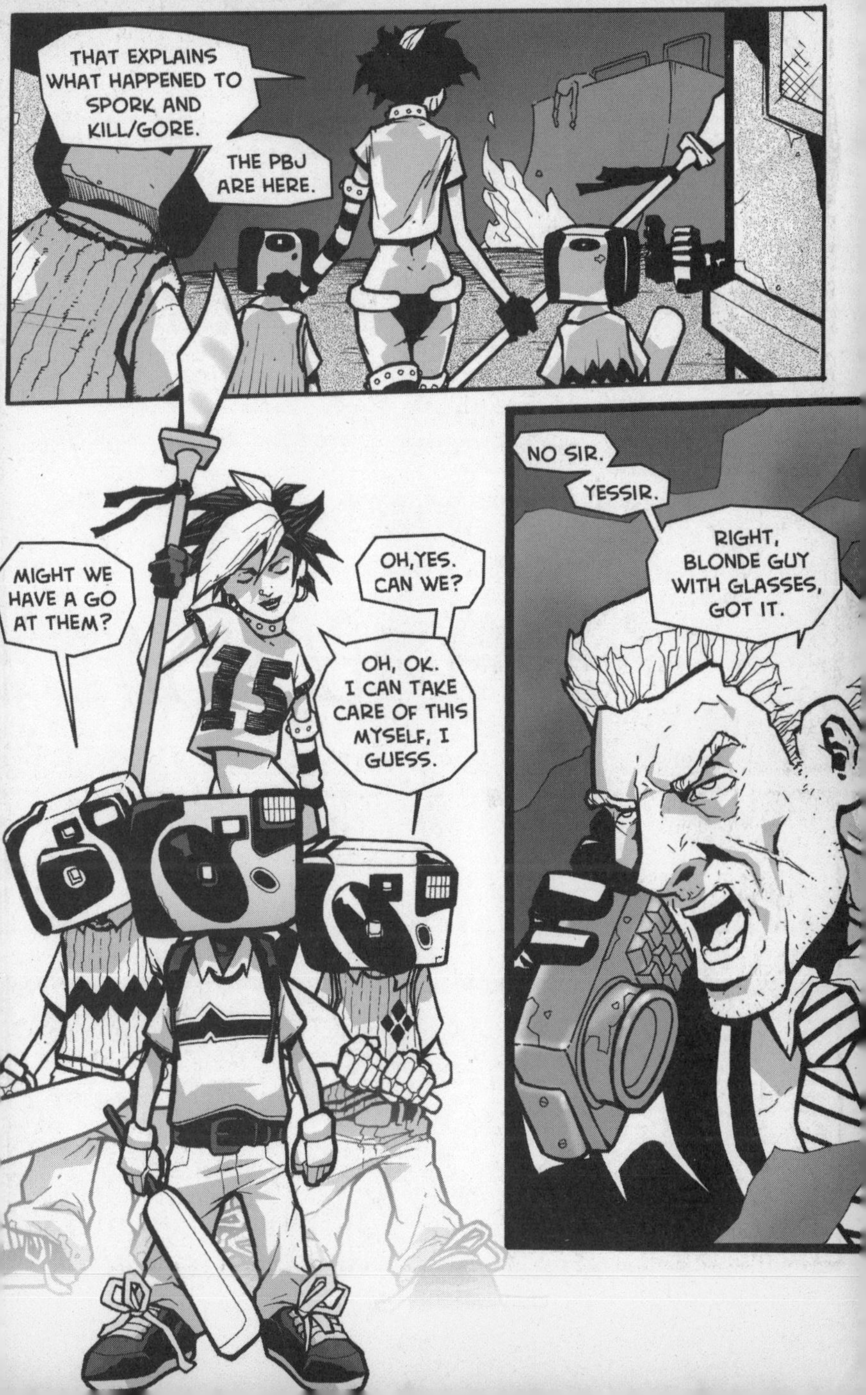
THAT EXPLAINS WHAT HAPPENED TO SPORK AND KILL/GORE.
THE PBJ ARE HERE.
MIGHT WE HAVE A GO AT THEM?
OH,YES. CAN WE?
OH, OK. I CAN TAKE CARE OF THIS MYSELF, I GUESS.
NO SIR.
YESSIR.
RIGHT, BLONDE GUY WITH GLASSES, GOT IT.

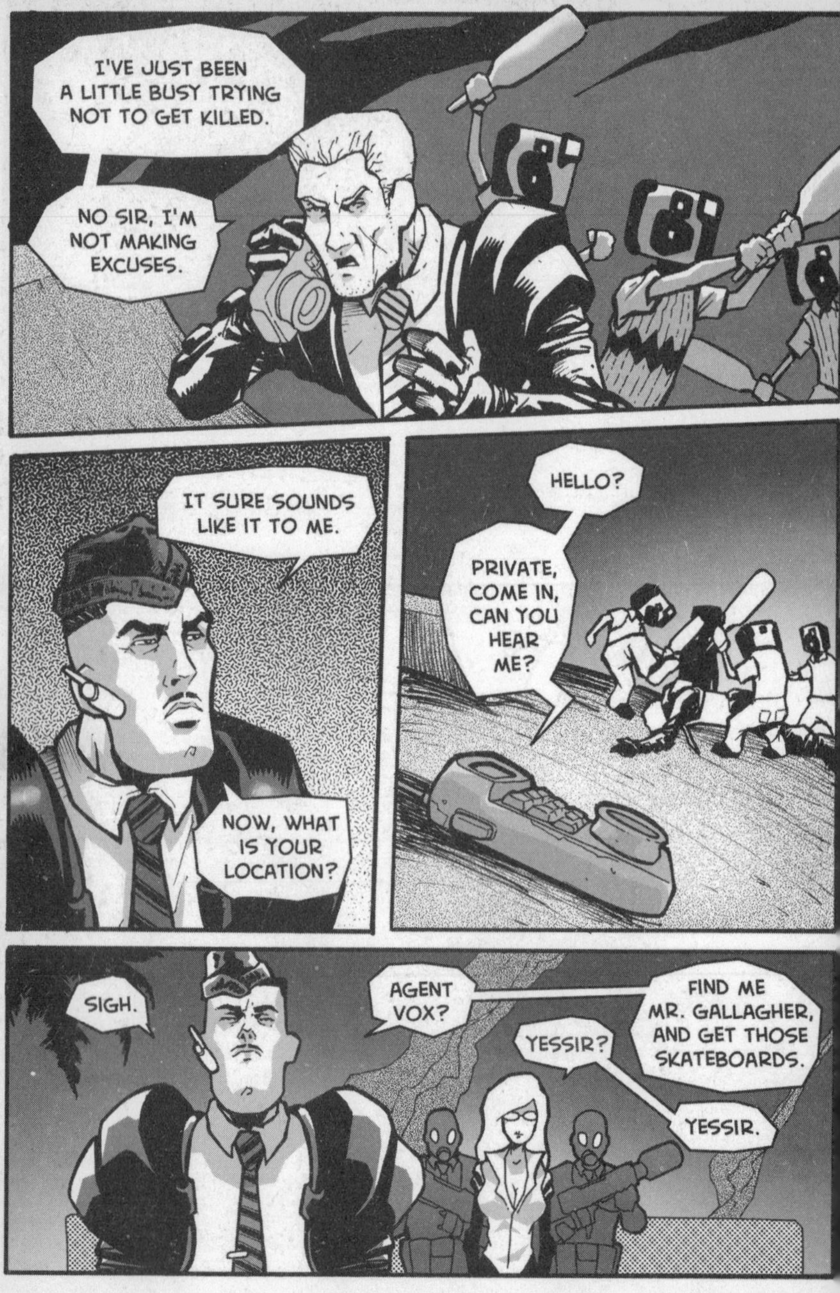
I'VE JUST BEEN A LITTLE BUSY TRYING NOT TO GET KILLED.
NO SIR, I'M NOT MAKING EXCUSES.
IT SURE SOUNDS LIKE IT TO ME.
NOW, WHAT IS YOUR LOCATION?
HELLO?
PRIVATE, COME IN, CAN YOU HEAR ME?
SIGH.
AGENT VOX?
YESSIR?
FIND ME MR. GALLAGHER, AND GET THOSE SKATEBOARDS.
YESSIR.

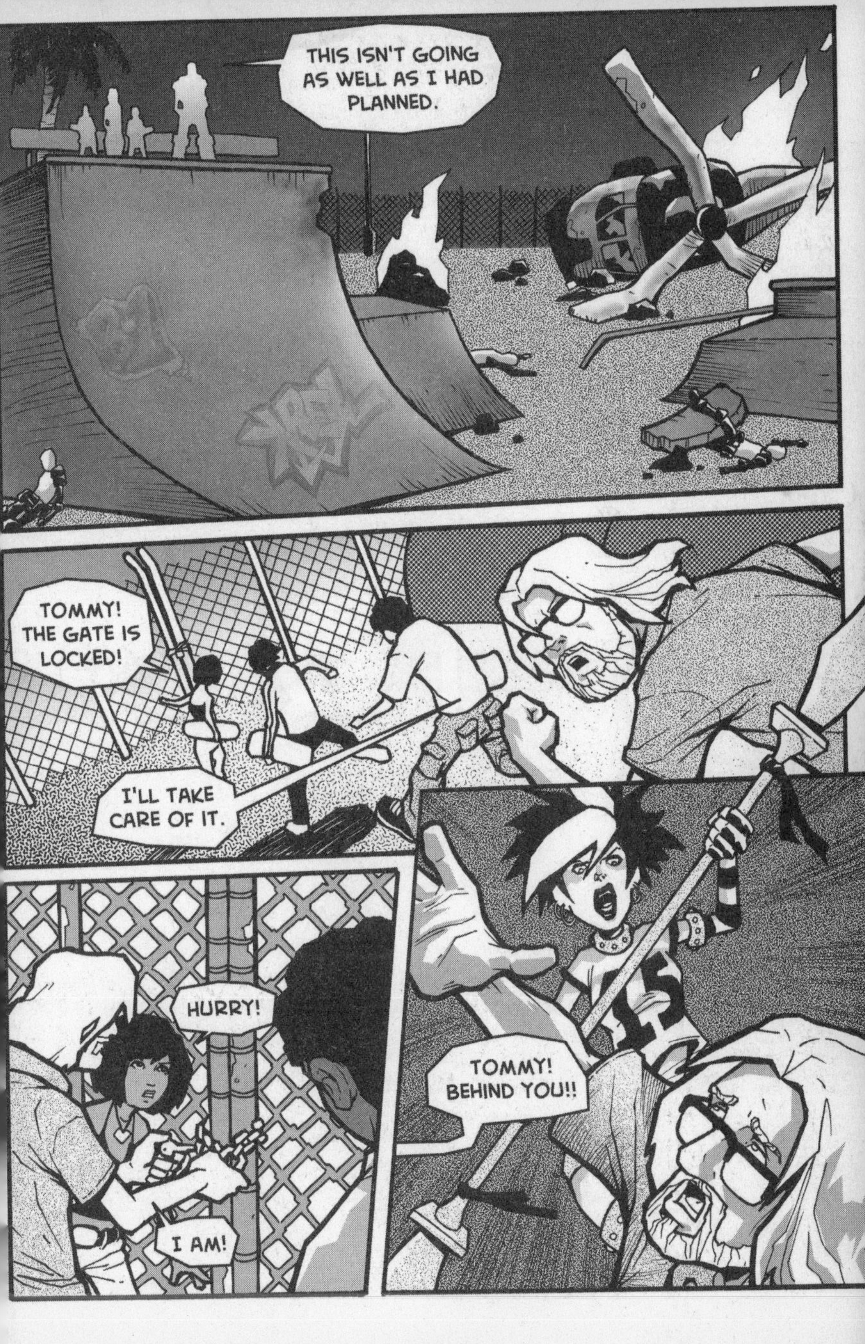
THIS ISN'T GOING AS WELL AS I HAD PLANNED.
TOMMY! THE GATE IS LOCKED!
I'LL TAKE CARE OF IT.
HURRY!
I AM!
TOMMY! BEHIND YOU!!

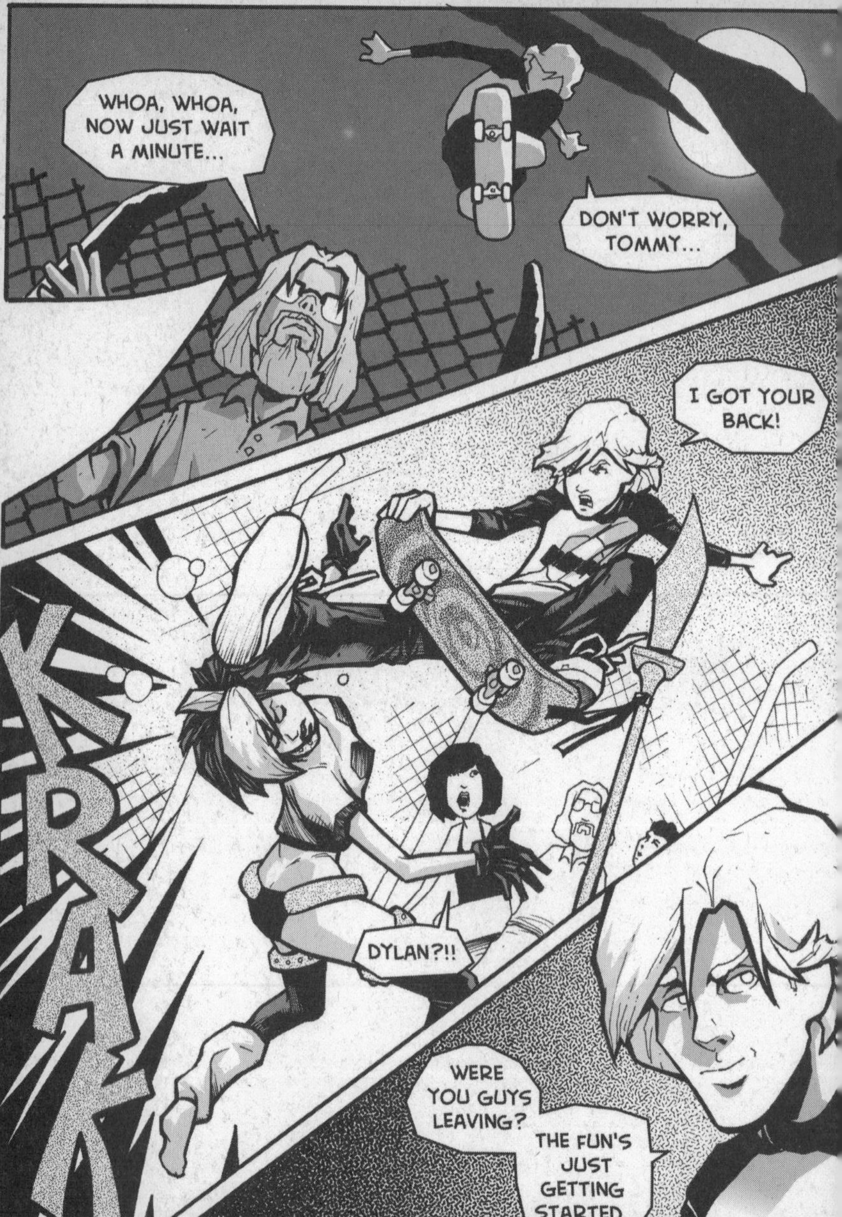
WHOA, WHOA, NOW JUST WAIT A MINUTE...
DON'T WORRY, TOMMY...
I GOT YOUR BACK!
KRAK
DYLAN?!!
WERE YOU GUYS LEAVING?
THE FUN'S JUST GETTING STARTED.

to be continued...

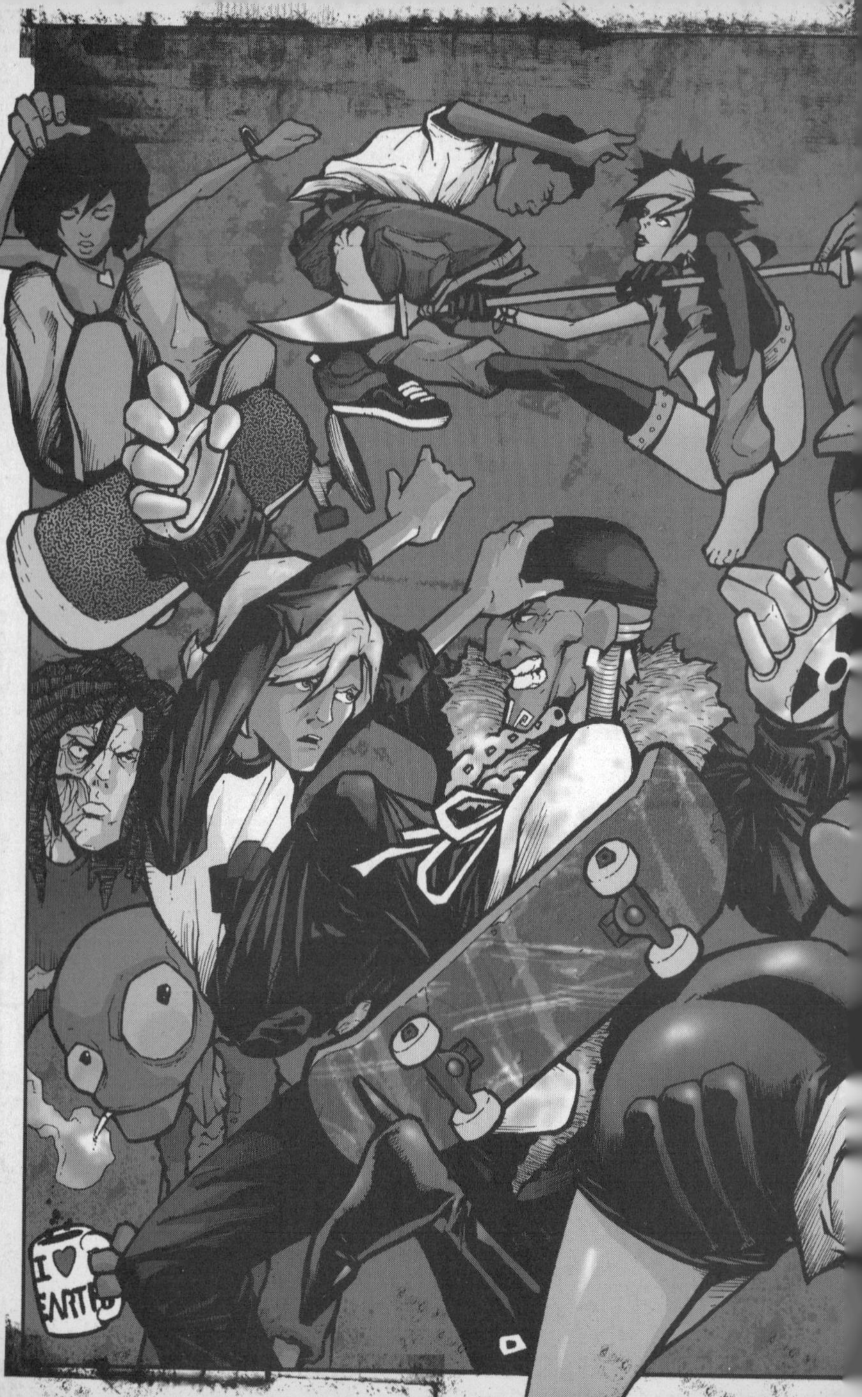
I ♥ EART

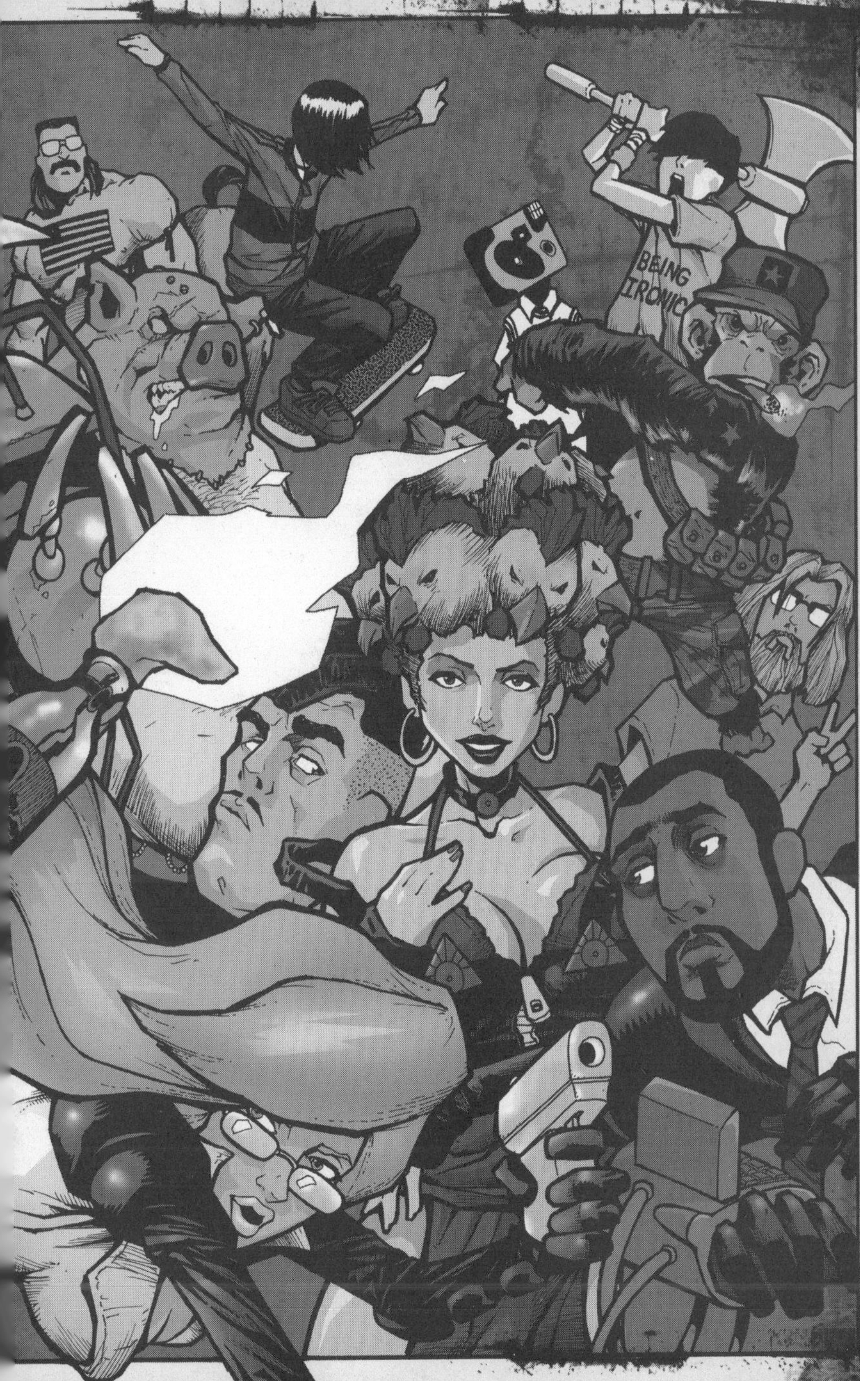
BEING IRONIC

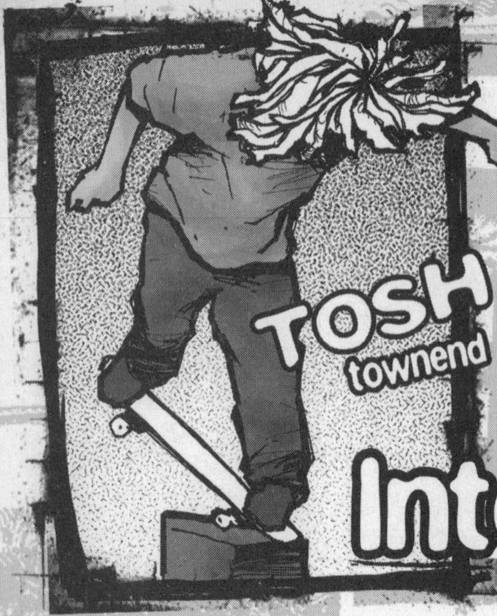
TOSH
townend

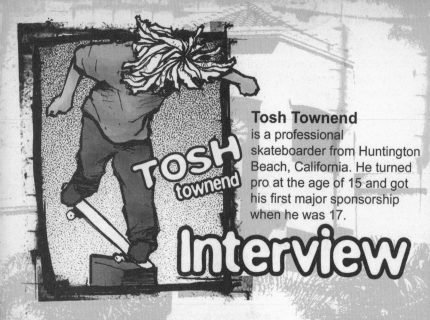

Tosh Townend is a professional skateboarder from Huntington Beach, California. He turned pro at the age of 15 and got his first major sponsorship when he was 17.

Interview

What's the life of a pro skater like?

busy...traveling all the time..

How do you become 'pro'? Is there a test or something?

ha, ha, ha. No, you just start off as an amateur, become known & prove your skills and then when your sponsor offers you a pro deal you turn pro.

What drew you to pursue skating professionally?

my dad had boards around the house and I started skating when I was young.

What is the best part of being a pro? The worst?

The best part is getting paid to do something that you love...the worst part is stalkers who drive by your house, honk and drive away.

Where do you see your career going, what do you have planned for 2007?

Touring with the Element team, promoting my new pro shoe, the Weenabago Projekt II, video by the homies Sin Habits, and lots of of skating.

Who do you hang with or skate with, or do you prefer to skate alone?

I skate with my homies all the time or sometimes with a filmer or photographer.

What board/trucks/wheels do you skate on?

Element Tosh model deck/Independent trucks Element Tosh 50mm wheels.

What do you do when you're not skating?

Surf, hang with friends, take Mexico trips getting the best barrels of my life.

What has been your favorite place to visit and why?

Japan because I went there for 7 days with the Benji Weatherly Project and we got to surf, snowboard, skate.

scene from 'The Weenabago Projekt'

I know some kids who look up to you, did you have any role models when you were coming up? Which skaters around today do you like?

As I was coming up I always liked the way Andrew Reynolds skated. And today Pat Pasquale is a new up & comer.

What was your role in the production of 'SkateFarm'?

My role is to let the artist Barzak know what looks correct. Such as skateboarding tricks and the input I give will make it legit.

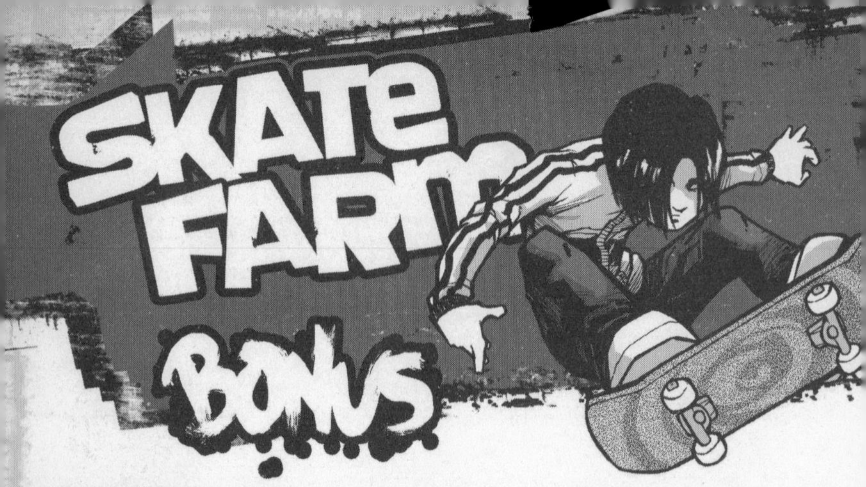
SKATE
FARM
BONUS

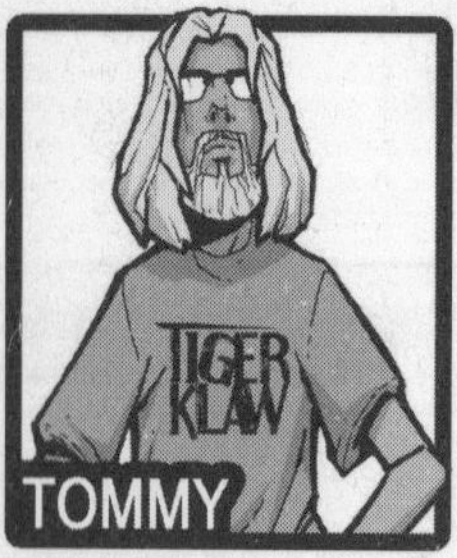
TIGER
KLAW
TOMMY

Tommy was abandoned at an early age and grew up in various foster placements and group homes in the southern California area. He took to surfing, and found acceptance within the close-knit community of surfers. His surfing led him to try skateboarding when he couldn't get to the water. Skateboarding is where Tommy really excelled, and he became a local celebrity and international sports hero, with his own brand of clothes and skateboarding equipment he named 'TigerKlaw'. With his financial success, Tommy opened up a skate park that was free to the publi and celebrated for it's annual skate camp.

Tommy retired from competition skating to focus on the skate park, which has becom a real passion of his. Within the park and the camp, Tommy feels he has created an environment of safety and family that he searched so long for as a kid. In providing that for others, Tommy has become a pillar of the community and mentor for the local kids

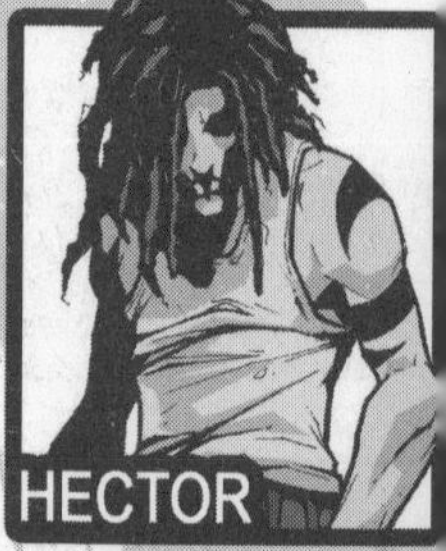
HECTOR

Hector was the youngest member on Tommy's first pro skate team, so the two go way back. Hector always looked up to Tommy and tried desperately to emulate his success, but never did. Since Hector couldn't be Tommy, he settled for being his best friend and the two have been inseparable since their teens.

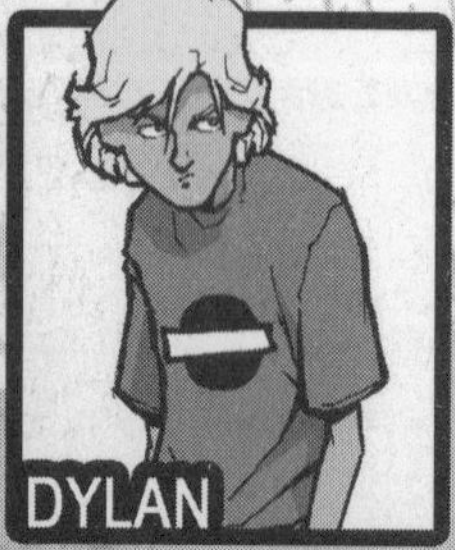
DYLAN

Dylan has worked for Tommy for about a year, doing odd jobs around the pro shop, during which time he developed a tight friendship with Tre. Although not a pro and without even a flow deal, Dylan has always had a raw skill that Tre is trying to help focus and turn into a pro sponsorship.

Dylan's father was a widower who himself died tragically at an early age. Dylan and his younger brother where taken in by their uncle, who was in no position to take on that level of responsibility. Dylan's uncle, Aaron, sees Dylan heading down a dead e and tries forcibly to shift Dylan's life to what he thinks is good for his nephew, mostly resulting in heated confrontations and sometimes violence.

After a meager childhood, Tre realized a certain level of success as a young teen. He showed an early, natural skateboarding ability, and soon went pro. He has had his own shoe line, TreBonics, as well as several spots in videos and features in magazines. The skate brand that sponsors Tre is owned and ran by Tommy, who has been a good friend of Tre's since he first came onto the scene.

Tre never forgot where he came from or his supporters. He is fiercely loyal to his friends and those that do kindness to him. As soon as Tre began to earn any serious money, he bought a house and had his father and two older bothers move in with him.

TRE

Rosie is generally in a bad mood. She feels pressured to be someone she is not, nor wants to be. Everyday is a struggle to just exist on her own terms. Rosie has a relatively large family, but none that she is particularly close with. She has a small group of close friends that get her through.

Rosie's mother brought her along to check on Shin's grandfather one time, which is when Rosie and Shin met. They immediately hit it off, with skateboarding being an obvious common ground. Shin is attracted to her natural good looks and strength, unknown to Rosie, who just sees Shin as a friend.

ROSIE

Shin has won trophies, awards and recognition in every sport and subject imaginable, except skateboarding. He just can't seem to get the hang of it, a fact that infuriates and confounds Shin, to the point where he is obsessed with skating and going pro.

Shin's family has its origins in Japan, where his mother spends the better part of the year on business. A single parent household, Shin's grandfather has moved into their southern California home to help out. However, Shin's grandfather is in ill health, and has frequent visits from an in-home caregiver, who is Rosie's mother.

SHIN

Ali is the defacto leader of The Dirty Deeds, being the first and oldest of the 'Deeds. Ali's history is unclear at best, but it is believed that he comes from North African and Arab decent, and may be over a thousand years old. Whoever pulls Ali's strings has been keeping him alive and modifying him for some time now. Ali is a quick learner and has adapted to his surroundings and modern times, so his demeanor and dialogue offer no hint as to his origins.

What is known about Ali is that he is ruthless and impatient, at times seeming irritated and bothered by the tasks he is given and by the other members of The Dirty Deeds. He has cybernetic hands and forearms that he can alter at will to form various weapons. His preferred weapon seems to be some sort of energy cannons.

ALI BABA GANOUSH

UNMEDICATED SARA

Crazy and deadly, Sara seems to be the right hand of Ali and The Dirty Deeds. If someone needs to be killed or something needs to be done, chances are Sara will be the one to do it. Reports have indicated that Sara has appeared to try very hard to impress Ali Baba and seems to be constantly seeking his approval, though we have no indication that Ali does indeed approve or even like Sara.

Sara does not have any visible modifications like the other Dirty Deeds. Given her manic nature, it is surmised that any modifications Sara has received have been to her brain, which may explain her super human reflexes and agility.

KILL/GORE

Before Kill/Gore's time with The Dirty Deeds, he was an average 'good ol' boy' by the name of Ronnie Taylor. A severely near-sighted and struggling rodeo bull rider, known for spending long hours training, he went out to the ranch to work on his routine one day, and disappeared. Seven years later Ronnie reappeared, calling himself 'Kill/Gore'. The lower half of his body had been replaced with that of a horse. Kill/Gore either has no memory, or no interest in his former life and has made no attempt to reclaim it or contact old friends and family.

Kill/Gore seems to enjoy himself more than the other 'Deeds. Laughing wildly as he tramples and smashes his victims. It would appear that he does not work well with the other Dirty Deeds, at times observed in verbal conflicts with several 'Deeds. Why he remains with them is unknown.

SPORK

Spork is an amalgam of various body parts, both human and animal, with a little space age technology thrown in. Other than the obvious, little is known about Spork origins. Investigations have revealed that a religious cult went missing from the same town at the same time that Spork first appeared. It is unknown if Spork was a memb of the cult, or if the cult itself was combined to make Spork. While it all could just be coincidence, Spork does share beliefs that mirror that of the cult.

Spork's role in The Dirty Deeds seems to be that of an enforcer, a purely physical br While many PBJ agents have reported being lectured by Spork on their attire, lifesty personal interests, there is no evidence that Spork's opinion matters to the other 'De

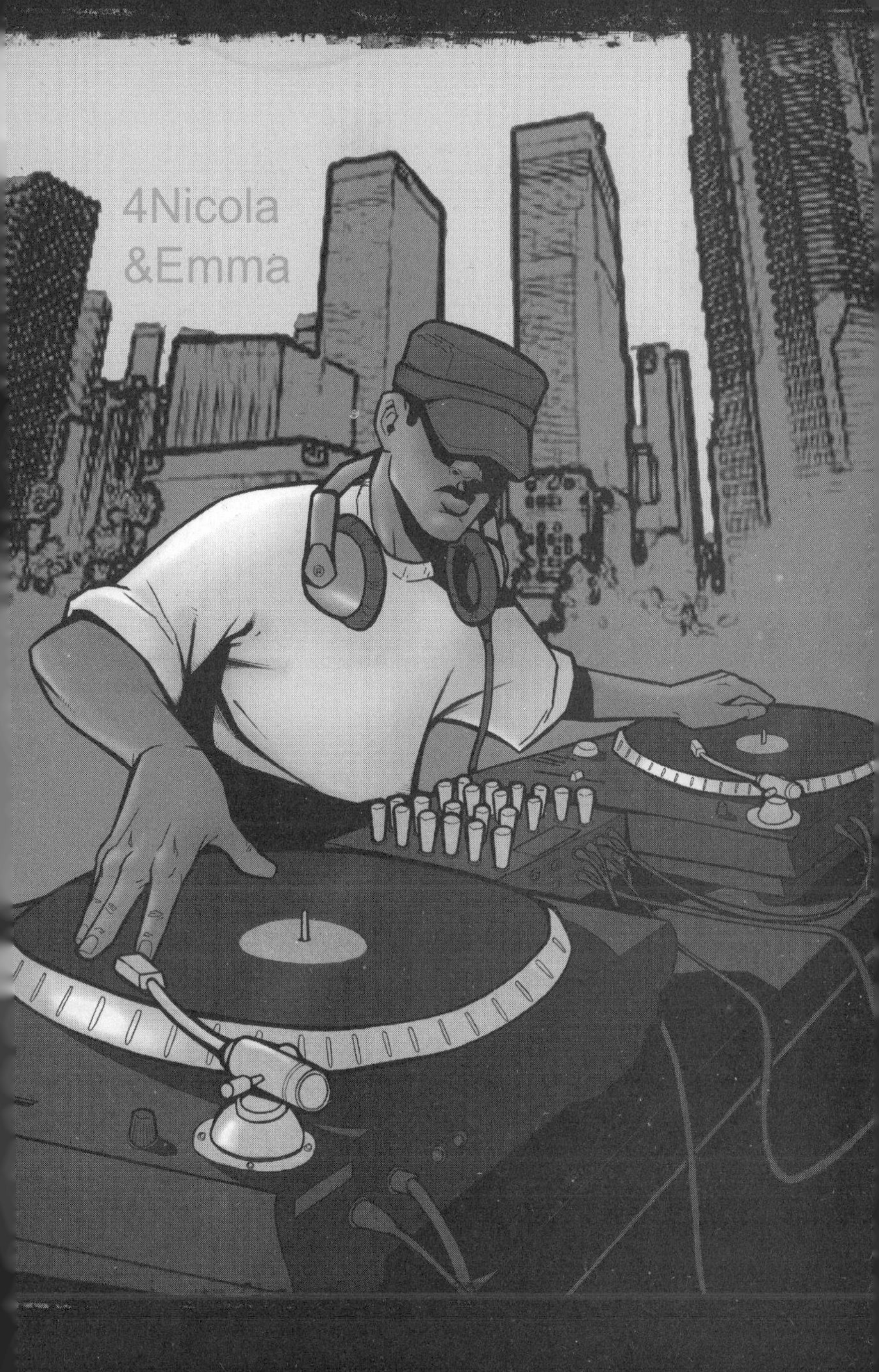
4Nicola
&Emma

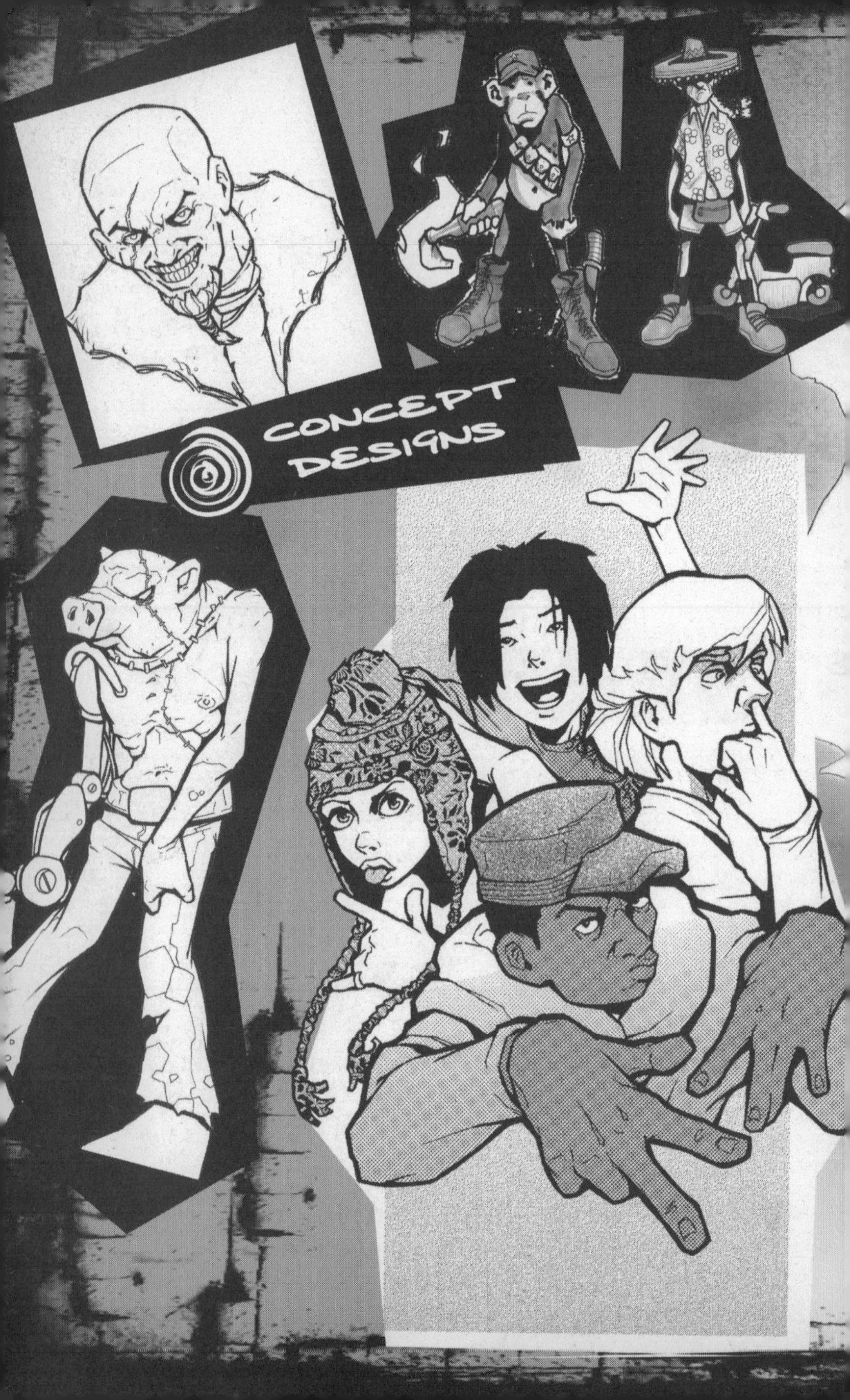
CONCEPT DESIGNS

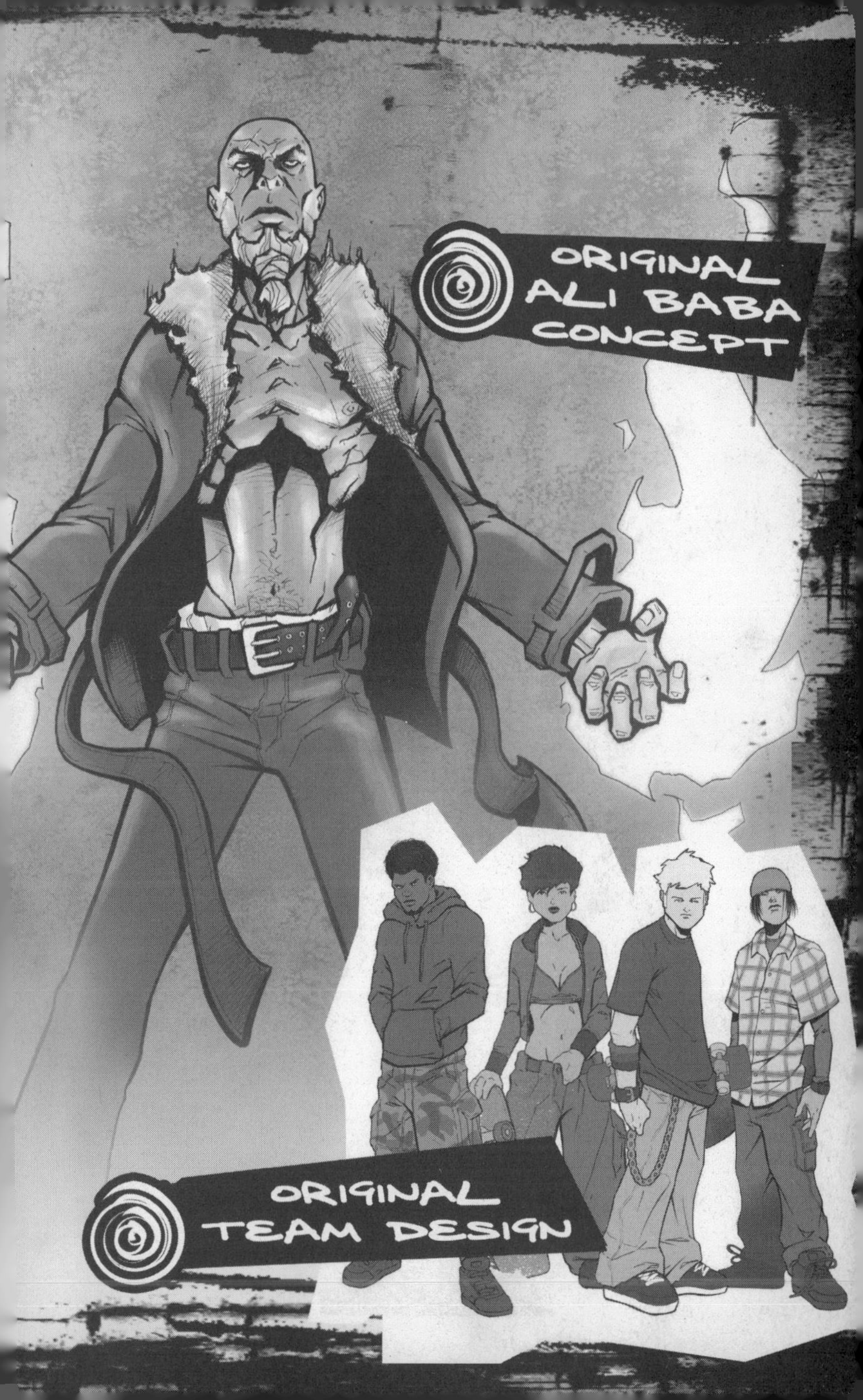
ORIGINAL ALI BABA CONCEPT
ORIGINAL TEAM DESIGN

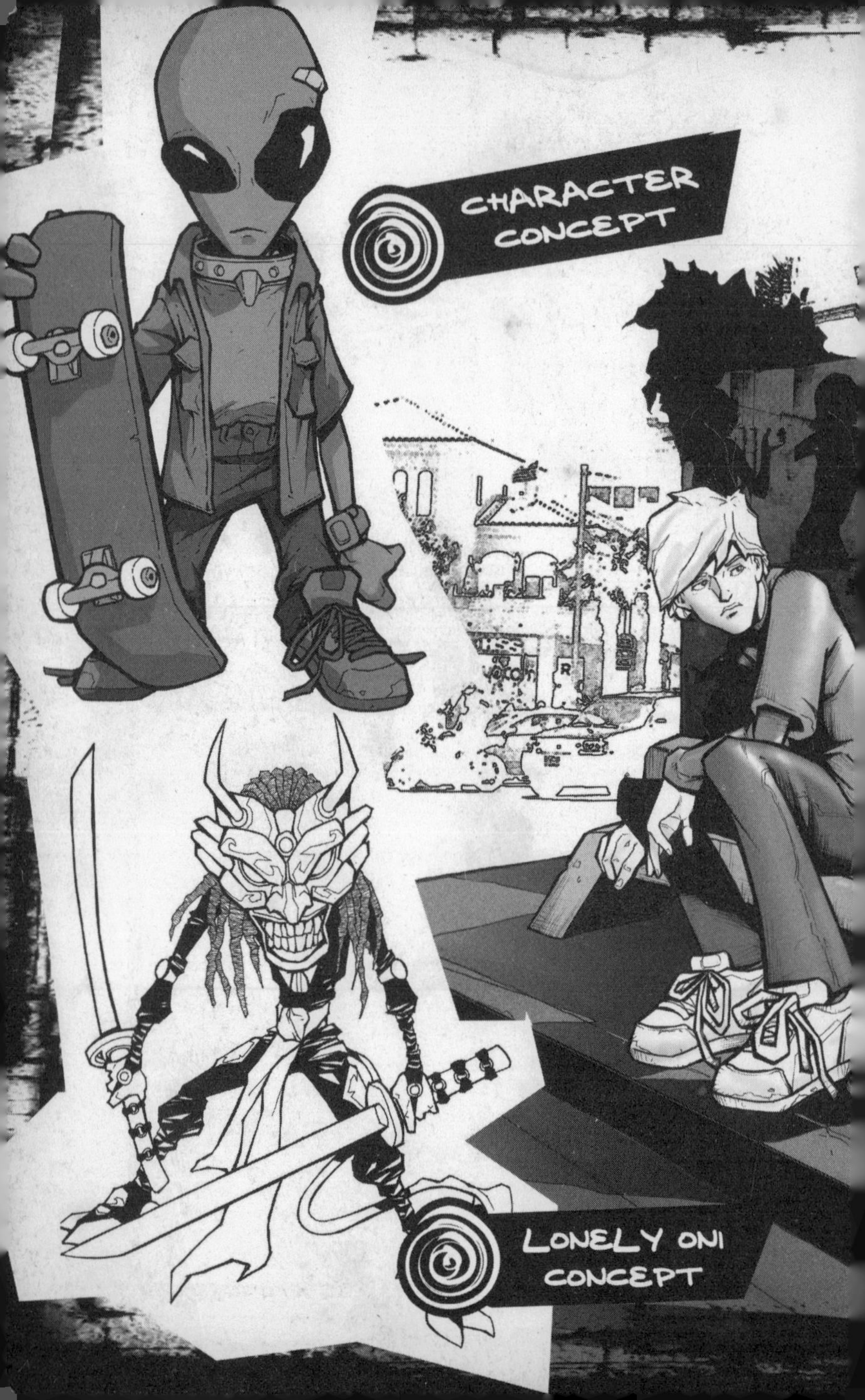
CHARACTER CONCEPT
LONELY ONI CONCEPT

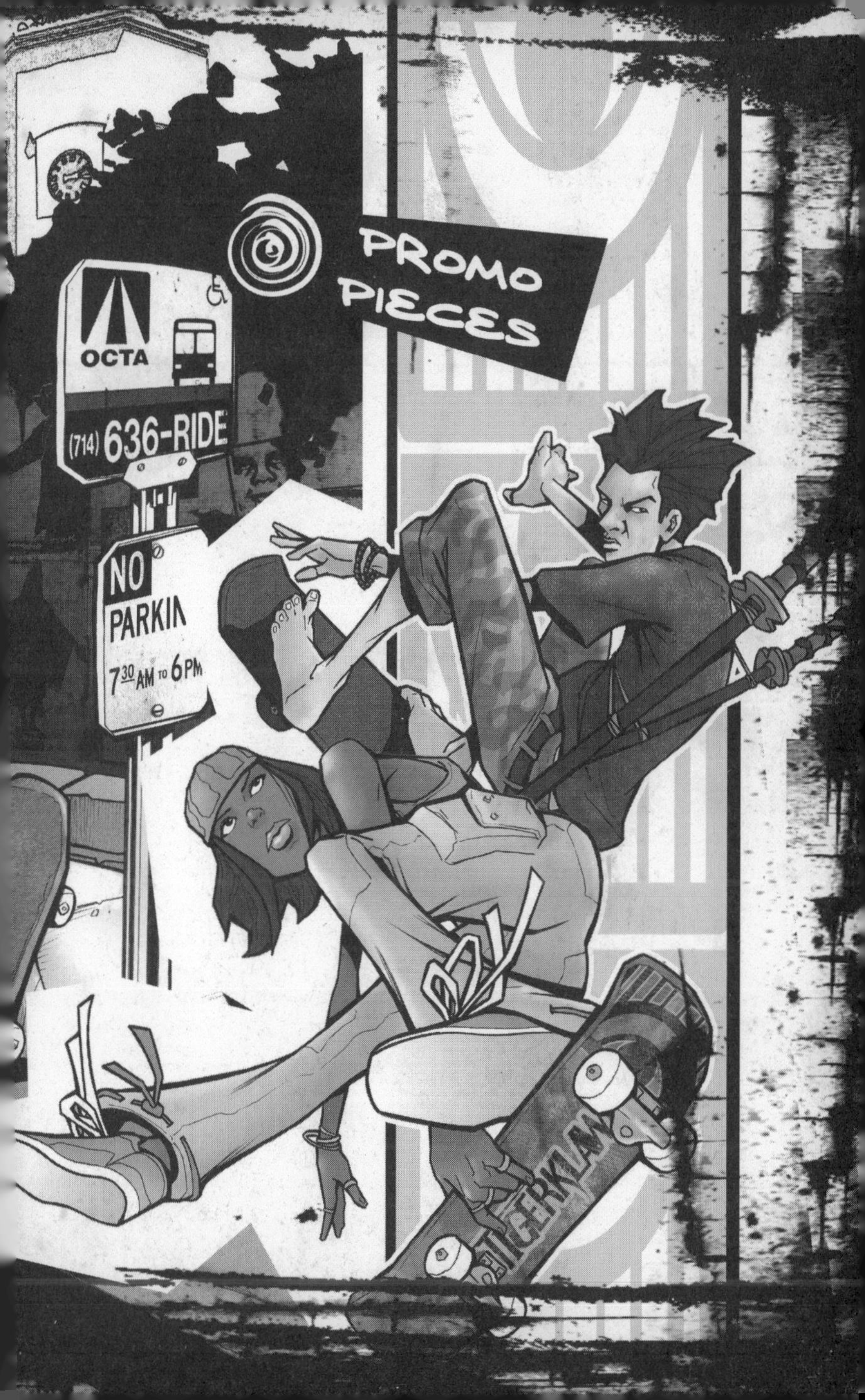
PROMO PIECES
OCTA
(714) 636-RIDE
NO
PARKIN
7 30 AM TO 6PM

SKATE FARM

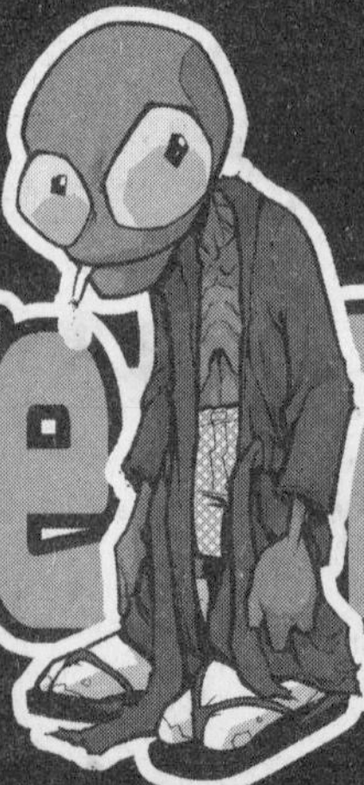

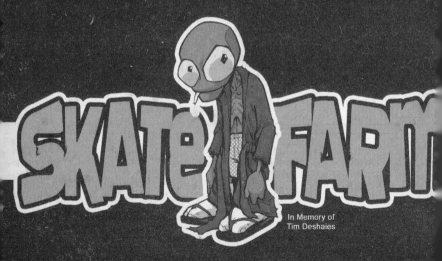

In Memory of
Tim Deshaies